The Limits of Analysis

THE LIMITS

OF

ANALYSIS

STANLEY ROSEN

Basic Books, Inc., Publishers

NEW YORK

Library of Congress cataloging in Publication Data

Rosen, Stanley, 1929–
    The limits of analysis.

    Bibliography: p. 271.
    Includes index.
    1.   Analysis (Philosophy)—Addresses, essays,
lectures.   I.   Title.
B808.5.R67   110   79-3138
ISBN: 0-465-04098-5

THIS BOOK IS DEDICATED TO

Francoise, Nicholas, Paul, Valerie, and Rex

Here, as usually in philosophy, the first difficulty is to see that the problem is difficult. If you say to a person untrained in philosophy, "How do you know I have two eyes?" he or she will reply, "What a silly question! I can see you have." It is not to be supposed that, when our inquiry is finished, we shall have arrived at anything radically different from this unphilosophical position. What will have happened will be that we shall have come to see a complicated structure where we thought everything was simple, that we shall have become aware of the penumbra of uncertainty surrounding the situations which inspire no doubt, that we shall find doubt more frequently justified than we supposed, and that even the most plausible premisses will have shown themselves capable of yielding unplausible conclusions. The net result is to substitute articulate hesitation for inarticulate certainty.

BERTRAND RUSSELL
An Inquiry into Truth and Meaning

CONTENTS

CONTENTS

ACKNOWLEDGMENTS

Some of the material contained in this book appeared in different form in *Kant-Studien* (section 2); *Theoria* (sections 9 and 10); *International Philosophical Quarterly* (sections 16 and 17). Sections 11 and 12 first saw the light of day, in a much inferior form, in *Heidegger and Modern Philosophy* (Yale University Press, 1978).

I owe a special debt of gratitude to David R. Lachterman, who read the entire manuscript with meticulous care and sympathy. He saved me from numerous errors, helped me to state a number of my points with greater clarity than I could have mustered without him, and gave me the benefit of his extraordinary erudition. Glen Helman read over several versions of Chapter Two. His steady advice and criticism saved me from more than one mistake, and were instrumental to my understanding of Kripke's work. Mark Wilson made a thorough and patient critique of material now included in sections 11 and 12, from which I learned much. While I am grateful to all the logicians and set theorists at Penn State who allowed me to audit their courses and seminars, I must single out Steve Simpson for special thanks. It is he who first made set theory intelligible to me, and he has been unstinting in his efforts to clear up technical problems, as well as to discuss with me a wide range of topics in the philosophy of mathematics. Thanks for practical help go to Stanley Paulson, Dean of the College of Liberal Arts; Carl Hausman, chairman of the department of philosophy; and Stanley Weintraub, director of the Institute for

ACKNOWLEDGMENTS

the Arts and Humanistic Studies, all of Penn State. I want also to thank the Institute's secretary, Shirley Rader, for unfailing efficiency; and my graduate student, David Roochnik, who prepared the bibliography and index. I am extremely grateful to Julia Strand and Arthur Krystal of Basic Books for a thorough reading of my manuscript, one that led to many improvements and the excision of numerous errors. Last and first, my thanks to Jane Isay, best of friends and editors, the incarnation of *phronēsis*, who has made a substantial contribution to the preparation of all my books, but especially to this one.

PREFACE

The following studies have their origin in a long-standing effort to grasp the foundations of discursive thinking. As a natural consequence of this effort, I have been concerned for a number of years with what is usually called analytical philosophy. A striking feature of this school is its celebration of rigor and lucidity, combined with a certain unwillingness to engage in self-criticism. Perhaps this reticence is a characteristic of every dominant academic school. It may also be a cause of decay. The strengths of the analytical movement, and its successful appropriation of the rhetoric of scientific enlightenment, have led to a general failure to understand the rhetorical nature of its own justification. There are signs that this failure is in the process of rectification. However, the signs are not yet strong enough to prevent the typical practitioner of analytical philosophy from succumbing to the temptation of confusing irony for a refutation of opposing views. Alternatively, the analyst is typically misled by the charm of his technical facility (or that of his masters) into assuming that a translation of other doctrines into his own idiom is tantamount to a refutation. And this despite strong warnings within the analytical movement as to the problematical nature of translation!

In any case, I myself do not believe that the limits of analysis can be defined, or the context of analysis translated, into analytical terms. For this reason, I do not believe that the title "analytical philosophy" is a good one. Philosophy is both synthetical and analytical, neither the one nor the other. As I hope to show, the enthusiasm engendered by the application of mathematical, or quasi-mathematical, techniques (like the functional analysis of the proposition) to the traditional problems of philosophy carried with it a misperception of the intrinsic nature of these problems. This enthusiasm for analysis led to the neglect, and even the suppression, of synthesis. To cite one important consequence, the attack against psychologism, although perfectly justified when accurately formulated, obscured the fact that analysis itself, as a cognitive function, cannot be understood independently of cognition. The visibility or "evidence" of formal structures points, to use appropriately old-fashioned language, in the direction of the subject as well as the object. Those who claim that semantics, or a doctrine of meaning, is the foundation of philosophy, cannot simply begin, as would the mathematician or logician, from the fact of evidence. They must first explain how it is possible for a sign or structure to "mean" something to someone. This in turn leads, not to psychologism, but to the recognition of semantical and ontological properties by which an intelligence perceives such-and-such a structure as "pointing to" such-and-such a meaning. The property of pointing cannot just be an element in the structure; in this case, structures would point to themselves, or require no interpretation. Similarly, the capacity to point out would seem itself to point to a unity of being and thinking, of a sort not amenable to structural analysis. The current popularity of pragmatic and constructivist doctrines among analytical philosophers is a clear sign of the inadequacy of a purely structural or "formal" account of analysis. What is the "structure" of pragmatism or constructivism? How does the philosopher of mathematics decide which interpretation of the ontological significance of mathematics is sound? And let the reader note: the ontological significance of mathematics is not a question of the range of values of its variables. It is a question of the nature of symbolism, *ordo et mensura*, the relations we choose to symbolize, and the fact that it is relations that we choose to symbolize.

In this book, I propose to investigate the adequacy of some contemporary analytical treatments of traditional topics, such as intuition, essence, unity, being, existence, and negation. I shall argue that the traditional problems associated with these topics have been ignored or distorted, rather than clarified or resolved, by their translation into the technical idiom approved by analytical philosophers. In the first three chapters, I take my bearings by the analytical literature, and attempt to develop my criticism from *within* the context of analysis. However, this cannot be accomplished by adopting the presuppositions of analytical philosophy. Since I wish to uncover and to study these presuppositions, my way of treating analytical procedures cannot be simply identical with that of the analyst. Furthermore, the analytical movement is not homogeneous, and it is necessary to shift perspectives in attempting to uncover assumptions shared by ostensibly conflicting tendencies. I have made very great efforts to understand analytical philosophy accurately, and my intention, even while developing forceful criticism, is to treat it more fairly than it sometimes treats its opponents. I want to emphasize that whatever criticism I direct against analytical philosophy as a form of scholasticism, is not directed against analytical thinking. For that matter, I have deep sympathies with the school itself, and to a certain extent, its enemies are my enemies. I have profited enormously from the long attempt to assimilate the doctrines and techniques of analytical philosophy. Nevertheless, I have fundamental criticisms. Analytical philosophy has failed to do justice to its own limits and context; it has therefore failed to do justice to itself. And this has important technical consequences within the analytical sphere.

In the last two chapters, I venture upon a somewhat more comprehensive development of my theme. On the basis of the initial, immanent analyses, I turn to the problem of thinking the context of analysis, rather than to that of arriving at the context from within. This problem is in a deep sense coextensive with the history of western philosophy. I have selected certain paradigmatic figures from the tradition, in order to illustrate the two most pervasive aspects of the problem. The first aspect is the attempt to validate analytical thought by a doctrine of the whole: the context of analysis is first and last our comprehensive understanding of the human enterprise. The second is the attempt to transform the dream-like features of this comprehensive understanding into the conceptual schematism of analytical thinking. My conclusion, baldly stated, is that the dream of Enlightenment, or full wakefulness, of which contemporary analytical philosophy is a kind of decayed epiphenomenon, leads us toward the ultimately destructive effort to transform the world into a concept. This effort has two consequences. The attempt to transform the conceiver into a property of his concept fails for technical as well as for psychological reasons. As a result, either the conceiver, as excluded from conceptualization, is ignored or else, and inevitably, he returns from the dream world to which he has been consigned, and gains his vengeance by *deconstructing* the conceptual structures of the analyst.

I write in the defense of reason. In order to contribute to this defense, I have tried, here as elsewhere, to rehabilitate old notions rather than merely to introduce new ones. This is to say that I have tried to do both, since these activities are inseparable from one another. It would have been far simpler to fly the revolutionary colors of analytical philosophy or its imminent opponent, deconstructivism. In my opinion, however, we live in a time of too many revolutions. One of the great defects of the analytical movement is that it was conceived, and to a considerable extent still regards itself, as a revolutionary break with traditional philosophy. There is too much commotion in our century.

Under these circumstances, a man who is trying to slow down may look as though he is running in the direction opposite to that of the crowd.

With this in mind, I make a final prefatory remark. Whereas this book cannot aspire to be a *ktēma eis aei*, it has not been written in a day. Considerable thought and study have been invested in its preparation. I am sure that it contains many errors. By a transcendental law of hermeneutics, reviewers are always wiser than authors, and I am confident that my errors will be pointed out to me. At the same time, without sparing me righteous criticism, the reader may perhaps consider that my intentions will not always coincide with his own.

It is my hope that this book will be of interest to reflective men, and not simply to professional philosophers. The nature of my subject, as well as the current state of philosophy, inevitably requires a certain amount of technical discussion. In conducting this discussion, I have tried to combine accuracy with lucidity, while avoiding oversimplification. To vulgarize the themes addressed in the following pages would be an affront to the reader. My goal has been to write in such a way that the non-specialist can move from step to step of each issue, even in those cases where he has no previous acquaintance with the terms and procedures of the specialist. At the same time, I have made every effort to satisfy the legitimate expectations of the specialist. In a very few cases, I have reserved some technical point for the notes at the conclusion of the book. The discussion of Casimir Lewy's work on modality in section 3 may be skipped by the general reader without any loss of continuity in the development of my argument.

The Limits of Analysis

CHAPTER ONE

Intuition and Analysis

Ｉｎ THIS CHAPTER, I shall introduce and defend the thesis that philosophy cannot be identical with analytical thinking alone. My reasons have nothing to do with a dislike of mathematics, a fear of precision, or the softness of a literary sensibility. There is, for that matter, no intrinsic incompatibility between mathematics and literary sensibility. The capacity to distinguish between distinct kinds of precision, as for example the numerical and the suitable, is a necessary prerequisite for philosophy. The limits of analysis stem from the nature of analytical thinking itself. One has to know the nature of analytical thinking in order to be able to spell out its limits. While a literary sensibility is no substitute for analytical competence, it is an always helpful and sometimes critical supplement. Analysis is a mode of cognition, and is therefore regulated by the judgment, intuition, or sensibility of the analyst. Knowing how to carry out a sequence of analytical operations is not the same as knowing the appropriate domain of application, nor is it the same as knowing how to start and when to stop the sequence. As I shall argue in detail, when we speak of "the dream of scientific objectivity," we are not merely employing a metaphor, except in the sense that all thinking possesses a metaphorical dimension. What we require, then, is a sense of rationality sufficiently extensive to cover the analysis of dreams and metaphors, and sufficiently precise to engage in this analysis without destroying its objects. The analysis of intentions is not coexten-

3

sive with the intention to analyze. If the intention is not rational, then neither are its consequences. Otherwise stated, knowledge of the nature and excellence of analytical thinking is neither acquired nor exercised by the application of rules, formal schemata, or axiomatic deductive systems. The task of the first chapter is to develop a notion of "intuition" that is both justified by ordinary use and not entirely at odds with the intuitions of analytical philosophers. As I shall argue, it is by intuition in this sense that we carry out our analyses.

1. Psychologism

Early in his interesting essay "Intuition and the Inexpressible" Renford Bambrough quotes and goes on to expound a famous remark by Wittgenstein: "Intuition an unnecessary shuffle."[1] The key to Bambrough's exposition is as follows. We often know something for which there is no procedure of proof or explanation:

> To say that we know it, without its being necessary or possible to give any reason for it, sounds dogmatic. To say that there is a faculty by which we acquire the knowledge that we do not acquire by any procedure may sound less dogmatic, but it is no more than a disguised way of making the same point again: that here is something that we know without the application of any procedure or the invocation of any faculty. [IE, 202]

Bambrough observes that what we know in this way includes "all the things that deserve to be called the foundations or ultimate grounds of all the rest of our knowledge." After a number of illuminating examples he turns again to Wittgenstein's observation and its lesson

> that we are liable to confuse the possession of a skill with knowledge of the truth of propositions. Because a skill can be partly expressed or displayed as knowledge of the truth of propositions, we are inclined to identify with this theoretical knowledge what should be seen primarily as a practice. [IE, 205]

Bambrough does not deny but rather asserts that we have what I shall abbreviate as non-procedural knowledge. And it should be emphasized that the foundations of knowledge are non-procedural (they do not consist of rules or routines). What he does deny is that such knowledge is propositional or theoretical, and so it would appear that it is acquired by an intellectual act such as intuition. I say "appear" because although Bambrough denies that there is an intellectual faculty of intuition, he does not say explicitly that practical knowledge is non-cognitive or non-intellectual.

Bambrough's failure to spell out his central point is reflected in the ambiguity of the Wittgensteinian passages on which it rests. In these passages there is a sketch of practical skill as the foundation of knowledge. Knowing is originally or fundamentally knowing *how to*. But the term *knowing* seems here to be an unnecessary shuffle for *doing*. There is a tension in Wittgenstein and his followers between recognition of a non-analytical mode of knowing and the equation of theoretical knowledge with propositional knowledge. The problem can perhaps be restated as follows. Either "knowing how to" is a consequence of intuition or it is amenable to routinization. Of course we can describe subsequently what we already know how to do. Thus Bambrough insists that "to hold that there may be inarticulate understanding is not to hold that there may be any understanding that could not be articulated" (IE, 212). This is true. But what is the cognitive value of an articulation of inarticulate understanding? To take an extreme counterexample, I can describe the barking of a dog, but this does not render the dog's barking a form of knowledge. And for that matter I can describe my own barking with the same negative results (think here of analytical doctrines of ethical statements as emotive, fashionable a generation ago). In less extreme terms and employing one of Bambrough's own examples, if I simply see that a given step in a logical proof is valid, is this seeing actually the consequence of the repeated activity of looking at steps in logical proofs or what are purported to be logical proofs? Nor does Bambrough withhold an explanation because none is available. Instead, like Wittgenstein, he strongly implies that the seeing of the step as valid is not a theoretical intuition but the exercise of a skill. This skill is not cognitive (although it is called "knowing") but a habit. We do it because we can do it, and we can do it because we have done it. But this is to reduce our recognition of the validity of a step in a proof to contingent happenstance. What if we had done things differently? If the reply is that things *cannot* be done differently, then surely we are entitled to some argument to establish this necessary link. For example, Bambrough might wish to say that the rationality of the act of seeing the validity of a step in a proof is the consequence of that act. But if the consequence is also an assertion, we return to the domain of propositional or theoretical knowledge, and the same question arises with respect to the propositional formulation of the content or consequence of the initial act of seeing the validity of the step in question. What does it mean to see that a given proposition captures the rational content of an antecedent act of seeing, which is itself understood as a practical rather than a theoretical activity? [2]

The strange thing about Bambrough's paper, and about Wittgenstein's remark, is that the paper, like its source of inspiration, talks regularly about the act of seeing how things follow from one another, or what to do next, without seeing that such talk contradicts the negative thesis concerning intuition. And it is Wittgenstein, more than any other philosopher of the twentieth century, with the possible exception of Husserl, who has provided such persuasive evidence of the need to supplement analysis with intuition. But Wittgenstein's apparent retention of his earlier notion of rationality as propositional, together with his semantical bias against the intrusion of psychological factors in the analysis of meanings, led him to deny the rationality of his own insight. Perhaps too it was Wittgenstein's anti-psychologism that prevented him from drawing an obvious consequence of his own doctrine: whether knowing what to do next is theoretical or practical, I know what to do next if and only if *I* know what to do next. Even if obedience to rules is social or political, the "we" of society or the political community is unintelligible except as an assemblage of "I's." The analysis of what I know is incomplete, and indeed, meaningless, if it makes no reference to how I know it, or that it is I who know it, namely, that meanings mean something only to knowers. Hence *I* become a problem in the attempt to establish the public or universal status of what I know. This problem is not resolved by pretending that it does not exist. In terms going back to Plato, the "What is X?" question cannot be totally severed from the "Who am I?" question.

Objections to Intuition

An appeal to intuition is faced with certain difficulties which can, I think, be stated more precisely than does Bambrough. I shall be discussing the role of intuition in analytical thought throughout the following pages. As a general introduction to the topic, I want to consider four related but distinguishable objections to the doctrine of intuition. (1) Intuition is more obviously connected to the perception of unities or syntheses than to the function of analysis, and explanations are more obviously analyses than syntheses. To perceive is one thing; to explain is something else. (2) An intuition seems to be a cognitive activity to which no structure corresponds. The act of perceiving a unity is distinct from the structure of the unity we perceive. Hence an account of the structure of the content of an intuition is not an account of intuition. Since a theory is an account of a structure, there can be no theory of intuition. (3) The absence of a definite structure corresponding to intuition is reflected in the fact that the word has many senses in everyday use, most of which are quite vague and have nothing to do with philosophical explanation. Talk about intuition is thus talk about a variety of metaphorical expressions for knowing "how to." (4) Intuition is a cognitive activity rather than a cognized or theoretical object.

6

Hence if it can be studied at all, it belongs to psychology, not to philosophy. Recourse to intuition within conceptual analysis is thus a fall into psychologism. These are the objections, all of which beg a number of questions, but raise points that must be considered, and in some cases granted. The two most important aspects of these objections are the conviction that philosophy is conceptual analysis and that the philosopher can and must ignore the conditions of conceptualization.

We begin with objection (1). The word *analysis* means a loosening or dissolving, and by extension, a division of a compound into its structural elements. According to Kant, every analysis depends upon a prior synthesis. If there had not first been a "putting-together" (whether by nature or the analyst), there could be no "taking-apart." This is so obvious that we may well ask why analytical philosophy tends to undervalue, and even to ignore, synthesis. In order to answer this question, it is not necessary to review the history of the analytical tradition. Nevertheless, a reference to Plato is in order. The paradigm of the genuine philosophical method is described in dialogues like the *Phaedrus* and *Sophist* as division and collection in accordance with kinds. Plato's general term for this method is *dialectic*, but he frequently uses the apparently narrower term *division* to stand for the method as a whole; this, however, is never the case with collection. The process of collection or synthesis is regularly described as a step in the comprehensive process of division. Unlike Kant, for whom synthesis functions in the very constitution of the concept by the transcendental ego, the Platonic dialogues do not begin with a transcendental synthesis of a concept, but rather with an opinion, or casually expressed thesis about a genus directly accessible to everyday discourse. Whereas for Kant, synthesis is the basis for analysis, in Plato the basis is opinion. If there are any "concepts" in the Platonic division, they emerge as a segment, species, or class falling under the initial collection. As one might express this, in Plato, synthesis is analytical. The analytical intelligence "stamps" individual objects with the seal that marks out objects of a definite kind, in the way that we stamp wax with a seal or signet ring.

Platonic dialectic is itself governed by the pervasive paradigm of counting and measuring as they function in everyday life. A simple example would be this: a collection of fruit is sorted out into kinds (apples, oranges, pears, etc.). Even if the genus to be divided is an abstract or general one like the arts or sciences, essentially the same procedure applies. We use a "measure" or form (in contemporary terminology, a set of predicates) by which to sort out each group within the initial collection. This measure is not a transcendentally synthesized concept but part of our general information. The curious feature of Platonic division is that it moves toward specificity by way of opinions. The sets of predicates employed at each stage of the division are treated as more or less

7

obvious, whereas the last step in the division, the class to be defined, is treated as the product of rigorous philosophical method. Plato does not call our attention to the fact that the use of conventional definitions can only terminate in conventional or contingent knowledge. He implies that the rigor of the method transforms conventional into natural definitions. And this rigor is supplied by the act of dividing, hence of counting the eidetic elements which compose the final definition. These elements are divided out from the initial compound and then reassembled in a final compound which is as distinct from the starting point as, say, the science of politics is distinct from the sciences. The eidetic elements are embedded within each other without losing their specific natures. So too they may be taken apart and recombined without loss of identity. In these respects, they are like the natural numbers. An element is a "number" and so too is a compound or sum of "numbers." Dialectic is thus a kind of arithmetic, in which to explain is primarily to take apart, and hence to exhibit the structure of the compound. By taking apart our opinions, we transform their elements into arithmological forms. In the same way, the "measure" derived from everyday life is transformed into an articulated concept.

Contemporary analytical philosophy is a curious blend of Kantian and Platonic fragments. In the present context, it is a fragment of Plato that lights the way of exposition. Analysis, to be sure, is articulation rather than dissolution. Nevertheless, if our intention is to provide a discursive account of a compound, we can do this only by dividing and measuring, or by counting in accordance with kinds. But what "counts" as a kind can only be determined by further acts of division. The standard by which I can count apples applies only to apples and not to some other kind of fruit. But what I consider the standard apple is initially an everyday perception or opinion as to what an apple is. The attempt to refine this opinion, say by the science of pomology, is again dividing or counting, in this case of predicates.[3] At some stage of the division, a sum of predicates is obtained that functions as the scientific, pomologically certified measure of membership in the class *apples*. If I ask how this pomologically standard set has been obtained, the reply can only be a "running-through" the steps in the division by which they were reached. The pomologist may in fact have had recourse to intuition at many or even all of the steps in this process. *But he cannot communicate his intuitions to me.*

In general, a unity or synthesis is presented to perception or intuition without a "spelling" ("counting") out of the elements in its structure. But perception, whether sensuous or intellectual, is neither explaining nor understanding. If we try to explain what we perceive, then analysis is necessary. We have to say something "about" the synthesis rather than to "bespeak" it by merely pronouncing its name. To say something about something is to predicate. Hence we see the link between the paradigm of arithmetic, or counting and measuring, and the doctrine of predication. Both are rooted in the apparent priority of dividing to collecting.

Suppose that we grant the priority of analysis to synthesis in the sense just sketched. It seems fair to maintain that an explanation is not so much a synthesis as an analysis. On the other hand, this scarcely licenses us to dispense with synthesis. Whether collections are transcendental or conventional, we have to perceive them as the appropriate starting point for analysis. In addition, we must see *where we are going*, or what will "count" as the successful resolution to the given exercise of analysis. "Counting" in this sense cannot be arithmetical in the sense of adding or summing by dividing off elements assumed to be identified by a standard or measure. Since the elements are not homogeneous, we have to know in advance the appropriate measure, and we have to see once we attain it the unity discovered by our measurements.

Analysis is the admittedly indispensable road to our destination, but it is no more the destination than it is the intention to begin the voyage. One could perhaps say that the destination is an articulated structure. But we know that we have reached the destination only when we recognize a given articulation as the *explanation* of that structure. We cannot see that an analysis explains a structure by performing an additional step in the analysis. At some point we must see that we are finished. And to see an analysis is not to analyze. It is rather to see an articulated structure as a unity, whole, or synthesis. Furthermore, to see the unity or wholeness of the structure is not to see it as a sum of parts. We can always add another element to a sum, or another number to a sum of numbers. There has to be some reason for our *not* adding another number to a given sum, and this reason is our intuition or perception that we now have *enough*. The judgment that an analytical exercise is appropriate is not the same as the arithmetical or quasi-arithmetical measuring of the steps in that exercise.

If to understand is to possess an explanation, and if an explanation is an analysis, it remains the case that an analysis is intelligible because it is also a synthesis. Explanation may be called "recollection" in the Platonic sense because it is the process of retracing, by the method of counting and measuring, the joints of an internally articulated unity, one prefigured within the initial formulation of the entire analytical exercise. In slightly more prosaic terms, analysis is never merely the application of rules. It is also at once a seeing of which rules to apply and how to apply them. This is what it means to say that analysis is also synthesis. And this is why it is false to say, as is at least implied by so much contemporary analytical philosophy, that we begin with intuitions and then replace them with ever more sophisticated analyses. Not only is it false to say this, but strictly speaking, it is meaningless. If "to mean" is "to provide an analysis," there is no analysis of analysis without ingredient intuition.

9

Without intuition, there is at each stage nothing to analyze. Intuition (of syntheses or unities) without analysis is mute, but analysis without intuition is inarticulate as well as blind: the sounds it utters cannot be distinguished from noise.

The second objection raised against doctrines of intuition follows directly from the preceding argument. To explain is to analyze or to articulate a structure. We grant that intuition is a regular element or dimension of explanation, since it is by intuition that we perceive the unity and appropriateness of the analysis. Let us then agree to refer to intuition as "the context of analysis." But there is no segment of the articulated structure that belongs to intuition as distinct or detachable from analysis. If a theory is understood in the contemporary sense as a *model* or a (semantical) interpretation of a formal structure, then it seems that there can be no theory of intuition. Intuition is an activity, not a set of rules for the exercise of an activity.[4] It is a "looking into" rather than an objective structure into which we look. We might conceivably be able to define a set of rules for looking "at" something, but there is no way to define the procedure for looking "into," because "into" implies a distinction between the exterior and interior of what we are looking at, hence between appearance and reality or accident and essence. Consequently, what we see when we look "into" is itself the basis for the construction of rules for looking "at." We can of course begin in any given case from conventional definitions of *at*-ness, polished to a specious gloss of precision by the languages of logic and set theory. However, the primitive concept of set theory, the epsilon-relation of "belonging to," is itself intelligible only on the basis of "looking into." We cannot look "at" the predicates of a set unless we know that they belong to the set, and we cannot know what it means to "belong to" by a definition.[5] On the contrary, we know what the definition means on the basis of our intuitive knowledge of the meaning of "belonging to." The same point is obviously true of predication as well. To say that something belongs to something is to say something about something. But to say something about something is to say that something belongs to something.

If theory then is the analysis of structure, there can be no theory of intuition. But if the identification of structure and the recognition of an appropriate analysis depend upon intuition, then there can be no theory of analysis. The objection that no structure corresponds to intuition, when taken seriously, leads to a modification of our conception of theory, not to the abandonment of intuition. As I shall argue in section 3, if theory is conceptual analysis, then a theory of analysis is a concept of *concept*, and it can be shown on analytical grounds (although it should perhaps be intuitively obvious) that such a concept is impossible without recourse to intuition. There are at least two ways in which to extend one's sense of theory in order to accommodate intuition. The first and in itself less satisfactory way is to provide a phenomenological description of the circumstances attendant upon the activity of intuition. While such a description proves nothing, it assumes that the circumstances being described are those of the intuitive act. The description must therefore be supplemented by the second method, which we may as well call recourse to "transcendental argument" or a demonstration that intuition is a necessary condition for the possibility of theoretical analysis. My reply to the first objection is in this sense a transcendental argument. It should be emphasized that the use of such arguments is indeed an extension of the usual analytical conception of theory, and not a procedure by which pre-theoretical intuitions are replaced by analyses.

It is not by chance that transcendental arguments are traditionally associated with the doctrine of self-consciousness. The absence of structure in the intellect is a necessary condition of its capacity to "look into" as well as "at" itself. This capacity of consciousness to look into itself is inseparably connected to its capacity to look into a formal structure, or to see the distinction between the essential and the accidental, the appropriate and the inappropriate. In terms that I shall try to make persuasive as this study unfolds, intelligence, and hence intelligibility, are functions of the detachment of structure from intellect. In decisive cases, "seeing" is seeing *nothing*, if "to be" is to be this or that form. Self-consciousness is one such case. The link between thought and its object, precisely as non-formal or lacking in structure, supervenes over, and is the condition for, the distinction between the individual analyzing intelligence and the content of the analysis. If the intellect were the same as the form it analyzes, it would not be intellect. If it were totally distinct from that form, there could be no intelligence of the form. Consequently the intellect must be both the same as and other than the object of cognition—a doctrine as old as Aristotle, although its fullest statement in modern times was formulated by Hegel. I mention Aristotle in order to make clear that the doctrine is intrinsic to the analytical tradition. But tradition to one side, the "look" of a form is meaningless except to the looker. A sign does not mean anything except to an intelligent being. If considerations of the well-formedness or internal structure of a sign could be totally sundered from the question of what it means to be intelligible, then semantics, however rigorous its mathematical format, would *have no meaning*. The distinction between sense and nonsense, and even the force of logical principles like that of non-contradiction, does not reside within linguistic axioms and symbols but in the intelligence that poses the axioms as "worthy of being believed" (the literal sense of the term). The intrinsic absurdity of attempts to show that the mind is a machine is that such a performance would have neither actors nor an audience.

There is no analysis, as distinct from a phenomenological description, of the

11

process by which we show something to someone. Yet it scarcely follows from this that demonstrations are conducted by no one for no one. The interpretation of a demonstration as both valid in accordance with appropriate rules and pertinent to the intention of the analyst is part of the meaning of any conceptual analysis. An adequate doctrine of meaning, or of formal analysis, must therefore account for the visibility of the form as looking to the theoretician as looker. And in fact this is exactly what a theory of meaning purports to do. The analytical techniques and formal structures it manipulates are not the theory of meaning, but the road leading to our recognition of what it means to "mean." To say that intuition has no structure of its own is to recognize the necessary condition for intelligence. A structure is visible, not to another structure, but to the intellectual capacity to perceive structure. So the second difficulty is transformed into an imperative addressed to analytical philosophers: become self-conscious. I am aware that they will take this imperative as a temptation to psychologistic corruption. In fact, the view which I am here defending would be rejected by one currently fashionable branch of analytical philosophy as a compounding of Frege's "original *Sinn.*" Let me make one or two remarks on this topic.

I am taking as characteristic of contemporary analytical philosophy the central emphasis upon semantics. However, I am in the process of arguing that Frege's distinction between sense and reference. paradigmatic in the subsequent discussion, involves us in the problem of understanding and cognition. A concept is a grasped sense, and there can be no concepts without conceivers. As I contend, the sense of "concept" is not intelligible apart from recognition of the contribution made to that sense by our cognitive processes. The critical reader might object that I have been seduced by Michael Dummett's interpretation of Frege, or one like it, and that the problems I raise concerning the relation between intuition and sense are all avoided by shifting to the translational doctrine of meaning associated with Quine and Donald Davidson. According to this objection, the concept of sense is indeed obscure; it muddies the clear water of formalism with mentalistic considerations, and it introduces superfluous theoretical entities called "meanings." The most influential attempt to avoid these ostensibly undesirable consequences stems from Quine's behavioristic interpretation of the context of analysis. It is this interpretation that has given rise to Davidson's attempt to construct a theory of truth for natural languages based upon the mathematical theory of Tarski.[6]

For present purposes, we can extrapolate the crux of Davidson's proposals to be that the meaning of a sentence in a natural language is given by its truth-conditions, or extensionally, rather than intensionally or by way of semantic entities independent of the recursively definable syntactic structure of the sentence. One may call this doctrine "behavioristic" (Davidson uses the term "empirical") since the task of establishing a sentence as true turns upon the observation of those circumstances in which native speakers assert a given sentence. The determination of these circumstances, or truth-conditions, enables us to "translate" the sentence from the object-language into its meta-linguistic equivalent (which may be the same sentence if the meta-language and the object-language are the same natural language). In slightly different terms, from the axioms and inference rules of our theory, we must be able to deduce a proof for a T-sentence that asserts that the sentence s in the object language is true if and only if p, where p is a sentence in the meta-language expressing the fact or event that is (presumably) asserted in the object-language by s. We thus start from certain assumptions about human behavior, e.g., the so-called "principle of charity" which holds that human beings normally speak the truth, i.e., what they suppose to be the truth. Hence, the principle contends that the beliefs of humans are very much the same, regardless of what language they speak, and therefore experience is both uniform and uniformly accessible. I note that this is an assumption, not just about nature, but also about mental experience. In any case, given the reliability of this principle, we then observe the behavior of persons as they speak a given sentence, or the circumstances under which the sentence is asserted, as well as the behavior of the speakers, and we assume that this is co-ordinate with their intention to assert a true sentence. Having thus obtained our truth-conditions, we proceed to apply our logical calculus to the sentence in question.

In short, Davidson takes for granted that our goal is to construct a theory, in the current logical or meta-mathematical sense of the term, that permits us, on the basis of publicly verifiable observations of linguistic behavior—yet buttressed by (what I call) "mentalistic assumptions" about linguistic experience and behavior—to deduce the precise circumstances under which the predicate "true" may be applied to any sentence formulable in a natural language. Some readers may wonder whether my critical analysis of the link between sense and cognition, and more specifically, intuition, might be rendered superfluous by adopting the Davidsonian program. At the risk of considerable oversimplification, but in order to point the way for what follows, let me say that I remain, on the point at issue, an orthodox Fregean. Or at least, I accept Dummett's interpretation of the issue as more accurate, and hence more fruitful, than Davidson's. To begin with the most general consideration, I deny that philosophy ought to pattern itself upon that reconstruction of science that one may perhaps still call "positivist." Science, we may agree, is the rational pursuit of truth, and a scientific explanation of meaning certainly involves logic and mathematics. The Davidsonian program begins with the assumption that such an explanation turns upon the application of logic to semantics. I, on the other hand, begin from the assumption that we must first apply semantics to logic. In

13

other words, we begin with a philosophical analysis of meaning and do not trim our analysis to fit the clothing of a given conception of logic and methodology.

This comment, as it stands, is much too general, but I hope to fill in the details as the argument unfolds. It is not hard to state the point at issue. Davidsonians beg the question of the nature of explanation, and so of theory. They assume that the context of analysis is either self-evident or given by analytical procedures themselves. Since there are conflicting analytical procedures (e.g., varying kinds of logic), this assumption is inadequate on technical grounds alone. Nevertheless, the same sort of objection might be made against the camp opposed by Davidsonians, which I shall call for convenience the Dummettians. However, the Dummettian program is, as I have already said, superior to the Davidsonian program because it explicitly recognizes the link between meaning and understanding. In addition to this, Dummettians have made cogent criticisms of the technical aspects of the Davidsonian program and with procedures like that of invoking the principle of charity. The problem is not simply in attempting to apply this principle in any given case. Any attempt to apply this principle amounts to building one's syntactic theory of truth upon psychologistic or mentalistic grounds. It is not simply the case that a speaker may be exercising irony, or engaging in outright deception, or involved in a ritual the sense of which entirely eludes us. The application of the principle of charity is based upon our own beliefs, and consequently our understanding of what it means to speak under such-and-such circumstances, or for that matter, to speak at all. The extraction of T-sentences is a meaningful process only by grace of our access to meanings, as for example those embodied in the concept of a deductive theory.

I am aware that Davidsonians are in general not so much anti-mentalist as they are anti-realist. But their fear of meaning-entities leads them to overlook the link between truth-conditions and meanings. Whether or not meanings are ontologically independent entities, a theory of meaning that makes no use of meanings is meaningless. The problem may be stated in two closely connected ways. Even if we knew the truth-conditions of every sentence in the English language, we would still need to know what any given sentence *means* in order to know what is being said to us, and hence to know whether the speakers are practicing irony, speaking incorrectly, and so on. This point becomes all the more important in the case of alien languages or radical translation. The other half of this objection begins with the fact that while we know the meanings of many sentences, there is frequently no way in principle that we can come to know the truth-conditions for these sentences. This point is made, for example, by Crispin Wright, who also notes that a theory of truth does not just characterize the semantic type of primitive terms in the object-language, but also contains base-clauses expressing what someone *knows* when he understands the predicate in question.[7]

These objections, general as well as specific, explicitly state or imply the admission that analysis is a cognitive process. The capacities noted and relied upon by Davidsonians—to speak and understand a language, to detect logical and syntactical structures, to apply the principle of charity without naivete, to know that people are talking and not just making noise—involve thinking and understanding in the heart of a theory of meaning. Truth-conditions can be extracted from this complex web, but they retain their meaning only within the format of a theory that is itself only informally intelligible. The context of analysis defines (and not recursively) the nature of analytical procedures. Model theory and recursive-function theory are theories, or have meanings, in senses that are neither model-theoretic nor recursively definable. To conclude this line of argument: a theory of truth that turns upon truth-conditions is unilluminating in the case of natural languages for two main reasons. (1) The concept of truth cannot be adequately captured in a theory of truth-functions; the term "truth" has too many senses (some of them incompatible) to be formalized, even though formalization of some senses is legitimate in mathematical analysis. (2) In many, perhaps in most, cases, we cannot know the truth-conditions of a sentence even though we know its meaning. Beyond this, emphasis upon truth as a property of sentences itself restricts our attention to one of many senses of "truth." This is bad, not because it is never wise to try to solve complex problems one step at a time, but because the step taken by Davidson is neither the first nor can it bear the normative weight that Davidson places upon it. In recognizing competent speakers, picking out structures, interpreting linguistic acts, wondering about the senses of "true," and looking for fruitful theories, including a theory about theory, we intuit and suppose, imagine and infer, guess and argue, or engage in a manifold and intrinsically ambiguous cognitive intercourse with the world. No good will come of beginning the attempt to understand this intercourse with the specious lucidity of a rigorously definable segment, if that lucidity is intended to illuminate the subsequent steps of our investigation.

In turning to the third possible objection against considering intuition within a philosophical analysis of semantics, it would appear that this difficulty has already been answered. Since philosophy is not simply equivalent to conceptual analysis, the ambiguity of the term "intuition" does not exclude it from playing a philosophical role. The Fregean doctrine of sharply defined concepts (those for which we can determine in each case whether or not an object falls under a given concept), while no doubt indispensable in mathematics, is itself too sharply defined to serve as the exclusive paradigm of philosophical reasoning.

Indeed, mathematics is not a sharply defined concept, as a glance at the literature of the philosophy of mathematics will show us. Nevertheless, I think it will be helpful to look more closely at difficulty (3). It will be useful to see at the outset that the manifold senses of "intuition" illustrate the impossibility of a univocal or sharp definition of "sense," rather than the philosophical inappropriateness of references to intuition. The crucial point is that what we often, and perhaps primarily, mean by "sense" is "intuition." No doubt the basic idea of "sense" is that of sense-perception. But the cognitive content of a perception is acquired directly, as if through the mere "presence" of the sensed object, and not by the mediation of discursive analysis. Of course, the epistemologist may claim that a categorial synthesis of sense-data is necessary for the perception of an object. Whether or not this is so, however, is irrelevant in the present context. The image of a perceived object is presented directly to consciousness, and not by an explicit application of discursive categories. It is no doubt right to say that sensation "makes sense" because we are beings who talk. But we do not reach the sense of our sense-perceptions by way of talk. On the contrary, talk begins with the perception. Furthermore, although we can describe our sensations in various ways, ranging from poetry to science, the senses of our verbal descriptions are not the same as the senses of our perceptions.

The Husserlian science of phenomenology is basically an extension of sense-perception. That is, it attempts to describe, and so to make sense out of, the content of each state of consciousness as "intended" by the conscious agent. In non-technical language, we perceive the contents of consciousness as given to analysis, in much the same way that we perceive sensuous objects. The sense of the "givenness" of the content of consciousness, however, varies with the objects themselves. For example, a table in my study is not "given" in the same sense as a logical category, although I am able to capture the sense of each form of givenness discursively. What one may call the *homogeneity* of scientific discourse about senses does not obliterate, but is abstracted from, the *heterogeneity* of senses themselves. The fundamental difficulty faced by phenomenology is in my view precisely the impossibility of bridging the gap between sense *qua* intuition and the discursive activity of "making sense." In a way phenomenology is superior to what is usually called "analytical philosophy" because it begins with an explicit recognition of intuition as the basic mode of presentation of objects of discourse. Nevertheless, it shares the inclination of analytical philosophy to assimilate intuition into conceptual discourse.[8] In yielding to this inclination, it tends to blunt the differences, not expressible within the homogeneous categories of scientific description, of the very senses whose distinctness it elicits.

Our "sense that . . ." is as heterogeneous as "our intuition that . . ." because to a considerable extent the two terms are synonymous, and when they are not synonymous, they run in parallel paths. More specifically: either a sense is an intuition, or else the sense (say of a scientific analysis) is accessible to the intelligence via intuition. For example, something could "make sense" in a way analogous to sense-perception, without being reducible either to sense-perception or a discursive explanation of a scientific kind. I may have a sense that someone is lying. This sense has a cognitive content; it is not simply a feeling (like that of heat or pain) or a type of perception of a physical object. I may of course see a blush on the speaker's cheek or sweat on his brow. But these perceptions might mean that he has a fever, or that the temperature has affected him adversely, or that he is nervous for some reason having nothing to do with what he is now saying to me. Corresponding to my impression, which is neither a knowing how to do something (I may not know how to respond to the sense that the speaker is lying) nor a sensuous perception, but is rather a *psychic act* on my part, there is something understood, whether or not intended by the speaker, who presumably does not wish to signal to me that he is lying. What I understand is as distinct from my act of understanding as is the sense of the proposition "$2 + 2 = 4$" from the psychological circumstances of my conceiving it. To a certain extent it is an inference from an indeterminate concatenation of psychic acts, only some of which are identifiably linguistic. And to these acts there corresponds an indeterminate concatenation of senses or meanings.

I may infer from the look in a man's eyes that he is lying, and I can then state that I base my inference on that look. But the sense of the look is not the same as the sense of the statement. There is no determinate linguistic expression that captures the truth of my inference. To this extent I believe I am in agreement with the later Wittgenstein and his followers. There is no linguistic rule defining an effective procedure for determining the truth or falsity of the statement that looks of this particular kind show a man to be lying. But I hold that such a statement is rooted in a look or intuition of a *theoretical* nature in the literal sense of the term. I look at the look in the man's eyes, and thereby I *look into* the man. I understand something about him. The result is not practical knowledge (although I may put it to practical use), nor is it the result of repeated practice. It should not be forgotten that repeated practice must itself originate in a recognition of a definite kind; for example, in recognition of the fact that looks of a given sort are a sign that lying is taking place. I am quite sure that there is no definite or canonical linguistic account of looks of this sort. But it does not follow that my inference is subjective or idiosyncratic. The statement "the look in his eyes showed him to be lying" is intelligible to every normally experienced English speaker. (The phrase "normally experienced" is exactly as ambiguous as "normal speaker," the basis of so much contemporary "scientific" linguistic theory.) Furthermore, it is not uncommon for several

17

persons to observe the same look and to infer from it, quite independently of each other, that the speaker who looks that way is lying.

Examples of this sort are easily available to every reader. However, the analytically oriented reader may object that senses of this sort do not fall within the concerns of philosophy. He may grant a plurality of meanings to the term *sense*, just as he grants the initial role played by intuition, and hold that the plurality must be reduced to unity, just as intuition must be replaced by analysis. My reply is quite simple. I have already claimed that it is impossible to replace intuition by analysis. And I now add that a philosophical doctrine of sense must cover *all* applications of the term, not just those that are linguistically definite. "Sense" is not a sharp concept, and neither is "reference." If by "theory" is meant a definite and rigorous conceptual construction, then there can be no theory of sense or of reference. There is no rule by which to define what I mean when I sense that a man is lying, and yet what I mean by that sense is as much a part of the philosopher's concern as the sense of "the present King of France" or "transfinite recursion." In order to make sense, I must *have* sense, and there are no rules for this. I have been arguing this point in the form of a defense of intuition, but it needs to be emphasized that the term "intuition" itself has many senses. My argument cannot thus be intended as a "theory" of intuition in the constructive sense of the term. On the contrary, I am claiming that theory construction is possible only on the basis of intuition, and further, that analytical thinking is saturated with intuition at each step. A complete and exact science of semantics would then be a "looking" as well as a "talking." We can of course talk about what we have seen, but there is no argument in heaven or on earth that will take us across the gap from seeing to talking.

Frege and Psychologism

In considering the final difficulty, or the objection that an appeal to intuition is an instance of psychologism, I am aware that the issue of psychologism has surfaced at a number of points in my discussion of the three previous difficulties. I have nevertheless been persuaded that it was worth taking the difficulties in order. If some repetition seems unavoidable, it may be justified by the fact that my views run counter to those which currently dominate. Perhaps what I have to say will gain something in clarity from being stated in a variety of contexts. In this subsection, the theme of psychologism will be discussed primarily in terms of the views of Gottlob Frege.

In order to appreciate Frege's attack on psychologism, it is important to bear in mind the following historical situation. There are two main positions one may take with respect to the relation between the intellect and the beings, entities, or objects of cognition. The first is that the intellect grasps these objects as they are or show themselves, and is thus passive or receptive. The second is that the intellect contributes to the way in which objects show themselves, or in fact constructs them by imposing a definite structure onto them. The first position is usually called "Platonism." We may designate the second position as "Kantianism." On the point in question, as in so many other cases, contemporary analytical philosophy vacillates between Platonism and Kantianism. As I am about to show, this vacillation is also to be found in Frege.

One cannot make sense of Platonism or Kantianism without giving an elaborate account of the function of the intellect. This account will of course differ sharply in the two cases. In the first case, we require a description of the intuition of formal structure, whereas in the second, we need what Kant called an account of the *transcendental ego*, that is, of the principles of subjective activity or construction which are invariant from one individual intellect to the next. In both cases, then, we must present an account of the subject as well as of the object (or of the thinker as well as of the content of thought). And in neither case is an account of the object a satisfactory substitute for an account of the subject. Stated differently, we cannot give an objective or reifying account of the intellect or subjectivity. An attack on psychologism is one thing; a failure to explain the intelligibility of the object to the subject is something else.

A sense is a sense *to* an understanding. This is the condition for our ability to distinguish between the meaning of a concept or the truth of a proposition and the circumstances under which we as individuals come to understand the concept or the proposition. In making this distinction, I do not banish the sense of the concept or proposition from my intellect. Suppose that the capacity of many individuals to understand the same sense, and to demonstrate this understanding by publicly verifiable criteria, establishes the independence of the sense from the set of empirical phenomena constituting this or that individual's personal, historical consciousness. In this case, what has been refuted is *phenomenalism*. What still needs to be explained is how different individuals come to understand the same sense. Is it because of a Platonistic formal intuition or because of a Kantian transcendental synthesis common to all individuals having a discursive intellect of the human type? The ambiguous vacillation between Platonism and Kantianism in the senses just noted is a striking characteristic of the writings of Gottlob Frege. Frege takes "intuition" now as sensuous, now as conceptual. His critique of Kant is frequently a critique of phenomenalism, not of Idealism. His Platonism requires a doctrine of intuition quite different from the one he attributes to Kant, and indeed from the one actually held by Kant. We find no systematic defense of the requisite intuition, but only remarks pointing in its direction, with no explanation of how they relate to the rejection of intuition in his critique of Kant. To add to the confusion, Frege occasionally speaks as though he were himself a Kantian, and it has been argued, with considerable detail, that Frege "associated himself with a Kantian variety of Idealism."[9]

It is not part of my program to engage in a detailed study of Frege's critique of psychologism.[10] Nevertheless, in view of Frege's pre-eminent position in contemporary analytical philosophy, I want to consider briefly the main aspects of his approach to the problem. I agree on the whole that Frege never formulated a general theory of meaning. However, it is not always clear that Frege thought of himself as primarily a Kantian. Consequently, I do not find it fruitful to argue over whether Frege was a Realist or an Idealist, since the question, so phrased, implies that he was one or the other, and thus, a systematic philosopher in the sense that Sluga has rightly denied. It is highly likely that Frege was deeply influenced by the Neo-Kantian atmosphere of his time. One might perhaps also claim that Frege's "Platonism" is in fact a defense of objective truth in a sense reconcilable with Kantian Idealism. I myself find no such reconciliation in Frege's writings, nor indeed, any sign that Frege was aware of the deeper problem in the conflict between Plato and Kant. Before turning to passages illustrating the vacillation in Frege's philosophical convictions, I want to state very generally the central difficulty in his thought. Platonism rests not merely upon a doctrine of eternal objects, whether these are called Ideas, Thoughts, or Meanings, but also upon the direct intelligibility of these objects. We do not arrive at eternal objects which are independent of the discursive intellect by the process of constructing propositions in our finite, empirical consciousness. Conceptual construction is rather grounded in an intellectual intuition of eternal objects. In other words, one cannot be both a Platonist and a Kantian, because Platonic Ideas are not constituted by the transcendental ego. Although there are central passages in Frege which are normally taken as evidence of his Platonism, these passages do not contain any explicit, developed doctrine of pure intellectual intuition. They are in fact complemented by passages in which such an intuition is rendered impossible. This impossibility is loosely connected to the Kantian stratum in Frege's thought. But Kantianism is itself rooted in a doctrine of transcendental subjectivity. If Frege is a Kantian, then his eternal objects or "thoughts" must have been synthesized by the transcendental ego. And there is no doctrine of a transcendental ego in Frege.[11] Perhaps the clearest aspect of Frege's philosophical views is his rejection of phenomenalism. It may be that Frege sometimes confused phenomenalism and Idealism; certainly one finds striking examples of this confusion in present-day Fregeans. But this confusion apart, Frege's attack on phenomenalism gives us direct entry into his repudiation of psychologism.

In his introduction to *The Foundations of Arithmetic*, Frege exhorts us as follows:

Never let us take a description of the origin of an idea for a definition or an account of the mental and physical conditions on which we become conscious of a proposition for a proof of it. A proposition may be thought, and again it may be true; let us never confuse these two things. We must remind ourselves, it seems, that a proposition no more ceases to be true when I cease to think of it than the sun ceases to exist when I shut my eyes. [FA, xviii]

As the preface to a refutation of phenomenalism, this is well-expressed. The Idealist, however, would reply that the conditions of our consciousness of a proposition are distinct from the conditions of its intelligibility, and that these latter conditions depend upon the nature of pure thought and its categorial structure. The perception of the sun depends upon human physiology, whereas the continuous possibility of our perceiving it depends upon the unity of thought and perception.

A few paragraphs later, Frege says:

The historical approach, with its aim of detecting how things begin and of arriving from these origins at a knowledge of their nature, is certainly perfectly legitimate; but it has also its limitations. If everything were in continual flux, and nothing maintained itself fixed for all time, there would no longer be any possibility of getting to know anything about the world and everything would be plunged in confusion. We suppose, it would seem, that concepts sprout in the individual mind like leaves on a tree, and we think to discover their nature by studying their birth: we seek to define them psychologically, in terms of the nature of the human mind. But this account makes everything subjective, and if we follow it through to the end, does away with truth. What is known as the history of concepts is really a history either of our knowledge of concepts or of the meaning of words. [FA, xviiif]

Those who regard Frege as a Realist seem to have taken passages like these as attacks on Idealism. In fact, there is nothing in either passage that is incompatible with Realism or Platonism on the one hand and Idealism on the other. The problem is that these passages contain nothing that would enable us to decide upon the quarrel between Platonism and Idealism. For example, the Kantian would certainly agree that concepts do not "sprout in the individual mind like leaves on a tree." Since concepts are constituted by the transcendental ego, which in itself is not a human mind, Kant would distinguish between his doctrine and psychology. The most one could perhaps say is that Frege tends to distinguish semantics from epistemology, and that he is in this sense implicitly criticizing Kant.[12] However, this line of interpretation is not entirely compatible with the Fregean texts, and it is unsatisfactory in itself since it leaves unanswered the question of the intelligibility of a concept. This question may be approached by considering Frege's treatment of intuition, and thus his distinction between intuitive self-evidence and intelligibility via the application of a logical rule. I shall begin with this question rather than with that of Frege's critique of Kantian epistemology. It may be that clarification of the first will resolve the second.

There are two main senses in which we may be said to "intuit." The first sense of intuition refers to sensuous objects. This is the sense in which the term is normally used both by Kant and by Frege. The second sense of the term is exemplified in different but related ways by Plato and Husserl. In the Platonic dialogues there is reference to the intuition of pure forms or Ideas; in Husserl's *Logical Investigations* we find a doctrine of "categorial intuition" or the nonperceptual acts by which perceptions are constituted as objective unities, and by which these objective unities are bound together into logical relations.[13] For the purposes of the present discussion we can summarize this second sense of intuition as *conceptual* intuition. Frege regularly denies that we possess conceptual intuition, thereby signifying at least partial agreement with Kant but a rather decisive disagreement with Plato. Nevertheless, Frege disagrees with Kant on an equally decisive point. He distinguishes between the natures of arithmetic and geometry, allowing the role assigned by Kant to intuition in the latter, but excluding it from the former. According to Frege, intuition is (as Kant held) sensuous and presents us with a spatio-temporal object of experience. This causes no problem in the case of geometry since geometry is governed by special axioms. The axioms of arithmetic, on the other hand, are entirely general. In other words, we can count anything at all, including concepts. More comprehensively, arithmetic provides us with knowledge of non-sensuous and unintuitable objects, such as the number zero.

If intuition is sensuous, and allowing for conceptual knowledge of non-sensuous objects (such as concepts themselves), how are we presented with these objects? We do not "create" them as individual thinkers, and there is no reference to anything like a transcendental subjectivity in Frege. But if there is also no conceptual intuition, there seems to be no way left in which to apprehend these concepts. Frege provides two incompletely developed ways to refer to this apprehension, or rather, he alludes to two related procedures: definition and discovery. Since definition is not creation, and discovery is not intuition, it seems that Frege must defend the thesis that we understand concepts entirely by logical analysis or the application of rules. One could then say that we discover by means of definitions based upon the application of logical or analytically formulated rules. But this line of interpretation is contradicted by Frege himself.

As we read Frege's statements on the basic notions of his entire doctrine, we should take note of the tentative language in which he expresses himself, as opposed to the ostensibly rigorous mathematicism of some of his contemporary followers. According to Frege, "Concept and relation are the foundation stones upon which I erect my structure."[14] These are, however, logically simple or primitive, not amenable to definition.

> Kerry contests what he calls my definition of 'concept.' I would remark, in the first place, that my explanation is not meant as a proper definition. One cannot require that everything shall be defined, any more than one can require that a chemist shall decompose every substance. What is simple cannot be decomposed, and what is logically simple cannot have a proper definition. . . . On the introduction of a name for something logically simple, a definition is not possible; there is nothing for it but to lead the reader or hearer, by means of hints, to understand the words as is intended. [P. 42f]

What does Frege mean by "hints"? This is not a casually chosen expression, as it occurs again in the *Grundgesetze*. Although Frege claims that his ideography (*Begriffsschrift*) will make rigorously clear what he means by a proof, the same cannot be said of what he means by "concept" and "relation."

> The following remark may be made before we proceed. It is not possible to give a regular definition of everything; for it must be our endeavor to go back to what is logically simple and as such cannot properly be defined. I must then be satisfied with indicating by hints what I mean. [P. 151]

I have already asserted, and will later develop in some detail, that there can be no concept of "concept," if only because of the connection between predication and "belonging to," with the attendant impossibility of giving a noncircular definition of these terms. Frege does not put the point in this way, but what he says is entirely compatible with my own thought. My analysis, however, is not compatible with Frege's conception of conceptual intuition.

The same difficulty can be stated from a slightly different perspective. We begin again from the fact that Frege explicitly treats intuition as sensuous and empirical.[15] In this sense the content of an intuition is on a par with that of an "idea" or modification of some individual's discursive understanding; both are to be sharply distinguished from eternal truths or what Frege called subsequently "thoughts."[16] It is a striking feature of Frege's exposition of thoughts that he never adequately explains how we think them. He says that "to the grasping of thoughts there must correspond a special mental capacity, the power of thinking."[17] And he frequently says that thoughts are determinations or the contents of judgments, whether affirmative or negative.[18] The reader might be tempted to take "thoughts" as Frege's version of Platonic Ideas. In this case, already noted, one would have to attribute to Frege an unstated doctrine of conceptual intuition of entities independent of the intellect. However, Frege notes that "it would only be possible to compare an idea with a thing if the thing were an idea too." He then goes on to say: "Without offering this as a definition, I mean by 'a thought' something for which the question of truth can arise at all. . . . So I can say: thoughts are senses of sentences." And in a footnote, he adds: "In fact I use the word 'thought' more or less in the sense 'judgement' has in the writings of logicians."[19] We note that neither "truth" nor "thought" can be defined, and this again would suggest that thinking is at least more like intuiting than applying rules, with respect to its basic concepts. However, Frege's entire discussion leaves unanswered the question of whether the sense of a sentence is constituted by "a special mental capacity" or discovered by it.

This problem is perhaps especially evident with respect to the status of truths about non-sensuous objects or about other concepts. It is also manifested in the case of truths about sensuous objects. Consider this passage from "Thoughts."

> A thought is something imperceptible: anything the senses can perceive is excluded from the realm of things for which the question of truth arises. Truth is not a quality that answers to a particular kind of sense-impressions. . . . But do we not see that the sun has risen? and do we not then also see that this is true? That the sun has risen is not an object emitting rays that reach my eyes; it is not a visible thing like the sun itself. That the sun has risen is recognized to be true on the basis of sense-impressions. But being true is not a sensible, perceptible, property. [P. 5]

Again, this passage is compatible with both Platonism and Kantianism. But this is to say that Frege does not explain the distinction between perceiving the sun to have risen and thinking *that* the sun has risen. He says: "We cannot recognize a property of a thing without at the same time finding the thought *this thing has this property* to be true. So with every property of a thing there is tied up a property of a thought, namely truth" ("Thoughts," 5). But he does not tell us *how* we "find" the thought, or by what agency a property of a thought is "tied up" to a property of a thing. Is not the difference between a thought and a sense-perception the same as that between an eternal and a psychological entity? How is this difference bridged? The issue cannot be evaded by drawing a specious distinction between semantics and epistemology. Especially if Frege is supposed to be an ontologist, we have to know the nature of the "beings" which he calls *thoughts*. It is not enough to be told that they are eternal, independent of subjective and psychological factors, and so on. The same can be said of Platonic Ideas and Kantian concepts and judgments. The ontological doctrine is meaningless, a mere poem, unless we are told how these beings are known to possess the nature attributed to them.

To summarize, "truth," "concept," and "thought" are indefinable, and so not "sharp" concepts in the sense required for the application of the rigorous analytical method of Frege's *Begriffsschrift*. Because they are inaccessible to intuition, Frege cannot adequately explain how a rigorous method can begin from ambiguously selected notions. What objective evidence, other than the historical, empirical, or psychological fact that most individuals seem to understand these terms (and that many can be persuaded to use them in the Fregean manner) can Frege offer in defense of his starting point? If he begins from the assurance that the laws of logic and mathematics are eternal and objective, then he is availing himself of intuition, and of a sort for which he has no account.[20] Strictly speaking, Frege has not even refuted psychologism, in the weak sense approximately equivalent to phenomenalism. But he has said enough to make phenomenalism implausible. On the other hand, he has said nothing to refute Idealism, and nothing to justify his reference to thoughts in either a Platonist or Kantian sense. He expresses clearly his conviction that what is purely intuitive cannot be communicated, and so that even the intuitions of space which underlie geometry have an objective content capable of expression in laws, hence verbally.[21] On the other hand, he does not even claim to have "made the analytic character of arithmetical propositions more than probable, because it can still always be doubted whether they are deducible solely from purely logical laws, or whether some other type of premiss is not involved at some point in their proof without our noticing it" (FA, 102). As the context of this passage shows, Frege realizes that he has not entirely demonstrated the possibility of replacing the "self-evidence" of intuition by steps in a proof conforming to rules "which are laid down once and for all" (FA, 103). Nevertheless, this is his explicit intention.

Since, then, there is no conceptual intuition, we cannot be said to "discover" thoughts or eternal senses in that manner. At the same time, we do not "create" them by definition. Definition "is, it seems, often credited with a creative power, but really all there is to definition is that something is brought out, precisely limited, and given a name."[22] What does Frege mean by "is brought out"? So far as I can see, this expression is no more explained than is "a special mental capacity, the power of thinking" in the passage scrutinized above ("Thoughts," 3ff). Frege offers a metaphor by way of explanation: geographers do not create seas by drawing border lines on a map. Unfortunately this metaphor overlooks the fact that maps are already images or conceptualizations of the earth, constructed in accordance with human intentions and perceptions. Needless to say, neither a Platonist nor a Kantian would claim that man creates the seas. But the significance or *sense* of the seas may be man-made: this is the central question of both ontology and semantics, and Frege leaves it unanswered if not entirely unasked.

Since "concept" cannot be defined, whereas individual concepts can be analyzed, there must be an essential unity (or synthesis) to the structure of the concept which is pre-analytically accessible. I myself can find no other term to explain the mode of accessibility better than that of "intuited," in a sense very close to, if not identical with, the sense of Husserl's categorial intuition. Contrary to Frege, I believe that we intuit the unity of a concept as the precondition for subsequent analysis. By extension, we intuit the sense (as distinguished from the reference) of a concept: the sense that, according to Frege, is neither "subjective like the idea, nor yet the object itself."[23] Instead of explaining directly how we grasp the sense, Frege offers this metaphor: "The optical image in the telescope is indeed one-sided and dependent upon the standpoint of observation; but it is still objective, inasmuch as it can be used by several observers."[24] It scarcely needs to be stressed that the telescope is a human artifact, and so already embodies the principles of optics.

I am not, of course, trying to build a case on Frege's innocent use of metaphors. They serve only to embellish the picture that emerges from the many passages cited from Frege's writings. Frege is neither a Kantian nor a Platonist, but the balance of evidence suggests that he tends to formulate his views within a Kantian framework. In my commentary on the passages from Frege, I have tried to bring out the fact that Frege is forced, despite his intentions, toward a doctrine of conceptual intuition. Without such intuition, his doctrine makes no coherent sense, however brilliant and suggestive its parts may be. *We cannot create senses by definitions*, and we do not arrive at our definitions by analysis. On the contrary, we begin with our definitions. But the process of analysis of definitions does not itself "produce" the conclusion of analysis. "The truth is that they are contained in the definitions, but as plants are contained in their seeds, not as beams are contained in a house" (FA, 101). We then require precisely formulated rules that will take us in a progressive manner from the definitions to the conclusion.

Frege has already granted that there are no rules for obtaining definitions. To this I add that there are no rules for obtaining rules, or for seeing which rule to apply next, or that a given step in an analytical deduction is actually the *conclusion* to the procedure in which we are engaged. To state my conclusion in a way that includes, but goes beyond, this brief inspection of Frege: It is true that intuition is a cognitive faculty. *But so too is analysis*. It is an open question whether the structures elicited by analysis are eternal beings, altogether independent from the operations of the human intellect. But if they are, some explanation must be given of how these beings are apprehended.[25] We no more commit ourselves to psychologism by invoking intuition than we do by invoking analysis. And since the concept of analysis makes no sense except through the assistance of intuition—or differently stated, since eternal entities, thoughts, senses, or truths make no sense except as thinkable—the war against psychologism has to be fought at a much deeper level than in the superficial distinction between semantics and epistemology.

2. Structure

Structure and Form

One of the underlying themes of this book should be clear by now: analysis is a cognitive activity and it cannot be coherently understood except by recourse to intuition. There is a non-discursive *context of analysis*. Philosophers who demonstrate paradoxes or contradictions intrinsic to the notion of intuited senses are in fact demonstrating deficiencies in their own *concepts* of intuited senses. But concepts are discursive constructs based upon intuitions; they are not themselves intuitions. However, it does not follow from this that nothing can be said of intuition, or that what can be said must be formulated within a private language. There cannot possibly be a private language. The correct inference is that language cannot be contained within a "theory" in the contemporary analytical sense. There cannot be a complete mathematizing of language or of "sense," because mathematics studies formal structures, whereas there are fundamental senses of "sense" that do not correspond to formal structures. A detailed analysis of this last assertion now becomes necessary.

One of the more fashionable words of the last twenty years is *structure*. In attempting to understand the problems which it conceals, let us take our bearings by the following remark of Jean Piaget. Piaget lists two characteristics common to various versions of what he calls "structuralism" (a term that is employed in senses other than those considered by Piaget). These are

> on the one hand, an ideal or hopes of intrinsic intelligibility, based upon the postulate that a structure suffices to itself and does not require, in order to be grasped, recourse to all kinds of elements foreign to its nature; on the other hand, fulfillment, in the degree to which one has succeeded in reaching effectively certain structures, and where their utilisation makes evident some general and apparently necessary characters which those structures present despite their variety.[26]

Piaget further clarifies this general observation by specifying three moments of structure: totality, transformation, and self-regulation. Finally, he says, structures can be formalized.[27] In short, structures are combinations of forms, possessing a systematic character in that these combinations undergo transformations in accordance with rules exhibited by the structures themselves. The direct visibility of these rules is part of what Piaget means by "intrinsic intelligibility." Categorial or conceptual intuition is thus an essential ingredient of analytical structuralism. Those "friends of the forms" who are also friends of rules tend to disregard the impossibility of formulating a rule of self-reflection. In addition, "intrinsic intelligibility" is also connected to the ideal of formalization. Piaget speaks of "hope" but does not sufficiently reflect upon its significance. One can construct a system in which each new level arising from previous operations is amenable to formalization. But neither the fundamental intuitions by which we construct the system nor the totality of its results is actually capable of formalization. The eschatological nature of mathematics is veiled by the fruitfulness of the intermediate condition, a situation not dissimilar to that described by theology (a rather more self-conscious discipline than the philosophy of mathematics). No structures correspond to the cognitive activity of hope; yet Heraclitus is right to counsel us that without hope, we shall not find the "unhoped-for."

I begin with Piaget's statement because it corresponds very closely to the aspirations common to members of the formalist wing of contemporary analytical philosophy. The statement thus effectively introduces us to the notion of structure within its not always observed context of hope. The task lies in showing that the analysis of structure leads us inexorably to the context of hope. A structure, then, is a combination of forms.[28] It would therefore seem that an analysis of structure presupposes an analysis of form. But it is obvious that, on the contrary, the analysis of form makes use of the concept of structure. A form is a shape or pattern, literally the *look* of a thing, that is shared by a number of things and that therefore permits us to "divide and collect" (order and measure), i.e., to separate out the things of a given look and to gather them together into a single family or class that the look defines in the dual sense of distinguishing and uniting. We can see at once the nub of the matter. If form is the element of structure, then form cannot in turn have structure, nor can it have a form other than itself.[29] The atoms of formalism must be seen or intuited (although our vision is inflected by hope). Two questions immediately arise with respect to forms or looks. First: are they the looks of things or the consequences of our looking at things? Second: how is one look distinguished from another? As we have seen, the first question is touched upon, but not satisfactorily answered, by criticisms of psychologism in the Fregean style. It concerns the link between senses and concepts as the building blocks of theory construction, or more generally, the link between knowing and making. In this section, I am primarily concerned with the second question.

We obviously distinguish, whether as discoverers or creators, between two looks or forms by virtue of their differences. But the difference between F_1 and F_2 (as we may label our two forms) must reside within them individually, or in what I shall call their "internal articulation." We cannot be articulate about what we see unless what we see has within itself certain articulations. It makes no difference whether this internal articulation is made or acquired by the act of looking. In either case the articulations must be sufficiently constant with respect to F_1 and F_2 in order to tell them apart in something other than a merely numerical sense. In short, the difference in the looks of F_1 and F_2 must be such as to define separate classes and not simply members of the same class. If the differences are altogether arbitrary or "free poems" of the activity of looking, then there are no forms in the usual sense of the word and certainly not in the sense of analytical formalism, with its critical rejection of psychologism (or attempted rejection of Idealism). At the extreme consequence, the difference between F_1 and F_2 would not, under the previous circumstance, be determinably different from the difference between any two forms chosen at random. It would follow that difference makes no difference or that everything is permitted, and thus we establish not formalism or structuralism, but nihilism. If the requirement that the difference between F_1 and F_2 be other than merely numerical requires any justification, it is readily supplied by looking at the symbols themselves. The difference between F_1 and F_2 lies, if we take them as tokens, in their subscripts. We can distinguish them only as countably distinct members of the class of F.

If we disregard the subscripts, one F looks so much like another as to be indistinguishable from it in a determinate or consistent way. The F's (assuming them to be typed by the same machine or to possess no visible mechanically imposed variations) reduce to points or reiterations of a formal monad. If there were nothing but F's (and so, no numbers to fix their distinct spatio-temporal co-ordinates), there would not even be forms, but simply one look, repeated indefinitely; consequently there could be no difference between look and looker. The intelligibility of the subscripts, as a matter of fact, lies in their difference, not just from each other, but from the F's which they instantiate. Numbers are not just monads but classes of monads. They differ from each other by virtue of internal articulation (e.g., in the set-theoretical account, m and n are distinct by virtue of their member-sets), and it is ultimately these differences which enable us to specify, if not indeed to perceive, the diversity of F's. The difference between F_1 and F_2 is that of an internal articulation, as defined by the difference between the subscripts "1" and "2." I do not mean to suggest that this is the end of the story of the difference between F_1 and F_2. My point is rather that any two forms, however simple, can be distinguished or identified only by virtue of their *structures*. If a form lacks structure it is invisible.

If a structure then is a combination of forms, it is also true that form possesses structure. Another way of saying this is that there can be no such thing as a non-circular, exact, and complete analysis of a structure. At some primitive stage we have to see the structure as a candidate for analysis, and what we see is antecedent to, not the result of, the process of analysis. We may, of course, make an *ad hoc* technical distinction between structures and forms. But this is a

decision of the analyst and not altogether dissimilar to his activity of formaliz-
ing structures, which we may perhaps call the activity of *construction*. [30] To say
that X is a structure whereas Y is a form is a question of terminology and a
decision external to X and Y. But even if we grant that there are natural differences between X and Y corresponding to the differences assigned by a school
of analytical formalists to structures and forms, it is still obvious that one structure cannot be distinguished from another except by virtue of the difference in
their internal articulations. The articulated components may be of transformations as well as of forms, but the visibility of a transformation is dependent
upon the visibility of the forms it covers. Indeed, a transformation is itself a
form or a structure of forms. Forms then do not merely possess structure, but
structures also possess forms. The natural differences between X and Y are formal: they possess different looks. If we argue that some of the properties of these
looks, such as transformation rules, cannot be reduced to or understood as
forms, then it must follow that they cannot be understood as structures. And in
this case it also follows that the difference between structure and form, between
one structure and another, and the identity of any structure, and so the meaning of the central conception of formalist structuralism, are not themselves
structures. The domain of the first and last stratum of intelligibility of all
formalist doctrines lies outside the domain of the purely formal content of the
theory. The senses of that content cannot be expressed in purely formal terms.
There is no formal definition of the difference between a form and a structure.

Structuralism, then, in the version we are considering, is a theory consisting
of the following elements: (1) structures and forms; (2) the activity of looking at
(and so understanding) these structures and forms; and (3) the hope or ideal of
integral and complete intelligibility. The theory itself cannot be formalized. In
other words, the conception of a theory as a formal structure is radically defective. It is wrong to try to restrict any theory to its formal elements, since these
depend for their sense upon the non-formal context. What it means to understand is not explained by any formal rules or effective procedures. As Michael
Dummett has pointed out with respect to Davidson's theory of meaning, we
can know that the M-sentence " 'The earth moves' means that the earth
moves" is true, without knowing in particular what "the earth moves" means.
What is required, Dummett continues, is a knowledge of the proposition expressed by the corresponding M-sentence. [31] Dummett also sketches an "intuitionistic" doctrine of meaning in terms of provability or verification. He rightly
notes that a theory of sense has to specify both what the speaker knows and how
his knowledge is manifested. [32] However, Dummett uses "intuitable" to mean
constructible; he never alludes to the basic stratum of philosophical Idealism in
Brouwer's original version of intuitionism. The question of how we are to

engage in successful constructions is thus restricted to the essentially formalist conception of axioms and rules:

> A knowledge of certain axioms, taken together, issues in a general capacity, in this case to recognize of any sentence whether or not it is well-formed; and the ascription to the speaker of an implicit knowledge of those axioms is based on the confidence that he has a general capacity which embraces all the specific abilities which correspond to theorems derivable from that set of axioms.[33]

Dummet's term "confidence" is a pale version of Piaget's "hopes," but pale or vivid, it conceals eschatological problems. Even if it were true that a knowledge of axioms could issue in a capacity, there would still be required some antecedent capacity by which we acquire knowledge of axioms. Dummett apparently identifies "general capacity" with "specific linguistic abilities" by which our knowledge is manifested (p. 71). Once again, a linguistic ability is not a linguistic utterance or entity. It is not a rule. Dummett's "intuitionism" is closely allied to pragmatism. When he refers to the possibility that a language may require changing or having its rules of inference reassessed, he speaks of "needs felt in practical communication," but in such a way as to imply that these needs are exhibited for the philosopher of language in "a complex of linguistic practices."[34] But linguistic practice, as we have already seen, is itself embedded in non-linguistic cognitive activity. Dummett's failure to notice this vitiates his subsequent recommendation, which surely points in the right direction, that we construct a semantics which does not take, "as its basic notion, that of an objectively determined truth value at all."[35]

Dummett's intuitionism, then, is pragmatic rather than Idealistic. But this leaves unresolved the relation between practice and rules or axioms. On the one hand, Dummett speaks of a knowledge of axioms issuing in a general capacity to recognize sentences as well- or ill-formed. On the other hand, he grounds the changing of rules of inference in the feeling of practical needs. The first thesis is compatible with Idealism. But the second thesis, if applied to the first, weakens the axioms into conventional constructions based upon a primary praxis. Dummett provides no analysis of praxis; instead, he merely assumes that praxis is amenable to axiomatization. But the "structure" of praxis is much wider than any selected set of axioms. I am not contending that praxis is unreasonable. On the contrary, I would level this charge against Dummett's account of the linguistic situation. It is the pre-axiomatic reasonableness of praxis in my methodology that enables us to select (or construct) axioms in a rational manner. Analogously, technical terms have a rhetorical dimension that is reasonable or unreasonable in a sense other than applies to the explicitly analytical situation.

The etymology of the word *structure* points us in a more reasonable direction than does Dummett's quasi-mathematicism. The English word comes from the Latin *struo, struxi, structum*: to join together, build, arrange, or order. *Struo* is related to *sterno*, and thence to the Greek *stornymi*: to spread smooth or to level. Etymologically, a structure is an *orderly spread*, an arrangement of connected parts, constituting a smooth or level unity of a manifold.[36] These etymologies seem to suggest that structures are constructions rather than discoveries, but this is a question that does not concern us here. Our difficulty is this: regardless of whether it is nature or man who is responsible for our "spreads," there is an ambiguity in the notion of orderliness, suggested in the etymology by the appearance of "smooth." My reference to the etymology of structure is not intended in any playful sense. It is especially important, when discussing a teaching that itself constructs a sense of theory in accord with mathematics rather than on any historical foundation, to emphasize the role of history in the analysis of senses. Primitive linguistic use often underlies in a decisive way the meaning of our axioms or the contours of our speech habits. Ordinary-language analysis is very much to the point in philosophy, provided it does not forget to examine the theoretical sub-structure of contemporary usage.

The word "ordinary" is itself a crucial case. Ordinary language is ordinary in the precise sense of ordering our discourse. It is, or claims to be, the standard by which we regulate discourse or distinguish between proper and improper forms of speech. It thus claims for itself a political function analogous to the role attributed by Socrates to *phronēsis* (intelligent judgment). This political function is neither purely mathematical nor purely historical. The task of analysis is to penetrate the levels of usage to the level of regulative structure. Ordinary language claims to be a smooth or level spread, by which we may smooth out irregularities in discourse. Unfortunately, there are rough as well as smooth patches within the continuum of ordinary discourse. Whether this means that there are rough as well as smooth forms, or that ordinary discourse is discontinuous, with the rough patches corresponding to formlessness, is not clear. And the concept of smoothness, which is decisive for the meaning of structure in general and ordinary language in particular, would itself seem to be a rough rather than a smooth patch.

The answers to questions like "What is smooth?" and "What is ordinal?" cannot thus be acquired by pointing to one set of structures rather than to another (and certainly not by justifying a given set of axioms on the basis of academic ideology), since what counts as a structure or regulative structure is itself dependent upon what we mean by "smooth" and "ordinal." Smoothness, like clarity and distinctness, is a subjective term.[37] And so we come once more to a recognition of the total inadequacy of the critique of psychologism rooted in Frege. In saying this, I do not mean to deny that there are natural or objective structures. What I do deny is the view that the distinction between ordinal and non-ordinal structures is itself a structure (or a form). *Structures are not self-regulative.* Furthermore, in calling "smoothness" a subjective term, I do not mean this in a pejorative sense. Regardless of whether structures are primarily discovered or constructed, what counts as a structure in a given context depends upon the intentions, ends, or values of intelligence. If these intentions are themselves analyzed or reduced to structures, then the guiding hand of intelligence has been suppressed. The sense of one structure must be determined by the grasping of another, but the process is infinite and there is no grasping agent. Intention-structures will then be smooth or rough by the standard of some other intention-structure, and so on *ad infinitum.* I note in passing that formalist and ontological versions of structuralism share in the rejection of the subject or ego, thanks to their common fear of psychologism. The result is to transform the author and the reader into a transcendental ghost whose intelligence haunts the constructions of structuralism with the invisible light of subjectivity. Under such circumstances the perception of objective structure is an exercise in night vision or in the blind leading the blind.

Sense and Detachment

In the first section I argued that it makes no sense to talk of analysis apart from reference to intuition. I now add that it makes no sense to talk of the analysis of structure, and so of sense, if by "analysis" we mean merely the replacement of one structure by another. The Greek word *analysis* means a "spreading out" by means of a loosening or dissolving. This process which may be characterized as an "upward" motion is perhaps more of a pervasion into all directions or dimensions. If a structure is an orderly, smooth, or level spread, or if structures are legitimate or illegitimate depending upon whether they are smooth or rough, then what counts as a smooth spread depends upon the activity of spreading out, or of differentiating in the sense of providing smooth patches within the continuum of intelligibility.[38] This does not necessarily mean that structures are essentially projections or creations. It might be, for example, that structures are natural whereas smoothness and roughness are properties of looking at or into, i.e., of interpreting the significance of structures. Or perhaps what counts as a structure to the active intelligence is an interpretation of some more fundamental stratum of the world. In any event, the notion of smoothness is again common to the notions of analysis and structure. Analysis in itself does not determine structure, nor does structure determine analysis. Instead, smoothness determines or participates essentially in the determination of both analysis and structure. And what counts as smooth cannot be analyzed into structure.

33

I want now to restate this conclusion in another way. Let us consider the relation between a structure and its sense and assume that the sense is itself a linguistic expression. This is equivalent to the view that logical forms, taken as the expression of senses, are linguistic expressions. If the sense of a logical form is detachable from that form and is itself a linguistic expression, then it obviously has a formal structure which may again be formalized. If this were not the case, then sense, contrary to hypothesis, would not be a structure. But if it is the case, then we can never arrive at the sense of any given form, since each sense possesses a structure, the sense of which can again be formalized, and so on. One might wish to object that no regress obtains, since a formalized sense is just its own sense. But in this case we could never move from formalization to a sense expressed in a natural language. If the sense of an expression in natural language is the formalization of that sense, then the natural expression means whatever sense we choose to give to its formalization, or else it is meaningless.

If we assume that sense is not detachable from logical form, this form being a linguistic expression, then each such expression, as a form, must be formally distinguishable from every other form. Let us designate the initial form as F_1. If I ask the question "What is the sense of F_1?" and refer by that symbol to a structure in a natural language, or to some objective structure intended by an expression in natural language, then there must be a distinction between the linguistic expression F_2 which contains the answer to my question, and F_1 as the formalization of the natural structure for whose meaning I seek. We have here two distinct forms. And the answer to the question, "What is the meaning of F_1?" cannot simply be "F_1." If it were, we could not state the difference between any two forms except by repeating their names and trusting to the intuition of our interlocutor to grasp the difference. And in this case we could not teach the difference to anyone who did not initially see it.

The identification of the sense of the form with the form itself assumes that understanding is immediate intuition taking place in pre-linguistic silence. Even if it were true that understanding occurs as totally silent intuition, it is not true that explanation occurs in that way. The identification of form and sense is thus tantamount to the denial of the necessity of explanation. But this can scarcely serve as a theory of sense.

One may agree that senses are not linguistic expressions, yet insist that they are communicated exclusively by means of linguistic expressions. I have been contending that this is impossible. The distinction between an expression and its sense, even if made a posteriori in language, is extra-linguistic. In other words, language itself conveys us into the significant domain of silence. If there were nothing but language, and expressions referred only to other expressions, then talk would be indistinguishable from chatter, or the tuneless humming of

Nietzsche's "last men." Our attempts to imprison ourselves within a self-con-
structed linguistic horizon take place in silence. Doctrines like that of the later
Wittgenstein, which deny the semantical relevance of internal and partly silent
thought, as well as of intellectual intuition, terminate in the same denigration
of sense as do formalist structuralisms. I am not here simply making the point
that words refer to things. Some do and some do not. A doctrine of language
must also take into account that *silence articulates discourse*. This is evident in
the central role assigned by the science of linguistics to the notion of differentiation. The difference between one intelligible element of sound and another
is not a third element of sound, and the same may be said of the difference between two units of meaning. The analytical intelligence is loath to take
seriously the phenomenon of silence, just as it refuses to face up to the problem
of nothingness.

We can avoid total silence only by jettisoning doctrines that identify sense as
essentially linguistic. In order to overcome total dependence upon intuition, we
must have recourse to partial dependence. The integrity of the senses of
linguistic expressions depends upon their connection and detachment from intuitable forms. The thesis that sense and form are identical leaves us in the following situation. When asked for the sense of F, one man may say F and
another non-F. How is the questioner to decide between these two answers if
he does not just *see* the form? And if he does, why did he need to ask the question? But even if there could be some way in which to distinguish between F
and non-F, the distinction, as sensible, would be by hypothesis a linguistic
expression and consequently subject to the same problem as are the forms
themselves.

In order to develop the previous conclusions, it will be helpful to signal as a
technical term *detachment*, introduced with respect to senses and their linguistic manifestations. I use the term detachment here with respect to the absence
of structure. The detachment of structure from sense is a corollary to the identification of intuition as the context of analysis. The intelligibility of an element
of meaning or of a sound to which a meaning may be attached, depends upon
the detachment of these elements from their linguistic manifestations. There is
a difference between one element and another to which no structure corresponds. The linguist restricts his attention to the conventional character of the
given linguistic manifestation, or to the dependence of translatability upon the
distinction between meaning and linguistic manifestation. He pays no attention
to the fact that there is *nothing* between any two distinct elements. But the philosopher should recall that *omnis determinatio negatio est*. If sense and formal
structure are inseparably connected, then the exhaustive description of a given
element in no way explains the fact that it is different from another element. A
full analysis of this point will take us into the contemporary version of the at-

tempt to transform the problem of nothingness into a syntactical operation. Here we note only that the difference between one element and another, or between one set of predicates and another, must be seen or intuited. And there is no predicate in the usual sense corresponding to the "not" in the assertion that F_1 is not F_2.

One structure is detached from another; the senses of structures are detached from the structures themselves; and structures and senses are both detached from intelligence. It is at this last point that we exclude psychologism in its pernicious form. Intelligence cannot be a structure in any determinate sense, because its function is to apprehend and to evaluate structures. If thinking is ordering and measuring, thought is the orderer and measurer, not a mathematizable structure. This is much clearer in Aristotle than in contemporary "philosophy of mind." One has to distinguish between the various functions of the soul and the specific function of intelligence which apprehends formal structure. Modern "philosophy of mind" is rooted in modern psychology, that is, in modern science. In this context, the soul is ignored or rejected (usually on the basis of a "religion of mathematics"), and all functions of the organism are attributed to the organism *qua* body or at best to consciousness or "mind." As a result of this latter step, the "structures" of the soul are all transferred to the intellect, and indeed, to the single capacity of the intellect to perceive form. But the transformation has the result of turning our attention from the perception of form to the forms themselves. In the extreme case, this line of development terminates in mathematical models of the mind.

Since most contemporary philosophers of mind are Kantians rather than Aristotelians, I will expand the point in Kantian terms. Let us assume that the intellect (the transcendental ego) produces or constructs the structures it looks at and talks about. If this productive capacity is itself structured, the difficulty again arises of distinguishing between truth and construction. If to talk is to construct, then there is no distinction between a true and a false proposition. The distinction between truth and falsehood rests upon a distinction between what we say and what we say it about. But this distinction cannot be drawn unless we are able to see what we are talking about, independently of the discursive aspect of the given act of talking. The radical extirpation of intellectual intuition leads inevitably to a doctrine of language as creativity. One sees some of the background to this development in the teachings of Kant and his immediate successors. Of course, Kant does not identify the intellect with the structures constituted by the transcendental ego. These structures are expressions designating a higher unity, which Kant calls the "transcendental unity of apperception." But there is no intellectual intuition in Kant. The unity of apperception is a logical condition for the possibility of discursive thinking. It does not correspond to the apprehension of forms but is rather the *unity of predication* to which no form corresponds. Kant's Idealist successors transformed the unity of apperception into an absolute ego capable of intellectual intuition; but again, this intuition has no formal content. It is a kind of reflexive apprehension of the activity of thinking, something like Aristotle's conception of god as thought thinking itself. The move from the unity of apperception to intellectual intuition thus encouraged empirically oriented philosophers to reject the intuition of forms. The distinct notion, going back to Plato and firmly rooted in common sense, of the intuition of examples, intentions, consequences of acts, looks, and the like, as well as of the application of rules, was then reduced to the status of a non-cognitive praxis. Philosophers like Wittgenstein, as we have seen, came to deny intuition even as they were calling it to our attention.

In Aristotle, the cognitive intellect "takes shape" or "somehow becomes" the form of the thing it knows, because it has no formal structure of its own. In the Kantian tradition, the intellect "takes shape" in the sense that we cannot grasp its functions without assigning structure to them. Nevertheless, the activity of taking shape is not itself a structure. It is this *activity of taking shape* that Wittgenstein (intentionally or otherwise) transforms into non-cognitive praxis. I myself would suggest that the intellect is prior to its structures in something like the way that, for some linguists, the linguistic system is prior to its elements, or the capacity to speak a language is prior to our learning the structures of that language.[39] In any case, as I understand the situation, the phenomenon of intelligence depends upon a detachment of cognition from the formal structures it apprehends. To understand a structure is to be it *objectively*, in the Scholastic or Cartesian sense of that term: to incorporate or comprehend the structure as an element other than the agent of comprehension. Intellectual detachment is thus the non-geometrical space within which the intellect incorporates and ejects structures, and within which we "change our minds" and thereby discern ourselves as so engaged, or as different from the various structures we entertain. If the intellect were a structure, it could know and formalize itself. But the activity (or passivity) of knowing itself would be at the same time a transcendence of, or detachment from, itself. The act of knowing could not be strictly identical with what is known. For example, let S designate noetic structure. If the act of knowing S were the same as the state of being S, then there would be no difference between saying "S" and "I know S." Knowledge, or the sense of knowledge, would be unspeakable. Human intelligence is both intuitive and discursive. We can speak about the content of our intuitions and to a degree about intuition itself. But speech, to be rational, need not be propositional or analytical in the contemporary sense. Finally, senses are not linguistic structures, nor can they be fully expressed in linguistic structures.

The sense of a structure, although detached from it and so not itself a linguistic structure, is nevertheless determinable over an indefinite range of variations in linguistic expression. Speech approximates to structural sense. If this were not so, there could be no intelligibility (and not simply of a propositional kind). If I ask, "What is the sense of structure S?" and you know, then you can tell me. You can express the sense, or some aspect of it, in a linguistic or symbolic form. But your expression is not the same as the sense. The sense of S is not identical with the sentences you have uttered in conveying or expressing that sense. The fact of intelligibility is then an exhibition of the objectivity of senses. But it is not a license to overlook the detachment of objective senses from their linguistic representations. This means that no exact theory of sense is possible. The unity of sense and intellect which renders the former accessible to the latter is not accessible to a "theory" in the modern sense. All rule-governed formal structures are constructions rooted in the unity they seek reflexively to capture. To capture it, however, is to conceal or destroy it. In slightly different words, the attempt to achieve an exact theory of knowing or being leads inevitably to psychologism.

As an example of this, I want to consider very briefly the later work of Quine, for whom the first and last criterion of sense in philosophy (despite his rejection of "meanings") is science. To take a case of pivotal interest, the sense of "sense" is inseparable from the decision as to what exists. Quine settles the question of "what counts as evidence for existential quantifications" not on the "trivial but undebatable" sense of $\exists x$, but on "essentially scientific reasons" for allowing classes, attributes, etc. to exist or not.[40] But science is itself rooted in sense-perception, not in logic:

> Regardless of whether sensory atoms or Gestalten are what favor the forefront of our consciousness, it is simply the stimulations of our sensory receptors that are best looked upon as the input to our cognitive mechanism. [OR, 84]

This language sounds superficially like that of Kant's, except that Quine has no doctrine of the transcendental ego. Hence the status of our "cognitive mechanism" is suspect. This is obvious, since scientific explanation, which includes logic as a tool, must also be a function of sense-perception and "community-wide acceptance" or the language of the scientific community (OR, 86–89). A doctrine born in the desire for mathematical rigor thus terminates in conventionalism. One sees the role of rhetoric and ideology at the heart of analytical philosophy. But questions of fashion and custom to one side, how can we understand the current language of science? More fundamentally, how can the "scientific community" achieve agreement on the meanings of its sentences, especially if the notion of "meaning" is to be rejected?

I shall try to make my point in terms of Quine's own doctrine of the indeterminacy of translation. In my opinion, this doctrine must also apply to one's own language and for a reason given by Quine in another context:

> The crucial consideration behind my argument for the indeterminacy of translation was that a statement about the world does not always or usually have a separable fund of empirical consequences that it can call its own. [OR, 82]

For Quine, epistemology and semantics are a chapter in psychology. Or rather, psychology must itself be transformed into physiology:

> Semantics is vitiated by a pernicious mentalism so long as we regard a man's semantics as somehow determinate in his mind beyond what might be implicit in his dispositions to overt behavior. It is the very facts about meaning, not the entities meant, that must be construed in terms of behavior. [OR, 27]

And again:

> there are no meanings, nor likenesses, nor distinctions of meaning, beyond what are implicit in people's dispositions to overt behavior. For naturalism the question whether two expressions are alike or unlike in meaning has no determinate answer, known or unknown, except insofar as the answer is settled in principle by people's speech dispositions, known or unknown. [OR, 29]

I infer from all this that psychology must be transformed into physiology because the question of overt behavior and speech dispositions is itself rooted in sensory stimulations. In other words, science is a "construction or projection from stimulations like those we were meting out to our epistemological subject (OR, 83).[41] Since Quine is neither a strict Kantian nor Fichtean, the construction or projection of science depends upon the co-ordination between statements about the world and separable funds of empirical consequences. In other words, science depends upon sense-perception, whereas the *meaning* of sense-perception depends upon science.

Quine rejects meanings in favor of behavioral dispositions. Stated otherwise: such dispositions are offered as the basis for determining the meanings of utterances. But what is the meaning of dispositions, or for that matter, of overt behavior? Either these meanings are themselves rooted in a semantical doctrine of senses recalling mentalism, or they must be established by the currently fashionable procedures of science, in which case we have invoked a vicious circle. There is in fact no more reason to adopt a scientific account of experience than a metaphysical, poetic, or political one. If the scientific account of experience is itself confirmed by experience, then putting to one side the problem of the circularity of the meaning of "confirmed," sense-perception must itself be regulated by our cognitive mechanism. And meanings are thereby rehabilitated. But if sense-perception rules the cognitive mechanism, then the latter is powerless to construct determinately meaningful statements about perception. We must therefore either reject the thesis of the indeterminacy of translation or else apply it to our own language.

To bring this section to a close, the following remarks are in order. The structure we give to our linguistic representation of sense is conventional, contingent, or constructive, while the sense is not. On this point I might be considered a Fregean or Platonist. In a similar vein, theoretical linguists distinguish between the "formal units" or "expression-elements" of a language and their "substantial realization" as sounds and letters.[42] The combinational and contrastive functions of the formal units argue for a self-identical being which we may take as an example of how to conceive of the distinction between sense and structure. However, that distinction is not itself a structure, and the absence of reference involved, like the classical problem of nothingness, cannot be resolved by syntactical devices. On this point, I am not a Fregean or Platonist, but perhaps a Hegelian. As I shall show at length in the last chapter of this study, Hegel is the only thinker to have argued out to its conclusion the premises intrinsic to the analytical movement, specifically, the premises expressed in the thesis that philosophy is conceptual analysis. But the non-structural distinction between senses and their representations leads me to sympathize with the ordinary-language analysts on a crucial point. The term "sense" has a variety of meanings which cannot be covered by a single paradigm or captured in a purely formal theory.

3. Concepts

Sight and Touch

The main thesis of this chapter has been that it makes no sense to define philosophy as "conceptual analysis." In the first section, I argued that analysis is intelligible only with respect to intuition, that both are cognitive activities, and that the usual refutations of psychologism leave untouched the deeper problem of the relation between intellect and its objects. In the second section, I claimed that the concept of structure cannot be rigorously defined, and that intelligibility is rooted in the detachment of structure from sense on the one hand and intellect on the other. I want now to consider more closely the sense of "concept," which will complement the first section and conclude my argument against philosophy as conceptual analysis.

I begin with some very simple, but often neglected, considerations on the origin of the concept of "concept" in sense-perception, and work gradually toward a technical argument to the effect that there is no concept of "concept" as such. In other words, the concept of "concept" must be complemented by intuitions of root-relations like "belonging" or "possessing." This argument will be taken up again, in varying ways, in subsequent chapters.

What is a concept? The simplest reply to this question takes its cue from the etymology of the term. A concept is the result of our grasping something mentally. The comparison of the mind to the hand is at least as old as Aristotle, older, that is, than the technical terminology of concepts. Here, as in so many other cases, Aristotle begins with everyday language, the original manifestation of the phenomena in linguistic form. We normally refer to thinking as a kind of touching, seeing, or hearing. Less usual, but not altogether absent, are allusions to smelling and even to tasting. Of the possible paradigms for thinking, the most striking is probably that of the eye. There will be some differences in our conception of thinking, depending upon which sense-paradigm dominates our reflections. For example, in the metaphorical language of these paradigms, there is a distance between the eye and what it sees, whereas the hand is in direct contact with what it holds. Doctrines of thinking as constructing and transforming phenomena, or even of arranging them in accordance with categories, are closer to the paradigm of touch than to that of sight.

According to Aristotle the grasp of thought is receptive but not fundamentally productive.[43] The work of imagining and talking, or the production of images and speeches, is rooted in the antecedent presence within the intellect of what we imagine and discuss. The presence of the *what* is the basis for the subsequent development of predicative discourse, in which the central notion is *belonging to*. The way in which a predicate belongs to a subject is grounded in the structure of the *what* or essence present to the mind. But that presence is not itself a "belonging." The essence does not belong to, but (somehow) is, i.e., comes to be "in," the intellect. I say "in," although Aristotle does not explain how the intellect remains distinct from the form it contains, nor for that matter, how it contains a plurality of forms in any distinguishable state of thinking. The main point here is that "belonging" entails structure (this belongs to that), and the intellect has no structure (as distinct from the soul, to which the intellect "belongs"). If the intellect were structured, then the essence could not be present, or would be at least partially absent because it would be covered over by the mediating structure of presentation. The modern doctrine of concepts is inseparable from the view that the mind possesses structure or is active *qua* productive rather than passive, or active *qua* receptive in its fundamental work. In the strict sense, there are for this reason no "concepts" in the modern sense in Aristotle. Cognitive work conforms to the phenomena or things themselves. Such at least is Aristotle's intention.

However, at the crucial point, Aristotle says too little about the metaphor of the hand. Suppose for the moment that the hand does not shape the thing it grasps. It is also not quite right to say that the hand is shaped by what it grasps. The obtuseness of the hand allows it to approximate only to the shape of the gripped object, and then only in the case of objects of a determinate kind. How, for example, does the hand conform to the shape of water? The limitation in the metaphor of the hand no doubt accounts for Aristotle's greater use of the metaphor of the eye, as well as for his claim that vision is the noblest of the senses (although this latter claim also has something to do with the detachment of the object as seen from the body, and so takes into account the virtue of continence). But the importance of the hand and of the language of touch should not be forgotten: it is central to Aristotle's revision of the Platonic doctrine of noetic intuition.[44] If we rely upon the language of vision alone, it is impossible to overcome the separation between the intellectual eye and what it sees. And in modern optics and the physiology of the eye the fact remains that sight and touch must be combined to explain the phenomenon of vision. If the intellect is a hand as well as an eye, then it can no longer see the original apart from its grasp. On the other hand, the intellect may now be able to see with precision *what* it grasps, or the aspect of the original *what* that is caught in its grip.

There is a corresponding defect in the attempt to unite the metaphor of the hand and the eye. Touch is clumsier than sight: potentially we can see what we touch, but we cannot always touch what we see. This is closely connected to the problem of counting. If to be is to be touchable, as Lucretius maintained, then the horizon, and indeed vision itself, cannot exist. Stated otherwise, the counting that is appropriate to vision is more heterogeneous than the counting that is appropriate to touch. I note here in passing that this unification of hand and eye, with the consequent restriction of vision by touch, underlies the absence in Aristotle of the Platonic sense of unity as exemplified in the Idea of the Good. The Aristotelian intellect sees what it grasps and, like the hand, it grasps what is definite. Furthermore, it grasps these definite elements or units one at a time. There is no *metabasis eis allo genos*. In Plato the situation is more complex. Plato cannot explain, even in the metaphorical language of sense-perception, how the intellect sees the original. But he can allow vision of an internally articulated unity of genera. Although this vision is often expressed in myth, and indeed, by the dialogue form itself, it corresponds to our everyday experience of sensing, discerning, intuiting, or "seeing things whole."

Plato's relative neglect of touch in favor of sight has many consequences, among the most important of which is the development of a poetic as well as a mathematical ontology (and this despite the politically oriented criticism of poetry in the *Republic*). Poetry is the visual effort to repair the gap between original and image. It is in his poetic dimension that Plato attempts to rectify the defects of the principle of his mathematical ontology, namely, that *to be* is to be countable. And there is a close connection in Plato, not to be found in Aristotle, between poetry and mathematics, as is perhaps most obvious in the "likely story" of the *Timaeus*. It is no accident that Aristotle's not altogether successful attempt to suppress myth by logos leads also to a lower status for mathematics in his ontology. Furthermore, I would claim that the true love of mathematics is expressed philosophically, not by an Aristotelian sobriety and empiricism, but rather by Platonic poetics.

The restriction of sight by touch, or (to put it somewhat misleadingly) Aristotle's empiricism, entails a restriction in what it means to count. Stated simply, the unit of counting is the form, the definite content of each act of noetic grasping. The visual nature of Plato's intelligible cosmos is, I believe, inseparable from the link between Ideas and numbers. Platonic Ideas can "share" in each other like the natural numbers (whereas predicates cannot, but instead "belong to" their subjects as external to them). This "sharing" is the distant ancestor of the set-theoretical conception of transitive sets. Of course, Plato gives only poetical accounts of sharing, and hints rather than accounts. But even these hints open the possibility of our thinking simultaneously a multiplicity of formal units. I find no such possibility in the Aristotelian doctrine of thinking, which turns upon the identification of the intellect, at each stage of actualization, with a definite, "touchable" form.

The metaphors of sight and touch are instructive so long as they are not taken too seriously. In a very general sense, sight is more discriminating than touch and interferes less with the shape of its object, although it goes without saying that sensory illusion may arise in either case. Within the terms of our metaphor, the issue is complex. As has been noted, we pay for the greater formal definition of sight by a loss of security or control over what we see. And the security of touch is accompanied, not just by a narrower range of objects, but by an ambiguity with respect to the nature of the object securely within our grasp. If noetic vision is a receptivity or identification between the intellect and the form, then we see only what we touch. Not only is the untouchable invisible in this model, but we run the risk of changing the visible shape of what we grasp, especially in the case of the most delicate objects. Aristotle, of course, denies that this is a feature of noetic thought. But he gives no arguments in support of that denial. As a consequence, his shift in the "location" of intelligible form from a visual "heaven" to a partly tactile grasping of the intellect is the basis for the emergence of the modern doctrine of the concept.

In synoptically considering the historical development of the modern sense of "concept" from Descartes to Hegel, one discerns an increasing emphasis upon the security of our grasp of the discursively intelligible form.[45] Intelligibility comes more and more to be identified with talking, even while the role of the imagination steadily increases. This is because intuition comes to be understood as sensation rather than as formal vision. The imagination is crucial in constructing the form of the sensory content of intuition.[46] Stated with extreme brevity, since there is no noetic vision of the form, we must constructively grasp that form from sensation and account for it in the categories of discursive thinking. After Kant, the cognitive content of intuition is transformed into a pure intellectual intuition that sees, not objects, but itself. This, however, does nothing to change the basic situation with respect to objects, which come more and more to be known through *construction*.

In the characteristic maxim of the modern period, we know only what we make. And in this sense, so far as objective or discursive knowledge is concerned, touch triumphs over vision. In the extreme Kantian formulation, we grasp something by our various cognitive faculties, but we cannot see it as it is in itself. Grasping is no longer merely touching, but constructing the structure that permits us to know what we grasp. The ostensibly pure reception by noetic vision of the essential form has been replaced by the cognitive construction of the concept of the object that is thought. And we build with our hands, not with our eyes. As a result, we think the constituted concept, not the thing itself. The object is the project of the thinking subject.

This is the (essentially Kantian) basis of the intrinsic unity between the ostensibly opposed poles of contemporary philosophy, existential or fundamental ontology, and analysis. It is the necessary background for our immediate goal of understanding the contemporary use of the term *concept*. A concept is a mental entity, intuited or constructed, expressing a determinate content of discursively accessible thought. It gives us security over what we think in a way analogous to the security we derive from the object that is gripped by the hand. This concept may be a function in the Fregean sense, or it may be a non-mathematical "idea" corresponding to any possibly cognizable aspect of experience. In the former case the concept must have sharp delimitation or a truth-value for every argument. In the latter case the necessary sharpness of the concept is a matter of dispute, but this much can be safely said: the analysis of a concept turns upon the determining of its structural properties. Giving an account is thus also a counting, not merely in the sense of identifying graspable units of a graspable structure but also because, even in the case of "inexact" concepts, the paradigm continues to be the precision of mathematics. In my opinion, this is also true for much of ordinary-language philosophy, namely, that part which follows the program of replacing initial intuitions and the imprecision of ordinary discourse with the exact distinctions of a technical terminology or a constructed theory designed to remove the ambiguities of the pre-analytical situation. The model here is still that of the mathematical sciences.

Conceptual analysis in the contemporary sense is thus a product of what I shall call the Kantian revision of Aristotelian Platonism. Unlike Kant, the analyst normally disregards synthesis as the necessary antecedent for analysis. As we saw in the first section, the analyst might claim that synthesis is the result of cognitive construction, an analytical unity produced by the act of thinking, which is also a collecting based upon dividing. In this case, all possible objects of analysis must be regarded as the products of previous analysis. But this leads to an infinite regress of analyses, or to an inability to explain the unity of the circumstances under which any definite analytical procedure begins. If synthesis is analysis, then no account can be given of the world as the context of analysis. The doctrine of a linguistic horizon or framework is no substitute for an account of the world. We construct our frameworks within a pre-analytical context which is either rational or not. If it is, then it must be accessible to extra-analytical modes of cognition. If it is not, then neither is the activity of framework construction. In other words, the concept of rationality, as a concept, is itself a construction. In the absence of a transcendental ego, however, constructive activity cannot be distinguished from random behavior. Technical success is thus 'emptied of its sense or value, and philosophy is replaced by historicism or poetry.

A word should be said about concepts in Frege and Husserl since these philosophers are often associated with Platonism, despite their more obviously Kantian inclinations (see section 1). In a distinction common to the two, a concept has sense and reference. The sense of the concept defines its range or serves as the criterion by which we determine whether or not an object falls under that concept. By a slight extension, we may say that only those objects have sense that fall under concepts. The sense of the object is a product of the work of the subject. In Frege, this leads eventually to the notion of a hierarchy of concepts, whereas in Husserl, we are led in two different directions: back to the life-world and up to the transcendental constituting subjectivity. Differences between the two thinkers aside, both are characterized by their reliance at the initiating or intermediate level upon a rigorous methodology. Frege's methodology is determined by the needs of mathematics, or rather by the desire to establish the foundation of mathematics and to define proof in a completely rigorous manner. Husserl's methodology is determined by the desire to start from givenness: in the famous slogan, to return to the things themselves —a slogan understood by Husserl to refer to the intended contents of acts of consciousness. For Husserl, the reference of a concept is finally some content of consciousness, whereas for Frege, it is determined by a definition, except, of course, in the case of intuited primitive elements.

We may discern in Husserl and Frege the two sides of Kant, or by way of a slight exaggeration, the results of taking perception and categorial thinking as independent of each other, or of using each to construct a distinct philosophical method. Thus, for example, the Fregean methodology turns upon deduction, whereas Husserl's method is descriptive. For our purposes, the important point of contact is this: human beings do not think things in themselves, but objects via concepts, whether those concepts are "discovered" or "constituted." In order to be thinkable in its turn, the concept must be "objectified" or subsumed under a concept of a higher order. And in both cases, there is a necessary beginning in intuition, however unsatisfactory may be Frege's account of this faculty. As we have already seen, the element of discovery in Frege is compromised by his Idealist proclivities, or failure to think through the conflict between Realism and Idealism. In an analogous manner, Husserl's "Platonism" or doctrine of pure intuitable essences is "Kantianised" by his doctrine of subjectivity and transcendental temporality. For these reasons, the centrality of the paradigm of the hand, and the conception of thinking as constructing, is not seriously challenged by the Fregean or the Husserlian school.

Lewy on Concepts

A concept is then a grasping of some definite, and hence countable, object. To conceive is to have something in the "hand" or grip of the intellect. If philosophy is to be defined as conceptual analysis, it would seem to follow that we "have" a concept of a concept, or (odd as it may sound) a *having of a having*. If no conceptual content can be given to the metaphorical characterization of "thinking as having," then it becomes dubious, to say the least, whether one has the right to insist that philosophy is equivalent to a single instrument, namely, conceptual analysis. Casimir Lewy has recently emphasized that there is a difference between a concept (e.g., the concept of a female fox) and a concept of a concept (e.g., the concept 'concept of a female fox').[47] It is possible to have the former without having the latter.[48] Let us take our bearings by Lewy's distinction in order to consider further what could be meant by conceptual analysis. This distinction turns upon our ability to apply correctly words like "vixen" without being able to apply correctly synonyms of such words, e.g., "female fox." If I can use the name "vixen" correctly, but not the expression "female fox," and moreover if I can understand the question, "What is the analysis of the concept of being a vixen?" without being able to give a correct answer and finally without being able to apply correctly any word in any language that defines "vixen," then the distinction just noted obtains. I have the concept of a female fox, but not the concept of the concept 'female fox,' and I have the former in some sense (i.e., in a sense other than that obtained by a correct definition), because I can correctly apply "vixen," which is correctly defined (although not by me) as "female fox." In my own metaphor, I have hit the target of 'female fox' without knowing the definition of the target I have hit.

Lewy does not apply his analysis to the concept of a concept and the concept 'concept of a concept,' just as he nowhere explains exactly what he means by "concept" (although the target he hits is evident from his distinction between concepts and propositions on the one hand and words and sentences on the other). In my opinion, this distinction, and in a way very much like that drawn by Lewy, underlies all of analytical philosophy, and especially that part of it that defines itself as conceptual analysis without defining "concept." The assumption, in other words, is that we know how to apply the word "concept" in various ways without being able to define the expression "concept of a concept." But Lewy has also shown, and in my view decisively, that having a certain concept X is not the same as knowing how to apply the word "X" (in any language). This follows from his initial distinction. In one of his examples, it is logically possible to have the concept of mother while not knowing how to use the words "father" or "parent." Since a mother is a female parent, one has the concept of parent (in my metaphor, one has hit the target of the concept), but not the use of the word "parent" or its synonym in any language. The question then arises: if we accept Lewy's distinction between concepts and words or names of concepts, might we then apply it to the problem of knowing the answer to the question, "What is a concept?" in such a way as to make plausible the definition of philosophy as conceptual analysis? I contend that we cannot.

There is a crucial difference between Lewy's examples and what I shall call the reflexive case of the concept of a concept. In order to hit some target B, it is necessary to know (or to "have") some A as an "arrow" that strikes, but is not identical with or substitutable for B. The metaphor of the target is defective in the important sense that an arrow is not an instance of a target, but it does bring out a crucial aspect of Lewy's distinctions. These distinctions depend upon a discernible difference between the concept of vixen and the concept of female fox, between the concept of man and the concept of rational animal, or finally, between the concept of man and the concept 'concept of man.' In the reflexive case the distinction between the concept of a concept and the concept 'concept of a concept' turns upon our knowing in advance the answer to the question we posed, namely, what is a concept? For we cannot correctly apply the word "concept" (knowingly) unless we have the concept under which applications of that word fall. Even if there should be a range of senses to the concept 'concept of a concept,' no single sense can be understood without understanding the concept 'concept of a concept.' And therefore, it seems, we cannot distinguish *conceptually* the concept of a concept and the concept 'concept of a concept.'

Again, Lewy does not explain exactly what he means by a concept or by "having a concept." I have thus far assumed that "having" means "knowing," but this is circular, since "knowing" means "having." Let me say in advance that I will not myself furnish any analytical explanation of knowing *qua* having. I hold that no such analysis is available, apart from circular paraphrasing, and consequently conceptual analysis is rooted in intuitions which cannot be replaced by the process of analysis but which *regulate* that process. A concept, to repeat, is a having. What then does it mean to *have a having?* (The reader will observe in what follows, that the same or analogous arguments apply to the case of predication, which I shall treat separately in a later chapter.) Suppose for example that to have a concept of a vixen is to know something essential about vixens, or to know something about the essence referred to in English by the name "vixen." This is not just knowledge of the use of a word, but rather knowledge of something about the essence to which a word refers. Lewy's entire argument, of course, is directed toward the defense of essences, which are required for modal logic. Our study of his argument is thus a bridge to the next chapter, in which I shall take the work of Saul Kripke as a basis for presenting the link between intuition and analysis. Meanwhile, let us say that if there are no essences, there can be no sharp definitions, and so, no well-formed concepts. In slightly different terms, if the reference of a concept has an accidental composition, then either there is no difference between essences and accidents, and everything is essential, or we can say anything we like about anything. I do not suggest that this is a sufficient treatment of the status of essences in contemporary analytical philosophy. But it is perhaps enough to justify Lewy's distinction. Even accidents are defined by the fact that objects *have* them. It is therefore an essential property of an object to *have* some properties. I shall develop this point in the following chapter.

Meanwhile, let us go a step beyond Lewy and say that there is a difference between the essence of a vixen and our concept of that essence. And we should make a distinction here between the concept of a vixen, in the sense of the essence itself or some aspect of that essence, and our conception of that concept, i.e., the psychological, linguistic, and historical circumstances of our thinking that concept. This distinction is not made as such by Lewy, but it mirrors his distinction between words and sentences on the one hand and concepts and propositions on the other. The distinction is hard to draw in all cases, but it can be done in general.

Now the concept of a vixen is neither the word "vixen" nor the word "concept" (to restrict ourselves for the sake of simplicity to English), and it is certainly not an actual vixen. Similarly, the concept of a concept is not the word "concept." *It is rather an actual concept.* Perhaps it should be noted that we can reach this conclusion without knowing what a concept is, since it is a tautology to say that a concept of a concept is a concept. Thus the reflexive case differs from all non-reflexive cases in that it is a self-having, and so the having of a having. For this reason, the most obvious analysis of the nature of a concept, or of the concept 'concept of a concept,' is inadequate. We would probably want initially to say something like this: "to have a concept of X is to know (something about) X, and so to have a (or the) concept of a concept is to know (something about) what knowing is." But this will not do, because in order to know (something about) what knowing is, we must first know (something about) what knowing is. And even if the "something about's" here are distinct, it is what they are about, i.e., the essence "concept" or "knowing," that we must know, not just hit, in order to know that we have indeed hit upon an appropriate "something," or in order to know that the something we know is indeed a strike upon the right target. To have a concept of a concept is already to know what knowing is. The ostensibly subsequent step of having the concept 'concept of a concept' is thus not really distinct from the antecedent state. As Lewy points out in another connection (while distinguishing between simple and unitary syntactical elements), we cannot know the concept 'concept of a concept' without knowing the concept named by the word "concept" (Lewy's own distinction is slightly different; I am adapting it to the present case.)

I have developed my point on the basis of a contemporary analytical text, but it is already visible in Socrates' effort to define knowledge in the *Theaetetus*. However, Lewy's discussion is more useful to us because he speaks regularly of concepts, a term never employed by Socrates, although there are some senses of *logos* that approximate to this term. Conversely, Lewy's concepts approximate to certain features of the traditional Platonic Ideas and Aristotelian essences. Whatever may be the case with the term "concept," the notion of "having" is central in analytical thinking from Plato and Aristotle to contemporary set theory. A has *b*, whereas *b* belongs to A. This schema has two main senses. First, we say that a set has members, a function has values, or an object has properties. Second, we say that a man has knowledge: a knower has a *logos* or a concept of a form or structure. These senses cannot be the same, as is perhaps intuitively obvious. We can, of course, objectify a knower, if we attempt to make a formal analysis of the act of knowing. But the analysis is not the same as the activity whose structure it ostensibly exhibits. We may also note that a form has properties. Thus, to have a concept of a form is to have a having, in a sense distinct from that which is applicable to the having of a concept of a concept. If a concept is itself a formal structure (or a formalizable entity), then to have a concept of a concept is to have a having of a having in both the first *and*

49

the second senses. It is to identify with, or "possess," a structure of a concept, but by a process that cannot possess structure. And the process (knowing the concept 'concept of a concept') is the same state as the possessing.

The difficulty may now be put as follows. On the one hand, the two senses of having are intuitively distinct. On the other hand, if we know what we are saying by calling philosophy "conceptual analysis," then the two senses must be the same. This is because knowing is having in the second sense, but this in turn is to "have" in the first sense. The *activity* of knowing is not a formal structure. But if knowing is having a formal structure, then knowing cannot be an activity. This is a somewhat compressed form of the motivation underlying the disappearance of the subject in post-Fregean conceptual analysis. Unfortunately, it leads to the loss of consciousness, in more than one sense of the term, on the part of analytical philosophy. It should also be emphasized that the problem surfaces initially in Plato and Aristotle. Noetic intuition, or pure knowledge of form, is marked by an absence of self-consciousness, at least in the *nous*. This is not the place to develop the point, but in both Plato and Aristotle there is also non-eidetic intuition or cognition. The restriction of knowledge or rationality to the cognition of structure or the possession of a concept results in the effective elimination of self-consciousness from the analysis of knowledge. And so the ancient doctrine that the intellect becomes the object of cognition is unconsciously rehabilitated in contemporary analytical philosophy, whether in Platonist or Kantian accents. This is true even in the case of recent attempts to reduce the mind to the body, or to explain the former in terms of the latter (what one could perhaps call contemporary Spinozism). In this case, knowing must be a constructing by the physical organism of a physical artifact. That is, there can be no intellect distinct from the physical fact of an instance of knowledge, otherwise the mind-body dualism would be re-established. The distinction between the physical organism and the knowledge-artifact simply recreates the dualism, and in fact, multiplies it, since there is a distinction between what I know and me as knower. We have here the previously noted puzzle of the two senses of "having," reproduced at the level of two distinct bodies (the knower and the known) which must nevertheless, at the instant of cognition, be the same body. By acquiring a concept of knowledge, the materialist also acquires an "abstract entity" and thereby refutes himself. Or else he acquires a having of himself as having, without an explanation of "having" *or* a concept of the 'concept of concept,' and so lacks an explanation of knowledge.

If to know is to be able to define a formal structure, and hence to "have" it, the structure must be both the same as and other than the knower. The two senses of "having" must be both distinct and indistinguishable. It does no good to suggest that they are indistinguishable in some sense other than that in which they are distinct, as I have already shown. So it is not merely the case that in order to acquire knowledge of knowledge, or the concept of 'the concept of a concept,' we must already have that concept. The problem is much deeper. It is in principle *impossible* to have the aforementioned concept because, in any discursive or analytical sense, *there is nothing to have.* In order to distinguish "having" in sense two from "having" in sense one, we have to see that, in sense two, "having" is not a concept at all, but an activity performed with or upon concepts. Now I believe that everyone sees this initially or that the distinction is intuitively clear. But the analytical philosopher tends to overlook this as soon as he notices it because he supposes that to notice differences is already to conceptualize, and therefore to be on the road toward the replacement of initial intuitions with analyzed concepts. In the present case, however, this is obviously not true, even though, puzzlingly enough, we seem to be employing concepts in referring to two senses. But as I am arguing, not all senses of "sense" refer to concepts.

In sum: anyone who cares to say something in sense two of knowing what he is saying, about "having" in the first or conceptual-structural sense, must begin by making the distinction between the two senses if he is to say anything at all. This distinction, however, is between two senses of "sense," and not just between two "senses" or semantical entities. Stated in one last way, whereas "knowing X" is arguably the having of a concept, whether in the sense of an essence or a linguistic expression, it is also the case that knowing or having the concept 'knowing,' or in effect having the concept 'concept of a concept,' is the having of a universal which is an instance of itself. The universal *qua* universal must be a particular, whereas *qua* particular, it must be a universal. I suggest that this is a vitiating contradiction, at least within the confines of analytical thinking.

CHAPTER TWO

Essences

4. Predication

BY NOW we have seen that the relation of "having" (or of "belonging to") is primitive, whether in the sense of class membership or in the act by which we predicate something of something. It is primitive because we must understand it in advance of each analysis of any meaningful utterance. We do not arrive at the definition of the relation via a step-by-step construction employing elements which, together with the construction they constitute, are intelligible without recourse to an understanding of the relation ostensibly defined. Analytical constructions proceed by way of propositions, and it is impossible to intentionally utter a meaningful proposition without an understanding of what it means to say something of something. We may of course talk to one another in a pre-analytical context without conscious reflection upon our successful use of the "having"-relation; but in this context it remains true that we proceed by seeing that something belongs to something. I have been using the name *intuition* to refer to this capacity to see, and I have argued that the primitive status of "having" makes it impossible for us to "have" an analytically constructed concept of concepts (see section 3). One could then state the conclusion of Chapter One as follows. The definition of philosophy as conceptual analysis fails at the outset to eliminate the traditional doctrine of intellectual intuition in the characteristically Platonic (or in our time, Husserlian) sense of a pre-discursive (or antepredicative) "seeing" of formal structure.

It has already been suggested that vision is not the only possible or desirable paradigm for the capacity designated by intuition. The term is admittedly defective in that its etymology expresses a "looking at" or "into" some entity. Nevertheless, the term is part of tradition, has marked advantages of familiarity in everyday speech and, with appropriate qualifications at certain junctures, may usefully be employed as a portmanteau-word designating a variety of cognitive activities which cannot be rigorously specified. To employ an *ad hoc* technical distinction, "concept" refers to analytically defined constructions of the discursive intellect. We have a *notion*, but not a concept, of intuition. "Notion" is an intentionally vague term selected to cover a wide range of mental contents incapable of rigorous definition. The fact that meaningful talk depends upon intuition does not mean that intuition is inaccessible to meaningful talk. Rather, it is true that "meaningful talk" is a wider term than "conceptual construction." In my present terminology, concepts are constructive representations of notions. This is why we speak today of "theory-construction." Some notions are amenable to conceptualization and others are not. But even in the case of the "sharply defined concepts," there remains a non-conceptual residue (or substratum) of notions, such as that of intuition.

I have emphasized in the previous chapter that we do not intuit forms or formal structures only. For example, I have an intuition of myself to which no structure corresponds. It seems likely that the majority of cases in which we exercise our intuition do not involve formal structures. This is no doubt the reason for the erroneous contemporary view that the task of a philosophical theory is to render intuition superfluous by supplying the initially absent or revealing the initially invisible structures. Also, it is probably true that historically the most important role of intuition has been its association with the doctrine of essence, and in the various controversies surrounding that doctrine. I shall now argue that we cannot do without essences, but also that essences cannot be defined by way of predicative discourse. Essences are accessible to the intellect only with the assistance of intuition. This does not mean that we cannot speak about essences or utter meaningful predicative assertions concerning them. It means rather that (1) predicative discourse itself depends upon intuition; and (2) that a defense of the doctrine of essences must finally (though not exclusively) rely upon *reductio* or "transcendental" arguments in the previously defined sense of stating conditions without which essences are inaccessible to discourse, and circumstances which render discourse impossible except by reference to essences.

What I shall now try to demonstrate is that analytical philosophy has not eliminated the traditional doctrine of essences. With this end in mind, I find myself compatible, on at least one point, with an influential species of analytical philosophy that, for purposes of convenience, I shall call the *Kripkeans*, after its most distinguished member. Unfortunately, the Kripkeans, despite their frequent recognition of the necessary role of intuition, do not articulate that role in a coherent manner. It seems that their procedure is vitiated by a reliance upon intuition joined to the belief that intuition is merely a preliminary to conceptual analysis and scientific investigation. The situation here is in part analogous to that of the later Wittgensteinians, who repudiate intuition while at the same time demonstrating its pervasive role in their analytical procedures. It should be understood, however, that I am not calling for a "theory" (in the contemporary sense) of intuition. Instead, I am calling attention to the intuitive dimension of theories.

In this section, I introduce the problem of essences by way of Aristotle, with special attention to his doctrine of predication. I want to say just enough about this doctrine to make clear that the attempt to define essences by sets of predicates, without intuition, leads to conventionalism or the denial of essences. In section 5 I shall consider some reasons why we cannot dispense with essences. Section 6 is devoted primarily to an analysis of Saul Kripke's use of intuition and imagination. I shall argue that there is a confusion in Kripke's published lectures between the intuitive *qua* phenomenological and the epistemological, or a vacillation with respect to the "given" that deforms his defense of the meaningfulness of a doctrine of essence. In section 7 I examine Kripke's doctrine of individual essences and conclude that his arguments on their behalf are failures. In general, then, the main theme of this chapter is as follows. Neither modern science nor contemporary logic refutes the traditional doctrine of essences. We have a notion of an essence, but not a concept. Since discursive analysis depends upon essences, we see again that the context of analysis is not analytically definable. What we need to do is not to dispense with analysis, but to open our eyes.

Aristotle is both the founder of modal logic and the first to present us with a detailed doctrine of essence. The connection between the two doctrines is immediately obvious. One cannot speak of the distinction between necessity and possibility if there is no distinction between the essential and the accidental. It is also obvious that essence, intuition, and predication are crucial elements in Aristotle's analysis of being and non-being. Consequently, what we have to say about essences in the present chapter will serve as a bridge to later discussions concerning the link between Aristotle and contemporary analytical philosophy with respect to the fundamental problems of unity, being, and nothing. My purpose is to show by an analysis of contemporary procedures themselves how their internal inconsistencies or other shortcomings invite us to return to a reconsideration of the metaphysical tradition. To some extent, these problems

arise from an acceptance of certain aspects of Aristotle's doctrine, such as predication, and a rejection of others, such as intuition. The implicit "Aristotelianism" of contemporary analytical thought, *despite the radical changes in
logic*, allows me to dispense with an exhaustive treatment of Aristotle. My goal
is not historical or scholarly, and I am not advocating a return to Aristotelianism, since part of my criticism of contemporary analytical philosophy is
also a criticism of Aristotle. But I believe that a reconsideration of the metaphysical tradition can prepare the way for genuine progress. And what I mean
by genuine progress is a satisfactory understanding of the philosophical problems, not the construction of a technical resolution to these problems. For
reasons which I am in the course of explaining, I believe that there cannot be
any technical resolutions to fundamental philosophical problems. But this has
to be shown in a technical way.

According to Aristotle, technical and scientific knowledge is of the "through
what" or cause.[1] Knowledge arises when we can answer the question: why does
one thing follow from another in such-and-such a way? More precisely, knowledge explains why one thing *belongs to* another. The "owner" of the property
or predicate is then the subject of predication, a secondary substance or species-
form. A second kind of knowledge is contained in a definition of the essence of
that form.[2] This kind of knowledge is intuitive. A scientific demonstration
"points out" the essential properties belonging to the substance.[3] This "pointing
out" follows the schemata of the categories, or the classification of the essential
attributes of a substance.[4] The categories may themselves be divided into substance and all the others which classify properties of substance.[5] The verb "is"
then points out a substance as a thus-and-such, i.e., as the owner of a given
(and in scientific knowledge, essential) property. But it does not exhibit directly
the substance. The substance, the subject of essential predication, is accessible
through sense-perception or intellectual intuition. Predication states which
properties are "present" in, or belong to, the substance, or which properties
are "absent" or do not belong to it. Consequently one must first intuit the substance in order to make a predicative assertion about it.[6]

We cannot say something of something until we see *what* we are talking
about. But the *what*, the substance or species-form, paradoxical as it may initially appear, is not the predicatively expressible structure of owner and essential properties. Predication follows an order of posterior and prior. If "this"
belongs to "that," then "that" is logically prior to "this" in the sense that the
owner is logically prior to his property. But, as Aristotle says, "there is no order
in the substance. For how could we be compelled to intuit (*noēsai*) posterior
and prior?"[7] The unity of the substance is not reducible to the discursive list of
its element-predicates. For example, "man" is not composed of "animal" plus
"two-footed."[8] Nor is the unity of substance like a point or monad, since then

55

we could not distinguish one substance from another. It is rather an entelechy and kind of nature.[9] That is, it is an "actuality" or completed being, the owning-dimension of the full presence or essence that becomes the task of a scientific definition to describe.[10] In predicative knowledge, the essence *qua* owner has just been shown to be other than, and the condition for the possibility of identifying, its essential predicates. So we have an impasse in the doctrine of predication. We need to see the essence in order to identify those of its properties that are essential. But what is it that we see, other than its properties?

To know is to state the "through what." Discursive knowledge is thus analytical; it can tell us why a man is a such-and-such, but not why a man is a man. There is no (discursively accessible) cause or ground "through which" a man is a man. To ask for this is not really to ask for a cause but to request a statement of identity. The man *qua* substance or owner of properties must first be evident via intuition before scientific inquiry into his nature can begin.[11] We can restate the problem as follows. If "to be" is "to belong to," as it is in scientific knowledge, then "being" becomes a syntactical operator on a par with negation or "non-being."[12] Since there is no discursive account of what it means to belong to, or since there is no purely discursive explanation of essential predication, the difference between being and non-being in such knowledge is conventional. If there are no essences and hence no intuition of essences, there is no *de re* necessity. But if there is no *de re* necessity, what could we possibly mean by *de dicto* necessity? Of *what* are we speaking when we speak of necessity? As a matter of fact, it really makes no difference whether we are speaking of beings or propositions. The unity of a proposition, or the "ownership" by a subject of its predicates, or of a range of values by a function, presents us with exactly the same problem as that of the unity of a being. There is no discursively accessible "through which" to serve as the ground of unity or essential identity.

In order to complete this sketch of predication, I want next to show briefly how the problem of intuition points ahead to the problem of non-being. I can do this by expanding and documenting my earlier remark about the "presence" and "absence" of properties in a substance. In the *Metaphysics*, negation and privation are defined with respect to a unity, i.e., a substance that serves as the subject of predication. Negation may take two forms. The first and simple form is the assertion that unity does not belong to the given subject. The second form is the assertion that unity does not belong to a given genus. This means that negation takes the form "S is not *p*" where S is deprived of the unity of which *p*-ness is intrinsic, or by the absence of *p* (literally, *apousia* means "away from the substance"). In the case of privation, the absence of *p* disqualifies S from being identified as a given species within a genus. As Artistotle says, "the difference is present in the unity, apart from the content of the negation."[13]

This raises the problem of the distinction between difference and otherness.[14] The differences are present in the unity of the genus, and so differentiate it into species. The unity of the genus thus continues to hold, even though within it, one species is not another. In privation, the unity of the genus is present concomitantly with the absence of the negated difference. Is the unity of the genus then the same as the unity of the species? If not, how can distinct unities be defined by negations? For our purposes, we need look only at the simplest or most accessible version of this problem. If negation, whether in its simple or complex form, refers to the absence of a property from a substance, then affirmation must refer to the presence (*parousia*) of an attribute in a substance. The "absence" in question is not of the subject of a negative predication, at least not in the case of genera and species, where scientific knowledge is involved. In this type of negation, the privation characterizes the substance,[15] which itself remains, even in the absence of the negated difference, as the unity of its genus, represented here by the definite exclusion of a single specific identity. Similarly, Aristotle says that the difference is present (*prosesti*) in the unity of the genus.[16] I arrive at the term "presence" or *parousia* to designate the presence in substance (*ousia*) of an affirmed property by joining together Aristotle's use of *apousia* with the technical distinctions just noted. And in fact, Aristotle explicitly contrasts *parousia* with *apousia* and *sterēsis* in Book 5 of the *Metaphysics*, in the chapter on "Cause" or "Ground".[17] Furthermore, in the *Physics*, Aristotle speaks of the *parousia* and *apousia* of contraries in a substratum. There can be no doubt, then, that the usage is Aristotelian, even though the term *parousia* is not always employed by Aristotle to designate affirmative predication.[18]

An affirmative statement does not "bespeak" the substance itself, but speaks about it via the presence of a property. Essential negation, then, or privation, is co-ordinate to essential affirmation. If privation is the absence of a property, then the presence of a property is obviously the actualization of a potentiality (viz, the privation) inherent in the unity of the genus. The presence is an actuality. But the substance must be both present and unspeakable, underlying as it does both the affirmation and the negation. Aristotle regularly speaks as though actuality (*energeia*) and substance (*ousia*) were virtually synonymous[19] in the sense of species-form. Yet it now looks as though there must also be an actuality of the essential properties.

In sum: scientific knowledge is for Aristotle knowledge of form (exactly as it is for contemporary formalists). Since no form corresponds to pure absence or nothing, Aristotle is led to define nothingness as negation. We may say "S is not *p*" when we mean "S is non-*p*" or that the property designated by *p* is absent from the being or substance designated by S. This in turn is possible only because the substance in question is itself present. So there are two different senses of "present." First: substance, as the owner of its properties and so as the criterion for the distinction between essential and accidental predications, is present to intuition. Second: the properties owned by the substance (as classified by the table of categories) are present and accessible to predicative speech. The sense of negation is thus dependent upon the senses of the two terms S and p, which are related syntactically in such a way as to exclude ownership of p by S. It is therefore taken for granted here that we understand what it means for something to belong to something, and hence that we grasp the essence in advance of our predicative analysis. Furthermore, whereas S and p are both "present," in however different senses, there is no presence co-ordinate with the "not" or "non-" in a negative predication.

In this sketch of the Aristotelian doctrine of predication, I have emphasized the notions of "presence" and "absence" (corresponding crudely to affirmation and negation) in order to underline the dependence of predication upon intuition. The discussion of essences will require us to pay special attention to "presence." However, "absence" will take center stage later on when we try to come to grips with the problem of nothingness (see section 11). Meanwhile, as a transitional remark, I note that intuition plays a ghostly role in contemporary analytical philosophy thanks to the distinction, made central by Frege, between sense and reference. In my discussion of Saul Kripke, the pivotal figure for the balance of this chapter, I shall be claiming that the distinction between sense and reference is rooted in an intuition of the presence of an object, and of objects as interrelated within a world. This is a point that has been rightly emphasized by phenomenological thinkers since Husserl and Heidegger. But the point follows without any reference to "world" merely from reflection upon what it means to refer. To say that the sense determines the reference leaves unexplained how we refer because, as Michael Dummett has pointed out, "to say of any condition whatever, that one knows what it is for an object to satisfy that condition, presupposes that one has the conception of referring, by some means, to a particular such object."[20] In other words, unless we are creating the objects of our discourse, linguistic distinctions alone will not connect our terms with their objects. In mathematics we may assume simple objects corresponding to names a, b, c, . . . But in meta-mathematics or in philosophical interpretations we have to know what we are talking about, and we do not learn this by further talk. Dummett suggests that ostension may be the origin of reference, but adds that the suggestion is not as important "as the fact that, for an account of sense of this kind," namely, his version of the Fregean account, "*something* must serve that purpose." I agree. But apparently I disagree with Dummett in my contention that what we require is intellectual intuition.

Kripkeans accept a kind of intuition that can only be designated "intellectual" (although they so far as I can determine, do not employ that adjective). Saul Kripke, as we shall see, distinguishes between how we come to be acquainted with, and hence know, an object, and the actual intrinsic structure of the object. This distinction is between the epistemological and the logical. Kripke's terminology already suggests something misleading, namely, that he accepts the intuition of objects but not of logical forms. I think it can easily be shown that this is not what he means, or at least not what he explicitly says. But it is worth noting from the outset that, when Kripke is not doing mathematics, but is instead philosophizing (the distinction is his own), he tends to be extremely careless about his terms and formulations. A central ambiguity in the distinction between the epistemological and the logical, as I shall claim, is that Kripke normally associates what he calls the "phenomenological" with the epistemological situation. But sometimes, and in crucial cases, he distinguishes between them. As a matter of convenience rather than as a sign of adherence to any doctrinal school, I shall use the term "phenomenological" to stand for the pre-analytical *presence* of objects in their interconnectedness and identifiability. Thus logical structures as well as objects related by such structures are "present" in the sense just defined. The phenomenological presence, whether obtained from Aristotle or from Husserl, is the basis and content of intuition. There are of course differences between the classical and the contemporary versions of phenomenological presence. But in this context, we can perhaps emphasize the similarities, and in this way cast light on the defects of the Kripkean analysis of the connected doctrines of essence and intuition.

We saw in the previous analysis that the term "essence" is normally used to translate the odd Aristotelian expression *to ti ēn einai*, "the what it was to be."[21] In the cause of brevity, we may say that, by "essence," Aristotle means basically *eidos* or form. And the form of something is literally its *look*, hence the immediate link between essence and intuition. In other words, Aristotle's doctrine of essence rests squarely upon the principle that being is knowable. To be is to be something, hence to be countable via the form which is the unit by which we may count. But the unit is a measure, and therefore distinguishable from all other measures. The marks by which one unit is distinguishable from another constitute its form or look. Just as in the case of Plato, thinking is both counting and seeing, or both *logismos* and *noēsis*.[22] Let us note that the show of things to the intellect is not perspectival: Aristotle is not guilty of psychologism. Being is knowable because of an underlying unity between the knower and the known. To say this is to say something more than that we know things as they are, or that we discover concepts and formal structures rather than invent them. Platonism or Realism entails the thesis that we have the *power* or intellectual capacity to become "somehow" (Aristotle's term) the form of what we know. Form and intellect actualize together. Hence the term "look" (which may refer either to the act of looking or to what we see) expresses the "belonging together" of being and thinking in a way that obviates the need to postulate the production of the world by human subjectivity. To anticipate, Kripke's distinction between logical and metaphysical necessity amounts to a separation of the form *qua* countable from the form *qua* look. And this in turn is rooted in the separation of thinking from being. To think in the genuine sense is to "calculate" the logical structure; to see the looks of things is to engage in epistemology or phenomenology (remembering that Kripke sometimes uses them interchangeably). Hence the doctrine of "possible worlds" or the logically conceivable is separated from metaphysical intuition and joined to the imagination. In this case the role played by the pre-analytical or common-sense situation becomes radically blurred.

According to Aristotle, things may be initially classified by their looks. The essence or form of a family or class of things is the look shared by all the individuals concerned, making for both an identity and a difference between the individual and its essential look. The individual *has* a definite look that identifies it as belonging to such-and-such a family, and that is the basis of essential predication. On the other hand, the look *has* an indeterminate number of individual instances. So the relation of *having* is not symmetrical. The sense in which an individual lion has the look of the family belonging to lions is not the same as the sense in which the lion-look has instances. In contemporary language, we have a hierarchy of types or orders. Perhaps it does not need to be emphasized that the phenomenological distinction underlying this logical point is the difference between looking at an individual lion and observing the lion-look. What should be emphasized, however, is that there is no way to explain discursively how we distinguish in the activity of looking, except after the fact. In order to see the lion-look, I must look at a lion (initially). I can then list two sets of properties, one belonging to the lion-look and one to the individual instance of that look. *But the two sets are distinguished by the antecedent act of bi-polar looking, not by two antecedent sets of discursively acquired properties.* If seeing the lion-look were the same as seeing the individual lion, then there would be no difference between the individual and its species. Otherwise stated, each lion would be an essence. But in this case, there could be no distinction between essential and accidental properties. We could never arrive at the notion of an essence. The example of identifying the individual lion as an essence is intelligible only because we imagine to ourselves that the lion-look is just like a physical lion. If it were, however, we would not know what is meant by "just like." Those who deny that "phenomenological looks" permit a doctrine of kinds or essences are then faced with the problem of talking away the initial looks of things. But they can do this only by referring to the initial looks which already serve as the basis for a distinction between "appearance" and "reality" or "surface" and "deep" structure. It makes no sense to talk of "reality" or "deep structure" unless we know the appearances or surfaces that they ostensibly explain. Since these appearances and surfaces make up the everyday or commonsense world inhabited by analyst and metaphysician alike, the denial of the significance of initial looks is finally impossible. Kripke recognizes this, but he is not consistent in honoring his recognition. For him, the residents of possible worlds are just the residents of *this* world. Consequently we must start with the looks of things. However, as I pointed out above, and as we shall see at greater length, Kripke divides these looks into logical and epistemological components; the net result is to transform intuition into the imagination. Kripke assumes that we can imagine a lion to look other than as it normally does while still being a lion, or that we can imagine what looks like a lion not to be a lion. And this is to separate the logical essence from the phenomenological look. The imagination of phenomenological variations replaces the intuition of the "phenomenological look." It remains to be seen whether this makes sense. We note here only that the initial look is the starting point, not the fantasy, and it is also the terminus of our fantasies, or what we intend to explain.

For Aristotle, the look of a lion is determined (primarily) by its essence. The individual lion is "present" to perception and calculation because the essence is "present" to intellectual intuition. These two senses of "presence" are the basis for any subsequent acts of imaginative variation. For example, I can be mistaken in what I see (e.g., I can take a stone for a man) only because I take one look for another, both of which are visible within the everyday or pre-analytical world. Mistakes in the everyday world are rectified, in the last consideration, not by logical analysis or imaginative variation, but by taking another look. Needless to say, my point is not that life proceeds in the everyday world as a discontinuous series of gazings. But the desired continuity cannot be supplied by discursive calculation, by counting and measuring. The continuum is a reciprocity of looking and talking. When I contend that we can say only what we have seen, I do not overlook the capacity to guide one's vision by speech. The important point is this: the presence of the look to the looker allows the transition from the phenomenological to the logical aspects of the look. In this sense logical analysis is rooted in intellectual intuition. There is, however, a further point to be made here. My emphasis upon "looks" and "seeing" is justified to a considerable extent by ordinary experience. But that emphasis can also be misleading, and once again we may be instructed by ordinary experience (thereby illustrating what I meant above by "taking another look"). It is more or less true that, for Aristotle, vision is the most important of the senses. As such, it serves most frequently (but not exclusively) as the paradigm for thinking and intuiting. However, Aristotle's word for intellectual intuition is *noēsis*, which does not express etymologically the paradigm of vision. Philologists have shown that the word may have been derived from "sniffing" the tracks of the quarry.[23] It is true that *eidos* directly suggests the paradigm of vision. Nevertheless, technical or abstract terms must have some origin or other, and it is theoretically quite dangerous to explain the sense of a technical term simply in terms of its etymology. (If this were legitimate, then "analysis" would mean "loosening" or "dissolving" rather than explaining or tying together.)

A look is a show. But shows may have non-visual elements as well. Consider such idiomatic English expressions as "I sniffed out his meaning," "I hear you talking," "You touch upon the nerve of the matter," and even "Victory was so close that I could taste it." Each of these expressions turns upon a kind of intuiting that invokes sense-paradigms other than that of sight. But even granting that vision is the paramount sense-paradigm for Aristotle, it cannot be true that noetic intuition of forms or essences is analogous to the quasi-physical act of seeing a picture or image in our imagination. It follows from our earlier remarks that if essences were pictures or visual images, we would still have to look at them and their instances in order to "see" the identity. And this is not the same as visual seeing, even if what we look at are visual objects. The essence of a lion is not a picture of a lion, any more than a photograph of a man is the essential man. If the photograph is a revealing one, we may learn something essential from it about its subject. But the process of learning is something in addition to merely looking at the photograph. Similar remarks might be developed about the other sense-paradigms. To say "this looks just like that" requires us to understand the meaning of "just like." And this understanding is not explicable in terms of solely "gazing upon."

There is, then, something intrinsically ambiguous about the notion of intuiting a form. The ambiguity is partly removed by speaking of the cognitive grasping of essences, but here we pay the price of shifting from the language of the eye to that of the hand. At least the term "essence" cannot be etymologically explained as a picture. But essences are indeed confused with pictures when intellectual intuition is confused with the visual imagination. For example, Hilary Putnam, when he believes himself to be talking about Idealism, is actually describing phenomenalism. As a result, arguments presented by him to refute Platonism serve instead to support it.[24] If by "mental object" we mean a picture or construction of the imagination, then intuitable essences are no more mental objects than they are what Putnam calls "concepts." The Platonist and the Aristotelian will therefore both agree with the following observation by Putnam:

> Someone who identifies conceptualization with linguistic activity and who identifies linguistic activity with response to observable situations in accordance with rules of language which are themselves no more than implicit conventions or implicit stipula-

tions . . . will, it seems to me, have a deeply distorted conception of human knowledge. [MLR, 41]

Putnam is a partial Kripkean with Platonist or Aristotelian tendencies, of which he is unfortunately unaware. And this historical oversight is not without theoretical consequences: it leads to his confusion of intuition and imagination. As a result, Putnam actually rejects essentialism, despite his apparent agreement with important elements of Kripke's views (MLR, 162f).

Putnam accordingly holds that "natural kind words" (the contemporary version of Aristotelian species) are not defined analytically, but have their meanings determined by "core facts" or a list of stereotypical properties, together with a test by which experts can determine whether a given individual is or is not a member of that natural kind (MLR, 143, 148ff). Needless to say, Putnam does not reflect seriously on the meaning of "nature," which he assumes to be the object of scientific investigation. He therefore begins with the phenomenological situation (objects and elements in the everyday world), which is not merely subjected to, but is already conceived in terms of, the analyses of empirical science. We can therefore state the difference between Putnam and Kripke as follows. Kripke accepts the intuition of logical essence, even though he separates logical structure from the phenomenological looks of things. Putnam rejects intuition (or believes that he rejects it), and so moves from phenomenology to history. That is, his phenomenology is in fact a scientific historicism: the history of scientific theories. For Putnam, what I call "presence" is the moving finger of time.

At the risk of sounding anachronistic, I am tempted to suggest that the Aristotelian thesis of intellectual intuition is an implicit transcendental argument. There is no possibility of a direct demonstration of the act of intuition in the sense of a discursive analysis of that act. This is because intuition is the necessary precondition for discursivity and, as an act, it has no structure. The case of intuition is in a deep sense analogous to that of temporality. The attempt to analyze the structure of temporal flow leads to the dissolution of the present into the past and the future. The present moment seems to have no independent form of its own, but is defined by its emergence from the future and disappearance into the past. Nevertheless, the notions of past and future are unintelligible except in terms of the present. It is thus not by chance that traditional philosophers have spoken of an intuition of the present in terms suggesting an intuition of eternity. To take another example, there is no non-circular demonstration of the principle of non-contradiction, at least in non-dialectical logics. Aristotle defends this principle in various rhetorical ways, including *ad hominem* arguments, but in the last analysis our decision on the "soundness" of this principle depends upon our intuition of rationality. In Aristotle, this intuition is closely connected to his belief that to speak meaningfully is to say something of something, or to predicate. And the same intuition dominates contemporary analytical philosophy, despite the revolution in logic since, say, Frege, Russell, and Whitehead. A simple example will suffice to make this clear. In set theory, sets may be formed, with suitable qualifications to avoid antinomies, from defining properties or from statements of predication. A predicative statement is one which says something about something, i.e., it claims that a certain property belongs to a certain individual (of whatever kind, natural or abstract). The statement is either true or false. Analogously, the Cantorian notion of a "formula in x" restates the predicative assertion in the language of mathematical functions. So a formula $P(x)$ defines a set A if and only if the members of A are exactly those objects a such that $P(a)$ is a true statement. In other words the values of the function $P(x)$, for a suitable domain, are predicative statements. So the statement-form "x is a lion" contains the predicate "———is a lion." All values a of x for which the statement "a is a lion" is true, form a set, namely, the set of lions. This is basically the Fregean functional analysis of propositions.

The question then arises: under what circumstances are predicating statements true? How do we know that a is indeed a lion? And the problem is at this level exactly the same for Aristotle and for the Fregean (or Kripkean). A mathematical model claims to be a *picture* of how we ought to reason in everyday life. But the picture does not tell us how we ought to decide that such-and-such properties of a given lion, say Leo, belong to his essence. According to the doctrine of predication, essences are defined by a set of predicates. But the defining predicates are themselves identified as essential by recourse to the essence. What we need, then, is a model that pictures the essence. We need a phenomenological model. Aristotle does not provide such a model, but he does admit the capacity of intellectual intuition. This capacity is peculiar in the sense that it has no formal structure. We cannot construct a picture, model, or blueprint of the activity of seeing essences. Since it is apparently also impossible to construct a model of the essence, the temptation is naturally great to dispense with both essences and intuition. The result is historicism or conventionalism: "essences" are replaced by stipulative definitions, and the philosophical task of grounding our knowledge in experience, or in things as they show themselves, is abandoned. Despite the apparent rehabilitation of essences and intuitions by the Kripkeans, this task is not taken up again, thanks to the ambiguous attempt to distinguish between the logical and the phenomenological. Kripkean essentialism fails for the same reason that Fregean Platonism fails. No coherent account is offered of the unity of being and thinking. The absence of such an account may be due to a fear of psychologism, or to the conviction, based upon modern science, that the initial appearance of things conceals a deep structure.

In either case, the problem remains of fitting together the conceptual or logical structure and the looks of things. It is not always apparent that this is the same problem as making the distinction in the first place.

5. Are Essences Necessary?

At this point in the discussion there would seem to be good reasons for wishing to dispense with essences. Is this possible? Or is the question of the necessity of essences already its own answer? There are various ways in which to defend the doctrine of essence. Without going into great detail we might say that we just intuit essences and would therefore be falsifying our experience if we denied them. People who are certain that they have seen a ghost do not always lose that certainty merely because they are unable to persuade the majority of their neighbors, or indeed, offer evidence of any kind. I do not believe that this reason is quite as insubstantial as it seems at first glance, but it would take us too far afield to defend it. Another class of reasons may be represented by the following argument: if there are no essences, then everything is accidental, in which case it makes no difference what we say or do. Reasons of this sort tend to be unpersuasive. In the first place, if there are no essences, then there are no accidents. Second, the accidental is not self-evidently synonymous with the valueless. But third, even if it were, that would not be a sufficient reason for holding a doctrine of essences; at the most, it would justify our pretending publicly that essences exist.

I turn now to two reasons why philosophers sometimes hold a doctrine of essences despite the difficulties involved. The first reason is one which I myself accept, and I regard it as binding upon reasonable men, whether Aristotelians, Kripkeans, or not. The second reason is Kripkean, and has to do with the nature of quantified modal logic. I have no objection to this reason, as I have no objection to quantified modal logic. But in itself, it would not be sufficient to move me to accept essences. However desirable such a logic may be in itself, the question of the existence of essences is prior to the question of that desirability. I do not suggest that the reasons I am about to give are the only reasons for defending essences. I claim only that the first reason is decisive, and that the second reason is central to a leading school of contemporary analytical philosophy. Before I examine these reasons, let me restate the connection between predication and how we identify things of any kind or modality.

A thing x, in order to be the theme of any discourse, must be identifiable within the universe of that discourse. We invariably say that x is what it is (even in the minimal case in which we say that x takes values a, b, c . . .) by virtue of possessing certain marks or properties, for example, the property of conforming to a definite mathematical operation. These marks or properties define x or distinguish it from non-x, i.e., from things of other kinds (as for example the complement of x). In short, x "has" some set of predicates p_1, . . . , p_n. The question again arises: what do we mean here by "has"? The pertinent case is the one in which one party of the investigation holds that p_1, . . . , p_n are essential predicates of x. Let us first consider the thesis of the other, anti-essentialist party, or as I shall call it, the *conventionalist* thesis.

The conventionalist, to begin with, is under the impression that he is denying the existence of essences. I say "is under the impression" because at least some essentialists (myself included) draw a distinction between essence and existence (although the character of English makes it sometimes awkward to insist upon or even to make it). From this standpoint, it is an error to affirm the existence of an essence (see section 9). For if essences do *exist*, it becomes very hard to distinguish between the essential and the non-essential aspects of the existing individual. Leaving this point behind for the moment, the conventionalist thesis amounts to one form or another of the thesis that objects are identified by collocations of properties, where the collocations in turn depend upon stipulations, definitions, linguistic use, points of view, historically changing conceptual frameworks, and so on. In sum, the way or ratio of the ostensibly essential presentation of properties is a linguistic convention. The conventionalist wishes to deny that we have access to, and indeed that there are any necessary connections between objects and their observed properties. The conventionalist, then, denies that objects are necessarily identified by this or that property; but he does not deny that *we necessarily identify objects by means of their properties*.

Let me emphasize this conclusion. In order for the conventionalist thesis to hold, there must be identifiable objects. And objects must be identified either by some kind of intuition, in which case essences are granted, or else by predicative discourse, in which case objects have properties. So the discursive denial of the essentialist thesis entails the specification of properties as *belonging to* those objects. The conventionalist denies only that any analysis of "belonging to" (by which we might establish the necessary connection of any property to any object) is possible. The "way" in which an object shows itself is then due to the "way" in which the subject looks at the object. At this stage the conventionalist may be transformed into an Idealist. Let us assume that he is not. The ways of the subject and object, then, do not constitute an account of the phenomenon of "belonging to." There is a missing link between the phenomenon of belonging and the circumstances to which we attribute the *sense* of the phenomenon of belonging. But the phenomenon of belonging is not itself missing.

If objects are unthinkable except as having properties, then "having" and "belonging to" themselves belong to the essence of objectivity (cf. section 3). And since there can be no analysis of "having" and "belonging to," we must intuit this essence. Conventionalism is thus a peculiar species of the intuitionist branch of essentialism.[25] It cannot be a discursive denial or refutation of our intuition of "having" and "belonging to," because such a refutation would be self-annihilating. To restate this conclusion as a thesis of essentialism, the notion of a logically necessary connection, or of essences, is intuitively founded, even if we cannot state discursively what any essential property might be. If I have understood him correctly, this is the thesis of Saul Kripke. It does not, of course, follow from this that Kripke is an Aristotelian, or that he would accept my argument as I have formulated it. Nevertheless, there is a kind of allegiance between Kripkeans and Aristotelians because Kripke provides arguments intended to justify the doctrine of essences that are not incompatible with modern science. I add that I see no reason why Kripke could not accept my thesis concerning the essentialist nature of conventionalism, and certainly none for his disagreeing with me about the intuitive status of "having" and "belonging to."

So much for the first reason in defense of essences. It boils down to this: we cannot talk intelligibly about objects, or for that matter about linguistic expressions, unless we can intuit the necessary connection of properties by which these objects or expressions are defined. *Reference depends upon intuition.* This is why there can be no comprehensive theory of reference; such a theory would require a model of the act of intuition. By way of transition from the first to the second reason, I reiterate that the distinction between *de re* and *de dicto* necessity is sometimes employed in an effort to preserve modal logic without essences. But this is altogether in vain since we still need to intuit the necessity of the connections in our utterances. Let us turn now to the second reason in defense of essences. I shall discuss it primarily with respect to modal logic, making necessary a note about logic in general. In non-modal contexts, when applying mathematical logic to philosophical problems, it is customary to interpret open sentences with one variable, e.g., "$x =$ Aristotle" or "———is Aristotle" as properties (or predicates) of individual objects. So "being Aristotle" is a property of the man called "Aristotle." And in this case it seems likely that "being Aristotle" is a necessary property. To turn to modal logic, there is a compelling reason why Kripkeans defend a notion of individual essences. And this is that in intuitive interpretations of Kripke's semantics for quantified modal logic, crucial use is made of "the idea of one and the same individual existing in different possible worlds."[26]

The distinction between syntax and semantics is a familiar one to professional philosophers and linguists. "Syntax refers to the purely formal structure of the language . . . semantics refers to the interpretation, or meaning, of the formal language—the truth or falsity of a sentence in a model is a semantical property."[27] Kripke's semantics, stated generally, is a model of quantified modal logic that tells us under what circumstances the sentences of the logic are true or false. However, this semantics is itself a set-theoretical structure or, in other words, possesses an exclusively set-theoretical meaning. Quantified modal logic becomes philosophically interesting, and controversial, not as an exercise in set theory, but only when we give it an intuitive interpretation by which it is applicable to questions of meaning, truth, and thereby the natures of things in the world. The intuition suggested by Kripke is that of possible worlds.[28] Before going on to consider this notion at length I want to state very briefly the sense of this intuition for Kripke's semantics. A property belongs necessarily to an individual if and only if there are no logically conceivable states of affairs under which the given individual might lack that property and remain the same individual. Kripke calls these states of affairs "possible worlds." This notion traces its philosophical pedigree back to Leibniz, but there is an informal source, clear from many of the examples in the literature: science fiction. This is not irrelevant to the confusion between intuition and imagination that also marks the literature of modal logic. In any case, the intuitive interpretation of quantified modal logic requires us to distinguish between necessary and contingent (or possibly otherwise) properties, and hence to attach a meaning to the notion of an essence of individuals. If we so wish, we may enrich our logic with natural kinds or sets, in which case these kinds or sets become objects and possess essences. But there is no need for us to take this step. Only individual essences are required to be meaningful for quantified modal logic. We may or may not accept essences of natural kinds. Hence it is wrong to call Kripkean essentialism a form of Aristotelianism.

It is easy to see that application of both universal instantiation and existential generalization within modal contexts commits us to essentialism. To take instantiation first, it is a logical truth that every individual is identical to itself:

(1) $$(\forall x) \ \Box \ x = x$$

If there are no individual essences, then there are no necessary properties of individuals. Hence it would be true that

(2) $$(\forall y) \sim \Box \ (y = x)$$

whereas it would be false that

(3) $$\sim \Box \ (x = x)$$

68

and consequently, universal instantiation would fail. In any given instance, nothing would be necessarily identical to an object x, even though (by the logical truth (1)) every object is necessarily self-identical.[29]

The case of existential generalization (EG) is associated with a famous objection, or series of objections, to quantified modal logic by W. V. Quine. These objections have been discussed often and extensively; for our purposes I shall restrict myself to what is for us the main point.[30] According to Quine there is an intimate connection between substitutivity (i.e., given a true assertion of identity, one of its terms may be substituted for the other in any true assertion *salva veritate*) and quantification. To put an open sentence with a singular term into quantified form is to say that there exists something having the property predicated by the sentence of the denotation of its singular term. If that term is p, and there exists an equivalent term q, then the sentence must be true whether p or q stands in the referential position. However, consider the following inference:

(4) $\qquad\qquad\qquad \Box\, 9 > 7$

(5) $\qquad\qquad\qquad \therefore (\exists x)\, \Box\, (x > 7)$

By the principle of substitutivity, we must admit that "9" may be replaced *salva veritate* by any co-referential term. But

(6) $\qquad\qquad \Box$ The number of planets is greater than 7

is false. The number of planets is only contingently 9; it could conceivably have been some other number, say 5. Therefore we cannot apply existential generalization to (6), which would yield (5) falsely.

According to Quine, "———is greater than 7" and "——— is the number of planets" each follows analytically from '9,' depending upon the way in which we specify '9.' Hence the modal operators characterize ways of speaking about objects, not about the objects themselves. In other words, the standard interpretation of the modal operators is *de dicto*. As is indicated by their positions outside the scope of the quantifiers, when this occurs, the operators apply to propositions, not to the objects that are the values of the variables within the propositions. Hence, when the modal operators occur within the scope of the quantifiers, as in (5), referential opacity results because substitutivity cannot be uniformly applied *salva veritate*. We can avoid this dilemma by introducing the distinction between *de dicto* and *de re* necessity into our semantics. But this commits us to essentialism. And essentialism, as Quine sees it, is a philosophically disreputable doctrine.

The standard replies to Quine's objections either reaffirm essentialism, by making explicit the *de dicto/de re* distinction, thus introducing a distinction between proper and improper substitution-instances of x in (5) (e.g., Hintikka,

Smullyan), or they claim that existential generalization in modal logic commits us to trivial senses of essence rather than to philosophically disreputable ones (Marcus, Parsons).[31] Since the first way regards essentialism as a significant philosophical doctrine, we may ignore it here. But we ought to look a bit more closely at an example of the second way, in order to fill out our sketch of the kinds of reasons presented to repudiate essentialism by contemporary analytical philosophers. It is neither feasible nor necessary to refute every possible version of the second way in order to defend essentialism. For basically the same kinds of arguments come into play against various efforts to "neutralize" the role of essences in quantified modal logic. Perhaps the main point is that the issue is philosophical, not mathematical.

In a widely-cited paper, Terence Parsons wishes to show that quantified modal logic (1) has no essential sentence as a theorem, (2) does not entail that an essential sentence be true, and (3) allows the formulation of meaningful essential sentences but is itself not committed to their truth.[32] Points (1) and (2) hold good within what Parsons calls a *maximal model* of quantified modal logic as interpreted by Kripkean semantics in its pure or set-theoretical form. But these points are irrelevant to the question of the philosophical application of Kripkean semantics, and we may disregard them here.[33] Let us restrict our attention to point (3). According to Parsons,

> although a system of quantified modal logic can assert, deny, or be neutral with respect to the *truth* of essentialism, it cannot be neutral concerning the *meaningfulness* of essentialism, for quantified modal logic simply *is* that symbolism within which essential sentences are formulable. Thus, in order to guarantee that all of its formulas are meaningful, any system of quantified modal logic must provide a meaning for each essential sentence. [EQML, 84]

In my opinion, one has only to read Parsons's statement to see that it is implausible. By Parsons's distinction, all sentences containing references to essences could be false without disturbing the meaningfulness of quantified modal logic. However, what would be the philosophical function of such a logic? The most that could be said is this: the interpretation of the logic shows that any attempt to state a doctrine of essences is false. But since no such attempt could be true, the term "false" ceases to convey any meaning. I conclude that, in this case, the logic has no philosophical function. One ought perhaps to conclude that it is intrinsically self-defeating to try to formulate essential sentences in a symbolic calculus. This is presumably not the conclusion toward which the champions of quantified modal logic are working.

Before I turn to a second approach to Parsons's point (3), I should remark that others may hold that it is initially quite plausible. Kripke himself makes a similar distinction and argues primarily (if not exclusively) for the meaningfulness of essentialism. There is, however, a fundamental difference between the two cases. As I have noted, it is compatible with Parsons's thesis that quantified modal logic has no interpretation by which it can be applied *meaningfully* to the actual world. The meaningfulness of the interpretation (and of the logic) turns upon a philosophical decision concerning the meaningfulness of the doctrine. And this in turn requires a basis for distinguishing between true and false sentences about essences. That basis cannot be the philosophical neutrality of the logician. Kripke's defense of the meaningfulness of essentialism may have been motivated by his semantics. But it is not explicitly designed to sterilize quantified modal logic of any philosophical significance. It is rather an attempt to establish the philosophical reputability of essentialism. This becomes especially obvious from Kripke's appeals to intuition, imagination, and the like. His goal is not merely technical or calculative. He is trying to connect an intuition about the world (in my language, about the "looks of things") with an intuition about logical structure. This attempt is not always coherently expressed, but it is philosophical in a way that Parsons's is not. In a slightly different formulation, Parsons's intentions are restrictive and defensive. But Kripke's intentions are expansive and constructive. If I may risk a conjecture, Parsons is afraid of the illicit reputation of essences, whereas Kripke is not. The concept of meaning for Kripke is not an end in itself, but a doorway into the more capacious concept of truth.

Parsons makes the following claim. The modal logician who denies essentialism can render harmless the meaning of his essential sentences by making them all false in all possible worlds (EQML, 85). But this requires the falsehood of such sentences as

(7) $(\exists x)\,(\exists y)\,(x$ is nine $\&\ y$ is seven $\&\ \Box\,(x>y))$

i.e., of sentences asserting "that there be things, nine and seven, such that in every possible world *these* things are such that the first is greater than the second." Here then is the sentence that Parsons would allow to be true, and one that according to him causes no difficulties for the modal logician:

(8) $\Box\,(\exists x)(\exists y)\,(x$ is nine $\&\ y$ is seven $\&\ (x>y))$

i.e., it is required that "in each possible world there be some things or other such that the first 'is nine' and the second 'is seven' and the first is greater than the second."

At first glance, we seem to have nothing more than a retreat from *de re* to *de dicto* necessity. However, if this retreat is to preserve meaningfulness for essential sentences, then we must claim that it is intelligible to say that numbers do not necessarily preserve their essential identity in all possible worlds. Is this claim meaningful? At the very least we can say that Parsons has not avoided committing quantified modal logic to essentialism by any technical operations internal to the logic as interpreted by Kripkean semantics. On the contrary, he has given a philosophical interpretation to the semantics. That is, he has incorporated into the semantics a controversial thesis about the nature of numbers. Let us distinguish between natural numbers and the objects by which we represent them in this world. As Alvin Plantinga points out, the fact that number theory can be reduced to set theory in various ways does not entail the conclusion that numbers are (in each world) the specific objects or constructions to which they have been reduced.[34] Plantinga goes on to draw various absurd consequences from Parsons's assumption. If I understand him correctly, he does not quite state the following criticism of Parsons's procedure. Parsons's assumption, as I hold, is not simply absurd in the sense of improbable or virtually impossible. It begs the philosophical question at stake by attempting to transform it into a question of translation, or a methodological choice between *de dicto and de re* expressions of necessity. The meaningfulness of (8) depends, contrary to Parsons's denial, upon "general considerations" (EQML, 81) or upon philosophical discussion of a fundamental sort concerning the nature of number. And this in turn raises the question of intuition. Stated as simply as possible, I reject Parsons's assumption because it violates my intuition of natural numbers. Therefore, I deny that we can affirm (8) at the same time that we deny (7). I may of course be mistaken. But the issue has to be argued in a philosophical context, not a mathematical one. The issue cannot be avoided by shifting from one mode of technical translation to another.

Let me try to state this in another way. What is wrong with contemporary discussions of modal logic is that, despite their frequent presentation in a thick wrapping of mathematics, they are surprisingly superficial from a philosophical standpoint. In the next section, I shall illustrate this criticism with respect to the central notion of a *possible world*. An extraordinary amount of technical ingenuity is expended upon the formalization of assumptions which are themselves virtually unexamined. Equally superficial is the practice of adopting those assumptions that facilitate formalization. It is conceivable (in the sense of "imaginable") that Parsons or someone else might devise a way of employing *de dicto* necessity without committing the absurdities flagged by Plantinga. But *de dicto* necessity would still be rooted in an intuition of the necessary connection of terms within our linguistic concepts. The first step is to get straight on the philosophical nature of our concepts and our capacity to conceptualize. The construction and interpretation of logics is at best the second step. And the interpretation of a logic is a philosophical decision, not just a technical exercise in meta-mathematics. We can of course give a mathematical interpretation to a calculus, just as Kripke gives a set-theoretical interpretation to quantified modal logic. But as philosophers, we must also give an interpretation to our set theory.[35] Kripke does just this in his use of the "intuitive" interpretation of his semantics as referring to possible worlds.[36] Unfortunately, he gives little or no critical attention to the philosophical sense of "possible world." He rather assumes that a certain meaning of "possible" is intuitively sound, and then proceeds to spin his web of examples on the basis of that assumption. But terms like "possible" and "intuitive" carry too heavy a philosophical burden to pass unanalyzed by philosophers.[37]

6. Intuition and Imagination in Kripke

Possible Worlds

The notion of a "possible world" is philosophical and theological, not mathematical. Its use in contemporary accounts of essentialism and modal logic would suggest that the term is either a self-evident component of everyday reflection, or that it can be defined easily and clearly on the basis of mathematical conventions already in use. However, anything can be mathematized, even our fantasies. The sense of "possible world" that seems to be taken for granted in the literature embodies a confusion between intuition and imagination. I believe it will be illuminating to preface our analysis of Kripke's terminology with a brief historical note.

The contemporary revival of essentialism is sometimes presented as a revival of Aristotelianism. I myself have argued that there are points of contact between the classical ontological doctrine of essence and the views of the Kripkeans. But there is also a radical difference between the pagan Aristotelian doctrine and the teachings of the Kripkeans. The sense of "possible world," and so of "intuiting" *qua* imagining, employed by the Kripkeans is not Aristotelian but Judaeo-Christian. Aristotle's essences are not possible logical structures but natural kinds, and nature in the sense of kinds or species is for him eternal. The Kripkeans may be somewhat playfully assimilated in the Ashʿarite sect of the medieval Islamic theologians known as the Mutakallimūn. They (the Kripkeans) wrongly believe themselves to descend from Leibniz. It is true that Leibniz makes central use of the notion of possible worlds. It is also true that Leibniz distinguishes between "truths of reason" (or logical truths) and "truths of fact" (or truths about nature). This distinction no doubt underlies the contemporary Kripkean distinction between logical and epistemological necessity. But in the Kripkean version, the world is not merely radically contingent; it could have been created in accordance with natural laws totally different from those which obtain in this world (so long as these laws do not violate the principle of non-contradiction).

Leibniz's doctrines differ significantly from those of the Kripkeans, as was pointed out by Hidé Ishiguro.[38] For Leibniz, a possible world is one which God could have created, and so which exists as an idea. But in Leibniz's notion of "possible," natural necessity is not totally sundered from logical possibility. Ishiguro notes:

> It may indeed be possible to describe a world in which some of our natural laws do not operate and others do. If we can still use our concepts to describe this possible world, we know where we stand. But where the natural laws diverge from those of our world, we must work out fully the consequences it has in individuating the entities and properties in that world. It is not obvious that any property can be meaningfully ascribed to objects in all possible worlds, including those worlds which have different natural laws from ours. And if assumptions of certain laws of nature are surreptitiously involved in our thoughts about all possible worlds, then to be necessarily coextensive in worlds which share *these* natural laws does indeed collapse into logical equivalence. [PLL 66]

And again:

> We can conceptually distinguish logical necessity ('true in all possible worlds') and physical necessity (or what Leibniz calls 'hypothetical necessity', necessary given the initial conditions of the world), but their mutual relation is a very complex one. Logical necessity and physical necessity (in the sense given above) are intricately intertwined in our thoughts about possible worlds. [PLL 93]

In sum: "it follows that all talk of coextensiveness of properties presupposes identification of entities which have the properties, and the latter is dependent on certain assumptions about nature" (PLL, 93). The moral to be drawn for the contemporary discussion seems plain. First: the defense of a logical conception of "essence" as distinct from a "natural" *qua* empirical essence depends upon a philosophical doctrine concerning *nature*. Second: whereas we may imagine some property to be missing from an object in our world, it does not follow that it is logically possible for that object to remain the same without the given property. These issues are already involved in our approach to the phenomenological presence of the pre-analytical world.

The fundamental question, then, is whether the world is radically contingent. Could God have created a world totally different from this one, with the sole proviso that the principle of non-contradiction continues to hold in every possible world? Those who take the affirmative on this issue are not Leibnizians but Mutakallimūn. I quote at some length from Maimonides's *Guide of the Perplexed*, Book One, Chapter 73: the Mutakallimūn

> are of the opinion that everything that may be imagined is an admissible notion for the intellect . . . The whole world is involved in this method of admissibility as they practice it. For whatever thing of this kind they assume, they are able to say: it is admissible that it should be so, and it is possible that it should be otherwise; and it is not more appropriate that one particular thing should be so than that it should be otherwise. And they say this without paying attention to the correspondence or lack of correspondence of that which exists to their assumptions. For they say of the existent things—provided with known forms and determinate sizes and necessarily accompanying modes that are unchangeable and immutable—that their being as they are is merely in virtue of the continuance of a habit. In the same way it is the habit of a sultan not to pass through the market places of the city except on horseback, and he has never been seen doing it in a way other than this. However, it is not held impossible by the intellect that he should walk on foot in the city; rather it is undoubtedly possible, and it is admissible that this should occur. They say that the fact that earth moves toward the center and fire upwards or the fact that fire burns and water cools is in a similar way due to the continuance of a habit. It is, in consequence, not impossible from the point of view of the intellect that this habit should undergo a change so that fire should cool and move downwards, while still being fire . . . At the same time they are unanimous in holding that the coming-together of two contraries in the same substratum and at the same instant is impossible, cannot be true, and cannot be admitted by the intellect.[39]

This is sufficient to convey the flavor of the doctrine Maimonides is examining. By way of criticism, he replies:

> Now it is a true assertion that none of the things that they consider as impossible can be mentally represented to oneself in any way whatever, whereas the things they call possible can be. Yet the philosophers say that when you call a thing "impossible," it is because it cannot be imagined, and when you call a thing "possible," it is because it can be imagined. Thus what is possible according to you is possible only from the point of view of the imagination and not from that of the intellect.[40]

The doctrine of the Mutakallimūn rests upon the assumption that what the philosophers (i.e., the Aristotelians) hold to be a form constituting a substance is in fact an accident. In other words, they draw a distinction between logical and epistemological necessity. Still more accurately, there is no epistemological necessity because there are no essences. The Kripkeans draw the same distinction, yet suppose themselves to be defending the meaningfulness of a doctrine of essences. This is because they in effect define an essence as that which in a given object cannot be imagined to be otherwise while the object remains identical to itself. Little wonder, then, that they are unable to provide any example of an essential property.

The Kripkeans assume that logical possibility is independent of natural necessity. This assumption vitiates the sound procedure of beginning with objects from the actual world in the attempt to define an essence by means of the doctrine of possible worlds. As Ishiguro makes clear, the relations between logical and natural necessity are so complex that it would be folly to entrust their separation to the imagination. Furthermore, to do this is to open a Pandora's box. For I can imagine a situation in which the principle of non-contradiction no longer holds. Nor is it out of the question to suppose a world in which what we can imagine, i.e., our capacity of imagination, is altogether different from what is actually the case. One thing I cannot imagine, as it happens, is a world in which one may break off any of a wide range of properties without altering the nature of the object deprived of the property, or the world in which the object resides. I cannot imagine this in a sense different from my capacity to imagine that the laws of logic no longer hold, or that imagination is altogether different from what it actually is. This incapacity derives from a set of views concerning nature. I have a set of beliefs about what is naturally possible, and these beliefs are in turn rooted in my intuitions of the everyday world or what I have called phenomenological presence. Intuitive beliefs in this sense are not affected by imaginary variations on things as they are. On the contrary, what we are able to imagine, and the various senses we are able to attribute to the term "imagination," depends rather upon our intuitions about what is phenomenologically present. I do not say that logical analysis plays no role in our reflection upon phenomenological presence. What I say is that logical analysis must not be placed in the blind hands of fantasy.

So much for the historical note. Let me make a fresh beginning with the following question. How do we refer to objects, states, and events whose logical or conceptual structure we are concerned to establish? In Kripke's own terms, there is a difference between "fixing the referent" and "defining the concept" (NN, 340). Keeping in mind that the sense or concept can determine the reference of a term only if we are first able to refer to a particular object, I can say that "orange" will mean an oblate spheroid, a citrus fruit, etc., but this in itself must be preceded by the grasping of an object to be called "orange." Once I have fixed the reference of the name "orange," I can then go on to determine the concept. My initial grasp of the object is clearly not effected by means of the concept, which I do not yet have. To this it might be added that each subsequent grasping of any object, whether or not we possess concepts for these objects, is effected via some sort of perception, whether sensuous or intellectual, and not by a direct application of our concept as a sort of criterion of identification. There are two distinguishable issues here. First: how do we perceive an object *qua* object? Second: how do we fix the referent of some particular term, say "orange," prior to having a concept of that object? Kripke does not raise the first question. He never alludes to a synthetic function of the transcendental ego by which an object is presented to the discursive intellect. Instead, his approach is casually commonsensical, and in this sense, quasi-Aristotelian. As we shall see, the advantages accruing from this tincture of Aristotelianism are soon dissipated by a conceptual carelessness about the initially given situation. At the start, however, there is no philosophical justification of the phenomena. Objects are given. Some we no doubt perceive sensuously and some we may conceive; in other cases, such as the state of pain, we feel it directly. In the case of most objects, how we fix the referent is for Kripke misleading, either altogether or in part. Kripke calls this initial referring activity the "phenomenological" but also the "epistemological" situation.

Now it is true that, according to Kripke, this initial situation has to be clarified and corrected by a combination of empirical science and logical analysis. But the confusion of the phenomenological and the epistemological amounts to the identification of the initial situation as a scientific construction. Instead of starting from a commonsense beginning, we start from the object of epistemology. Differently stated, commonsense is defined by contemporary science. For example, if Kripke were to assert that we start with the simple perception of an orange, we could reply on his own grounds that initial perceptions are frequently misleading, and that it is empirical science (optics, physiology) that explains and clarifies perceptions. The intuition of, say, the essence of the orange must therefore precede the perception of the orange as an object of scientific analysis. There is, so to speak, a whole dimension of being antecedent to the dimension of scientific analysis, and the latter is a construction arising out of the former. Our philosophy of science must therefore be grounded in our ontology of the given; to this extent, I agree with Husserlian phenomenology, although it should be added that Husserl's doctrine is an excessively formalized version of a Platonic teaching. If there is no pre-scientific intuition of natural essences, then the constructive character of the initial situation will guarantee that the essences at which we arrive are also constructions. As I read Kripke, he sometimes acknowledges the regulative character of the pre-scientific intuition and sometimes he denies it. One could say of him what was said previously of Frege: he vacillates between the need for intellectual intuition and for a transcendental ego.[41]

Kripke's distinction between fixing the referent and defining the concept shows us how the problem of intuition surfaces in his doctrine: intuition is required in the fixing of the referent, which is in turn the precondition for the defining of the concept. But the ambiguous nature of the situation within which we fix the referent compromises our initial intuitions, which are often replaced by logical intuitions consequent upon the process of concept-definition. In order to bring out another side to the problem, I must introduce a second Kripkean distinction, that between the *logically necessary* and the *epistemologically a priori*. If *"a priori"* means "known without recourse to experience," then we can have *a posteriori* knowledge of necessary truths. Kripke gives two kinds of examples. The first is a computing machine that answers our question whether a certain number is prime, a number which has not previously been calculated. Our belief in the response of the machine is based upon our knowledge of the laws of physics and the construction of the machine. So our knowledge of whether the number is prime, which is necessary, is also *a posteriori*, although it might have been known *a priori* without the use of a computer (NN, 261).

The second example should be discussed at somewhat greater length since it plays a prominent role in Kripke's reflections. We may believe, he observes, that a table is made of wood, not ice, for a variety of reasons, all plausible, and so conclude that it is not made of ice, thereby reasoning in an *a posteriori* manner. The appearances could conceivably be deceiving; it is possible (says Kripke) that the table is actually made of ice. Note that Kripke is speaking here about logical possibility, not about physical possibility based upon our knowledge of physics.[42] This means that Kripke takes for granted the possibility of detaching logical from physical possibility: to say that it is possible to detach logical from physical possibility is to beg the question at issue, since the assertion is formulated on the basis of an acceptance of the theoretical doctrine at issue. Kripke goes on to say that we can imagine that what looks in all plausible ways like a wooden table is in fact a table made of ice. But

> given that it is in fact not made of ice, in fact is made of wood, one cannot imagine that under certain circumstances it could have been made of ice. So we have to say that though we cannot know *a priori* whether this table was made of ice or not, given that it is not made of ice, it is *necessarily* not made of ice.[43]

Kripke's argument, which is basic to his doctrine, is symbolized:

(9) $\qquad\qquad P \supset \Box P, P, \therefore \Box P$

Some comments on this example are in order. First, it is relatively easy to think of counterexamples, given the terms of Kripke's own doctrine. For instance, the stuff from which a table is made may itself consist of unstable atoms (or perhaps these atoms are subject to perturbations from rays projected by insidious Martians) such that the table is not now made of material of the same kind as it was when it was originally produced.[44] Second, the invocation of imagination makes it impossible to distinguish between plausible and implausible possibilities. We might imagine that the table is actually a leprechaun, disguised to look like a table as part of some elaborate hoax by the race of little folk. My point is that there is no more reason to imagine that the table is made of ice than that it is a leprechaun. We can always find out whether the table is made of ice. But if the disguise is perfect, then the ostensible ice is actually wood, and the imaginative hypothesis loses all relevance. The imagination plays no relevant role in the task of determining the essence (if any) of the table. It serves only to confuse the investigation. Finally, in asking what stuff the table is made of, Kripke takes for granted the presence of the table as object, or rather, he overlooks it. The ontology of appearances is thus covered over by (basically) scientific epistemology.

A third example of Kripke's distinction between the logical and the epistemological is this: in our pre-scientific experience we identify light as, say, whatever affects our eyes in a certain way. Similarly, we identify heat as what causes a certain sensation in us. But these are contingent properties; even if we all went blind, light would not cease to exist, nor would heat cease to exist if people were insensitive to it. However, when we discover through scientific investigation that light is a stream of photons, or that heat is molecular motion, then we have defined an essential, i.e., necessary property of light or heat (NN, 324ff). Kripke's main purpose is illustrated by contrasting the cases of light and heat with that of pain. Before we turn to pain, however, let us note Kripke's own peculiar insensitivity to the difference between the phenomenological and the epistemological. For surely, if there were no people (or sentient beings of our sort), there would be neither heat nor light. These words describe phenomena, not scientific entities independent of experience. The photons and molecules might exist without people, but that is quite different from the existence of heat and light. And it could also be argued that even the existence of the photons and molecules, which are theoretical constructions, is dependent upon the existence of theorists.

This aside, given that science correctly informs us of the nature of light (as a stream of photons), it is necessary that light be a stream of photons. But let us next consider pain. According to Kripke, "pain is not picked out by one of its accidental properties; rather it is picked out by the property of being pain itself, by its immediate phenomenological quality." Here Kripke makes the distinction between the phenomenological and the epistemological, albeit still in terms of science (stimulation of certain fibers within the brain). The initial perception is then not superseded by logical analysis. So "the reference of the designator," i.e., the name "pain," is "determined by an essential property of the referent" (NN, 340). In cases where fixing the reference and defining the concept are the same, then, even though science investigates the cause (e.g., excessive heat or light) and the inner structure (e.g., the central nervous system) of pain, the essential nature of pain *qua* pain is not conditional upon scientific investigation. This result figures prominently in Kripke's reflections on the mind-body problem. What counts for us, however, is that in some cases the immediate phenomenological situation is logically or metaphysically sound, whereas in others it is not. In my terms, Kripke notices the presence of pain, but as pain, not as presence. In his own terms, pain is an exception to his general rule covering natural kinds, states, events, and so on. The general rule is that science tries to find the nature, and so the essence, of natural kinds (NN, 329f). It does this by the investigation of "basic structural traits." Therefore, nature is for the most part *a conceptual and logical construction or reconstruction of the phenomenological situation*. But how can this be if we begin in a pre-scientific sense from the phenomenological situation?

In quasi-Aristotelian language, our intuition of pain is not just a feeling, but also the grasping of an actual essence. For Kripke, however, in the case of natural kinds or Aristotelian essences, "the way the reference of a term is fixed should not be regarded as a synonym for the term." (NN, 328). Here the phenomenological situation does not agree with the logical situation. There is no allusion to the presence of the look of the natural kind as antecedent to, and constitutive in, the epistemological act of fixing the referent of the term. For Kripke "it is an empirical matter whether the characteristics originally associated with the kind apply to its members universally, or even ever . . ." (NN, 329). But Kripke engages in no philosophical analysis of experience. Most of the time, "experience" is what science tells us it is. But sometimes it is something prior to what science tells us. Otherwise stated, nature is sometimes a logical construction, but sometimes it is not. How then are we to account for this structural incoherence within nature? How do we justify logic and science? It cannot be on the basis of the initial phenomenological situation, if that is either a consequence of logic and science, or else logically and scientifically incoherent. In sum: Kripke cannot explain intuition via science and logic because, by his own account, science and logic are based upon intuition. But the circumstances giving rise to intuition are themselves usually explained in terms of science and logic. Clearly, we need some careful account of intuition. But this is precisely what Kripke does not give us.[45]

Kripke's Use of "Intuition"

We can, I think, distinguish three different senses in which Kripke speaks of intuition. First: intuition suggests to us a particular theory, for example, a theory about logical necessity or essences. Stated more positively, intuition is the ultimate judge of whether a logical theory is meaningful or true. Second: intuition is equivalent to imagination; it tells us whether a particular property is necessary or contingent, or plays a fundamental role in our decision on this status of the property. Third: intuition is indistinguishable or not distinguished from imagination; it erroneously identifies properties to be necessary that science, together with intuition in the second sense, shows us to be contingent, and that are to be replaced by necessary properties. Before giving examples of these three uses, let me repeat the central point of our investigation. Michael Dummett, as I have noted, raises the question: how do we refer to objects? By a process of elimination, we found that Kripke's answer to this question is: by intuition. This is mandatory because Kripke is not concerned with *de dicto* necessity or the modalities of propositions. He is talking about beings in the world or *de re* necessity. We have also seen that intuition cannot be explained by science or logic. Not merely does it lack any structure, but it is itself the basis of science and logic. Therefore Kripke, whether he is aware of it or not, is concerned with *the traditional metaphysical thesis of the unity of being and thinking*. It is not possible to rehabilitate the doctrine of essences in a radically new form, defined by contemporary logic and analytical devices. It is, however, possible to beg all the interesting questions. We would be wrong to demand of Kripke what we ourselves admit to be impossible: a detailed analysis of intuition or thinking. But we have the right to expect that he recognize the problem, formulate it in a coherent manner, and that his use of "intuition" be consistent with the requirements of the problem. These uses must be consistent with each other, and they must refer to a cognitive faculty that is adequate to the distinction between the phenomenological and the epistemological. Intuition cannot be a product of logic, but it must be "regulated" by the natural elements as well as the web of natural elements of the original (phenomenological) situation. Conversely, these natural elements and their web must be initially free of the subjective distortions or inadequacies of what Kripke calls the epistemological situation. In a word, intuition must be of natural essences, not of conceptual constructions. And if they should be of conceptual constructions, then we require a Kantian doctrine of the transcendental ego.

Let us now scrutinize some examples of the three senses of "intuition" in Kripke. First: intuition functions to certify the meaningfulness of a theory. Thus he insists that the notion of a necessary property has "intuitive content" and goes on to say:

> Of course, some philosophers think that something's having intuitive content is very inconclusive evidence in favor of it. I think it is very heavy evidence in favor of anything, myself. I really don't know in a way what more conclusive evidence one can have about anything, ultimately speaking. [NN, 266]

The term "intuitive" refers here to a logical doctrine about necessary properties. At the same time, to say that a theory has "intuitive content" must mean that it also has properties, i.e., theoretical properties. And these are necessary in the very direct sense that the theory could not be what it is if these properties were other than they are. A theory asserting the meaningfulness of necessary properties would not be the same theory if we imagined it to be denying the meaningfulness of necessary properties. But the act of imagining that the theory has other properties than it actually possesses is distinct from the act of intuiting the theory as sound. Thus the term "intuition" is used in the extension of the passage just quoted to combat those who object that the distinction between accidental and necessary properties is unintuitive. Such an objection is based upon the belief that the question of essential properties is identical with the question of identity across possible worlds. This in turn requires necessary and sufficient conditions of identity, which are very difficult to find, especially for material objects, human beings, and instances of natural kinds. In this context, Kripke makes an important point. Possible worlds are stipulated, not discovered by looking through telescopes and so on.

We can stipulate something about an object already identified or at hand in this world (and here we see the "commonsensical" nature of givenness for Kripke). To take one of Kripke's favorite examples, suppose that Richard Nixon had lost the election of 1968. This supposition does not engender an infinity of possible worlds, each with a possible Nixon, through which we must voyage with an infallible criterion for identifying Nixon in each possible world as either the same as or distinct from the actual Nixon (NN, 344, n. 13).[46] In addition to what Kripke says on this point, we might add that human discourse lacks the creative power of the divine logos. A related observation is that it makes no sense to stipulate anything about an object that does not exist in this, the actual world, in the sense that it consists of properties altogether absent from this world (even from fiction or fairy tales). We could not even say that such an object exists, or is an object, since existence and objectivity are properties in this world. (For a discussion of whether an actual being possesses an essence *qua* individual, see section 7.) As for Kripke's remark about counterpart theories that "intuitively speaking, it seems to me not to be the right way of thinking about possible worlds," there are at least two other uses of "intuitive" in sense one in "Naming and Necessity" (NN, 267). The first concerns the "intuitive bizarreness of a good deal of the literature on 'transworld identification' and 'counterpart theory.' " The other is an assertion that "one of the intuitive theses I will maintain in these talks is that *names* are rigid designators" (NN, 289, 270).

So much for the first sense of intuition. In its second sense, intuition is either equivalent to or essentially connected with imagination, and plays the crucial role in determining whether a property is necessary or contingent. This is the standard role assigned to intuition in Kripke's lectures, and there are too many examples of its use for us to consider them all. I shall select some sample passages for analysis and comment. Take the following assertion about the possibility that Nixon might have lost the election of 1968.

There may be a problem about what intuitions about possibility come to. But if we have such an intuition about the possibility of *that* (*this man's* electoral loss) then it is about the possibility of that. [NN, 268]

Despite a slight syntactical obscurity in this passage, it is clear that the property of winning the election of 1968 adheres accidentally to Nixon. In this case, our intuition tells us not merely that a theory about necessary properties is meaningful, but also that a certain property of the actual Nixon is not necessary. By Kripke's own formulation of the case, intuition must also be able to tell us that a certain property is necessary. This use of intuition is connected to the imagination as follows. Kripke refers to the objection that the trans-worlder doctrine comes to the same thing as his own doctrine. He says: "if we can't imagine a possible world in which Nixon doesn't have a certain property, then it's a necessary condition of someone being Nixon" (NN, 268). In this passage, it is Kripke, not his opponent, who replaces "intuition" by "imagination" with respect to Nixon's properties, and specifically, the property of winning the election of 1968.

In general, Kripke distinguishes between the epistemological question and the logical question. The first question is this: is Nixon, as we suppose, a human being, or is he an automaton? (Note that there is no distinction here between "epistemological" *qua* scientifically verifiable and "phenomenological.") The second question is "whether Nixon might not have been a human being, given that he is one" (NN, 269). We might want to ask: is this epistemological or logical? However, the formulation of this inquiry might easily mislead us. The same property is both known and characterized by a logical modality. It is not therefore the case that Kripke sets himself the task of dividing all properties into two classes, the necessary and the accidental. But neither does he begin by dividing them into the epistemological (whether *a priori* or *a posteriori*) and the logical (whether necessary or contingent). His method may be characterized as argument by counterexample. We ask ourselves with respect to each individual object and each property of that object: can I suppose or imagine the object to be the same individual, on the assumption that the property in question is absent or changed into its contrary? Very frequently we can imagine that the specified change would not alter the identity of the object. But occasionally, if rarely, we cannot imagine this. In these cases, Kripke claims, to change the property would be to change the identity of the object. Hence these properties are essential.

As soon as we generalize Kripke's procedure in this way, it becomes clear that the imagination (or capacity to suppose) is for him either synonymous with, or itself judges, the intuition. For in the case of any given property, we are at the mercy of our imagination. We must therefore distinguish between logic as a technical discipline and a theory about the application of logic to the actual world. As a technical discipline, logic deals with the application of rules to well-defined expressions. It is not concerned with the imagination. But the interpretation of logical calculi as regulating arguments about the world rests upon our pre-analytical understanding of the world. If we put to one side question-begging attempts to mathematize "meta-philosophy," we have to ask ourselves: what counts as a sensible argument about the objects in the world? As our examples have shown, Kripke holds that we turn to our intuition. But in the implementation of intuitively-approved theories, it is our imagination that rules.

Someone might claim that he is indeed able to imagine that Nixon, or a table, might lack a property imagined by Kripke to be essential, and yet remain the same object. It is not some technical application of logic that decides the issue here, but an appeal to the imagination (occasionally called "intuition"). We may of course call it "logical intuition," but the appeal is the same. To state the point as broadly as we can, if it is intuition or imagination that certifies theories as sound, then there are no logical rules by which intuition or imagination is regulable. Even if Kripke were to invoke the principle of non-contradiction, he would still be appealing to our *intuition* of this rule, or our ability to imagine its non-validity. One striking feature of the whole corpus of literature on the interpretation of quantified modal logic is its theoretical unimaginativeness. It is silently assumed that intuition and imagination are governed by the very rules of logic that we ought to be trying to establish as sound or unsound on the grounds of intuition or imagination. Specifically, I am not aware of any consideration of dialectical logics in the discussion of essences by Kripkeans. What modifications, for example, would be required by the use of Hegelian logic? If we are told in reply that our common sense or "robust sense of reality" (Russell's phrase) excludes Hegel's logic from the outset, then we in turn must say that common sense is here a catch-phrase concealing a philosophical ideology. The bizarre examples of Martians, blue gold, and tables made of ice are in fact a smoke screen for logical and imaginative orthodoxy. The appeal to the imagination is therefore finally spurious, all other questions about such an appeal to one side. In saying this, I do not retract my initial criticism that the appeal to the imagination is irrelevant to the determination of essences. But if we are going to appeal to the imagination, then we must actually do so. And in this case, to sink into the vernacular, all hell will break loose. The carefully controlled whimsicality of the Kripkean use of imagination will be swept away by a genuinely revolutionary openness of horizons.

I turn now to cases in which Kripke uses "intuition" in the second sense with respect to ostensibly essential properties. One such case refers to the *substance* of which an object is made.

> But could anything be this very object and not be composed of molecules? Certainly there is some feeling that the answer to that must be 'no.' At any rate it's hard to imagine under what circumstances you would have this very object and find that it is not composed of molecules. A quite different question is whether it is in fact composed of molecules in the actual world and how we know this. [NN, 269]

What precisely is Kripke arguing here? If an object is in fact made of molecules, we know this *a posteriori* or empirically, and our knowledge is also contingent upon the reliability of science. However, Kripke also seems to be claiming that, if the object is indeed made of molecules, then it is necessarily made of molecules. In this second case, the court of appeal is neither science (epistemology) nor logic, but the imagination. Kripke is asking whether or not my imagination confirms his own on the point in question. The answer is "no." I can imagine cases in which one would have the very object without its being composed of molecules. One such case has already been mentioned with respect to the table. But whatever I can imagine, how is that relevant to the question of whether the table has an essence? As we also saw previously, it is relevant only upon the assumption of the detachability of logical possibility from natural necessity. Now I can imagine that this might be the case, but that does not make it so, or even possible that it is so. What we require is an argument to the effect that what I can imagine, is possible. Kripke supplies no such argument. Like all Ashʿarites, he is assuming the radical contingency of the created world. But this is a theological assumption, not an argument.

In addition to a thing's substance, Kripke gives two examples of essential properties. The first is a thing's *origin*; the second is the property of *being an x*; for example, it is an essential property of a table to "be a table" (NN 322, n. 57; cf. pp. 314, 320). An example of "origin" is a person's parents. Kripke illustrates this via the present Queen of England (NN, 313). He defines "parents" as "the people whose body tissues are sources of the biological sperm and egg." And he claims that if Queen Elizabeth had been born of completely different parents, she could not have been the same person:

> in what sense would she be—*this very woman?* One can imagine, *given* the woman, that various things in her life could have changed. . . . But what is harder to imagine is her being born of different parents. It seems to me that anything coming from a different origin would not be this object. [NN, 314]

I make two comments in passing. First, Kripke's language is usually quite tentative. He seems to be inviting us to agree with his intuitions rather than to be demonstrating the soundness of a theory. Second, Kripke does not concern himself with the givenness of the woman as a presence within the world. But if we merely perceive her, then the question of her mode of givenness is transformed into the scientific question of the nature of perception. Since we can imagine science to be wrong, we can also imagine the doctrine of perception to be wrong. However, the main point is perhaps this. Kripke suggests that we cannot imagine Queen Elizabeth to be who she is and yet have different parents. And this use of the imagination is logical, not epistemological. However, I take him to mean, not that we cannot imagine ourselves to have been born of different parents (something that is in fact possible), but that we cannot imagine ourselves to be the same person under this circumstance. There is then a conflict between the imagination and logical intuition, at least between the imagination and Kripke's logical intuition, or the logical intuition of someone who accepts the same logical rules as does Kripke. But Kripke does not distinguish between the imagination as an instrument or regulator of logical intuition, and the imagination as an obstacle to logical intuition. In different words, Kripke distinguishes between the logical essence of the individual and the individual as person. If I were king, I would be a different person. But I would not (or need not) be a different individual unless I had been born of parents other than my own. (See section 7 for a discussion of Kripke's doctrine of individual essences.) From this we observe that intuition and imagination are used as virtual synonyms. We try to imagine the object as the same, despite the absence of a given property. If we fail, then we infer that the property is necessary or essential. If we succeed, then we infer that the property is contingent. So everything depends upon the power of our imaginations. This power cannot be restricted in advance by logical rules because it is up to our imagination to verify such rules. One could say that we intuit the rules which regulate the imagination. But verification of our intuition must be by way of imagination: suppose that such-and-such a rule did not hold?

To anticipate: if Kripke is right in his denial of the logical identity of the mind and the body, then there is no reason on his own grounds why we cannot imagine ourselves *qua* mind to have been incarnated in some body other than our own. If the imagination is to be restricted, it must be by intuitions concerning things as they are, intuitions which give rise to those logical rules we deem acceptable. Since I can imagine anything at all, either the imagination is irrelevant to the task of establishing essences, or it must be governed by intuition in a sense distinct from imagination. We can offer various discursive justifications of our intuitions, but we can never demonstrate them in a non-circular manner. To say that y belongs essentially to x is to know prior to the assertion that y is part of the essential x. This is awkward, but there is no getting around it. We do not learn the fact contained in a predicative statement by asserting it. In

Kripke's formulations, the initial looks of things are assimilated into the epistemological aspect of experience. Hence it is subjective and must be corrected by logical intuition. But if the initial looks are subjective, *what is the conceivable objective content of logical intuition?* It must be logical intuition that tells the act of imaginative variation: "thus far and no farther." The content of this intuition must be independent of the imagination.

In the third sense, intuition, or its surrogate, imagination, erroneously identifies certain properties as necessary which later turn out to be contingent. The example discussed by Kripke is that of gold. Members of a given community of speakers use "gold" as the name for a certain kind of thing. This thing "appears" to have certain properties, such as its yellow color; and we use these properties as identifying marks of gold. But, as Kripke's imagination tells him, we might find that we are wrong about all these initially perceived identifying marks. Again, we are to "suppose" that circumstances caused us to perceive gold to be yellow, whereas it is actually blue. Or we might find empirically that iron pyrites are yellow, but not gold. The net result is that science corrects our initial understanding of the essential properties of gold. We do not, incidentally, change the meaning of the term "gold"; instead "we *discovered* that certain properties were true of gold in addition to the initial identifying marks by which we identified it" (NN, 316).

Kripke then makes the same point in the case of tigers. The general sense of these examples is as follows. In the pre-scientific situation, or what Kripke calls here the "phenomenological" situation, we arrive at a concept of natural substances or kinds by a direct reliance upon the looks of things. Note that this is not the epistemological situation. Nor are terms or concepts defined by sense-perception alone. We intuit the looks of things, although obviously intuition relies upon sense-perception and therefore assumes that it grasps the kinds it discerns within sense-perception. This reading is borne out by Kripke's own language. In the pre-scientific situation we do not know the "internal structure" of, say, tigers, but we "suppose" that

> tigers form a certain species or natural kind. We then can imagine that there should be a creature which, though having all the external appearances of tigers, differs from them internally enough that we should say that it is not the same kind of thing. We can imagine it without knowing anything about this internal structure—what this internal structure is. We can say in advance that we use the term 'tiger' to designate a species, and that anything not of this species, even though it looks like a tiger, is not in fact a tiger. [NN, 317f]

We have to distinguish here between the case of an automaton constructed, let us say, by Martians, that looks exactly like but is not a tiger, and the case in which (as we imagine it) some animal looks exactly like, but is not, a tiger. As it happens, I can imagine that the first case is possible, whereas, although I can imagine the second case, I cannot believe that it is possible. Kripke identifies the possible and the imaginable because of his assumption that the "natural" or "created" world is radically contingent, or that logical and physical laws are sharply separable. Since he presents no arguments in support of his theological or metaphysical thesis, the issue must be decided on the basis of imagination; namely, my own (or the reader's). It is not an issue in logic, not even in modal logic.

On the other hand, Kripke grants in the example of the tiger (and in some others) that we imagine that things form species in accordance with an inner structure, species which we initially identify on the basis of their *looks*. In quasi-Aristotelian language, we have an intuition of what looks like an actual essence. However, we are wrong, or only partly right. Our initial phenomenological intuition or imagination is then corrected by another kind of imagination buttressed by natural science. This other kind of imagination is intuition in the second sense. But the initial kind is intuition in the third sense. So in Kripke's terms, phenomenological intuition must be corrected by science plus logical intuition. Again, logic is distinct from nature *qua* what shows itself initially; obviously enough, "nature" in the scientific sense is already a logical-conceptual construction. However, the initial intuition that tigers form a species, or that gold is a natural element having essential properties, is for Kripke not wrong. What is wrong here is the identification by intuition of the properties ostensibly defining the essence in question. Here Kripke associates himself with Hilary Putnam:

> cats might turn out to be automata, or strange demons . . . planted by a magician. Suppose they turned out to be a species of demons. Then on his view, and I think also my view, the inclination is to say, not that there turned out to be no cats, but that cats have turned out not to be animals, as we originally supposed. The original concept of a cat is: *that kind of thing*, where the kind can be identified by paradigmatic instances. [NN, 318f]

Now I must say candidly that I find it absurd for analytical philosophers, who are ostensibly "tough-minded" about traditional metaphysics, to take this kind of argument seriously. For it turns upon the *possibility* of cats being demons, and not just on our capacity to imagine that cats are demons. Logical possibility is identified by Kripke with metaphysical possibility, and this in turn is distinguished from epistemological or natural possibility in the scientific or empirical sense. For Aristotle, logic is not a part of metaphysics, but a method. The nature of an essence can then not be determined, or even established as possible, simply on the grounds that what we imagine does not violate the principle of non-contradiction. And as we have seen, such a procedure is not even justifiable on Leibnizian grounds. The shocking thing, of course, is not that contemporary Kripkeans deviate from Aristotle or Leibniz, but that they present no grounds whatsoever in justification of their procedures. It is taken for granted that metaphysics is imaginative speculation on contemporary logic. Sometimes this amounts to an unwitting acceptance of metaphysical principles implicit in the logic; sometimes metaphysical principles are accepted as a basis for logical reflection, but with no awareness of what commitments have been made.

This aside, in the example of the cat, the species turns out to be one of demons, contrary to our initial expectation. However, it remains a species. In this important sense, not fully noticed or at least not discussed by Kripke, we were right to rely upon our intuition of the phenomenological situation. The looks of things are a guide to their families or kinds. And this in itself gives us a basis for distinguishing between phenomenology and epistemology. In conclusion: I have already noted that Kripke's views descend from Semitic theology. Just as there is in the case of the medieval theologians, there is a tincture of Aristotelianism in Kripke's theological doctrines. The mixture amounts to this: we (sometimes) intuit essences on the basis of the initial looks of things, but we are *never* in a position to state with logical necessity that this or that property is an essential predicate of such-and-such an essence. However, on the main points, Kripke is not an Aristotelian. Kripke, like the entire Fregean tradition, rests within the Kantian version of the Semitic presuppositions concerning the radical contingency of nature. Contrary to the apparent thrust of Kripke's entire argument, there is no intellectual intuition of the essences of natural beings. Instead, there are inadequately explained intuitions of logical essences or concepts. Instead of the Hebraic God, we are faced with the *deus absconditus* of the constructive intellect. This amounts to the assertion that logical essences or concepts are possibilities, not actualities (and in the sense that they do not violate the principle of non-contradiction).

7.   Individual Essences

Modern logic, and not just quantified modal logic, has a heavy investment in the thesis of individual essences. Although I want to show that Kripke's arguments fail to establish that there are individual essences, my purpose is not to rule these out of court. The question of individual essences is an enduring metaphysical problem, and it cannot be solved by the devices of contemporary analytical philosophy. In other words, it is my view that logic is not metaphysically neutral, but already embodies a variety of philosophical presuppositions. Some of these are for the sake of calculative convenience, some express scientific ideologies, and others are apparently invisible to the masters of the *technē*. Let us make a fresh beginning by recalling the following passage from Kripke's lectures:

> I am not suggesting that only origin and substantial makeup are essential. For example, if the very block of wood from which the table was made had instead been made into a vase, the table would never have existed. So (roughly) *being a table* seems to be an essential property of the table. [NN, 351, n. 57]

Kripke denies that general names like "cow" and "tiger" express properties, "unless *being a cow* counts trivially as a property" (NN, 322). Is there some difference, relevant to the discussion, between being a cow and being a table? The difference between a natural and an artificial kind is obviously of importance in its own right. It might bear upon the present discussion in this way: whereas natural kinds have internal structures independently of human production, artifacts are whatever we want them to be. However, Kripke draws no such distinction and indeed uses an artifact in referring to the ostensibly necessary property in question. Tables and cows are on a par if the world is radically contingent. Kripke might perhaps accept (although he does not offer) the following argument. Just as men produce and may radically modify tables, so too "nature" produces and may radically modify cows. In any event, it is not the evolution of tables or cows that is at issue since evolution as such is in the domain of the *a posteriori*. What counts is this: if *x* is a cow, then it must have certain properties, and so too with tables.

If then *being a cow* counts as a property, so too must *being a table*. We thus reach the conclusion established previously by reference to the procedures of logicians. Given *x*, where *x* is any object at all, then *being an x* is a necessary property of that individual. The formula

(10) $(\exists x)(\phi x)$

is then derived legitimately from "F*a*" where "———is an F" is a property of an individual *a*. More precisely, from "A*a*," where "———is an A" is a property of an individual *a*. But how does "being an *x*" or "A*a*" give us any information about the individual *qua* individual? For example, suppose we try to solve this problem by adapting to our purpose a device taken from Quine. In his discussion of how to reduce proper names to definite descriptions, Quine suggests that names like "Pegasus" (or "Socrates" and "Aristotle" to add two others) can be replaced by the predicate "pegasizes," or as we might put it

"———is (a) Pegasus." In this event, a sentence like "Socrates exists" might be analyzed as

(11) $(\exists x)$ (x is a man & x socratizes).[47]

So if we adapt these procedures to the present context, "———socratizes" is an instance of the property-schema "being an x." However, if we transform our familiar individual into a predicate, whether peculiar ("socratizes") or familiar ("———is Socrates") have we not recast him into a species of which we have ostensibly identified (thus far) a single instance? But in this case, we cannot identify the individual by means of the predicate since we constructed the predicate out of the individual. In slightly different terms, what is the distinction between the individual and the species-predicate? Obviously enough, the individual is a human being, whereas the predicate is not. But many individuals are human beings. Since we now have no basis for picking out "Socrates" as a unique individual, (11) succeeds in transferring our attention from the individual to a general case of conjunction of predicates. And it is no longer clear how we identify the value of the variable x in (11). If we say that "Socrates socratizes," it no longer makes sense to say that "being Socrates" is a necessary property of Socrates. The property is now being used to identify both an individual and a species-essence.

In my opinion, "being an x" refers to *two* properties: "being" and "self-identity." Whereas it seems intuitively obvious that self-identity is a necessary property, the same is not the case with "being." For all x, to be an x is to be an x, and necessarily so. But this is not the same as saying that for whatever x that is (=exists), it is necessarily so. Of course, we may attempt to talk the problem away by claiming that "to be" is here an incomplete expression standing for "to be an x," so that the two assertions are actually the same. The only question is then whether they are to be understood *de dicto*

(12) $\Box \, (\forall x) \, (x = x)$

or *de re*

(13) $(\forall x) \, \Box \, (x = x)$.

(See section 9 for further discussion of this ostensible solution to the problem.) In the meantime, we can say if "being an x" is the logical property of identity, it does not individuate, and so cannot belong to an individual essence as individual. It is clearly not the same to be a cow, a table, or Richard Nixon; yet "being an x" in the sense of self-identity is the same for all. At first this seems to be of no significance for Kripke's argument. A cow cannot be a cow without being a cow. If Richard Nixon had been Harry Truman, he would not be Richard Nixon. However, there is the following difficulty. "Table" and "cow" are general names, i.e., names of *kinds*, whereas "Richard Nixon" (taken as a covert definite description) names a unique individual. So "being a table" is true of *all* tables, whereas if "being an x" can take the argument "Richard Nixon," it does not mean "being *a* Richard Nixon" (since this would at once convert Nixon into a species), but "being *this* individual named Richard Nixon."

Now of course, we might distinguish individual cows by using names, as in "Elsie the cow." It is not usually done, but we might also name tables. But then there would be no difference between "being a cow" and "being Elsie the cow." Does this matter? Why could not "being Elsie the cow" be a necessary if trivial property of Elsie the cow? The difficulty is perhaps suggested by Kripke's own procedure. If I am not mistaken, he never says that "being Richard Nixon" is a necessary property of Richard Nixon. Instead he asks: what properties must be predicated of Richard Nixon in order that he be Richard Nixon in all possible worlds (states of affairs)? It is true that he begins with Richard Nixon as given in this world, "phenomenologically" or pre-analytically. Still, his purpose is to determine what properties of this Richard Nixon cannot be imagined not to obtain, without this Nixon ceasing to be Nixon. So we want to know what properties are necessary for being Richard Nixon, and (I claim) we are not told anything if someone replies: one such property is "being Richard Nixon." Or alternatively, we are told too much, since the expression actually refers to (at least) two properties, one necessary and the other contingent.

Why is this different from being told that "being a table" is not a necessary property of being a table? Because what we mean, even if we do not intend it, is that among the properties of *this* table (and Kripke here is talking about a specific table) is the necessary property of belonging to the general class or kind: *tables*. And exactly the same is true, of course, of cows. But it is not true of Elsie the cow *qua* this Elsie, and it is not true of Richard Nixon *qua* this individual man. We are now at the heart of the problem of individual essences. Are there *any* properties that we must predicate necessarily of Nixon *qua* Nixon? Are there properties that must hold true of him, given that he is the individual that he is, not as member of a kind or species, but as that unique individual? In a religious vein, we might say that God created the unique soul of Richard Nixon. However, once an omnipotent God is brought into the discussion, it is hard to see how one would limit His powers of creation, even by the principle of non-contradiction. The problem here is exactly analogous to reliance upon the imagination. Furthermore, when God says "I am that I am," he is not mentioning a necessary property of his uniqueness as an individual but indicating that his uniqueness is a mystery, inaccessible to analytical or predicative discourse. If Richard Nixon says "I am that I am Richard Nixon," is he mentioning a necessary property of his uniqueness or suggesting that his uniqueness is not necessary but contingent? How could we designate the essential Richard Nixon, save by listing those unique and contingent properties by which he is distinguished from every other individual?

With this in mind, we turn to the other two necessary properties suggested by Kripke: origin and substance. To begin with origin: is it true that, given the biological definition of "parent," Nixon could not have been Nixon had he sprung from parents other than his own? Suppose we grant Kripke that this is true. What follows, evidently enough, is that living beings depend for their biologically transmissible properties upon their parents. But this dependence is a necessary property of an individual *qua* member of a natural kind. What we mean by "the unique individual, this Richard Nixon" is surely something else. Suppose now what is conceivably true: that we are able (or will be), by purely biological means, to distinguish every unique individual as that individual. (On this assumption, the difficulty of distinguishing between origin and substance becomes quite obvious.) Is the essential Nixon the biologically unique individual, uniquely generated by his parents, Mr. and Mrs. Nixon? For my part, I do not see that anything has been accomplished by this supposition toward identifying an essential property of the unique individual known to us as Richard Nixon. My reason, stated very generally, is that this unique individual is not and could not be known by his unique biological recipe, even assuming that this were available. We recall that the question is logical, not epistemological. But the logical question is precisely that of our capacity to distinguish this individual as the same in all possible states of affairs or worlds. In order to make this distinction, we have to know something distinguishing or individuating. So far our assumptions indicate that the recipe of the unique individual would serve to identify *the wrong object*. We say that someone knows Richard Nixon if he knows *who* Richard Nixon is, not *what* Nixon is. Who is Nixon? He is a Californian, a Quaker, a graduate of Whittier College, a former senator, an ex-president of the United States, a whipping-post for Saul Kripke, and so on. And all of these are contingent properties, as Kripke would grant.

Thus far (the situation will change) we cannot argue against Kripke's specific point that Nixon's parents could not have been other than who they were as biological individuals. But we can certainly argue that they might have been completely different *persons*. To be a person is not to be the same object as to be a biological individual of such-and-such a unique recipe. Unless one is a total physiological determinist, it makes no sense to claim that for logical purposes, we have located the essence of Nixon *qua* Nixon by identifying his parents or his unique biological recipe. This is what I mean by saying that this procedure identifies the wrong object. And Kripke himself seems to argue in the spirit of my point, with respect to such individual persons as Moses, Isaiah, Aristotle, or Nixon. Neither does it make any difference to Kripke whether his definition of "parent," or for that matter of the science of genetics, is actually true. His thesis is that, given science, given the definition, given that x and y are this Richard Nixon's parents, then the fact that they are so is a necessary property of this Richard Nixon.

I have contended that if all we knew about Richard Nixon was his ostensibly unique biological recipe, we would know nothing about Richard Nixon. But Kripke may reply that I am missing his point. Whatever we know about Richard Nixon, he might say, depends upon his having the exact parents he actually had. I grant this contention. I grant for all human beings that whatever we know about them depends upon their having the exact parents they actually had, or possessing a unique biological recipe. What I claim is that this is a necessary property, not of a unique individual, but of a member of a natural kind. It is the property of a species.

Suppose that Nixon's biological recipe is XYZ. Suppose too that the science of physics is able to give a unique formula for each table, and that the formula for a certain table, named "Samuel," is X'Y'Z'. If we know both formulae, do we know anything more about Nixon than we do about Samuel? We do, only if we can prove that there is a necessary connection between XYZ and those properties uniquely designating the individual to whom we refer when we answer the question "Who is Richard Nixon?" But if we could do this, then we would have refuted Kripke, since he claims, with some hesitations, that whatever is true of the individual, except for his origin and substance, might have been otherwise. Moses might not have led the Hebrews out of Egypt, Aristotle might not have become a philosopher, Richard Nixon might not have gone into politics, and so on. Perhaps I should emphasize again that the point is not epistemological. I am not arguing about what we happen to know about Nixon, or even how we know it. I am arguing about whether there is anything which, if we did know it about Nixon, would be logically necessary of him to be the individual who he is.

As far as I can see, Kripke's case comes down to the question of an ostensibly unique biological formula (a convenient way of referring to both origin and substance). And I can now introduce a further argument against that case. A formula, even if actually or epistemologically unique, is an abstract generalization, like H_2O. There is no logical reason (in Kripke's sense of "logical") why we could not imagine some other human being, say Richard Nixon's clone or identical twin, or a Doppelgänger produced by a demon, as having the same biological formula. As Kripke himself has shown us, what science can actually or possibly do or know is irrelevant to (what he calls) the logical situation. The situation is that it *is* possible to imagine, in two different senses, someone other than "this" Richard Nixon having been born to Nixon's parents and possessing Nixon's epistemologically unique biological formula. Assuming current genetic theory to be true, identical twins have exactly the same biological formula. Differences between them arise from mutations, all of which are contingent. So it is logically possible to conceive of two individuals with the same biological formula, with or without contingent mutations. And if the mutations occur, although it is perhaps inevitable that they must, which ones actually occur is contingent. So whether or not modern genetics is right, we can imagine that there are two or more distinct Nixons having exactly the same parents and the same biological recipe.

But this is not the end of the story. The Kripkean (as Glen Helman has pointed out to me) has still another construction that can be given to the master's argument. This construction follows from Kripke's view that "under appropriate qualitatively identical evidential situations, an appropriate corresponding qualitative statement might have been false" (NN, 333). In other words, if there is a property necessarily predicable of an individual as this unique individual, it cannot be qualitative.

> This table itself could not have had an origin different from the one it in fact had, but in a situation qualitatively identical to this one with respect to all the evidence I had in advance, the room could have contained a *table made of ice* in place of this one. [NN, 332f]

So there might have been two distinct individuals with the unique biological formula of Richard Nixon. But (the argument goes) it is logically impossible for two Nixons to have been born at the same time, to have issued from the womb simultaneously, occupying the same spatial position, and so on. The uniqueness of Richard Nixon's origin, then, is not the uniqueness of his parents, nor of his genetic and biological formula, nor for that matter that he is made of flesh, blood, bone, and sinew, but the quantitative spatio-temporal coordinates of his birth.

If this is the right interpretation of what Kripke means by "origin" as a necessary property, the first thing to be said is that the substance out of which something is made cannot be a necessary property in itself. All human beings are made of flesh, blood, bone, and sinew, and more than one might have been made of biologically indistinguishable constituents. Second, I can imagine a possible world in which space has more than three dimensions, or circumstances under which Martian scientists arrange for the molecules of two biologically identical Richard Nixons to integrate at the instant of birth, so that both of them emerge from the womb at the same time, with no spatial differentiation between them, and then bifurcate again. Or to use one of Kripke's own arguments, if the mind or soul is logically distinct from the body, then there is again no reason to accept even the minimal property of an ordered quadruple of spatio-temporal co-ordinates as belonging necessarily to the individual *qua* individual. The quadruple in question is perhaps a necessary property of the body whose birth it tickets (although I have just given a counterexample), but it is a contingent property of the mind or soul inhabiting that body. We might imagine circumstances under which evil demons or supremely intelligent Martians had snatched away Nixon's soul one instant before it was about to be incarnated in what is its actual body. We might also imagine two souls in the same body, since souls or minds presumably have no spatial co-ordinates. And arguments like these can easily be constructed to fit all cases. The shift from qualitative to quantitative properties does not work. Simply stated, qualities are logically distinct from quantities, and if an essence is anything, it is a quality.

Here then are two major difficulties with Kripke's defense of individual essences. First, the suggested necessary properties identify the wrong object. Second, they are not necessary, if to be necessary means that we cannot conceive of circumstances under which they are absent while the object remains the same.[48] This raises a further point. Despite all differences between Aristotle and Kripke, both suffer from the same weakness with respect to knowledge of individuals. If rational discourse is restricted to predicative assertions of the kind amenable to analytical study on the model of mathematics, then nothing rational can be said about individual human beings or events. To take a specific case, it is not necessary to Kripke's argument for Aristotle to have been a philosopher or Hitler a murderer: "both . . . might have lacked these properties altogether" (NN, 289). It seems to follow from Kripke's analysis that Aristotle might have been a Hitler or an Alexander the Great, and that Hitler might have been an Aristotle or a Heidegger. To borrow an expression from Kripke, I find this intuitively bizarre. However, what is required to remove the bizarre element is not a more sophisticated modal logic, but a more sophisticated notion of what it means to be rational.

I shall close this section with a final observation about Kripke's views. In his lectures he denies that there is a "bare particular" or a propertyless substratum underlying the qualities of an object (NN, 272). This is reminiscent of Socrates' denial in the *Theaetetus* that an object is a unity other than the sum of its properties, although I note immediately that for Kripke (as for Hilary Putnam) an essence cannot be defined analytically by a conjunction or logical sum of its predicates. Once again Kripke's example is Richard Nixon. Since some of Nixon's properties are essential, and Nixon is not an essence distinct from his properties, in what sense "is" Nixon his properties? Kripke denies that "a particular is nothing but a 'bundle of qualities', whatever that may mean." and he adds:

if a quality is an abstract object, a bundle of qualities is an object of an even higher degree of abstraction, not a particular. [NN, 289]

Nixon, a table, or any other individual, *has* properties. But the individual cannot be described as either "nothing but a bundle" or as an essence lurking behind the bundle. So the table "has" properties but must not be identified with the set of its properties, "nor with the subset of its essential properties." In this case, what does Kripke mean by "has"? His initial response is as follows:

> Don't ask: how can I identify this table in another possible world, except by its properties? I have the table in my hands, I can point to it, and when I ask whether it might have been in another room, I am talking, by definition, about *it*. [NN, 272f]

If Nixon (or a table) is not, but has, a bundle of qualities, and this bundle is an abstract object, then Nixon must "have" or participate in at least one abstract object. What is the relation between this abstract object and the essence of Nixon *qua* Nixon? Since the abstract object consists of Nixon's properties, if it is not his essence, then that essence must be something other than his properties. What could this be, unless it is a "bare particular," a propertyless substrate, or an invisible essence? One might reply: it is Richard Nixon, who is other than his properties but not therefore propertyless. But this is to make Nixon identical with his essence, and so to deny him contingent properties. We seem to have two relations: (1) the relation between the object "Nixon" and its properties; (2) the relation between the object "Nixon" and the bundle of its properties. If (1) is predication, what shall we say of (2)? Kripke has already denied that it is identity. Besides, as we saw earlier, "being Nixon" is for Kripke almost certainly an essential property. Identity cannot therefore be the same as the "being" of Nixon, with the latter "being" understood as the relation between the object and the bundle of its properties. Perhaps Nixon "is" the ratio or way in which his properties combine. But this is merely to say that Nixon both is and is not his properties, without explaining the sense of "is." I think it is more compatible with Kripke's general thesis to say not only that the unity of an object is *not* the same as the sum of its properties, but also that this unity is a not further analyzable and intuitively necessary aspect of the object's essence. Nixon is *not* identical with his properties. But neither is he identical with his essence. To list or sum up his predicates does nothing in itself to define his essence. So even if we can say that his essence includes the ordered quadruple of the spatio-temporal co-ordinates of his birth, there is nothing we can say of an analytical or predicative nature about his unity, except that it is essential to him. Perhaps this is what Kripke would mean by saying that "being Nixon" is an essential property of Nixon. But whether it is or not, it provides us with our transition to the next chapter.

CHAPTER THREE

Existence
and Non-Existence

8. The Ontological Copula

THE THEMES of this chapter may seem initially arid and unfamiliar to the general reader. My intention in the following pages is to show that the prevalent analytical treatment of the central questions in ontology is inadequate. "Ontology" is a professorial word, coined by german academicians in the eighteenth century, which means something like "the science of being." Ontology, then, is a branch of philosophy in which we attempt to give a rational account of whatever exists. This account may restrict itself to the development of a table of categories, or basic properties of whatever there is. Or it may try to go deeper, and to say something about the nature of Being, the source or principle of whatever there is. In this sense, Being is not a table of categories; instead, the categories are consequences of the activity of Being, or the way in which Being manifests itself. The first, if not the most important, question in ontology is then, not "What is there?" but "What do we mean by a *science* of being?" In the analytical tradition, going back to Plato and Aristotle, the tendency is to take one's bearings by definite, countable things. The most comprehensive version of this tendency is to be found in Aristotle's *Metaphysics*, where "to be" is to be something, namely, some specific individual (even if in the extended sense of an essence of a family of individuals). It is this tendency which explains Aristotle's famous remark: "being has many senses." When Aristotle speaks of "being *qua* being," he is referring by a short-hand expression to the set of properties which mark whatever exists, and so ultimately to substance or essence. Note, however, that substances come, so to speak, in various kinds.

In the twentieth century, we have essentially two kinds of ontology, analytical and fundamental. The latter is derived from the thought of Martin Heidegger, and attempts to articulate a science of Being, albeit in a sense of "science" different from (if related to) the usual meaning of the term. As I shall be primarily concerned with analytical ontology in this chapter, let me make a general remark about fundamental ontology. Partisans of this way of philosophizing seem to me to commit one of two errors. Either they attempt to give a fully developed, conceptual account of Being, or else, when this attempt fails (as it must), they lapse into quasi-silence of a peculiarly garrulous sort that attempts to make a theoretical virtue of what they call the covering-over of Being. One sees a complex and partly obscured version in fundamental ontology of the same erroneous procedure that marks analytical philosophy. The ontologist begins in accord with the paradigm of conceptual rigor that marks modern science, but is unable to carry out his enterprise because, in the sense that I have tried to make clear, there are no concepts adequate to his enterprise. As a result, he rebels against conceptual thinking, and looks for a new way of explaining Being that is adequate to the peculiarity of Being. Lest the reader suppose that this last step ought to meet with my approval, allow me to register the following reminder. I am not advocating a new way of thinking, and I am certainly not arguing that we must begin our philosophical work by rejecting analytical procedures. What I advocate is that we begin in a variety of ways, and so remain faithful to the deep reasonableness of the Aristotelian adage that "being has many senses." The rejection of analytical thinking is an erroneous inference from the principle that Being conceals itself in its very activity of presenting itself via beings or individual things. However, just as analytical thinking is saturated with intuition, so too is intuition (in a sense broad enough to encompass the insights of fundamental ontologists) saturated with analytical thinking.

Now I turn more directly to analytical ontology. Up to a point, I agree that a critical part of ontology is semantical. We have to decide what we mean by "being" and "non-being." Central to this investigation is the question whether there is a distinction to be drawn between "being" and "existence." I shall put the point as simply as possible. Even if we grant that being has many senses, it may be the case that one such sense corresponds to what fundamental ontologists mean (or try to mean) by Being. Or again: it may be impossible to spell out the properties of individual existing things without invoking a fundamental distinction between "existence" as a property of an individual instance of an essence, and "being" as the mode of presentation, the nature, of essences. This consequence necessarily follows for those who take modal logic seriously, although I am not aware that modal logicians concern themselves with the distinction in question. In any case, we must not be corrupted by inadequate standards of analytical rigor. The views that I shall be opposing either explicitly deny the difference between "being" and "existence" or tend to ignore that difference. Hence the most direct formulation of my goal is that I want to show why we must draw such a distinction, and to do so on analytical grounds. It will follow directly that an incorrect analysis of "being" as "existence" leads to an inadequate treatment of "non-being" as "non-existence." A second goal of this chapter is to contribute to the rehabilitation, within the context of analysis, of the most perplexing of all philosophical problems: what do we mean (if anything) by "nothingness"? Whereas I shall indulge in some concluding speculations on this initially odd topic, I arrive at this topic by very specific analysis of altogether usual procedures in contemporary philosophy. My argumentation will proceed from the inside to the outside. By this I mean that, as usual, I try to arrive at a somewhat richer account of the context, and so of the limits, of analysis than is usually offered. However, I argue that we are led to this richer account by the nature of analytical thinking itself. In one last formulation, I am neither here nor elsewhere an opponent of analytical thinking. On the contrary, I regard myself as a loyal practitioner of philosophical analysis. But this is not the same as to say that I accept the rhetorical presentations of contemporary analytical philosophy. Neither, then, am I bound by their self-imposed scholastic restrictions.

The traditional analysis of the copula distinguishes three main senses: identity, predication, and existence. It is a consequence of this analysis, together with the rejection of essences, that the traditional term "being" has been dropped in favor of, or assimilated into, "existence." The rehabilitation of essences by contemporary modal logicians has not, so far as I can see, been accompanied by a renewal of the distinction between essence and existence, or being and existence. Certainly one of the main reasons for this is the fact that, by "essence," modal logicians normally mean "'logical possibility" in the sense of what does not violate the principle of non-contradiction. As I observed in section 6, this usage is based upon a radically narrowed interpretation of Leibniz. In the pre-Leibnizian tradition deriving from Aristotle, an essence is an *actuality*, not a possibility (and this Aristotelian doctrine is itself a reinterpretation of the Platonic Idea). When Kripke, for example, speaks of "logical or metaphysical necessity," he does not mean a necessarily actual being which is logically distinguishable from its existing instances, but rather something which is possible *qua* not self-contradictory. It is necessary only hypothetically, namely, *if* there are essences. Kripke has certainly not proven that there are essences, however much quantified modal logic may require them. To state the point in another way, Kripkean essences are neither beings (as distinct from existing things) nor existing things. It is therefore unclear from the outset exactly what Kripke could mean by asserting (hypothetically or otherwise) that "essences exist." The "way" in which something (ostensibly) exists necessarily or essentially is defined by the properties it must possess in order to preserve its identity in all possible worlds. It therefore looks as though the "existence" of an essence is reducible to identity and predication. This is not a very substantial sense of "existence."

It follows from Kripke's mode of analysis, whether he intends it or not, that the problem of essences turns into the problem of a criterion of identity for a given entity. This is so regardless of the fact that Kripke begins with actual individuals "existing" in this world. I put "existing" in quotes because it is easy to show the insubstantial nature of the term in Kripke's analysis. There may be no problem about identifying Richard Nixon or a table in our everyday, pre-scientific experience. But identification in this sense amounts to a kind of knowledge by acquaintance. It certainly does not provide us with the "identity" of the essential properties of Nixon or the table. We vary imaginatively the (known) properties of *this* Nixon in order to identify his essential properties, thereby establishing his essential identity. Despite certain indications of Kripke's to the contrary, I am unable to see that this identity could be for him anything else but a set of predicates. The "existence" of Nixon, or anything else, is for Kripke, just as it is for Quine, a matter of science. The perceptually given, for example, depends upon the sciences of optics, physiology, and so on, to say nothing of logical analysis, in order to be certified as *existing*. Hence, even though Kripke apparently affirms essences whereas Quine denies them, the term "ontology" may be used within a Kripkean perspective in exactly the sense given it by Quine. Ontology is concerned with the answer to the question: "What is there?" And it draws its answers from the mathematical and empirical sciences, not from common sense, the phenomenologically given, or any other pre-analytical mode of experience.

Quine's ontology, then, and by extension, Kripke's, is an expression and a consequence of the rhetoric of the modern scientific ideology. I find no extensive attempts by either thinker to justify that rhetoric, with the single exception of some of Quine's early papers on ontological topics. I mean it only as an informal and introductory paraphrase of Quine's position when I say that he seems to believe himself to have disposed of traditional philosophy by the fact of modern science and the technical exercises in which he analyzes the sense of "existence" and "non-existence" appropriate to the first-order predicate calculus and certain associated technical innovations of Frege, Russell, and Carnap. It would be accurate to say that this is a circular and self-justifying procedure, but I shall try to study at least the crucial steps in Quine's procedure in due course. But let us continue our preliminary survey of the terrain. What does Quine mean by "is" in the expression "on what there is"? The simple reply is "exists," but this is only the surface of a deeper problem. Quine's scientism leads him to the view that we can only say what exists when we are speaking precisely or with philosophical responsibility within a scientific theory. There are, as it were, two axioms governing the ontological dimension of theories. These may be simply stated as (1) no entity without identity; and (2) to be is to be the value of a variable in the first-order predicate calculus under a given interpretation. To be, thus, is to be countable, and to be countable is to be an object. But to be an object is to be identifiable, and this means to possess identifiable properties. The properties, however, are not countable, i.e., do not exist within a theory, unless they are taken as objects, that is, as sets. But sets are themselves defined by properties which must lack objective status within the given theory.

We thus reach this curious situation. Quine's axioms amount to a contemporary version of the basic thesis of the Platonic-Aristotelian tradition: to be is to be countable, but we count by unit-measures, and these are not countable. Quine's inclination not to quantify over predicates, except when forced to do so by the exigencies of mathematics,[1] looks like a version of Aristotle's distinction between unit-measures or species-essences and existing individuals. It thus looks as though Quine ought to accept a distinction between being and existence. Such a distinction might be explained by analogy with the theory of types or the hierarchy of ordinals, to mention only two examples. Objects might be said to "exist" within an order-type, where the type provides the "being" of those objects. In any case, Quine would not take his inclination in an Aristotelian sense. This is because he assumes that predicative constants do not refer, but rather function like logical constants in modifying the truth-conditions of an expression. And this in turn is because (whatever Quine's doubts about meaning and reference) his paradigm of existence, and hence of meaningful reference, is that of the definite or countable object, in the sense of some existing particular, to which we refer by a name. It is the quasi-scientific conviction that only objects, i.e., spatio-temporal things, are "real" (res) that leads Quine to reject quantification over predicates. This is no doubt why Quine has been called a "realist." Nevertheless, I do not think that the appellation is deserved.

The referential capacity of the name-variables in the formal language of a theory depends upon the properties of the elements in the universe of the interpretation. Given Quine's distinction between the ontology of a theory and the meta-linguistic criterion of ontological assumption, a theory's ontological commitments are a merely technical affair, to be determined by the domain of the values of its variables. What counts ontologically is how we identify the objects constituting that domain. But those objects cannot be furnished by pre-scientific experience, since this would reduce to the level of farce the elaborate insistence upon formalization. In this case the formal language of our theory would tell us less than our pre-theoretical inspection of the objects under scrutiny. If we try to resolve this problem by a meta-meta-linguistic criterion, we have generated an infinite ascent of theories, or in effect said *nothing* about what there is. We might follow my earlier suggestion and call the meta-linguistic criterion covering the immediately preceding linguistic level the *being* of the existents within the language of the theory. But this would transform Quine into an Idealist, and would raise the question of the ontological status of the capacity to construct ontological levels. Here then is another curious consequence of Quine's procedure. If existence depends upon the interpretation of a formal language, and this in turn depends upon the not yet existing properties of the objects of that interpretation, then Quine's "existents" are only *possibilia*. The definition of "what there is" is a criterion for identifying logically possible, but not metaphysically actual, things. As scientists, we cannot rely upon common sense or the pre-analytically given to answer the question: "What is there?" The scientific ideology common to Quine and Kripke leads them, by slightly different paths, to place possibility higher than actuality. It leaves them both without a non-circular account of actual existence. And this is, finally, because neither accepts the distinction between essence and existence. Kripke's failure to identify an essential property is a consequence of his conception of existence as radically contingent, i.e., of his *rejection* of essences. Quine's rejection of essences, conversely, leads to the assertion of an empty concept of existence.

In the previous chapter, I distinguished between phenomenological presence and the scientific or epistemological reconstruction of presence. In this chapter, I want to distinguish between the unity of what is phenomenologically present and the sum of its analytical properties. Without such a distinction, neither Kripke nor anyone else will ever be able to find an essence. But the being which we may also designate as *unity* (to be distinguished from "identity") can be established without any reference to essences. One way to do this is to consider the structure of the basic unit of linguistic intelligibility: the proposition. In the next section, I shall exhibit the ontological unity intrinsic to both the statement of natural language and the propositional function of Fregean formal languages. This will lead to a criticism of the analysis by Frege and his followers of existential statements. And that in turn will lay the groundwork for the discussion of the analysis of statements denying existence. My preliminary formulation of the situation may be summarized as follows. Contemporary analytical philosophy, and especially in its formalist versions, tends to be an ontology of possibility, but with no way of grasping the actual. This is trivially obvious from the reliance of analysts upon the paradigm of science. To simplify but not to distort a complex story, the account given of "reality" by science at any stage is false. What is ostensibly not false is the method by which we continuously improve upon the sequence of falsehoods. Ontology is therefore identical with logic. But as Leibniz himself pointed out, truths of reason are not the same as truths of fact. A scientific ontology seems to lead inevitably to the thesis that to be is to conform to the principle of non-contradiction. However, this takes us only as far as possibility. It does nothing to establish actuality.

My own approach seems to me to be more in keeping with philosophical analysis than the scientism of Quine. My question is not "What is there?" but "What does it mean *to be*?" I cannot hope to provide a comprehensive answer to this question. But I hope to be able to give a better analysis of the question than is normally provided by contemporary analysts. The first step is to explain why the copula must have an ontological sense in addition to those of identity, predication, and existence. I have already argued that existence is defined analytically in terms of identity and predication. Quantification is permissible on the basis of the identification of a domain of objects by way of their properties. We may disregard the doctrine of essences and restrict ourselves to the case of stipulative definitions. Here the objects of an interpretation are defined by linguistic conventions. However, the conventional nature of these definitions governs the ontological commitments of the language of the theory, not the intelligibility of the interpretation or meta-language. We are committed to saying that "there are such-and-so's" on the basis of our linguistic conventions. But the intelligibility of these conventions is not itself a matter of convention. Nor is this intelligibility a matter of which logic we choose to employ. The intelligibility of the concept of an object depends upon our intuitive grasp of the sense of "belonging to," which is *then* defined formally as a relation. It is not the construction of a formal definition that makes the relation intelligible. And even if we abolished objects from our logic, the concept of logical consequence already contains the intuitive or synthetic sense in which a conclusion "belongs to" its premises.[2] Every attempt to construct a meaningful statement, one which asserts a proposition, and so possesses a truth-value, depends upon our capacity to see how the elements we manipulate fit together in an appropriate manner. A well-formed formula is not simply the result of a mechanical application of rules. We have to see (whether directly or in the oblique form of a program for a machine) which rule to apply at each stage of the construction, and still more fundamentally, why the application of these rules to those symbols produces, not just a string of symbols, but a structure conveying a meaning within a given calculus.

Here is another version of the same point. To say that *a* exists is, in itself, analytically meaningless. The "cash value" of the assertion lies in our capacity to identify *a*, i.e., to distinguish it from non-*a* or to distinguish those values of *x* (in some definite context) making the statement ϕx true. We do this by saying something *about a* that serves as its identifying mark. What we say might be symbolized either as $a \in b$ or as $a \subset b$, depending upon whether we are talking about members of a set or subsets of a set. In either case, as is clear from the fact that *a* is a subset of *b* only if the members of *a* are members of *b*, we are required to prove the existence of *b*, and consequently to identify it. So if "exists" means "belongs to a set," we come at once to the requirement of defining the set by means of its predicates. We form one set from another pre-existing (and larger or equal) set by the axiom of comprehension. But the axiom of comprehension is a version of the doctrine of predication. Having defined the set by comprehension, we then prove the uniqueness of the set by the axiom of extensionality, or the principle of identity. The analytical treatment of existence, which employs set theory as its paradigm, transforms existence into identity and predication. So there is no independent concept of existence, not simply in the formalist wing of analysis, but in any version that restricts rational assertions to predicative statements, or more accurately, that attempts to explain predicative statements predicatively. Set theory is guided by Cantor's notion of the construction of sets from previous sets, and it was developed for mathematical purposes. So if the question "What is there?" is equivalent to the question "How many sets do we want to have?" then "since there are no ways of constructing individuals," we settle the question of how many individuals to admit "by arguments of simplicity and elegance." And "it turns out that for mathematical purposes there seems to be no real need for individuals other than the null-set."[3] Little wonder that set-theoretically oriented ontology is unable to cope with actual existence.

I draw the following conclusion from the preceding remarks. There is a radical confusion in the analytical treatment of existence. Either the sense of "exists" is rooted in the intuitive sense of "belongs to" or it turns upon our definitions of identity and predication. In the first case, "is" (as in "*x* is *y*") cannot mean simply (if at all) "exists," since that term is defined in the manner summarized by the second case. The analytical sense designated by the term "exists" is then rooted in the *ontological* sense of the copula. But in the second case, "exists" has no independent sense. The most that could be said, within a formalist ontology, is that sets exist. The great debate over the truth, or even the sense, of this assertion is enough to establish the ambiguity surrounding the concept of existence in analytical philosophy. However, let us assume that sets do exist. What then? Sets are not objects of perception, validated as genuine by empirical science. Either they are intellectual objects or human inventions. In the former case, we have "Platonism," or the distinction between two senses of "exists." The first sense refers to perceived individuals and has no analytical or ontological status. The second sense is that of *essence* or *being* in the language of the philosophical tradition. In the latter case (that sets are human inventions) we have Idealism, and the consequence that we ourselves produce ourselves, presumably as agents of the transcendental ego. Or else we arrive at Nietzschean perspectivism and the subsequent indistinguishability of existence from chaos. In sum: ontology is either Platonism or a consequence of how we talk. But if the latter, what is how we talk a consequence of?

If "exists" is defined in terms of identity and predication, it is also the case that identity and predication depend upon each other for their definitions. Simply stated, we cannot predicate something of x unless we can identify it, but we cannot identify x analytically except on the basis of its predicates (even if these are as primitive as subscripts or superscripts). I infer from this that there are two distinct kinds of identity. We identify some x initially, as the entity of possible predicative analysis, by an intuition of its *unity*, which is the same as intuiting its distinctness from other possible subjects of predication. This sense of identity is reflected in the axiom, $a = a$. A perception of the unity of a is the necessary prerequisite for the operations of reflexivity, symmetry, transitivity, and replacement within quantification. These operations define what we mean by the relation of identity; they do not define what we mean by unity. The unity is the domain of the relation. We may attempt to analyze identity further by means of some version of the axiom of extensionality. This attempt leads to the conception of identity in the second sense, namely, as a one-to-one mapping of the predicates of a and b. (We can speak of a mapping of the members, but in order to determine what are the members of a and b, we still require access to their predicates.) In this sense identity is an equality, namely of two sums of predicates (or of not further analyzable members). So b is the same as a because a and b are sets defined by the same properties (and hence sets containing the same, i.e., equal, members). It is worth noting that use of the axiom of extensionality requires us to quantify over predicates or sets. The identity of a, which consists of the members having a definite set of predicates, is equal to the identity of b, because the predicates defining the members of b are exactly the same as those defining the members of a. The identity of a and b, in this second sense of equality, involves the *unity* of the identifiability and sameness of the predicates of their members. So identity in the second sense assumes both predication and identity in the first sense, namely, unity.

I believe this is as far as we need to go in examining the usual definitions of identity. I claim that if there is no distinction between unity and identity, the definitions of identity and predication are not merely circular but *unattainable*.

"Identity" is an unsuccessful (and presumably unwitting) attempt to analyze unity. As analysts, we attempt to establish "scientifically" or "rigorously" the unity of an entity by establishing its identity via the entity's predicates. However, we require a pre-analytical intuition of the unity of an entity in order to recognize that such-and-such predicates belong to it. It follows that a whole is not the same as the sum of its parts. We cannot arrive at the unity of a whole by listing the set of its predicates, even upon the very rash assumption that the list is complete. Instead, we begin our analyses, as for example with assertions of the form "consider x," with a reference to the unity of x. The phrase "consider x" is short-hand for "there is an x," and the sense of "is" here is ontological. This is what I mean by the ontological copula. "There is an x," understood ontologically, is not the same as, or equivalent to, "x exists," where "exists" is understood in the ways just canvassed. The analytical tripartition of identity, predication, and existence amounts to an interpretation of the famous Aristotelian remark: " 'being' is spoken in many ways." This remark is true. But it does not follow that there is no sense of "being" to correspond to the *unity* of the three senses. Even our canvass of the logical and set-theoretical representations of identity, predication, and existence has shown that these concepts are not independent of one another.

The belief that logical analysis disposes of the sense of the question "What is being?" or that it answers this question by citing the three aforementioned senses of the copula, is a myth. To say that a term has three (or twenty-seven) different senses does not explain how we recognize these as senses of the same term. To attribute this sameness to the historical accident of a family of natural languages is not very persuasive. We see this by inspecting the procedures of formal languages. These procedures confirm, because they exhibit, the ontological perceptions intrinsic to the Indo-European languages. As I shall show in the next section, this is true whether or not we fail to represent "is" explicitly in our symbolism. Languages which lack the ontological perception of *essences, being, unity,* and (as I shall argue later, *nothing*) are not just different; they are ontologically defective. If, however, ontology is the study of the questions I have just listed, then there can be no possibility of exchanging Indo-European languages for others which provide us with an alternative "understanding" of the world. There is no alternative understanding of the world. To understand the world is to see the structure of the world. But this structure is both more simple and more complex than analytical philosophers would have us believe. The failure of analytical philosophy to do justice to the structure of the world encourages those who reject the attempt to understand altogether, or who believe themselves to be understanding when they are actually enjoying. It is part of the task of understanding to understand what it means to enjoy, but that does not reduce understanding to enjoyment.

9. Unity and Existence

In the *Theaetetus*, Socrates refers to the doctrine of simple elements as a dream, and subjects it to some criticisms which, as I shall contend, are unsatisfactory. This is because the criticisms are based upon an acceptance of the same principle that underlies the doctrine of elements itself. A brief inspection of this dream will serve to introduce the problem of unity, and to illustrate how this problem is concealed or ignored by contemporary analytical philosophy. Socrates' criticisms are unsatisfactory because they rest upon the dream that thinking is analyzing, or coextensive with *dianoia* and *logismos* (discursive and calculative thinking). Our inability to arrive at simple elements by analytical devices leads us to exclude unity from the domain of philosophical discourse, or to equate it with totality *qua* sum of analyzed parts. Socrates thus insists that knowledge of a whole is the same as knowledge of the sum of its parts. This raises the question of how we are acquainted with the relevant whole. For Socrates, or more generally, for Plato in his analytical moments, the whole is furnished by ordinary experience. The "unscientific" character of this mode of givenness is ostensibly overcome by the application of *diaeresis* or analytical dialectic. The empirical object is replaced in the process of analysis by the scientific, mathematical, or eidetic structure. Despite all the changes that have occurred since the fourth century B.C. with respect to science and the knowledge of genesis, Plato's procedure, or what seems to be Plato's procedure, is in a deep sense not much different from that of contemporary formalists. A crucial difference, of course, is that for Plato, the eidetic structure elicited by analysis is actual, "being" in the fullest sense, not an expression of logical possibility. In other words, what is necessary or possible is defined with respect to the actuality of the eidetic structure, whether this is intuited or grasped analytically.

The transition from ordinary experience to formal analysis is not a mark of empiricism so much as it is an expression of a distrust of experience. This distrust seems to enter modern philosophy with Descartes, who begins his *Meditations* with a universal doubt that is in a curious way reminiscent of the present-day lucubrations of modal logicians. What if the world has been created by a malign genius with the intention of entirely deceiving us? I pass by the implications of this universal doubt with respect to Descartes's supposed reliance upon the veracity of God. Whatever one may think of the *cogito*, it is intended to provide us with a first step in constructing a method with which to combat the possible malignancy of nature, or the cause of nature. Descartes's analytical method is designed to overcome the unreliability of ordinary experience by extracting its mathematical structure. Platonic *diaeresis* seems to be associated with an analogous distrust of genesis. In Plato, as in contemporary analytical thinkers, there is a curious ambiguity surrounding the link between a reliance upon one's robust sense of reality and a conviction that the real is accessible only through a rigorous methodological reconstitution of everyday experience. The radical form of this conviction is the rejection of psychologism, in which case it seems irrelevant to the philosopher how he comes to be acquainted with the object of analysis (or formal reconstitution). If the rejection of psychologism is thought through to the end, then the pre-analytical situation seems to be altogether dispensable to the formalist. Philosophy converges steadily upon, and in fact is soon indistinguishable from, mathematics. The religious conception of the radical contingency of genesis combines with Platonic formalism and modern science to produce the contemporary view that logical possibility and hypothetical necessity are equivalent to metaphysics, which in turn makes "nature" dispensable, at least for the philosopher. This is also the line of thought underlying the widespread conviction in our time that science is a kind of poetry.

The equation of reason with analysis and the attack upon psychologism lead, then, in the case of many of Frege's partisans, to a disregard of the mode of givenness of the object. As I have been presenting the problem, these trends lead to a rejection of intuition even as the analyst is making use of intuition. And as we have seen, our formalist techniques seem to render us oblivious to the intrinsic contradiction between a robust sense of reality and the fantasies of the student of science-fiction. But the rejection of intuition, or its unreflective use, leads in turn to the invisibility of unity, and so to the transformation of being into existence. When we read documents from the history of philosophy in this perspective, their unity as well as their complexity inevitably evade our analytical devices. In the case of the *Theaetetus*, such a perspective leads us to overlook, or to reject as literary trimming, the rhetorical and poetical accounts of the psychology of the philosopher. The ultimate problem of the *Theaetetus* is the way round the aporia intrinsic to the equation of the whole with the sum of its parts. However, as students of analytical thinking, we take our bearings by the aporia itself. Analytical thinking, rigorously and consistently understood, requires simple elements. Yet if we restrict ourselves to analytical thinking, simple elements are impossible. This is the problem of Socrates' dream. Let us now explore some of the details.

Socrates follows his criticism of the doctrine of simple elements by constraining Theaetetus, against his initial inclination, to agree that the whole (*to holon*) is the same as the "all" (*to pan*) or sum of its parts. We may be inclined to sympathize with Theaetetus and to find this identification disturbing. To begin with, it is in conflict with our ordinary experience (or robust sense of reality). There are wholes, like organic unities, that do not readily, if at all, lend themselves to analysis into countable parts. And there are wholes, like an army or a city, that surely cannot be adequately understood as a sum of elements. One might suppose that Socrates means something harmless here, namely, that *if* one counts up the parts of a given whole, their sum cannot designate a unity other than that of the whole. This of course assumes that the whole has parts. If the view is in fact harmless, it is not what Socrates has in mind. He identifies the whole and the sum of its parts in order to illustrate the thesis that knowledge of the parts is knowledge of the whole. I pass by the obvious counterargument that one does not know what an army is simply by knowing how many soldiers it contains. More interesting to us is the following reason why the identification of the whole with the sum of its parts is disturbing. If there are no simple elements, or "clear and distinct" boundaries to analysis, in what sense can we say that there are wholes? Here the weakness of anti-psychologism surfaces in a particularly sharp manner. It is no doubt true that the expression "clear and distinct" is subjective in its implication. However, without a clear and distinct intuition of a unity in the sense of a whole, how can we know that we have arrived at a sum of "parts"?

In considering this question, we distinguish between two senses of "simple." The first sense is "having no parts," and the second is "not subject to further analysis." Points, or Aristotle's mathematical units, may serve as examples of the first sense of "simple." But we cannot distinguish one point from another, except with reference to a matrix of spatial co-ordinates. If a whole is the same as the sum of its parts, and if these parts are simple *qua* not themselves having any parts, then wholes themselves become indistinguishable from each other, or reduce to points. Or else all wholes are systems of spatial co-ordinates, an alternative which, for all practical purposes, reduces to the first inversion. This is enough to enforce the conclusion that if there are wholes, and if wholes are sums of their parts, then these parts cannot be simple in the first sense of the term. (Compare this to the discussion of structure in Chapter One.) Now let us consider the second sense. We may define "simple" as that which is destroyed by analysis, or else immediately replaced by the act of analysis with some structure other than the one to which we initially addressed ourselves. This formulation could be improved, but I trust that it conveys my point with sufficient clarity. To use Socratic language, take the form (Idea) *man*. No doubt there are various attributes which one would have to state in the process of explaining what one means by "man." But the sum of the terms in our explanation of "man" would not be the same as the unity of the whole form *man*. In arriving at what we call the defining (or essential) attributes of "man," we certainly do not dissolve the form into its constituent elements. In contemporary language, if there is such a thing as the concept of man, all analyses of this concept must proceed with respect to an apprehension of the significance of that concept as a unity. This does not mean that the significance of the concept as a unity is the same as the results of our analysis. There is more than one analysis of the concept of man, yet it does not follow that there is more than one concept. Furthermore, analysis is not a random procedure. The intelligibility of the analytical procedure derives from our seeing, and seeing as significant, the complex unity we are analyzing. Different analyses are the result of different perspectives of the concept of man. If it were contended that there is a different concept corresponding to each perspective, then the sense of unity I have in mind would be a feature of each distinct concept in turn. The unit of analysis does not take shape as a consequence of analysis. On the contrary, it "measures" or guides each step of analysis. I have been arguing that analysis is annihilation unless we can see what we are doing: seeing is not analyzing, any more than knowing is the summing of parts. In order for parts to "add up" into a whole (and thus to become genuine parts), they must be seen as parts *of* a whole. We may be inclined to call this "of" or belonging-relation by the name of predication. But the act of seeing a whole as a unity is not the same as seeing a collection of elements.

On the basis of the second sense of "simple," we may offer an approximate definition of wholes as articulated unities of other articulated unities called "elements." By way of anticipation, I claim that the unsatisfactory features of this definition arise, not from the fact that some other analysis of the whole is superior, but from the fact that no analysis can ever be adequate to the task. To go more slowly, the articulations within the whole and its elements make possible the application of analytical techniques; the unities guide this application. In shifting from our apprehension of the comprehensive unity to its ingredient or element-units, we shift from one structure to another. At each level of structure, the unity of the whole is visible as the basis for analysis, yet it cannot itself be analyzed without dissolving the unity of that level. In a sense, the attempt to analyze the unity is like trying to include the ordinal of a given level within a proper sub-set of that ordinal. If thinking is identical with analyzing, then unity at each level is invisible, which is to say that ordered structures are unthinkable, as must be "wholes" and "parts." (The unity of an ordinal is not the same as the sum of its defining parts; the same considerations apply to ordinal numbers as to any unity.) In other words, unless there are simple elements that cannot be replaced by further analyses of their ingredients, but must be perceived as a unity that *regulates*, and so is antecedent to, further analyses, there cannot be any sums of elements counting as wholes. Each ostensible whole is merely a resting stage of an infinite process of analysis, consequently each stage is incipiently collapsing or actually unintelligible. Instead of saying that we think such-and-such, or know that such-and-such is so-and-so, we can only observe that, as we speak, this is how things look to us, or how we use terms, how we speak now.

Socrates' failure to distinguish the two senses of "simple," and his consequent rejection of the intelligibility of simple elements, leaves equally unintelligible his claim that a whole is the same as the sum of its parts. For we do not know what "same" means here. It certainly cannot mean "in one-to-one correspondence," since that requires us to conceive, and indeed to construct, two distinct sums. Put otherwise, the concept of one-to-one correspondence is itself a unity distinct from the co-ordinate x's and y's of sets X and Y. When I see that X and Y are the same, I see something other than the one-to-one correspondence of their individual elements. It therefore seems to me that the entire discussion of knowing in the *Theaetetus*, if we take it out of its dramatic context in the usual style of analytical interpreters, is unintelligible because Socrates never alludes to intellectual intuition of unity. In the analytical sections of this dialogue, he takes it for granted that thinking, and hence knowing, is *dianoia* or discursive analysis.

Whether wholes are forms or functions, they cannot be the same as numerical sums. Not even the unity of a sum is the same as the sum of its units. A relation of order is not an element in the domain of the relation. No number is an element of itself. And yet, forms, functions, or relations are not nothing. To illustrate this point I refer to the basic or "simple" structure of the proposition. From Aristotle to Strawson, ordinary-language analysts have normally explained this structure as a combination of subject and predicate. In the formalist or Fregean analysis, the symbol for the predicate or concept comes equipped with a number of blanks (the number depending upon the nouns in the sentence from which the concept has been extracted) into which name-variables may be inserted. It looks here as though the ordinary-language distinction of subject and predicate is no longer retained. What we actually have is a reinterpretation of this distinction, or a disregard of the surface grammatical structure in favor of a presumably deeper analysis which entails the application of the mathematical concept of the function. Subject and predicate are redefined, but not dropped entirely from the logical analysis of the structure of the simple proposition. In the Strawsonian analysis, to take a recent contrasting interpretation, the structure of ordinary language rather than of mathematics is paradigmatic. The basic form of the proposition is symbolized as ass (i, c) where ass ( ) expresses the function of a propositional combination, i is the symbol for a particular (the subject) and c for a concept (the predicate).[4] For our purposes there is no significant difference between the Fregean and the Strawsonian analyses. But perhaps the point I have in mind is easier to visualize in Strawson's schema.

In this schema, we have a symbol, "ass ( )," which designates the combination or unity of subject and predicate, but (as Strawson emphasizes) *not a concept*. I presume that Strawson does not mean to deny that a function is a concept, but wishes instead to distinguish the uniform application of this concept in all propositions, that is, uniform as distinct from the concept symbolized by *c* and combined with *i*. We can already see that if the function of combination is a concept, and is present in every proposition, then the unity and intelligibility of a proposition depends upon a concept that cannot be the sum of its parts. But this is the least that can be said. The unity and intelligibility of each proposition seems to be the same in all cases; it is both internal and external to the individual case, as one might say. In order to make clear the consequences of this odd fact, I remind the reader of a feature of Aristotle's doctrine of predication, discussed in section 4.

Aristotle's doctrine of predication is at many points the same as Strawson's. But even where they differ, e.g., Aristotle's doctrine of substance (*ousia*), the net result is the same. The species-form or "substratum" of predication is grasped by intellectual intuition. Yet it does not seem to be directly accessible to discursive thinking. What we say of an *ousia* is either an affirmative or a negative predicate: a *parousia* or an *apousia*. These predicates "'belong to" the *ousia* in a "way" that must be seen as the precondition for discursive analysis. Those who attempt to distinguish between essential and accidental attributes by recourse to criteria of linguistic use are simply not paying attention to the problem. A criterion of essentiality cannot be based upon how we normally define our terms. And in fact we define terms by a process that depends upon the perception of unities. To say that *p* belongs to *S* is not to explain what "belonging" means. It does not distinguish between "seems to be" or "usually goes together" or "cannot be otherwise." And even if it did, to say that *S* cannot be otherwise than *p* is not to give an analysis of *ousia* as the unity of *S* and *p*.

Strawson does not seem to suspect that his analysis preserves the Aristotelian doctrine of the *ousia* as present but inaccessible to the predicating or analytical intelligence. The presence of *ousia* is not the presence (*parousia*) of its attributes. In fact, Strawson's "ass( )" provides us with a phantom linguistic reification of Aristotle's ontological copula. Just as a set of predicates, affirmative or negative, is not the same as the *ousia* it is intended to designate, so too the assertion of combination is not a sign for the unity intrinsic to the meaning of a proposition. Even worse, since Strawson claims that the combinatorial function is not a concept but a sign of general linguistic activity, if we take him at his word it must stand for the human capacity to create meanings rather than to refer to them, which is presumably unacceptable to Strawson. Furthermore, if philosophy or rational thought is conceptual analysis, then since the combinatorial function is not a concept, "general linguistic activity" must be inaccessible to rational, i.e., analytical thinking. In the midst of Strawson's sober analyses, we find a Fichtean version of Aristotelian *ousiai*.

In turning now to the formalist analysis of the proposition, one discerns in the Fregean schema that the problem is perhaps obscured by the technical ease with which concepts are distinguished from their instances, and by the ease with which the logical analysis of statements charts the functional relation of the variables. We may thus forget that the unity to which I am addressing myself is already present in the statement that we subject to mathematical analysis. If that analysis removes the unity, it destroys rather than translates accurately the sense of the statement. I refer to the unity underlying both the surface and the deep structure, or the precondition of any analysis. This aside, nothing is said to explain the unity of instance and concept, the Fregean version of Platonic *methexis* and Aristotelian *hyparchein*. This makes sense from a mathematical standpoint. The mathematician is concerned with operations and constructions. He wants to be told how to use the epsilon-relation or how to subsume instances under concepts. The transfer of mathematical techniques to philosophy certainly facilitates our analyses in one sense. But it covers over rather than removes the philosophical problems. The invisible or inaccessible *ousia* now lurks in the language of functions and variables. By concentrating upon operations and constructions, or upon rule-governed activity, we disregard or conceal the underlying problems of unity and being. It seems to me that this cannot be called a resolution of the problems so much as thoughtlessness.

I want to illustrate the unity of the proposition in terms of the analytical doctrine of existence. The analyses of Frege and his successors begin with the assumption that to be is to be countable or nameable (as in the case of uncountable sets) and thus "objectified." This assumption represents one-half of a more complex situation in Greek philosophy. In the contemporary doctrine, the question of "being" is replaced from the outset by the question of existence. Contemporary scholars have engaged in much disputation as to whether Plato and Aristotle distinguished between the ontological and existential senses of the copula. This dispute can be regarded as a mark of the bad effect of analytical devices upon common sense. How could the distinction between forms and instances be preserved if there were not a parallel distinction in the copula? In the case of Plato, I can be very brief. There is a quite clear distinction in the *Theaetetus* (185C–186B) between "essence" or *ousia* and "existence" or instance in the domain of genesis (*estin*). What "exists" is the sensuous instance of the form or kind we wish to define. The instance, in other words, is countable by virtue of its form. Furthermore, the *ousia* becomes accessible to us by way of sense-perception. This, of course, is the meaning of the so-called doctrine of recollection. We are "reminded" of Ideas by our basically sensuous experience of (countable) particulars in this world. There are, then, no Ideas of non-existing things (a point of interest to contemporary modal logic).

This is the basis upon which Aristotle builds his own doctrine. But it would not be easy to point to a passage in which Aristotle explicitly distinguishes between "being" and "existing" (no doubt because he takes it for granted). He does, of course, distinguish between *ousia* or species-form and sensuous individuals. But it could be objected that sentences often translated with the verb "exists," as for example "Socrates exists," actually mean, upon analysis, that Socrates is an instance of the species-form "man."[5] In my opinion, even if this is the correct analysis, it makes the distinction I have in mind. As with Plato, the difference between "being" and "existence" corresponds to the difference between *ousia* as species-form and *ousia* as concrete individual. The famous passage[6] in which Aristotle says that the expressions "one man," "man," and "existing man" all refer to the same thing, does not contradict this point. Aristotle is arguing here that unity and being do not have distinct reference. He is not asserting that there is no fundamental difference between the species-form and the individual.

And this, I think, takes us to the heart of the difficulty in Aristotle. Whereas the senses of unity are the same as those of being, there are manifestly different senses of being, and the most dramatic difference is that between the species-form and the concrete individual or "subject." The unity of a species-form cannot possibly be identical with that of a concrete individual, if "identical with" is taken extensionally. I am not sure that we can say anything at all about whether the unity of the species is the same as the unity of the concrete individual. For "unity" *qua* common to species and individual unity is not amenable to analysis. But we must say that the unity of the species is not the same as the extensional identity of the concrete individual. The distinctness of the species-form is that of the unit as measure. It is not that of a number or sum of units. *"Being" in the primary sense* (irregardless of what stand we take on "exists" in Aristotle) *is uncountable because it is the measure of counting beings in the secondary sense.* The easiest way in which to explain this distinction in English is to use the terms "being" and "existence." But whatever terms we use, the situation remains the same.

The situation, as I have emphasized, is ambiguous. To begin with, it is worth noting that, just as in the case of Plato, the species-form is picked out via sense-perception. Only "existing" things have essences. Investigation must begin with the *that*, or with what exists.[7] In the *that*, we pick out what exists by intuiting the "what" or *ousia*, and this in turn enables us to count or collect together the individuals. It is possible to count individuals because there are many of each kind. But the unity of the species-form must be both the same as and other than the unity of the individuals. It is the same because to be a man is defined by the species-form. It is other because the individual is himself a sum of attributes, accidental as well as essential. (This indicates the difficulty in saying that the unity of the species-form is "the same as" the unity of the individual.) And what are we to make of the fact that there are many distinct species-forms? We might wish to say that these are countable in the same way that individuals are countable. But since counting proceeds by a measure or kind, which is also a species, it would follow that species-forms are collectable into one species; and this, of course, Aristotle regularly denies. The harsh truth is that there is no plain answer by Aristotle to this problem of the unity and multiplicity of *ousiai* or species-forms. I note in passing that if "being *qua* being" is understood as god, who is defined as thought thinking itself, it is still the case that the species-forms are distinct from god, and related to pure thinking by a *pros hen* or "with respect to" relation, not by unity. If god is taken as the unity of *ousiai*, then Aristotle is transformed into Hegel (by way of Neoplatonism).

Aristotle's *ousiai* are the ancestors of contemporary predicates. Those who, like Quine, have reservations concerning the quantification over predicates are therefore renewing the ambiguity in the Aristotelian situation, but with the added difficulty that they deny the *ousia* as an essential unity. This denial underlies the possibility of "objectifying" at a higher level the predicates of a lower-level language. The shift to "substantiality" takes place as a linguistic device, and at the convenience of the analyst. So whether we are ancients or moderns, if there is no distinction between "being" and "existence," a grave problem arises concerning the ontological status of predicates or concepts. For we must now assume that "exists" means "is quantifiable." Existentially quantified statements are built up from atomic statements of the form Fa. But the legitimacy of quantifying Fa depends upon the knowledge that there is an individual with the property designated by F. Since Fa is atomic, it is not possible to analyze the a further, or to assert its existence meaningfully except by describing it via another property, say G. In this case, Fa is complex. So it looks as if we cannot arrive at existing elements by analytical devices. Instead, we must apparently stipulate them in one way or another. This is the simplest formulation of the background for the two main approaches to existence-statements, which we may represent by way of Russell and Strawson. I want to make one or two remarks about each representative, merely to exemplify the relation between the problem of existence and that of unity.

Let us take Russell first. He begins with the assumption that names denote the objects for which they stand. Therefore, a proposition containing a name as a subject-term must presuppose the existence of the object it denotes. But a singular existence-assertion, e.g., "Socrates exists," is meaningless. In order to have a meaning, such a statement must be capable of being negated. However, since names denote, "Socrates does not exist" is self-contradictory. Similarly, "Socrates exists" is redundant; the predicate adds nothing to the subject (and here is the ghost of the Kantian contention that existence is not a genuine predicate). I suppose it has been pointed out on numerous occasions that this interpretation rests upon the assumption that Socrates *does* exist. Yet the fact that he exists cannot be meaningfully asserted. This distrust of pre-analytical givenness is inherited from Russell by Quine, and continues to be visible in the next generation, of which Kripke is perhaps the most distinguished representative. I do not know why these men regard themselves, and are regarded as, realists or anti-conceptualists. The doctrine in question is self-evidently a version of Kantian conceptualism, not to say Idealism. Modern science begins not simply as empiricism, but also as Platonism. Under the influence of Kant, it begins the process of reinterpretation culminating, not in hard-headed realism, but in historicism and poeticism.

Russell then introduces the Fregean notion of the propositional function, and (as he claims) shifts from the surface grammatical form to the deeper logical form. "Socrates exists" then becomes "there is at least one x such that x is a human and x is named Socrates." The name becomes an element of the predicate; failure to pick out an x with such a name no longer cancels the meaning of the statement. "Exists" is then defined as "satisfies a propositional function." But this amounts to saying that existence is defined as the belonging-relation of an element in a set or an instance of a concept. So part of the Aristotelian doctrine of predication (something belongs to something) is retained, but in the guise of quantification-theory, which replaces the *ousia* by a propositional function.

Let us add a word about definite descriptions. They are built up on the basis of atomic statements and propositional functions. The question whether there exist any so-and-so's denoted by expressions of the form "the so-and-so" is avoided in the familiar way. The expression "the so-and-so" is translated as "there is a unique x such that (say) Fx and Gx." It is obvious that the meaning of this statement depends upon the assumption of the existence of an a with properties designated as F and G. Yet that assumption, as we have just seen, is analytically meaningless. This difficulty cannot be avoided by recourse to a highly developed sense of reality. For we presumably talk only about real objects as existing. But this looks circular. If to exist is to be real, and to be real is to exist, then the question of existence must be settled empirically or by stipulation, rather than by the shift from grammatical to logical form. If all that can be said of "exists" is finally that it is synonymous with "something," where "something" is defined by the epsilon-relation or as an instance of a concept, then we still need a criterion for distinguishing between real and imaginary concepts. Besides, is it really satisfactory to explain existence by means of concepts? If "real" means "empirically available," are not all concepts unreal? In this case, how can an instance of what is unreal be called "real" by virtue of being such an instance? In short, if we need to be directly acquainted with existing things, this must transpire either by sense-perception or by intuition. In the latter case, we return to Aristotle; in the former, by an indirect route, we are led to Strawson.

Strawson, of course, dispenses with intellectual intuition, and subsequently (by intention) with *ousiai* or simple elements. He takes it for granted that we know the meanings of our utterances and the intentions of our acts in a publicly certifiable manner. The public manner is not simply through sense-perception since we can "carve up" (a phrase of Dummett's) or "articulate" the world of objects in various ways. Furthermore, there are unending sub-articulations within each comprehensive articulation. We see here the link between Strawson and Quine, as for example in the latter's criticism of understanding translation on the basis of a doctrine of reference. Reference is relative to the language or the interpretation of our theory. Each carving or articulating produces a context of discourse. The meaning of *exists* depends upon the particular context of discourse. In place of the ostensible dangers of intellectual intuition, or of infinite imaginary objects, Strawson substitutes an apparently unending number of senses of "exists." This is Kantian conceptualism rather than Aristotelian ontology, but without a transcendental ego to provide limits.

The Strawsonian approach, which resembles if it is not based upon the later doctrines of Wittgenstein, seems to raise as many difficulties as the Russellian approach. In the first place, what is to prevent us from coming eventually to senses of "exist" which are virtually private, as for example those shared only by members of small groups of specialists? We cannot rely upon sense-perception to furnish existing objects since the perceived continuum can be articulated in various ways, some of these by specialists, with the result that they will be unintelligible to the general public. In the second place, Strawson's account seems to oversimplify the problem of distinguishing between real and imaginary objects. What if I begin a story by saying: "Once upon a time there was a millionaire . . ." Am I not referring to an empirically existing object by a signal that no such objects exist? Third and most comprehensively, how do we account for the unity of our initial grasp of "exists," which leads us to distinguish its various senses? To be told that these senses have no unity but possess instead a family resemblance is to assume that knowledge of the whole is the same as knowledge of the sum of its parts, with the fatal addition that we deny the whole from the outset. We soon come to the need to stipulate by rules or criteria of some kind "what exists." And this seems to be the procedure of mathematics, not of ordinary language. Unlike Aristotle, the ordinary-language philosopher has not learned the decisive lesson of everyday life. The unity of the units of experience cannot be explained analytically or constructively. Strawson fluctuates between Aristotelian and Kantian procedures, and this produces no clear formulation, let alone resolution, of the status of existence.

Having said this, I should add that I find Strawson's procedures far more sensible than those of the formalists. The distinction between ordinary language and scientific discourse, far from challenging the integrity of science, provides, or rather preserves, the only possible ground for the sense and value of science. I have been criticizing the *senselessness* of the formalist analysis of existence. The suppression of intuition and the affirmation of mathematical concepts of "theory" lead to a deconstruction of ordinary experience every bit as radical as that of the French post-Heideggerians. My central illustration of this has been the existential proposition, which purports to be talking about "something," i.e., a unity. But what is the principle of that unity? It cannot be the x or name-variable, since the x is neither this nor that. The bounded or quantified x possesses a contingent unity as defined by its predicates, say F and G. But these cannot stand for the source of unity, since either or both may be false, i.e., fail to be instantiated (since we do not yet know the difference between real and imaginary predicates). This leaves nothing but the propositional function itself, which, like the Hegelian Absolute, is common to all purportedly existing instances of unity. And we still do not know what it means to exist. The function of unity is then common to meaningless, or finally, uncountable and unnameable units. The suppression of the difference between being and existence leads, not to clarity about existence, but to its disappearance. We can explain neither unity nor existence, since both are modifications of being or *ousia*, which is in turn inaccessible to analysis because it is uncountable and unspeakable.

As for Strawson's schema, it seems to simplify the justification for quantifying over predicates by remaining closer to ordinary language. There is no temptation to quantify the function of combination, which is cleanly distinguished from the predicative function of specifying concepts or properties. At the same time, his schema is self-defeating, since it separates the combining function from the predicate *qua* sign of a concept. If it is the predicate that combines, and if a predicate specifies a concept, then why is combination not a concept, and indeed, the same concept as that which combines with the particular? On the other hand, if combining is a non-conceptual function of predicates, then we return to the distinction between predicate and *ousia*. Quine's analysis, to which Strawson objects, is an adaptation of Frege's. He transforms simple predicates into nouns with two-place predicates. Thus "Socrates swims" becomes "swimming is performed by Socrates," or "Performs (swimming, Socrates)." In this notation, only nouns are quantifiable, but the combining or unifying function is even less visible than in Strawson's paradigm. We are, so to speak, led by the hand to insert subject-terms in exactly the right slots. These instances can never be confused with their predicates or concepts. But the hand that leads us is invisible, at least to analytical thinking.

The invisible hand of unity cannot be explained in the Aristotelian style of co-ordinating the senses of "one" with those of "being." For Aristotle, we can explain why something is something else, because there is a specific "through which" or cause in each case. But we cannot explain why something is itself, since "there is one *logos* and one cause in all cases."[8] We cannot explain the unity of the species-form because this just amounts to sameness, and to say that something is the same as itself is just to say that it is itself. By the same argument, "is" in the sense of "exists" may be applied to every subject. And this corresponds to the interpretation of "exists" and "is identical with" as permissible but *vacuous* predicates.[9] They add no new information about their subjects. Nor, I add, could they, since information is defined as the result of analytical or predicative thinking. The concept of vacuous predicates points directly toward my interpretation of the inaccessibility of Aristotle's *ousia*. Since the primary sense of "being" is *ousia*, and since *ousia* is primarily *eidos*, the analytical account of an *eidos* is always of its properties or predicates, and never of the unity of those properties. The problem of the essential unity of an *eidos* or subject is thus exactly the same as that of the unity of the proposition, except in the case of the intuition of essence (see section 4).

10. Socrates' Dream

I have been arguing throughout this book that philosophy is at each step both intuitive and analytical. In order to give a reasonable account of analysis, one must give an account of something other than analysis. The dream of describing the world in terms of an alphabet of simple elements must be supplemented by an account of dreaming. In this section, I begin such an account, or provide some notes toward the elaboration of such an account. I begin with a remark about Aristotle. Aristotle distinguishes between a "whole" and an "all" with respect to two main features: the unity and the position of the parts.[10] A whole is not a point but an internally articulated or, so to speak, "well-ordered" unity. Because the nature of the unit is to be "a kind of origin for number,"[11] it is not necessarily the case that the unity of the whole is also a sum of natural parts. For example, pleasure is an activity and a whole in the sense that it is complete at every moment.[12] One might analyze the experience of pleasure, and Aristotle does this at some length. But the analysis of the experience of pleasure is not the same as the experience of pleasure. I believe that we can sharpen this formulation. Pleasure itself, as distinct from both the concept and the experience of pleasure, is a unity in the sense that, as Aristotle says of an element, "it is indivisible in its form into another form."[13] The analysis of the concept of pleasure is thus rooted in the experience, not of a concept, but of pleasure itself.[14] Such an analysis can never capture the unity of pleasure itself as it shows itself within the continuum of our experience of that unity. On the contrary, we measure the experience, and consequently the analytical construction of the concept, by the unity.

The example of pleasure is intended to suggest something about the manner of accessibility of simple elements or units of measurement. One does not have to be an existentialist to point out that life is a kind of unity of unities, none of which is equivalent to a set of analytical predicates.[15] Since analysis is an activity of living beings, in order to make sense out of analysis we must be able to speak rationally about life. In this section I want to sketch briefly the existential and the logical components of Plato's treatment of Socrates' dream. These remarks are not addressed to philologists, but to philosophers. I hope that they may be of interest to those who are concerned with the question of how to read a Platonic dialogue. However, my main purpose is to call attention to some features of Platonic rhetoric, as a kind of antidote to the analytical rhetoric which provides so much of our professional sustenance. It is a widespread superstition among analytical philosophers, who include some of the most articulate and polemical rhetoricians in the academic community, that rhetoric is not a part of philosophy. I disagree. Rhetoric is the art of speaking, and this includes the capacity to address problems that are not amenable to analytical resolution. Similarly, it includes the attempt to persuade the student that philosophical problems *are* capable of analytical resolution, although there is certainly no analytical evidence of such a resolution. The context of analysis is a dream, not an analytical discourse. I am not objecting to its dreamlike quality, but rather to the absence of any doctrine of the proper mode of analyzing dreams. The following remarks touch upon Plato's presentation of the context of analysis. I regard this presentation as paradigmatic. Nevertheless, I shall offer one or two suggestions for modifying the Platonic paradigm in the light of lessons learned from the history of philosophy.

The first thing to be said is that the Platonic dialogue is a daydream of the whole. It is counter to the late Wittgenstein, whose remarks, like the epigrams and paragraphs of Nietzsche, remind us of monologues in search of a dialogue. Neither Wittgenstein nor Zarathustra is capable of dialogue. Both must reject their disciples (apparently without the disciples' awareness) because the context of a discursive community is for them illusory, a chaos or nothingness to be felt, not spoken. For Plato, on the contrary, the whole is accessible to *logos*.

However, just as Wittgenstein's complex thought may be vulgarized by reducing it to techniques of conceptual analysis, the same can be said of Plato: *logos* means here ratio or harmony as accessible to speech, and cannot be reduced to "logic." In other words, *logos* includes *mythos*, or the variety of ways in which humans communicate to each other via symbols that are detachable from their meanings. In still another formulation, the dream of analytical elements is also the dream of an alphabet as the unity of these elements. But how we talk about elements is not simply identical with how we talk about the alphabet. Plato suggests this distinction in the following way. In the dialogues, there are four main appearances of the example of the alphabet: these occur in the *Theaetetus, Sophist, Statesman*, and *Philebus*. [16] Socrates is the main speaker in the first and the last, whereas he is replaced by the Eleatic Stranger in the second and third. In the *Sophist* and *Statesman*, the Stranger introduces the example of the alphabet as an illustration of the analytical method, one that is in sharp distinction to mythical or pre-analytical thinking. As the Stranger observes in the *Statesman*, the function of the example of the alphabet is to illuminate the *technē* of politics, or to provide waking knowledge, not dream knowledge (278e4–11). The context makes clear that the dream knowledge in question is the myth of the reversed cosmos, previously told by the Stranger (cf. 277 A–C). [17] Basically the same situation obtains in the *Sophist*. The example of the alphabet prepares the discussion of the communion of kinds, or the analytical resolution of problems raised by children or old men who have come late to learning (251B). This passage in turn serves to contrast the analysis of elemental relations with the doctrines of Parmenides and the other pre-Socratic thinkers who spoke in a "popular" (or "relaxed") and "mythical" way about the number and kinds of beings (242C).

The alphabet serves the Stranger as a paradigm for sober, analytical, or waking thought. He concentrates exclusively upon the letters as elements of syllables. In the case of Socrates the situation is more nuanced. In the *Philebus*, where the discussion turns initially from pleasure to unity and plurality, Socrates introduces eidetic numbering, diaeresis, or the analysis of formal structure as a gift of the gods (16C). He describes this method in language that is both mythical and analytical. The example of the alphabet, which Socrates employs to clarify his initial statement, is very soon converted into the story of Theuth, the Egyptian god who first saw the unities or letters in the infinite continuum of sound (18B). In the *Theaetetus*, Socrates speaks of a dream rather than a myth, but the point is the same (201E). To the analytical intelligence, dreams are myths or fairy-tales. In fact, Socrates refers the dream to some unnamed source; this is his usual procedure of attributing myths to gods, poets, or the ancestors. Socrates provides us with a different context of analysis than does the Stranger, a context more like that of the dialogue form itself. This makes me think that those who identify Plato's "mature" position with that of the Stranger, and as a tacit criticism or repudiation of Socrates, are mistaken. Such an identification is based upon an interposition of the oversimplified rhetoric of contemporary formalist analysis onto the Platonic dialogue. We note further that in his development of the paradigm, Socrates, exactly like the Eleatic Stranger, focuses exclusively on the letters and their combinations into syllables. He does not treat discursively the paradigm of the alphabet as a unity of letters. To express this point in modern language, there is no reduction of theory to a formal language. In slightly different terms, the language, as well as its interpretation, is metaphor or myth. We are left to infer Socrates' attitude toward the alphabet from the dramatic context. Plato, whether in his Socratic or his Eleatic manifestations, accepts both the necessity of simple elements for discursive thinking, and the impossibility of giving a discursive account of their nature.

An account of the nature of simple elements would explain not merely their simplicity as detached elements, but also their unity within an alphabet. This is impossible, and the effort to engage in such an analysis leads us directly into the heart of a Hegelian or dialectical logic. The unity of the elements in an alphabet cannot be analyzed into still simpler elements. Hence the temptation arises to explain the elemental relations as "processes." To employ a metaphor, formal logistic and its language of mathematical functions, if carried to its end, transforms formal elements into moments like those of the motions of the physical world, described by the Calculus. The functions themselves are not moments in the process (hence the reluctance to quantify over predicates must be extended to functions) but metaphorical representations of that process as absolute activity. German Idealism and Hegel are thus an alternative consequence of Leibniz, and a consequence that in my opinion goes more deeply into the philosophical nature of formal calculi than does the doctrine of the formalists. In Plato, the language of myth is required as a supplement to the language of analysis. In the modern epoch, thanks to the initial stimulus of Aristotle, myth is transformed into metaphysics, which in turn undergoes a dual transformation into transcendental or Idealist ontology and formalist analysis. But formalist analysis is not self-conscious. I have been arguing all along that the relation of the formalist to experience is inconsistent: it amounts to an acceptance of everyday experience together with the attempt to reconstitute experience formally. And this in turn is the result of a dislike of metaphysics or transcendental ontology. Oddly enough, the wish to remain faithful to everyday experience is better served by transcendental ontology than by formalist analysis. I would make a similar comment about Greek philosophy. Plato's use of myths is a safer basis for fidelity to everyday experience than is Aristotle's rejection of myth. That rejection arises from Aristotle's belief that he has resolved the problems of unity, multiplicity, and hence non-being, by his doctrine of predication. This Aristotelian belief is the ancestor of contemporary analytical philosophy. But at least Aristotle retains intellectual intuition. The contemporary analyst has no such doctrine. Since a formalist justification of formalism is impossible, the analytical philosopher is inevitably placed in one of two alternative positions: Hegelian dialectics or Nietzschean celebrations of chaos. We should not be deluded by the present dominance of analysts in the English-speaking academy from recognizing this process of transformation. It is happening now, and those with eyes to see will see it.

Now let us return to the situation in the *Theaetetus*. This will enable us to study, in a relatively accessible manner, the aporiai underlying all references to ontological alphabets in Plato. As I have been contending, these are also the aporiai of analytical thinking in general. The *Theaetetus* is especially interesting to us because in it, Socrates converses exclusively with mathematicians, in pursuit of a quasi-mathematical definition of "knowledge itself" (146E). The search for this definition is inspired by Theaetetus' discovery of how to divide, not the infinite continuum of sound, but that of the numbers. Theaetetus is unable to transfer his mathematical technique to the problem at hand. He finally remarks that he once heard someone else refer to knowledge as "true opinion together with *logos*" (201C–D). Socrates makes a very illuminating comparison between this definition and hearsay evidence used by skilled lawyers to obtain a conviction when there are no eyewitnesses to the crime (201A–C). As we may restate this, the stories told by gods, poets, and the ancestors provide us with the general picture in those decisive cases where there are no formal structures for direct inspection. In all these cases, there may be true opinion but not technical or epistemic knowledge.

Socrates' distinction brings to mind an analogy between seeing and epistemic knowing. Hearing, as he now indicates, is like dreaming.[18] In exchange for Theaetetus' memory or dream, Socrates will recount one that he has himself heard. We are altogether in the realm of "hearsay" (201D). Neither Socrates nor Theaetetus, themselves characters in a Platonic dream, have dreamt the dreams they mention. It would be going too far to say that they are only tangentially involved in the proceedings, yet both have been transformed for the moment into symbols of a message from a deeper stratum of experience. Socrates "seems to have heard" people defending the doctrine of simple elements. The emphasis upon hearsay apparently disregards the visual content of dreams. But the difficulty lies precisely in recollecting this content, or in translating it into public *qua* scientific discourse. If the dream were merely reported, it would become public in another sense, like a Socratic myth or a Platonic dialogue. The analogy between seeing and knowing is therefore incomplete. We also know what we hear, even in those cases where there is nothing to see, or, stated more cautiously, where there are visible forms but invisible combinations of these forms. I want to emphasize that this metaphor is intended to work in both directions: seeing the whole depends upon hearing (or something like hearing), but hearing also depends upon seeing.

The image of the dream must be connected to the previous figures in the *Theaetetus* of the wax tablet and the aviary, introduced by Socrates to facilitate the analysis of knowledge. These are the functional equivalents to Wittgenstein's fables and examples. They are the consequence of the imagination, not of analysis. And this means that there is a Platonic version of the doctrine that human thinking participates in the work of revealing the truth. As we already noted in conjunction with diaeresis (or "concept-formation"), thinking is productive as well as theoretical or (as it is called in the *Sophist*) acquisitive. If dreaming produces the unity of the whole, or better, contributes to making that unity visible, then the logic we require for the analysis of that unity is, so to speak, psychoanalytical rather than mathematical. This is another way of calling attention to the deficiencies of extreme anti-psychologism. It is obvious from the nature of the dialogue as daydream that thinking is productive in the sense just mentioned. That it is not productive in the sense of a creation *ex nihilo* follows from the Platonic Ideas and doctrine of nature, including the nature of the soul. Those who fear the language of dreams and psychoanalysis should remember that the study of the internal structure of mathematics is not the same as the study of the soul *qua* mathematician.

It now becomes necessary to indicate the nature of the technical *aporia* in the content of the dream. According to this dream, we can name each element as distinct or separate in itself (*auto kath' hauto*), but we can say nothing more about it, not even that the element exists or does not exist, since that would be to attach being or non-being to it (201E). This is, so to speak, the grandfather of Quine's reluctance to quantify over predicates. We cannot even say of the element that it is "same," "each," "alone," "this," and so on (202A). Some philosophers have supposed that the problem Socrates raises here is solved by the Stranger in the *Sophist*. My view is quite different. I cannot go into all the details, but the main point is easy to state. The difficulty concerning the simple elements is exactly the same as that which applies to the doctrine of "greatest kinds" and their combinations. In order to say, and thus to think analytically, the element *x* by itself, it is necessary, as Socrates observes, to combine two elements, *x* and *itself* (note that if *x* is just the element of "selfhood" or sameness, the problem is even more peculiar). But this gives us the standard Platonic formula for the Idea: *auto to x*. So too in the *Sophist*: "same" is a distinct kind, as are "being," "other," "change," and "stasis," to restrict ourselves to the Stranger's examples. The analytical explanation of the meaning of the assertion "change is not stasis" requires us to postulate a communion between "change" and "same" with respect to change itself, and then between "change" and "stasis" via "other." But how, in logical or ontological space, can we (or a divine intelligence) distinguish between the "sameness" of change itself and "same" as the logically distinct form to which "change" must be related in order to "be" itself via a further relation to "being"? If the answer is that all these relations subsist eternally as the ground of logical discourse, then I reply that it is discursively impossible to separate these elements and their relations. I mean by this that what we "separate" in our statements are aspects of an eternal web as we intuit it, not the elements of the web itself.

Any attempt to formulate the doctrine of the community of kinds, whether these are taken to be simple elements or ontological paradigms, provides us with evidence, not of that doctrine, but of another. I refer to the doctrine that elements are like letters in the alphabet, but that the alphabet is the unity of differences, or a self-differentiating whole, to be conceived on the model of genesis, or what Plato sometimes calls *eros*. And this means, I think, that it becomes impossible to distinguish intelligence from the elements it differentiates. The "psychoanalytical" interpretation of *eros* is, or leads to, a peculiarly Hegelian logic of being and nothingness, not as predicates (whether vacuous or otherwise), but as the disturbances constituting the inner excitation of the whole. And indeed, if we cannot quantify over predicates, or are free to do so at a level of discourse one step higher than that in which they function as predicates, how is this different from the view that "predicates" are disturbances or differentiations in the continuum of discourse? Let us recall the puzzle of the "altogether not" in the *Sophist*. Whatever we may say of a simple element is actually an assertion about a compound of elements. If negation is the cancellation of a predicate, but a negation in relation to a subject defined by other predicates, then the denial of simple elements is like the cancellation of all predicates. If it is improper to say that predicates "exist," then such a cancellation is easy enough to imagine. In this case, with respect to what subject does the comprehensive cancellation occur? Surely there is no other candidate than the compound or syllable. One might try to suggest another candidate, like "logical space" or even "the receptacle." [19] But anything we say about these candidates is itself woven together from syllables. If the syllable has no letters, or if the letters are invisible, then the syllable itself collapses internally, or becomes a letter, and is hence itself unknowable. Socrates in fact points out this consequence in the *Theaetetus* (205E), but since he does not distinguish between the two senses of "simple" that I noted previously, and because he makes no explicit use of dreaming or intellectual intuition here, but restricts knowing to analyzing, he cannot solve his own puzzle. The assertion of simple elements is then unintelligible, whereas the denial of simple elements amounts to the assertion of the altogether not.

Socrates criticizes the doctrine of simple or unknowable elements (202Dff), but he never repudiates the associated definition of knowledge as right opinion together with *logos*. Instead, he says that the definition is "likely" (202C–E, cf. 201C). As I have been arguing, this means, not that the doctrine of simple elements must be rejected, but that it cannot be explained in its own terms. One odd sign of Plato's manner of presenting the issue is that none of the main uses of the alphabet-paradigm makes mention of *words*. The speakers either restrict themselves to letters and syllables, or proceed directly from these to statements. Words appear only as strings of syllables, not as distinct structures in the paradigm of meaning. But this vitiates the force of the paradigm, as is immediately obvious from one of Socrates' own examples. We may allow that names refer to elements, and that explanations are constructed from names. But words are not formed by combining the names of syllables. We could say that the name of the syllable formed from the letters S and O is SO. Hence the name "Socrates" might be woven together from the names SO, CRA, and TES. But the meaning of the name "Socrates" has nothing to do with the names of its syllabic constituents.

The word is the crucial mediation point between elements and statements. If the word had no elements, then we could not understand it. But we understand it in the context of statements. Words then become "simple" elements of statements, which in turn may perhaps be called "simple" elements of *logoi* or connected accounts. There is a kind of circularity of explanation here but, I think, an altogether necessary one. At the same time, the circle is not quite the famous "hermeneutic circle" of the Diltheyan or Heideggerean schools. That circle arises upon the assumption that meaning is at each level either discursive or defined by the perspective of the interpreter. I mean neither of these. The situation I describe is rooted in the non-analytical nature of the unities at each level of meaning, and this has nothing to do with the perspective of the interpreter. These levels are not established by "myths" in the sense of historical constructions. The context of analysis is always the same in its general features. To take my own example, unity *qua* wholeness does not alter its nature from one historical epoch to another. And yet it cannot be explained in a purely analytical way. It points beyond analysis to a universal dimension in which formal characteristics are embedded in an unformalizable process. Plato exhibits this process in his myths; I call these "general pictures" which combine hearsay and direct visual (or intuitive) evidence. As is obvious from Plato himself, these general pictures in no way interfere with the development of mathematical analysis. On the contrary, they give sustenance and sense to this development. But the peculiar feature of these general pictures is that they can be expressed only in terms which vary from telling to telling. It is as though one generation of art critics after another each attempts to interpret an extraordinary masterpiece. The masterpiece remains the same, and hence controls the perspectives of the critics. Nevertheless, the accounts of the critics will certainly vary from generation to generation. The universality of the context of analysis is accessible only to the specific language of poetry, fables, hunches, examples, or dreams. Thus the temptation to equate general pictures with transient or historical creations is very great. It amounts to the confusion of the critic's account with the masterpiece he is interpreting. Nevertheless, the philosopher is not quite an art critic. He must find a way to resist that temptation without falling into the opposite temptation of formalism.

I close this section with a last extended remark about Plato. The problem in the dialogues, as I see it, is this. They provide us with materials for a general theory of the context of analysis. But the explicit treatment of thinking is always in terms of a paradigm of analysis of compounds of simple elements. This leaves us with a blurred picture or what seem to be two discontinuous levels of human spiritual activity. Let us call these activities mathematics and poetry. Hegel's dialectical logic is the attempt to unify these two activities. Now Plato in my opinion quite intentionally omits to suggest anything like a dialectical logic. But very few readers are able to rest content with a blurred picture. The temptation is very great to bring the picture into focus. There are basically three ways in which to do this. The first is to reject the poetical elements and to emphasize analysis. The second is to reject the analytical elements and to emphasize the poetical dimension. The third is Hegel's way. The great difficulty I myself face in developing an explicit account of my own position is that I am advocating that we *leave the picture blurred*. This inevitably looks like slovenly thinking to members of at least two out of the three aforementioned schools that have responded to the Platonic situation. It now looks as though I am somehow a member of the "poetic" school. But this is reductionist thinking. Poetry and mathematics are what they are, and both are necessary. However, the common ground from which they spring is neither a poem nor a set of axioms.

If the Platonic alphabet is regarded exclusively as a sum of elements, then there can be no analytical distinction between the whole and the all. But if it is regarded exclusively as a self-differentiating unity, there can be no analytical logic. I infer from this dilemma that the whole is both the same as, and other than, the all. Hegelian logic, far from being an eccentric fantasy of speculation, is suggested to us by common-sense considerations of simplicity, unity, and wholeness. But the same considerations of common sense lead us to add that even a dialectical logic depends upon the capacity to distinguish formal elements. If such distinguishing is analyzing, it is also intellectual intuition: even more, it is vision in cooperation with hearsay evidence. I therefore conclude that philosophers must be lawyers and psychoanalysts as well as mathematicians and poets. This is my emendation of the program for educating philosophers as put forward with tongue-in-cheek by Socrates in the *Republic*.

11. Non-Existence and Nothing

In section 9, I offered a preliminary criticism of the analysis of "existence" stemming from Frege (to summarize a school of thought by the name of its most distinguished recent representative). The main purpose of this criticism was to defend the traditional distinction between being and existence. I want now to continue the criticism begun in section 9, but from the vantage-point of a still more peculiar difficulty. To put the question in its most provocative form: if there is a distinction between existence and being, are we entitled to speak of a parallel distinction between non-existence and nothing? In more subdued form: what do we mean by "negation"? Is there a sharp conceptual difference between the negation-sign as it appears in, say, non-p, or in "p or non-p," and in the negative quantifier? What is the connection between a negative fact and non-existent objects? If we grant that it makes sense to speak of the ontological copula, are we not committed to the apparently absurd consequence that it makes sense to speak of the non-ontological copula? In other words, if we deviate from the Fregean analysis of existence, do we not run the risk of hypostasizing nothingness? Questions like this could be multiplied, but enough has been said to indicate the general topic of the present section. I want to preface the main part of this discussion with an extended "methodological" remark.

A failure to distinguish between "being" and "existence" leads to a confusion over the status of abstract objects. One may therefore make the following objection against attempts to paraphrase away the existential status of predicates or concepts. Not even the strictest nominalist denies that we construct or imagine, and hence conceive of, abstract objects. The general approach of those whom we may call the anti-Meinongians, after Alexius Meinong (1853–1921), a kind of extreme Platonist, is to admit that there "are" abstract objects in the imagination while denying that they exist. In so doing, however, they grant the distinction between being and existence, but fail to notice this because of an obsession with spatio-temporal existence. No Platonist to my knowledge, whether ancient or modern, holds that Ideas or concepts exist in the sense of spatio-temporal individuals. (If any do so, we may safely repudiate them here.) The disagreement between Platonists and anti-Platonists, or between

Meinongians and anti-Meinongians, is not on this point. The two camps in fact agree that abstract objects may be conceived, whether or not they link such conception with intuition. For example, in a recent discussion, Charles Chihara develops the position of what he calls the "mythological Platonist" who makes no decision as to whether abstract objects exist. "It is enough that such objects can be conceived."[20] But this is also enough, as Chihara does not seem to notice, to grant the thesis of the non-mythological or actual Platonist who insists upon the difference between "exists" in the sense intended by Chihara, and "is" in the sense that Chihara must grant if he is to allow the conceiving of abstract objects at all. The pivotal thesis of Platonism, as the term is normally used, is that certain kinds of abstract objects "are" conceivable, i.e., that they have *noetic* being, not spatio-temporal existence. It would be more appropriate to refer to someone who attributes spatio-temporal existence to abstract objects as a mythological Platonist.

This brings me directly to the methodological point. If we are told that we imagine that there are abstract objects, and imagine ourselves to be referring to them, whereas in fact abstract objects do not exist and we are actually referring to something else, the reply is as follows. First, the objection confuses "imagining" and "conceiving," in a way reminiscent of Kripke's confusion of imagination and intuition. I repeat that the conceiving of abstract objects is not at issue. We are, if we are "imagining" at all, not imagining that we conceive of abstract objects, but (ostensibly) that they exist. However, the Platonist is *not* imagining that abstract objects exist. If to imagine is to form an image, the Platonist may imagine that he perceives a spatio-temporal instance, say, a grazing cow, of an abstract object, "the Idea of the cow." But he does not imagine that the Idea of the cow is grazing before his eyes. The term "Idea" is perhaps needlessly provocative in this context. The Platonist's reply may be emended very simply. If we cannot conceive of a non-grazing cow, or in other words, have a conception of cows in general, then there is no way in which to conceive of an individual cow as existing, since "existence" is defined as the subsumption of an individual under a concept. However, a parallel situation obtains in the case of non-existence. If I perform a mental operation, the content of which is expressed in the statement that "there are no unicorns," then I possess the concept of unicorns. To say that unicorns are imaginary animals is not the same as to say that the concept of unicorns is an imaginary concept, in the sense that we "suppose" ourselves to be thinking the concept of unicorns but are actually thinking something else. Exactly the same holds for the concept of a golden mountain or a round square. The concept of a round square is especially intriguing, precisely because I *cannot* imagine it or provide a geometrical construction. I hold no brief for round squares. I agree that a round square is a self-contradiction, unimaginable and unconstructible, and therefore "thinkable" only in an extremely tenuous sense. Nevertheless, I contend that I am thinking it in some tenuous sense precisely because I am able to deny not merely that round squares exist but that they are even imaginable. The attempt to imagine a round square is intelligible in a way that disappears if I am told that I am not thinking about round squares at all, but about something else, say, an imaginary conflation of squares and circles.

All attempts to resolve ontological problems by recourse to paraphrase suffer from the same defect. This defect was the subject of a paper by William P. Alston. If a given sentence (1) seems to commit us to the existence of undesirable entities, whereas a sentence (2) is an acceptable paraphrase of the meaning of (1) but does not make mention of the undesirable entities, then (2) has exactly the same, if any, ontological commitments as (1). Otherwise (2) could not be an acceptable paraphrase of the meaning of (1).[21] As Alston puts it:

> whether a man admits (asserts) the existence of possibilities depends upon what statement he makes, not on what sentence he uses to make that statement. . . . It is a question of *what* he says, not of *how* he says it. Hence he cannot repudiate his admission by simply changing his words.[22]

This formulation is perhaps not sufficiently nuanced, but it makes the right general point. Admission and assertion of possibilities are two distinguishable cases. I may assert something that I do not admit, and did not intend to admit, because I misspoke or did not understand the precise meaning of what I said. However, this does not significantly alter the issue at hand. If I intend to refer to a square circle, or rather, to the concept of a square circle, then in some sense I am doing so by virtue of the fact that this is my intention. (On the other hand, if I intend to refer to an existing square circle, or to the geometrical construction of a square circle, then I am mistaken.)

I am about to argue that an analysis of "does not exist" is inadequate if it does not keep the road open for a pre-analytical sense of "nothing" or "nothingness." I use alternative terms because of the admitted peculiarity of the sense under discussion. There is a puzzle about "nothing," which is obvious from our attempt to choose the right name for the puzzle. However, the fact that we are puzzled is itself evidence of the significance of the term(s). If we think that we understand some problem or puzzle, and if we are able to describe what it is that we do not understand, then it is not a satisfactory explanation to be told that we did not correctly believe ourselves to understand what it is that puzzled us. No one can believe himself to be thinking of something without actually thinking of that which he believes himself to think. This case is parallel with that of pain and pleasure; it seems not to be, however, when we analyze "thinking" in terms of "predicating" or "constructing." It should go without saying that to believe oneself to be thinking something is not the same as to possess knowledge of the nature of something. The example of the round square is pertinent here. I am entirely at ease with the proposition that round squares do not exist, and further, that nothing can be known of their nature, since they have no nature. Depending upon how the term "concept" is defined, I am prepared to grant that there is no concept of a round square. To say, however, that I am not thinking of a round square at all, when I suppose myself to be doing so, but rather of, say, the null-class, is not acceptable. This sort of talk confuses mathematical convenience with philosophical analysis. Or still more accurately, it confuses an account of thinking with the manipulation of well-defined analytical operations. There is undoubtedly something extremely odd about the notion of a round square. The notion is so odd that it would be absurd to concoct a doctrine of thinking or being in terms of it or others like it. One might want to say that the expression is incorrectly formed, given the meanings of its constituent terms. This, I think, is sound. But in deciding upon the incorrectness of the expression, I am "somehow" thinking the expression and in a way that is not easy to explain. What *is* easy, however, is to deny that, in expressing the phrase, I am *intentionally* referring to the null-class. I am aware that what I intend is of no interest to the logician or (except in dispositional terms) to the analyst of reference. But I hold that this lack of interest is an error. It turns away from the odd cases and encourages us to resolve them by a calculative device.

To come now to the crucial instance: if I am puzzled by nothingness, my puzzlement cannot be resolved by the assurance that I was actually thinking about something, and so was falsely puzzled. It does no good to point out to me that "-ness" is a suffix designating a positive abstract quality, or that I am inconsistently using an abstract term as though it were both the name of something and yet without any reference. This last response, for example, itself raises the question of what we mean when we say that a term is *without any reference*. It comes down to this: the various attempts to talk away the puzzle of nothingness by technical paraphrases all begin from the fact of puzzlement. But they ignore the fact of puzzlement as a "psychological" irrelevancy. Hence they do not in fact analyze the act of thinking involved in this puzzle, but provide us with a "theory" of successful reference based upon a combination of bafflement as to how to deal with puzzles and the conviction that puzzles are opportunities for technical ingenuity. This mode of philosophical analysis leads to scholasticism and self-hypnosis. It accounts for the frequent and vulgar occurrence in which the analyst purports not to understand what the traditional philosopher is saying. And finally, it produces a generation of uneducated technicians who have been conditioned actually *not* to understand anything said to them in a dialect other than that of their school.

One consequence of the Aristotelian truism that " 'is' has many senses" is that there can be no monolithical theory of reference and no homogeneous ontology. The expressions "——— exists" and "——— does not exist" mean different things in different contexts. The difference of the contexts cannot be removed by paraphrase. To a considerable extent, this has been recognized by the ordinary-language analysts. Thus, the old claim that statements like "Socrates exists" tell us nothing new about Socrates has been rejected as inadequate, since Socrates might clearly not have existed. Again, the statement that "Santa Claus exists" has often been used as a paradigm for the ostensibly meaningless set of assertions that non-existent objects exist. But the problem is readily overcome by reference to the context of the assertion, not by paraphrasing it or translating it into the first-order predicate calculus. There is no real difficulty in explaining what we mean by statements like "Santa Claus exists" or "the present King of France is bald" until we attempt to impose onto them excessively rigid doctrines of reference. In the best cases, ordinary-language analysts actually look at what we normally say, rather than referring to the convenience of a preferred formal language. As Strawson reasonably says, "neither Aristotelian nor Russellian rules give the exact logic of any expression of ordinary language, for ordinary language has no exact logic." [23] In a similarly reasonable vein, Strawson observes that it is not expressions but speakers who refer, and consequently sentences beginning with uniquely referring expressions can be understood with respect to the context of use. Unfortunately, as we saw in section 9, Strawson pushes this reasonableness to the point of philosophical unreasonableness. He adopts a modified version of the Aristotelian doctrine of predication in order to explain the form of a proposition or sentence. This is connected to his attempt to explain the senses of "is" in terms of the context of use. On the one hand, he does not see in his analysis of the form of a statement the presence of ontological unity. On the other, he does not see that same ontological unity in the open set of uses or contexts of use of "is." The shift from the demands of a formal calculus to the contexts of use in natural language is reasonable, as far as it goes. But it requires a supplement to the ordinary doctrine of predication.

So much for the methodological remark. We are entitled to analyze statements of non-existence, but we must not analyze away the problem contained in the particle expressing negation. It should be clear that this problem is inseparable from that of existence. We can see this from a brief inspection of the usual distinction between negation and the negative quantifier. The negation-sign can appear as a prefix to a propositional variable, making it prior to the introduction of quantifiers. In this case, where p is a proposition formed by the usual rules of the propositional calculus, "non-p" means that the fact represented by p does not obtain. If p stands for "my dog plays the flute," then "non-p" means "it is false that my dog plays the flute." This is obviously different from the statement that "there are no dogs," which is also false, but for a reason other than that of the falsehood of "my dog plays the flute." Dogs do in fact exist, although mine at least is incapable of playing the flute. We can, then, distinguish between a negative existential and a negative fact. On the other hand, the statement that "there are no unicorns" is not merely a negative existential but also asserts a negative fact, namely, that it is a fact that unicorns do not exist. And conversely, "my dog plays the flute" is false because nothing exists that is both my dog and a flute-player. So the distinction between negative existentials and negative facts is not a rigid one. It seems to be relative to the depth of our analysis of the logical form of a proposition. But in ordinary-language analysis, the distinction between the propositional and the predicate logic is an artificial one. Facts are about things, and things either exist or they do not. The same point emerges from a quick look at a third type of negation. We may affix a negative particle to a term or predicate. In this case, where p is a predicate, "non-p" refers to the logical complement of p. One may assert "non-p" in this sense without being prepared to admit the existence of instances of non-p. On the other hand, the assertion of a predicate, whether positive or negative, is not a genuine assertion at all. Predicates are constituents of assertions which take some stand about the existence of instances. So long as we do not confuse the different uses of "not," which we are not likely to do in any event, we are entitled to conclude that the problem of non-existence is the deepest form of the problem of negation.

We may observe next that the problem does not surface in a simple contrast of affirmative and negative existential assertions, regardless of whether the subject-term is like "Socrates" or like "Santa Claus." This is easily illustrated by reference to "free logics" or related formal systems in which "existence" is introduced as a predicate.[24] The introduction of an existence-predicate, combined with a Meinongian distinction between existential and non-existential reference, raises no insuperable difficulties for the ingenious logician. But these various technical tricks all take place within a community of agreement as to the nature of what may exist, and hence rely upon the possible reference of negative existentials. To make existence a predicate in other words is just to overlook the difference between existence and being. This renders needlessly obscure the question of the status of abstract objects. But it also renders invisible the status of unity and the ontological copula. And, as I now suggest, it renders invisible the problem of nothingness. If a referring-expression points by definition to an object, then the expression "nothingness" has no reference. In this case, negation in its various forms must be explained syntactically, as a version of the Platonic-Aristotelian doctrine of "otherness," although brought up to date by the terminology of concepts and instances. If something does not fall under a given concept, it nevertheless falls under some other concept, and this latter fact enables us to express its non-participation. But this line of explanation does not explain what it means *not to fall under a concept*. There is no more an analytical explanation of "not belonging to" than there is of "belonging to."[25] The intelligibility of the belonging-relation rests, as I have argued, upon an intuition of being. By a parallel, although considerably more disconcerting, reflection, I suggest that the intelligibility of "not belonging to" rests upon an intuition of nothingness. It is easy enough to assert that " 'Nothingness' cannot be thought," and this assertion has been made since the time of Parmenides. It is quite superficial to suggest that the problem arises because of the commission of a grammatical error. As I noted in my discussion of paraphrasing, every attempt to remove the ostensible error by a syntactical analysis depends upon the antecedent intelligibility of what we are removing.

In order to illustrate this, it is worth inspecting briefly two attempts to explain away the problem of nothingness. The first is an example of ordinary-language analysis and the second employs set theory. According to the first analysis, the term "nothing" is a syntactical device known as a "subject-excluder."[26] One may well agree with the analyst that "expressions such as 'nothing' were coined to block gaps that would otherwise be filled by references to one or more of whatever sort of thing is in question."[27] And it is no doubt true that

> it becomes baffling if we insist that if Nothing can be spoken of it must conform to the rules for those subjects of discourse that it is designed to displace. . . . For this is to require that if Nothing is to be mentionable it must establish its credentials as a logical subject, identifiable and describable: we must be able to say that it is a so-and-so, and which so-and-so it is.[28]

However, none of this meets the crucial point. In the first place, the meaning of "exclusion" is exactly as ambiguous as that of "negation" or "not." We cannot exclude instances of a concept without knowing what it means to say that there are no instances of that concept. To say that the concept has no extension is just a fancy way of avoiding the issue, since we still need to understand what "no" means in the expression "no extension." This line of explanation is like trying to explain negation in terms of truth-tables, which themselves make use of the concept of falsity, and so of negation. The sense of "no" in "there are no so-and-so's" is derived in part from the defining property of the set of so-and-so's to which it applies. In any definite case, the negation requires us to think of every individual object as either a member or not a member of a given set. But this in turn requires us to understand the meaning of "not." And so, regardless of the criterion of membership we employ, the intelligibility of "not to be a member" turns upon the intelligibility of "everything" and "nothing."

The second proposed resolution of the problem of nothingness proceeds from the concepts of set theory. We may be tempted to say that "not" functions *semantically* to designate an absence of reference. I think this is right. But we may go on to say that the semantical role is played by the construction of a predicate from the null-set. And this I think is wrong. For in this way, we transform nothingness into a concept. According to David Wiggins, "logical orthodoxy finds a way of removing the apparently referential status of 'nothing' . . . by parsing" the propositions in which it occurs into not-$(\exists x)$ (Fx). The procedures of logical orthodoxy, however, in fact give referential status to the "concept" of *nothing*:

> this orthodoxy makes $(\exists x)$ $(.\ .\ .\ (x))$ a certain predicate of predicates of individuals. It is a predicate, here applied to the predicate F, which we may roughly equate with the higher-level notion of *instantiation* . . . On this account, not-$(\exists x)$ $(.\ .\ .\ (x))$, like $(\exists x)$ $(.\ .\ .\ (x))$, will also be a higher-level predicate or predicate of predicates of individuals. It will be the compound predicate of predicates, non-instantiation. And whether a man knows it or not, what he is thinking about and struggling for an account of when he thinks about *nothing* is precisely what this compound second-level predicate of first-level predicates stands for,

namely, "a third-order statement of the existence of a second-level concept" that, of course, is itself, as a cognized entity, a concept: the concept *nothing*, "even if nobody thinks about this concept."[29]

This orthodox statement of orthodoxy makes entirely clear the incapacity of analytical thinking to deal with the problem of nothingness. In the first place, we are assured that what we are actually attempting to think is the set-theoretical construction of the unit-set of the null-set. This is nonsense. All other difficulties to one side, one might wish to *avoid* thinking nothingness by shifting to the language of set theory. Such a shift, however, even if it were theoretically sound, could not tell us what we were attempting to think, but only what we *ought* to think. Putting this aside as well, the next thing to be observed is that we can translate "nothing" into either first- or second-order logic. In first-order logic, "nothing" is expressed as

$$\sim\!\exists x\ (x = x)$$

whereas in second-order logic, we would say

$$\sim\!\exists x \exists P\ (Px).$$

Strictly speaking (and how else should we speak when employing set-theoretical notions?), these two formulae have different senses. The first says that no things exist, whereas the second says that nothing exists of which any property can be predicated. It might be held that these two formulae amount to the same sense since existence and identity are to be taken as predicates in the second case. But this is not the point. If one distinguishes between essence and existence, and so between being and existence, as well as between unity and identity, then the second formulation allows the *being* of essences. The exhibited second-order negation thus fails to annihilate everything and is not an accurate transcription of nothingness. In other words, Wigginsian orthodoxy assumes that "to exist" is synonymous with "to have properties," thereby suppressing the distinction between being (or essence) and existence. It therefore rests upon the intelligibility of the belonging-relation, a point which I have already discussed at sufficient length.

My third objection to this analysis can be introduced by noting that the set of all concepts without extension is denoted as $\{\Lambda\}$, which is itself the extension of the concept "concept with no extension," where the concept is symbolized as $\{\{\Lambda\}\}$. And this is one way of writing the number "two." In order to explain the difference between *nothing* and *two*, Wiggins must of course provide a natural-language interpretation of his symbolism. I believe this amounts to an admission that the language of set theory is *less* perspicuous than natural language in cases like *nothing*. But even if this is disregarded, we are still in the presence of an attempt to give a "property-like" account of nothingness. The circularity of the attempt is plain from the definition of "nothing" as "non-instantiation." But worse than circularity is the motivation of the analysis. Whatever the syntactical and semantical obscurities involved in thinking, or even attempting to think, nothingness, they are not removed, but ignored, by recourse to extensionality. Nothingness is not a concept, even though we may have a *notion* of it. I remind the reader of my very informal distinction between a concept and a notion. A concept is something which may be more or less "sharply" defined. We can give a criterion for its extension. A notion cannot be sharply defined, and there is no criterion for its extension. Furthermore, in the case of the central notions of philosophy, there is no question of extension. Such a term is either entirely misplaced (as in the case of unity and perhaps being) or it takes our attention away from the crucial issue. Therefore, even if we distinguish fussily between use and mention, there is no "concept" of nothingness to mention, and nothingness, which we are attempting to mention, is not a concept. For if it were a concept, definable in the language of set theory, then it would necessarily have extension, and this extension could be "nothing" other than a short-hand way of stating "cases in which there is no instantiation," with the aforementioned faults accruing to such an approach. The sense of the short-hand expression is either not what we are trying to say, or it is itself circular, or so ambiguous as to require considerable interpretation.

What is the philosophical motivation underlying attempts to paraphrase the traditional problem of nothingness into the language of set theory? It is Platonism, not in the superficial sense given to this term in contemporary discussions, but in the deeper sense exemplified by the "axioms" of the determinateness and countability or nameability of being. If Frege is a Platonist in this sense, so too is Quine, and so then are all members of this community of the orthodox. For the sake of thoroughness, then, we must now look at Frege's account of negative existentials. Since that account is an aspect or consequence of his account of affirmations of existence, we shall be repeating one or two points made in section 9. In the nature of the case, however, this cannot be avoided, and will also have the advantage of a summary of claims that are bound to be regarded by the majority of analytical philosophers as controversial. According to Frege, it is impossible meaningfully to deny the assertion that "A exists."[30] In assertions like this, whatever value one gives to A, the object in question must itself exist or be experienceable, i.e., subsumable under one or more concepts. Frege thus equates the meaning of "exists" with that of "is experienceable." He also equates "is experienceable" with "is an object (whether concrete or abstract)." It makes no sense to say that something that one has experienced has not been experienced. "A exists" is then meaningful only if A has been experienced, and consequently "A does not exist" is meaningless or self-contradictory. (This is basically Russell's account as well.) On the other hand, if one asserts that "the object of representation B is experienceable," this may be negated, since there is obviously a difference between an experienced representation and the possibility of its referring to a real object. We may also note that, on Fregean grounds, it is impossible to put *nothing* into the slot marked (or filled by) A since *nothing* is to be explained via the negation of the existential quantifier, within which the variable x presumably ranges over some definite set of objects. I need repeat here only that this analysis fails to come to grips with nothingness which, if it negates at all, negates all sets, not just their members.

In "A exists," then, only definite, countable, or nameable instances are, for Frege, possible values of the variable A. Furthermore, Frege, like many if not all his successors, claims that "exists" or "is" adds no information to the mere assertion of some value for A.[31] This is the disastrous consequence of attempting to apply the language of functions to the philosophical analysis of natural language. All the serious problems disappear, to be replaced by the horizon of technical manipulation. Or rather, as I have been trying to show, the serious problems are concealed although still present in a concealed manner. With respect to the objection that Frege's claim erases the distinction between "exists" and "does not exist," as for example in the assertion "the largest number does not exist," Frege has a reply. He analyzes statements like the one just cited in such a way as to show that no objects (here, numbers) fall under the concept "largest number." The assertion "A exists" is understood to say that there is at least one thing such that it falls under the concept, or bears the predicate, A. If A is a proper name, e.g., "Pegasus," we can perhaps follow Quine's suggestion and speak of the concept "Pegasizing" or the predicate "pegasizes." [32] I deny that either of these could be explained without reference to the name "Pegasus," but pass over this point. More important is the fact that the Fregean analysis of "being," adopted in modified form by Quine and a generation of analytical philosophers, amounts finally to the Aristotelian contention that there is no opposite or contrary to *being* (or to "being a predicate"). This has interesting consequences.

In the statement "Pegasus does not exist," we are saying, along Fregean lines, not that there is no concept "Pegasus," but that there is not at least one object falling under the concept "Pegasizing." This of course assumes that we understand the concept "not" or its co-ordinate operation of exclusion. Furthermore, the concept "Pegasizing" cannot be said not to exist because it is thinkable and so experienceable. A concept can have sense without reference, or it can refer to some arbitrary object, say a^*, when there is no experienceable object falling under the concept. [33] This means that it is not concepts but existence-statements that possess contraries. If concepts exist (and for Frege, they do, as instances of higher-order concepts), then negative concepts do not. If concepts do not exist, then it must be impossible to think, name, or count them. But in either case, there is no logical contrary to a concept. And this is the same as the Platonic-Aristotelian doctrine that there is no contrary to "man," "horse," or "flower." Thus, for example, "not-man" means "something-other-than-man." The statement "negative concepts do not exist" must itself be subjected to the analysis by which "negative concept" is a concept having no instances or objects falling under it. In the Platonic-Aristotelian schema, there are contrary predications of "man" (roughly equivalent to "———is a man" in Fregean terminology) and the other subjects (i.e., objects), but this is explained by the doctrine of Ideas, forms, or essences, in which predicates (properties) do or do not inhere. The essence "man" (in Fregean terminology, "———is a man") cannot itself be properly negated. Frege's doctrine seems to be a still more radical version of the Greek doctrine, in that he transforms predicates (or the co-ordinate concepts) into *ousia*-like essences.

The correct analysis of "not-man," then, is not the negation of a concept, predicate, or essence. Just as *nothing* means $\sim \exists x\ (\ .\ .\ .\ (x))$, so "this is not a man" is analyzed as $\exists x\ (Tx\&\sim Mx)$ where $\sim Mx$ does not mean the negation of a concept, but rather that the x to which the statement refers does not fall under the concept M. We thus reach the "Greek" conclusion that what "is" in the proper sense of the term, has no contrary. If to be is to be experienceable, thinkable, or nameable, then "what is" cannot not be (whatever that means). One may destroy an individual man, horse, or other (non-abstract) object. But one cannot destroy the essence or concept *man*. It follows naturally that since what exists can be named or counted, concepts must be able to stand in for objects in higher-level quantification. I note in passing that the concept of hierarchy is essential in the mathematical version of analytical philosophy. This is in a way also "Platonic," except that the "Fregean" does not speak of an order of excellence but rather of abstractness or structural complexity. In contemporary thought, the concept of a concept is not "better" than a concept. But the concept of order is better than disorder or the absence of orderable concepts. It is not obvious, however, how it follows from this axiological principle that the universe is well-ordered or consists of a hierarchy of ordinal types. It is not obvious what the *constructible* universe of the set-theoretician has to do with the world of experience. This is the point at which profound metaphysical decisions are concealed. But getting back to the main point, how are we to understand the case in which a concept serves as an abstract object and is said not to exist in the sense of not falling under a higher level concept? It seems as though either the transformation of objects into concepts, or the hierarchy of order-types, is a *façon de parler*, in which case the result is nominalism. Or else the abstract object retains its identity as a concept, and consequently can no more fit into a negative existential statement than can that concept. Negation is the denial of existence when it occurs together with a quantifier, whereas quantification is in its affirmative existential form the assertion of existence. If we can quantify over concepts, whereas concepts have no contraries, or cannot fail to exist, then is not negation impossible in all these cases? And if negation is impossible, in what sense is affirmation possible?

The ontological "is" seems then to play a role in the Fregean doctrine as well as in the Platonic-Aristotelian teaching. It cannot be explained by the notions of identity or predication since these allow of negation. Precisely if, as for both Frege and his Greek ancestors, "is" or "exists" adds nothing new in the sense that it does not tell us anything about some *other* property of an object to which it is applied, then to say that concepts exist is not to predicate. Let us note that, for the Greeks, it is a truism that "is" tells us nothing about some other predicate; we have other predicates for other kinds of information. But it does not follow from this that "is" tells us nothing. Frege cannot make this distinction. Yet he is in the same situation as the Greeks with respect to the non-predicative status of "is" or "exists." To call "exists" a vacuous predicate is to beg the question, or to deny that it is a genuine predicate, i.e., it is to deny that we learn anything about an object via "exists." What, then, is the ontological function of "exists"? It is precisely the same as the function of ass (   ) in the Strawsonian analysis. It designates ontological unity *without being able to say that this is what it is doing*. To this, I add that "does not exist" serves to convey an intuition of nothingness or the absence of unity.

I offer one last illustration of the problem of nothingness in analytical philosophy. Suppose that we try to divide the universe of discourse into concepts and objects, but to explain negation in terms of facts rather than existence. We can adapt to our purpose here a passage from Wittgenstein's *Tractatus*. According to Wittgenstein, the negation-sign in a proposition corresponds to "nothing in reality."[34] In other words, it is neither the name of an object nor a sign denoting a fact or conceptual structure of objects. A proposition *p* is negated, not by "non" or by ~ but by "what is in common to all the signs of this notation which deny *p*."[35] I take this not as a reference to an extensional, "propertyless," or "non-instantiation" approach to negation, but rather as a directive to think of the negated fact as excluded from the universe of discourse by a set of denying facts. Whether or not this is right, Wittgenstein does not tell us what it means to "deny *p*." We might, for example, say that *q* stands for the conjunction of propositions corresponding to the facts which, taken together, exclude the possibility of the fact expressed by *p*. But how do we explain that *q* "excludes," i.e., contradicts *p*, without at the same time explaining that contradiction contains negation as an essential ingredient? Since there is *ex hypothesi* nothing in reality to which the negation-sign corresponds, how did it come to our attention, or better, how did we associate a concept with it? To ask this is not to fall into psychologism, or to confuse epistemology with semantics. This distinction is itself bogus, as I have argued at length in Chapter One. If we cannot understand a term as what it purports to mean, then it does not mean what it is supposed to. Stated more succinctly, I am not denying that we think negation, but insisting that we think it because of a reason that Wittgenstein has not succeeded in formulating. To continue: if the fact that *p* is not the case is equivalent to the fact that *q* is the case, then the assertion of *q* is part of an explanation of why *p* does not obtain, but it is not the whole of that explanation. We must first notice the absence of *p*. It is all very well to talk of "inferring" non-*p* from *q*. The question is how this is possible. No manipulation of present items will produce by itself an absence. Wittgenstein's account suffers from the same deficiency as its Platonic-Aristotelian ancestor.

This deficiency can be restated as follows. We assume that if a term has reference, the latter must consist of nameable or countable "somethings." Thus "nothing" can have a sense if and only if it has no reference. Yet, as we saw above, that sense is apparently intelligible analytically only through the construction of a reference or extension. How then do we actually identify the reference of a predicate in a false assertion? To say falsely that a so-and-so is such-and-such, is to misidentify a specific property. This seems to mean that the reference of a term can be something other than (and even in conflict with) its actual or normal reference. When someone mistakenly predicates *F* of *a*, it is fair to observe that in this case he does not know what he is talking about. If another observer, with access to the original or genuine situation, corrects the false assertion by saying truly that "not-*Fa*," he correctly refers to the property designated by *F* as absent from the object *a*; but he is presumably not referring to "absence" or nothingness as present. The initial speaker was erroneously referring to the absent property as present in *a*. Presumably he was led to do so by misidentifying a present property. In other words, he took the present property, not as itself, and not even as absent, but as *something else*. So the reference of his predicate is *not* the present property. But it cannot be the intended and absent property; if it were we could not distinguish effectively between true and false predication. An evidently false predication could be certified as true on the grounds that the reference was correctly intended by the speaker. In our example of the two observers, the distinction is artificially preserved by the *deus ex machina* of the second speaker, who is assumed to have access to the original situation. But no explanation is given of the mechanism of misidentification in the first case, or of how the second speaker certifies his access to the original. And it is upon these two factors that the analysis of "not" depends. If we are not prepared to allow the distinction between a true and a false predication to turn upon the intention of the speaker, and if our logic does not explain this distinction but simply uses it, then we are clearly in need of some explanation of this use external to both logic and psychology.

12.   Concluding Speculations

As the greatest philosophers have always known, the problems of being and nothingness are inseparably connected. Hence the continuous attempt by analytical philosophers to by-pass the problem of nothingness has crucial consequences for the doctrine of being. The paradigm for this attempted by-pass is to be found in Plato and Aristotle. At the same time, neither Plato nor Aristotle is an "analytical philosopher" in the contemporary sense. This is not the place to develop a comprehensive interpretation of the role of analysis in their respective teachings. Nevertheless, we have had to say enough about each of these great ancestors to make clear what they regard as the context of analysis. The doctrine of analytical thinking is rooted in the conception of intelligible form, and this in turn is inseparable from intellectual intuition. One way to summarize my entire argument thus far is to say that, when intuition is abandoned, rhetoric takes its place. But rhetoric unsupported by intuition deteriorates into ideology. In slightly different terms, the rhetoric of the scientific enlightenment is rooted in a doctrine of intuition, as one may quickly confirm by a reference to Descartes. The term "intuition" is today virtually without content, and is used as a synonym for "supposition," "imagination," and "fantasy." Logic was originally talk about the structure of intelligibility. Without intuition, however, it is merely talk about talk.

I said just now that the doctrine of analytical thinking is rooted in the conception of intelligible form. This is true; but it is also true that we cannot analyze forms without an intuitive understanding of what to do next. At the risk of oversimplification, we may say that there is a theoretical and a practical intuition. Without the first, there is nothing definite to think; without the second, there is no basis for deciding what to do. The net result is that the attempt to construct actuality by analytical tools has cut us off from the actual world. The great show of technical precision that constitutes the surface of contemporary analytical philosophy all too often conceals an empty interior. This is why, despite surface unanimity of orientation, there is as continuous a fluctuation of ideological fashions at the interior of analytical philosophy as there is in Parisian cafe philosophy. In the best cases, of course, there is a genuine attempt to face up to the perennial nature of philosophical problems, and to avoid the last refuge of scoundrels; school-jargon, Voltairean irony, and the arbitrary rejection of what one has been neither educated about nor permitted to understand. Lest this strike any reader as too harsh, I add at once that a blindness toward analytical thinking is to be condemned with equal firmness. There is no place in philosophy for the whirling dervish. But that place is created by the analyst who allows his intolerance toward "speculation" to narrow the focus of the philosophical enterprise beyond what the human spirit will bear. I am, then, condemning neither analytical nor synthetic thinking, but only a low form of scholasticism that blooms in all triumphant camps.

The glory of rationalism has its dark side, and this sometimes manifests itself as the incapacity to see in the dark. Traditional analytical criticism of the attempt to think nothingness proceeds as if it were an illicit "something." No sane man will quarrel with the assertions that we cannot list the predicates of nothingness, that we cannot imagine it (in the sense of constructing an image of it in our thoughts), that we can scarcely refer to it without employing definite terms, and so without apparently referring to some definite thing. One wants to ask: what is wrong with indirect reference? On which of Moses' tablets is it written that significant discourse always has an object or entity as its primary target? And yet, this does not go to the heart of the matter. For I venture to say that every moderately thoughtful man has violated the injunction of Parmenides. The most powerful and influential account of this violation in our time is without doubt that of Heidegger. I want to consider some aspects of this account, as a necessary supplement to the arguments of the previous section. I think it can be shown that Heidegger's doctrine, although extremely valuable, is despite its ostensible anti-Platonism still marked by a kind of Platonism.

Under ordinary circumstances, when someone asks us "what" we are thinking, if we cannot reply, we admit that we have not been thinking in the genuine or strict sense of the term. To a considerable degree, Heidegger would concur. The authoritative description in *Being and Time* of the encounter with nothingness makes this quite clear.[36] I restrict myself here to the essentials. The encounter with nothingness or, initially, with nothing (*nichts*) does not occur as a direct consequence of intentional thinking, i.e., thinking something (a *Seiendes*). Instead, it occurs via a mood or existential attunement with human existence (as *Dasein* may for all practical purposes be translated). The paradigm-case of this attunement is anxiety (*Angst*), which arises when we face up to the call of our conscience, and so turn away from inauthenticity or everyday anonymity. As everyone presumably knows by now, existential anxiety does not itself answer the question "what?" by naming a thing, state, or event about which I am anxious. Heidegger turns away from "objective" thinking to the experience of mood because, in *Being and Time*, he does not reject the traditional view, transmitted through Husserl, that to think is to think something. He is working toward a modification or extension of this view, and it is important to note that he begins by accepting it. Since being and nothingness are not "something," not this or that, whereas thinking in the traditional sense is thinking this or that, we cannot begin to think about being and nothingness by thinking them intentionally or directly, in the usual manner. We begin the presentation of the problem with the case of Being, as it will now be written, to avoid confusion with this or that "being." This, incidentally, is crucial for an understanding of Heidegger's "Platonism" (or anyone else's, for that matter): nothingness must be approached via Being. Being is "strict transcendence" of all beings or things (SZ,4). If it should be possible to think Being at all, then we shall require a new kind of thinking, a kind that is not thing-oriented, and which must therefore reply "nothing" to the question "what?" As is evident from the entire existential analysis of *Being and Time*, the move from beings to Being or the transition across the "ontological difference" presupposes the most extensive application of the thinking of things: this, that, such-and-such. We require an elaborate discursive, analytical, and quite traditional preparation for the new kind of thinking. An essential element in that preparation is the encounter with nothing (or nothingness) through anxiety; but this too is traditional and intended to be so. Heidegger is not inviting us to experience some new phenomenon. He is describing an experience that every normal human being has undergone at one level or another of his consciousness.

Whereas existential anxiety is not thinking in any usual sense, the meaning of the experience is accessible to traditional discourse. To go directly to the nerve of the matter, anxiety arises only within a world (basically, the world of everyday experience) that is already a web of articulations or senses, a web spun by the finite *Dasein* in its finite speeches, deeds, desires, and so on, and which can be spun because to exist is to "open" a world as the horizon of existence. In this sense at least, we "act" before we articulate. It should at least be noted in passing that this act of "opening" the horizon or projecting the world is not dissimilar to Wittgenstein's doctrine of the linguistic horizon. To express this point in terms that might be acceptable to both men, articulate discourse is an interpretation of the perspective in which we see. Although the perspective is accessible to articulation, it is also antecedent in the sense of a "transcendental" condition. Talking is not only interpreting; it is also *constructing*, or the face of construction, that is, so to say, the "interior" of our world. It is an anticipation of my main analysis, but one should raise the question here: what lies on the "outside" of the world? The answer is "nothing," and it is an answer that we are able to give by way of direct reference to the world. The most difficult question is whether the nothing "outside" the world is, like the world, finite.

We experience anxiety with respect to this world *as such*, or with respect to ourselves as "being in the world as such" (SZ, 186f). The "as such" points to the definiteness of the notion of "world" or of "being-in-the-world" that allows us to think it as the "before what" (*wovor*) of our anxiety. There is, then, a kind of "what" in the experience of nothing that enables us to move beyond attunement or experience as a pre-cognitive mood to the exposition of *Being and Time*, which identifies "nothing" as nothingness (*das Nichts*). Differently stated, in *Being and Time*, nothingness is indistinguishable from, if not the same as, the world "as such." We can no more think "the world as such" than we can think nothingness, at least in a way traditional enough to culminate in ontological assertions, however surprising their content. Every attempt to think the world "as such" results in thinking some aspect of the world: this or that. There is, however, a plausibility in the initial claim that we experience nothingness as anxiety. This claim cannot be verified by argument; the reader has to consult his own experience.

We must emphasize that by "nothingness" Heidegger does not mean absolute vacuousness or *nihil absolutum*. Anxiety detaches *Dasein* from its normal affective connections with things in the world by emptying these of meaning, not by erasing them (SZ, 343). Heideggerean existential negation is thus a version of logical or "Platonic" negation. It attaches a "non" to a *p*. The total negation of anxiety brackets (in Husserl's sense) the world with a "non" and so deprives it of existential sense. This is Heidegger's version of the phenomenological *epochē*, but with the important difference that "scientific" analysis is now lacking in motivation and sense. One could perhaps say that Heidegger's existential translation brings out the nihilistic implications of phenomenology, implications that are concealed by the same scientific rhetoric that initially motivated the great rationalist and empiricist traditions of the modern epoch. In the contemporary analytical school, existential significance is "bracketed" in "subjective preference sets" and other misapplications of set theory. Heidegger, however, retains the possibility of salvation, in however secular a form. In *Being and Time*, the "disconnecting" of the significance of the world is an encounter with the world "as such." The underlying idea is to be found in Hegel, and in different ways, in both Nietzsche and Marx: negation uncovers totality. However, for Heidegger, disconnection does not take us "outside" the world. Heidegger's transcendence is immanent and temporal. Anxiety reveals us as finite beings in the world, who, along with the world, are marked by negativity (*Nichtigkeit*) (SZ, 308; cf. 187f, 330). The nothingness is that of the world as such. In a Hegelian formulation, it is not empty, but contains what it negates: everything.[37] This is a point which, as far as I know, holds good throughout Heidegger's published work.[38]

After *Being and Time*, Heidegger comes to identify nothingness with Being.[39] There is, however, what one may call an anti-Hegelian demotion of human activity as the engine of negation. The "activist" dimension of *Being and Time* is replaced by a mood of submission or "letting-be," and man is now described, in a striking phrase, as the shepherd of Being, "the place-holder of nothingness."[40] At least in the first period of his thought, Heidegger's doctrine of negativity is not dissimilar to the constructivist interpretation of negation in analytical philosophy. It follows from the doctrine of meta-languages that both negation and affirmation of existence are to be explained as linguistic operations. Not only is negation a syntactical operator, but "there is" has a theoretical, and finally a linguistic sense. As Quine puts it, "this is why I have urged the inscrutability of reference; existence in its final estate is theoretical."[41] In his later period of ontological resignation, Heidegger tells us to await the next gift of Being rather than to choose, and so to construct, an authentic existence. However, there is no change in the doctrine of the finitude of Being, or of the identity of Being and nothingness.[42] Nothingness is therefore accessible to us in and through Being. Heidegger continues to reject the *nihil absolutum*. Despite his avowed rejection of Platonism, then, Heidegger continues to obey the injunction of Parmenides. The article in *das Nichts* is not a mere grammatical appendage, but answers to the "what" in the "before what" (*wovor*) of the anxiety described in *Being and Time*. *Das Nichts* is the nothingness "of" (subjective and objective genitive) Being.

Two comments, at first apparently contradicting each other, are in order at this point. First: the identification of the world with nothingness amounts to the doctrine of the radical contingency of the world, or the denial of nature in the Greek sense. Heidegger, like Saul Kripke, is an Ash'arite. The second comment: the identification of Being and nothingness is desubstantialized Platonism, but Platonism all the same. Our attempt to suppress the *nihil absolutum* leads to the "hypostasis" of nothingness. Nothing is filled up by the emptying of Being; hence nothingness is the replacement of substantiality. Kripke's doctrine of logical necessity is at least an attempt to think the thoughts of God as He thinks them, prior to the creation of the world. This metaphor comes from Hegel's *Science of Logic*; I mention it here as a preparation for the theme of Chapter Five, namely, that Hegel is the ultimate conceptual analyst. The Platonic-Aristotelian response to the problem of nothingness, then, is to attempt to replace it by paraphrase, at least for analytical purposes. Nothingness becomes otherness, and it is explained as syntactical operation. However, the attempt to carry through this syntactical interpretation must necessarily fail because the principle of otherness is a corollary of the doctrine that to be is to be countable or nameable. The last consequence of these principles is the set-theoretical interpretation of nothingness via extensionality. Heidegger seems to reject this "extensional" or Platonist approach to nothingness, yet in fact, he retains the crucial element. As finite, nothingness is the same as, or defined by, Being. Nevertheless, Heidegger is not a genuine Platonist because the only eternal Idea he retains is that of nothingness. But neither is he a genuine Hegelian, since man is demoted from the agent to the place-holder of negativity. If there are no positive Ideas, and if man cannot produce a satisfactory world by his own labor, is Heidegger not a victim of nihilism, or of the failure of western metaphysics to think Being?[43]

Let us recapitulate in the light of this question. Since it is meaningful to prohibit reference to the altogether not (*nihil absolutum*=Parmenides' *to mēdamōs on*), it must be meaningful to refer to it. And yet, to "what" are we referring? Certainly not to the null-set or the unit-set containing the null-set. I repeat: what lacks all predicates is not the concept *nothing*, but nothingness, the cancellation of all concepts, and so of all objects. To reject this nothingness in favor of any conceptual device, whether Plato's or some Fregean variant, is to turn from one nothingness to another, and so, at least in speech, from this to that. Yet the turn is also from nothing to something. So too the turn from the *nihil absolutum* to the finite *Nichts* takes place within a dialectical "is and is not." This leaves Heidegger in the same dilemma as that which is occupied by Platonism. On the one hand, we must think what we are warned is unthinkable. On the other, we must be able to describe the finite *nothing* since it is delimited, and hence possesses predicates. Analytical philosophy takes the second horn of the dilemma, but the attempt to carry through the predicative analysis leads us back to the nothingness without predicates. Heidegger, in my opinion, takes neither alternative. But this poses a new choice for him: either revert to Hegel's logic of contradiction (i.e., to a dialectico-speculative interpretation of "is and is not") or give up ontology. As his later work makes progressively more apparent, Heidegger chose the latter. But he does not abandon the "question of Being," and it remains true that he must provide some account of the new, post-ontological thinking which "bethinks" Being and nothingness while continuing to reject the *nihil absolutum*. Of course, as Heidegger regularly insists, his task is to pose the question, not to answer it. He is "on the way toward" the bespeaking of Being, *unterwegs zur Sprache*. In itself, this is fair enough. I agree that the fundamental philosophical problems can only be stated, not removed. But one cannot state them by giving unintelligible hints concerning a new way of thinking. The performance of the later Heidegger is especially disappointing in that his "hints" look more and more like bad poetry.

The distinction between the *nihil absolutum* and the finite *Nichts* is possible only when the former is drawn into our thinking. In just this sense, Hegel assimilates the Absolute into the process of thinking described in his *Science of Logic*, namely, the *nihil* contained in the religious expression, creation *ex nihilo*. I pointed out previously that the Platonic doctrine of the web of intelligible forms is already at the border of Hegel's dialectical logic. We now see further that the identification of Being and nothingness puts us directly into the heart of that logic. Interconnectedness on a comprehensive scale yields specific relations only by the intentionality of thinking. The attempt to analyze is not intelligible apart from the activity of the analyst. If we are to succeed at all in isolating "eternal" or "objective" forms, it will only be by a careful study of consciousness. Logic, despite its many virtues, is not the study we need for this purpose.

CHAPTER FOUR

The Whole

13. Intuitions and Dreams

AS I have regularly stated in these pages, my purpose is not to refute analytical philosophy, but to contribute to its revision. Thus far my strategy has been to show how the comprehensive problem of the context of analysis is intrinsic to the sense (or lack of sense) of specific technical devices which were constructed with the intention of dissolving that problem. For example, the semantical conception of "sense" proved to be inadequate to fulfilling the purpose of a semantical theory: to explain what we mean by "mean" without recourse to non-semantical terms. In slightly different language, we cannot explain what it means to refer without taking into account the intentions of the speaker, and this leads in turn to a reconsideration of standard criticisms of psychologism. To the extent that semantics is a rule-governed procedure, it needs to be supplemented by a doctrine of intuition. The rules and concepts of formal languages are not intelligible except on the basis of theoretical and practical intuition, by which I mean the capacity to see what is pertinent and to know what to do about what we see. The functional analysis of the proposition, the doctrine of predication, and the primitive relation of set-membership all depend for their intelligibility upon pre-analytical cognitive operations. It is not possible to "bracket" this dependence by doctrines of stratification, meta-languages, or hierarchies of order, since such doctrines themselves incorporate pre-analytical assumptions, such as what it means for something to "belong" to something (to mention only one). It makes no sense to say that pre-analytical assumptions are part of the methodology of theory construction, not of the scientific theory itself. The sense, truth, validity, or value of the scientific theory depends upon the sense, truth, validity, or value of the methodology or metalanguage.[1]

If to be scientific is to be reasonable, then it behooves the scientific philosopher to reflect upon the hierarchy of meta-languages, or rather, upon the mode of his reflection on this hierarchy. The act of constructing a hierarchy cannot be explained as itself falling within one level of the hierarchy. We do not define recursively our recursive activity. Rational men, whether they call themselves philosophers or scientists, are concerned, not simply with a progressively more complex (or sophisticated) series of analytical steps, but with the context of analysis. They are concerned with the whole. (For the difference between a whole and a sum of parts, see sections 8 and 9.) I want to say here a word about the whole as a logical problem. It is well known that no consistent axiomatic system containing a decidable set of axioms can express all of number theory or the truths of arithmetic. Furthermore, as Cantor's diagonalization-method and power-set theorem show, it is always possible to construct a set, within the axioms of classical set theory, that is larger than any arbitrary set. This is enough to establish that, whether the world is enumerable or not, there can be no mathematical formalization of its structure: that is, no formalization of the whole. On the other hand, Gödel's first incompleteness theorem shows that truth (in the arithmetical sense) and theoremhood or provability in any formal theory *are in no sense the same.*[2] Sentences can be constructed that are true in a theory, but which are not deducible from the axioms of that theory. The limitations of formalism, then, do not merely show that the whole cannot be captured axiomatically, but that *it is necessary to conceive of the whole in order to grasp the difference between truth and theoremhood.*

This point is given a phenomenological development by Robert Tragesser, in an interpretation of Gödel's paper on the continuum hypothesis. Gödel observes that debate about the truth or falsehood of Cantor's continuum hypothesis "clearly assumes a well-determined reality, a well-determined objective domain, deciding all sentences expressible in the language of set theory."[3] In Tragesser's Husserlian reformulation of Gödel's argument, we have a *prehension* of S, the domain of set theory, that is, "an inadequate or imperfect grasp" of S, "where the content of the grasp adumbrates or points to something beyond what is given" (PL, 17f). We therefore prehend S, and on this basis "one can find many paths promising more complete apprehensions of S possibly decisive for CH" (PL, 20). We continue the operation "set of," thus bringing more and more of S into determinate view (PL, 23). In my own language, we have an intuition of the whole, at least in the form of an indeterminate sense of the totality of well-determined objects. The philosophically crucial question arises, not in attempting to devise technical procedures for continuing the operation "set of," but in reflecting upon the indeterminate sense of totality. As I have tried to show in a variety of ways, the attempt to render this sense determinate causes it to disappear, or to be transformed into some sense other than the one with which we began.

In general, all formal reasoning, including the construction and testing of axiomatic systems, rests upon something less than a determinate concept, and something more than a vague apprehension, of the whole. It is therefore not true that contemporary logic and set theory confirm Aristotle's argument against a *summum genus*. Instead, contemporary mathematics has demonstrated that the *summum genus* must be conceived as a class rather than a set, or that our axiomatizations can approximately encompass the universe V to any arbitrary ordinal, but never include it entirely.[4] Important as this point is, however, it would be misleading to stop here. The problem of the context of analysis, or of the whole, is not one of the completability or incompletability of formalism. Even Tragesser's phenomenological interpretation of Gödelian Platonism does not go far enough (or alternatively, goes too far), since it couches the issue in terms of mathematical sets. I can bring out the difficulty as follows. It is often claimed that mathematics (or a large part of mathematics) can be reduced to, or constructed within, set theory. This does not mean that numbers and formulas are in fact (i.e., ontologically) sets, but that there are analogues to numbers and formulas among the sets we can construct.[5] It should be still more obvious that the things in the world of human experience are likewise not sets. Even if it were possible to find sets analogous to each thing we find in the world, it would scarcely follow that the properties of the things in the world would be equivalent to the properties of the sets, or vice versa. Their *mathematical* properties would be the same, and nothing more. Mathematized ontologies are engaged in the analysis of quasi-mathematical entities, or pure mathematical entities, on the basis of which assumptions are made about beings in the world. This is a non sequitur (except with respect to mathematical properties themselves). It is not by chance, or a temporary technical difficulty, that mathematically oriented debates about ontology take place within natural language. We talk about the senses of our sets, theorems, theories, and so on up to the general procedures for constructing metalanguages, hence of justifying notions of well-definedness or well-constructedness in a language distinct *by its nature* from that in which our constructions take place. There is no question here of a relation between meta-language and object-language. This way of conceiving the situation is based upon a fundamental misunderstanding.

This misunderstanding takes two apparently incompatible forms. The first is that philosophy must be radically presuppositionless; the second is that a theoretical language must begin with precisely defined axioms, terms, and principles of transformation. Both express the view that philosophy is, or ought to be, "scientific" in the sense that it mistrusts, and must methodically revise or reconstruct, the pre-scientific or everyday situation. I have already explained my objection to the second form at some length. We cannot begin a radical reconstruction of everyday experience except upon the basis of the presentation of the everyday. The dilemma of mathematical empiricism, so fashionable today, is that it wishes simultaneously to be guided by experience and to create a new domain that is radically distinct from experience. The new domain, or the theoretical "model," is far too limited, thanks to its precision, to explain our experience. As a result, we are encouraged either to mutilate our experience, or to accept a sharp discontinuity between theory and practice. However, the second alternative is merely a concealed form of the first. Human existence could scarcely be better defined than as the unity of theory and practice. The attempt to articulate this unity must necessarily fail if it is conducted in the language of sets, predicates, functions, and quantifiers. The language of traditional philosophy, and thus *the actual if now largely implicit* language of analytical technics, is altogether superior to formal languages due to the aforementioned attempt to articulate the unity of theory and practice. It is not the case that mathematics does not address the whole. The philosophical deficiency of mathematics is that it is incapable of reflecting upon, and so accounting for, its speech about the whole. I am in no sense advocating a dissociation of philosophy from mathematics. What I advocate is self-consciousness, or attention to the fact that the philosophical lessons we draw from mathematics cannot be expressed in quasi-mathematical dialects.

There is a deep quarrel at the heart of philosophy concerning the proper relation between two kinds of measurement. Pascal gave these kinds their most striking formulation: the *esprit géométrique* and the *esprit de finesse*. The initial version of this distinction is to be found in Plato, as for example in the *Statesman* (284E). The true statesman is an expression of the unity of theory and practice; since he is concerned with the whole city, he must know who are the experts and when their expertise is appropriate. He must possess the art of measuring the appropriate, fitting, or timely, and this art is not the same as the art of arithmetical measurement. It would be an oversimplification, but not a misleading one, to say that all the deficiencies of contemporary analytical philosophy stem from the absence of the *esprit de finesse*. One aspect of the *esprit de finesse* is the capacity to perceive the domains appropriate to each kind of measurement. I want to emphasize that each *is* a kind of measurement. Returning to my point that the conception of philosophy as presuppositionless is mistaken, I think that the error is immediately obvious. If philosophy had no presuppositions, it would have no beginning or would begin from nothingness. Those who claim to be free of presuppositions invariably start with the conception of a method, as well as a justifying rhetorical statement, in which all the presuppositions are to be found. I think it should be granted that philosophy always starts from a fundamental presupposition: the intelligibility of experience. Alternatively stated, we begin to philosophize because we wish to understand the whole. This attempt may take the form of physics or politics but the intention is the same. We are provided by our very being with measures and intuitions concerning the use of these measures. The root of the philosophical enterprise is measurement, but in the two senses distinguished by Plato.

Analytical philosophy is the latest form of modern scientific enlightenment. We cannot understand analytical philosophy simply by learning the now fashionable techniques, whether these be modal logic, set theory, or something else. This is of course not to suggest that we ought not to learn these techniques. It is, however, to insist that the significance of analytical philosophy lies in the doctrine of enlightenment, or in the conception of rationality devised by the founders of the modern epoch in terms of the new mathematical and experimental sciences. At a first inspection, one may infer that this notion of enlightenment has triumphed among analytical philosophers. However significant may be the disagreement of ordinary-language analysts with this notion, their position in the analytical movement is steadily dwindling. The serious challenge to formalism and technicism in analytical philosophy is not from ordinary language but from an amalgam of movements, all as obsessed with technical operations as the mathematical formalists. These movements differ among themselves with respect to the presupposition of the intelligibility of experience. For example, Husserlian phenomenology, in its authentic version at least, and despite any claims by Husserl to presuppositionlessness, is an obvious representative of the presupposition of intelligibility. At the other extreme, one finds thinkers like Derrida and Deleuze, who more or less explicitly reject this presupposition as a mark of anthropomorphism and traditionalist conservatism.[6] I have predicted on more than one occasion that analytical philosophy will succumb, sooner or later, to some combination of doctrines drawn from post-Heideggerean thought. It will succumb for two closely related reasons. First: it is technically incapable of addressing itself to the most fundamental philosophical problems. Second: it is incapable of justifying itself in any reasonable way, but (like all schools) must have recourse to political dominance in the academy. And amusingly enough, this is its Achilles heel. One cannot exercise political dominance without engaging in politics. But analytical thinking is inappropriate in politics. One requires rhetoric, ideology, and dreams. And the constellation of intellectual dreams now fashionable among educated persons is not compatible with the dream of analytical philosophy.

Analytical philosophy cannot survive in its present form. If it is to survive at all, it must begin to analyze its own dream. But the language of dream-analysis is not the same as that of set theory. The presupposition of intelligibility, and hence the devotion to the two kinds of measurement, is a dream about the whole in a sense corresponding to unity rather than to the sum of parts. This is an extraordinary phenomenon and it cannot be treated by ordinary measures. After all, mathematics is itself an extraordinary way of treating ordinary experience. Perhaps there are other extraordinary manifestations of rationality and the devotion to measure. And perhaps these extraordinary ways have already been discovered in the long history of human reflection. Perhaps we are not simply at the mercy of the latest Parisian fashion. Analytical philosophy in its present form was created by men who combined common sense and an extraordinary imagination. Unfortunately, their imaginations were directed to the wrong form of measurement. The devotion to intelligibility and measurement is not incompatible with the transcendence of common sense; and indeed, one cannot preserve common sense except by transcending it. Even sensible men disagree, and we regularly come to see that what was once regarded as foolish or even mad is actually quite sensible. It has to be admitted that our criteria for measuring good sense themselves change, and that there is no criterion other than intelligence for regulating this change. In advocating that we consider our dream of the whole, and so have recourse to dream-analysis, I cannot put forward a fabulous method, one that is free of presuppositions or braced by mathematics. What I propose is "speculative," and no doubt even dangerous, both in itself and certainly by the sterile criteria of analytical philosophy. Nevertheless, I wish it to be recorded that my proposals are made as an ally of analytical thinking.

The present chapter may perhaps be characterized as a contribution to philosophical psychiatry. The context of analysis is the dream of the whole, and the task of analysis is now with dreaming, or the generalized form of intuition. We have already met with some of the themes of this chapter in sections 10 and 12. For the sake of initial clarity, let us oversimplify a bit. Philosophy is the dream, not merely of the whole, but of a rational account of the whole. This is, to be sure, a traditional understanding of philosophy. However, as I shall argue, it is the correct understanding, and hence one which is wide enough to encompass those anti-traditionalists who, taking their cue from Nietzsche, deny, or attempt to deny, the whole and the traditional doctrines of intelligibility and reason. To say that philosophy is the dream of a rational account of the whole is to make two implicit statements. First: as a dream, philosophy can never fulfill itself, or thoroughly awaken into wisdom. Second: as a dream of wholeness, philosophy claims to be able to distinguish between dreaming and wakefulness. This second statement should not be misunderstood; the distinction in question may occur only as *a dream of wakefulness*. In this case, however, one should perhaps speak of a daydream. The conception of man as a daydreamer does justice both to the Platonic thesis of man as part-way between the bestial and the divine, and to Nietzsche's assertion that man is the unfinished animal. As I shall be interpreting the metaphor, one must give preference to Plato at least to this extent: Nietzsche's interpretation of incompleteness is itself either complete or a dream, no better than any other.

The whole is the context of dreamer and analyst. Suppose for example that the analyst is the formalist analytical philosopher who believes himself to be awake, whereas the dreamer, his patient, is in fact himself, dreaming the dream of analytical wakefulness. Our task, then, is to identify neither with the physician nor the patient, but to grasp the context. It may be objected that this is merely to dream a more comprehensive dream. However, I do not regard this as an objection. The more comprehensive the dream, the more faithful it is to the whole. The method we shall follow in pursuing this metaphor to its root, as we may hope, in wakefulness, is to consider three different versions of the dream of wholeness. The three are variations on a still more fundamental dream, namely, that the dream of wholeness transpires within an image-world, and so true wakefulness is, or would be, arrival via sound dream-analysis in the original of which the world is a copy. I shall examine these versions as they have been represented in the history of philosophy by Plato, Fichte, and Nietzsche. It may not be evident at the outset, but I trust it will become clear as we go, that these examples have been selected with an eye for the revision and expansion of contemporary analytical philosophy. Once again to indulge in an initial oversimplification for the sake of clarity, each of our three examples has an essential ingredient to contribute to the philosophical analyst. From Plato we learn that analytical construction must be regulated by an intuition of formal structures, the originals of which our linguistic propositions, formulae, and the like are only copies. Fichte teaches us what is in many ways the most difficult of our three lessons: the transcendental logic of self-consciousness. The lesson of Nietzsche is that of nothingness, or the relation between creativity and chaos. If we attempt to think the whole on the basis of any one of these ingredients alone, we fall victim to one of three parallel diseases. In the first case, sole reliance upon the original-copy paradigm leads to the impossibility of distinguishing between the original and the copy. This is why Frege's attack on psychologism must eventually be transformed into psychologism, if only in the disguised or unself-conscious version of the later Wittgenstein. In the second case, an excessively transcendental analysis of self-consciousness leads to unconsciousness, and so prepares the way for the unself-conscious transcendentalism of contemporary philosophy of mind, in which the phenomenon of self-consciousness is replaced by logic. In the third case, our confrontation with nothingness becomes a surrender to, or exaltation of, nothingness. We then ply our constructions on the sea of history, carried from one nowhere to another.

The following pages, then, are not to be understood as an exercise in philology. We are about to make use of three figures from the history of philosophy for our own purposes: self-knowledge or philosophical psychiatry. This is, of course, not a license for distortion. It is rather an explanation as to why I have chosen certain aspects of each of the three models for attention here. Our goal is to arrive at the root of finesse and geometry, and hence at their unity. In one sense, it is clear from the outset that we cannot achieve this goal. In another, however, we may hope that the journey will be its own reward.

14. Plato's Image of Images

Painting and Talking

My paradigm of the Platonic dream of the whole is the passage in the *Sophist* (233c10ff) in which the Eleatic Stranger introduces the distinction between icons and fantasms, or veridical and misleading images. There is a valid distinction between original and copy, introduced into philosophy by Plato, but it is a distinction that cannot be mechanically applied. There are no rules by which we can distinguish the original from the copy. To say this, incidentally, is not to contradict my previous emphasis upon the importance of the given. Our judgment concerning the given, or the interrelation of nature and human purpose, is as much a given as are the phenomena of everyday life. The order of excellence of my intentions is not a matter of theoretical deduction or construction. Those who love wisdom do not do so because they have constructed a theory about the purpose of human existence which certifies the love of wisdom as paramount. The actual situation is rather the reverse. In somewhat more concrete language, I can distinguish a tree from the picture of a tree with no difficulty, and it is clear that the tree counts as the original under all normal circumstances. But some circumstances are not normal and there are no rules by which we determine what is normal and what is not. The Platonic emphasis upon common sense and good judgment serves as the background against which such fantastic doctrines as the Ideas or pure Forms are developed. Plato does not explicitly instruct us how to balance the sensible and the fantastic. We have to do this by means of our tact or sense of the fitting. To this general remark I add the following specific explanation of my choice of texts. The discussion of Ideas, Forms, or grammatical categories is not intended by Plato to give us our bearings in thinking the whole. This is obvious in the nature of the dialogue, which, as I just noted, begins and ends with the normal or conventional. The homely example of the sidewalk sketcher, when carefully read and pondered, opens up the same deep problems as do discussions of being, nothing, change, rest, and otherness, with the added advantage that the example of sketching exhibits the continuity between the normal and the abnormal. In order to reach the depths, as Leo Strauss used to say, we must begin with the surface.

The sophist, as his name suggests and the dialogue makes explicit, is a kind of copy of the philosopher. We are of course led to believe that he is a fantasm or misleading copy, rather than an icon or veridical copy. What is the fundamental defect of the sophist? It seems fair to say, at least initially, that he is defective because he presumes to know everything, or because he is able to persuade young men that he knows all things (233a8–b2; c10). Does it follow from this that the philosopher actually knows all things? The Stranger says that he and Theaetetus are able to employ division and collection according to kinds (*diaeresis*) or dialectic "with respect to each and every thing" (235c6). This is enough to justify a suggestion. In the *Sophist*, Plato is exploring the possibility that there is a universal method by which its possessor can know everything. Since we are dreamers rather than philologists, let us say that this is Plato's "Cartesian" experiment. If the whole is the sum of its parts, then potential knowledge of every part, thanks to the true method, is potential wisdom. Now there is something immediately unsatisfactory about this hypothesis. The method is diaeresis, or the classification of forms. But how could the method tell us which of two pretenders is the philosopher, and which is the sophist? The contemporary reader may be inclined to settle the issue by checking the "arguments" presented by each, with respect to their validity. This will not do, however, and for a reason which I have already developed in an earlier context. Since, according to the Stranger, the nature of the original is first discerned within images and *then* submitted to diaeretical analysis, it is intuition rather than logical technique that identifies the original. But there is no reference to cognitive intuition in the *Sophist*.

Here is another version of essentially the same point. In Plato's dialogues, it is clear that there is an intimate connection between sophistry and politics, if only through the mediation of the orators and rhetoricians, who are students of the sophists. Furthermore, as is apparently confirmed by the *Statesman*, the sequel to the *Sophist*, politics and the political art are "things" to be defined by the application of division and collection in accordance with kinds. In the *Sophist*, however, there is a virtual silence concerning politics. This cannot be explained on the grounds that the art of politics is reserved for the *Statesman*. If our intention is to understand the sophist, it is not immediately clear why we begin with silence about his most obvious activity. The sophistic art of mimesis is by no means purely epistemic; his capacity to persuade the young is not just applicable to, but is itself, a political phenomenon. By disregarding the political function of the sophist, or considering him from a purely technical standpoint, the Stranger raises a doubt in our minds as to the efficacy of the diaeretic method. Is a technical analysis of *technē* the right way in which to come to grips with sophistry? The contemporary analyst might answer in the affirmative, but Plato (not to mention Aristotle) gives us sufficient reason for saying, if not "no," certainly "yes and no."[7] If the method of the philosopher is diaeresis or dialectic, then the sophist must imitate this method. But dialectic is called "the science of free men" by the Stranger (253c4–9). Even if the Stranger uses "free" here in an extra-political sense, it is still necessary to "divide" freedom into its political and non-political species. So we cannot avoid the problem of politics in thinking about the sophist. The city is an imitation of the whole, and politics is the great rival to philosophy, as is obvious from the opposition of nature and convention.

A very general and preliminary reflection upon the *Sophist* thus suggests a connection between analysis and politics. Dialectic is the science of the free man, but the free man is not himself dialectic, or a definition achieved by diaeresis. He is a *free man*. This is, to all intents and purposes, the rhetoric of the modern Enlightenment, only here restricted to a few remarkable individuals. If we become wise by knowing everything, and free by being wise, is freedom the same as wisdom? In other words, is the whole the same as the sum of its parts? I have already observed that the *Statesman* teaches us otherwise. The true or epistemic statesman knows how to weave men of opposite natures together into a whole, as well as to apply the art of the fitting or timely. Neither of these is a question of diaeresis, but rather of intelligence (*phronēsis*). Given the aforementioned definition of wisdom, may it not be the case that freedom stands to wisdom as unity to totality? We can put this in the form of a question. What is the relationship between *dianoia*, the dividing and collecting capacity, and *phronēsis*, which we may translate as "sound judgment"? What is the sophistical imitation of sound judgment? And finally, to draw all these questions into our overarching problem: what is the sophistical version of the philosopher's dream of the whole?

At least one aspect of the difference between the philosopher and the sophist turns upon the nature of persuasion. The philosopher claims to possess a technique by which everything can be defined. I think it is not unreasonable to attribute the following counterclaim to the sophist. Definitions presuppose stable beings or essences, whereas the truth is that nothing is stable, except for the very general motivations of human desire. The sophist thus claims to possess a technique by which things may be rendered desirable or undesirable. He too "defines" everything. We are moved to exclaim, with some indignation, that he defines by means of a faulty logic, but this simply begs the question. The distinction between a sound and a faulty logic (taking the term in its wide sense) turns upon the stability or instability of things. But this in turn depends in part upon intuition and in part upon our dream of the whole. The deepest struggle between the philosopher and the sophist is not at the level of logical analysis. Once we free ourselves from the most naive form of technicist rhetoric, there is no reason why a sophist might not have an extremely powerful capacity for logical analysis. I challenge those who think otherwise to prove their case by logical analysis alone. The only way in which to distinguish between the disputations of the sophist and the definitions of the philosopher is by *looking at the original*. But if the original is just a linguistic construction, or a speech-form, then we must have recourse to some other motivation for choosing this rather than that construction. Why not the motivation of desire? As a matter of fact, a very limited experience of the world enables us to state this point even more forcefully. If we have no intuition of the original, or no method of choosing between one dream and another, then the sophist's disputations or appeals to desire are in fact more persuasive than the philosophical analysis of linguistic expressions. As Theaetetus observes, no one would engage in dialogue with the sophists and pay them, if they did not promise to make their pupils skilled in argument about laws or customs and all political affairs (232d1–4). We can also raise the same question in an inverted form. If this is the characteristic claim of the sophist, how is he a rival and false image of the philosopher? We can answer this question, but only in the form of another problem. Logical analysis is obviously incapable of certifying originals because it is either itself a copy, or based upon a denial of originals. If there are no originals, or if these are inaccessible, then we can do whatever we desire. The "kind of doxic knowledge about all things" attributed to the sophist (233c10) can be distinguished from the philosopher's wisdom only if we can define knowledge, and perhaps not even then.

From considerations like these, I draw the following inference. The way in which we come to understand the context, and so the limits, of analysis is more like political judgment than it is like pure theory or technical production. It must be emphasized that I am *not* subordinating analysis to a political doctrine. I am rather calling attention to the peculiar and comprehensive nature of political judgment. In the exercise of this judgment, we decide what kind of life we ought to live, and therefore how to adjust the ambiguous relations between theory and productive capacity. But we do not exercise this judgment by theory or production in themselves. In the language of the *Philebus*, the good for man is neither pure intellect nor pure pleasure. In terms of the present discussion, the good is not a matter of pure analytical thinking. But if rationality is equated with analytical thinking, then we shall have no alternative but to decide how we ought to live on the basis of pleasure. This is the wider background of the technical discussions in the *Sophist*. It therefore remains invisible, or is disregarded as irrelevant to his concerns, so long as we obey the technician. The net result, however, is to render technically defined production (*technē*) itself unintelligible.

In keeping with the silence about politics, the *Sophist* presents the question of original and image in terms of art or mimesis. If there is no basis for a view of the whole, or as we may also say, of the good, then the distinction between what are called the "fine arts" and technical production can no longer be sustained. This is why analytical philosophy is soon transformed from "Platonism" to pragmatism, and thence to an appendix of the post-Nietzschean doctrine of creativity or world-making. The Stranger asks: what if someone claims to know, not how to say or dispute about, but to make and do all things by one art? Theaetetus interrupts to state his lack of understanding of "all," a term he previously used without difficulty (233d3–e1). Presumably the difficulty is this: whereas the mathematician knows all things *in potentia*, namely, as constructible or countable, only a god could claim to make everything. Furthermore, Theaetetus' difficulty arises as soon as the Stranger shifts from "all things" (*hapanta:* 233c4) to "all things taken together" (*ksynapanta:* 233d10, e3). There is an additional puzzle about the notion of taking all things together as a unity (233e2–234a6). The Stranger explains that he is thinking of a technician who makes all things quickly and sells them for very little money. This "joke" (234a1–6) is a hit at the reputation of the sophist, except for the reference to the small fees. It actually names the sidewalk artist who makes quick sketches for a pittance. Apart from the deeper implications of the metaphor, its rhetoric is significant. An essential aspect of the refutation of the sophist is *ridicule*. We cannot refute sophistry merely by checking the validity of the sophist's arguments. To say the least, we need to establish the meta-validity of argumentation, and this can be done only through an appeal to perceptions of nobility and baseness. The good is visible only to the good soul. This apart, the sidewalk sketcher, like any mimetic artist, copies an original which he has not himself produced. It is therefore begging the question to take this example as a true image of the relation between originals and images. We visualize ourselves as perhaps leaning over the shoulder of the painter, in order to compare his sketch with the visage of the model. But what if this act of "comparing" is itself a kind of painting? What is there in the cognitive process that enables us to compare our representations with their ostensible originals?

Suppose for a moment that painting is a metaphor for the intellectual intuition of originals. If seeing is immediate imitation (a kind of photography), the same cannot be said of our discursive interpretation of these photographs. Since we interpret pictures with words, the primacy of painting to discourse leads to the relativity of interpretation. Even in cases where we all "see the same things," we "make something different" of what we see. In order to bring out in full relief this important theme, I want to make a very general observation about the *Republic* and then discuss a passage in the *Philebus* that parallels the passage under analysis in the *Sophist*. I said that philosophy and politics are rivals. But the situation is more complex; there are in fact three rivals: philosophy, art, and politics. In the *Republic*, Socrates resolves this rivalry by a daydream about the good, and hence the just, life. Philosophers become kings, and are thus also the rulers, i.e., the *interpreters*, of poetry (the exemplificatory art, critical because it employs words). The same point is made in a more condensed way in the *Philebus* (38e12ff). Socrates discusses the processes of thinking in terms of the arts of writing and painting. He suggests that there are two "craftsmen" in the soul, a writer and a painter. Memory and sensation register affections in the soul, which are like the inscriptions of discursive accounts. No copy intervenes between the grasping and recording of these affections. After their inscription, the second craftsman, the painter, produces images (*eikonas*) of the words. These images are intelligible thanks to the words or speeches of the writer. In general, memory, the "savior of sensation" (34a10ff), holds together consciousness and furnishes sensations with meanings within that unity. So images (sensations taken apart from words) are judged to be true or false depending upon the truth or falsity of the "opinions and arguments" to which the memory gives us access. Recollection preserves memories, or recalls them in the soul as independent of bodily activity (34b2ff). So the truth or falsehood of our perceptions of the world of genesis depends upon a recollective access to some discursive domain of meaning which is prior to, and the original of, the likenesses of sensation, made by the painter-craftsman.

In the *Philebus*, then, painting does not stand for the intuitive apprehension of originals but rather for the perception of the physical world. And this perception, taken in itself, lacks discursive significance. Genesis is rendered intelligible thanks to the hermeneutic activity of the writer in the soul. Since there is no explicit reference to intellectual intuition in the *Philebus*, we are not told whether the writer produces these interpretations or records them on the basis of some original vision of his own. We are thus left with a problem, not an explanation of cognitive processes. It is more or less clear that "painting" must be subordinate to "talking." But what regulates our talk? The status of this problem is closely connected to the absence of politics as an explicit theme in the *Philebus*.

In the *Sophist*, then, painting stands for the technique, not of the soul, but of the sophistically ruled soul. At first the image seems faulty, since the sophist's technique is verbal, not pictorial. But a closer inspection shows that the image may be more accurate than we supposed. Painting may stand for "silent" speech; that is, it may designate speech without philosophical reason. Of course, the sophist believes himself to be interpreting the external world accurately. The world is one of desire and flux regulated by desire, not by cognitively accessible essences or forms. From the standpoint of the sophist, it would have been fairer that he be compared to the epic poet. But even from the standpoint of the Eleatic Stranger, there is finally something defective about the image of the painter. This image functions only upon the assumption that we, like the observer of the sketching-process, can make a direct comparison of the original and the image. If we cannot do this, it is not apparent how we may refute the artist's claim to make the whole.

It looks as though the Stranger is aware of our objection and takes a step to meet it. The painter, he continues, produces copies having the same names as their originals ("the beings"). When he exhibits these at a distance, he is able to trick the "mindless" children in his audience into supposing him capable of doing whatever he wishes (234b5–10). As for the sophist, the magic art that copies in words is able to deceive the young in general, and not just the mindless. The art of painting is thus presented as an image of the art of making verbal images. And this enables the Stranger to smuggle into the verbal image our ability to look directly at the painting and its original. The young, he says, can be tricked because they are "far from the truth of things" or lack experience of life. The "spoken likenesses" produced by the sophists thus act upon the young ears as though they were true speeches of wise men (234c4–7). We note that this statement emphasizes experience or youth, not perception or cognition. For nothing is said as to how we come close to beings by way of the discursive intellect or theoretical argumentation. The word which I just translated as "things" is *tōn pragmatōn*, literally, "affairs." If there is no intellectual intuition of originals, then we must have recourse to mature judgment in order to regulate the speeches of the writer in our souls. I am well aware that this raises a problem rather than removes all difficulties. But the task of the philosopher is to see how things are, not to invent "theories" that resolve artificially defined problems or puzzles and leave life as ambiguous as it was before the resolution of the puzzle. Some problems illuminate, and others darken, especially by the specious light of their solutions.

The problem we are inspecting also surfaces in the later, technical discussions of language in the *Sophist*. All that is required here is to mention the main point. According to the Stranger, a true account copies within a web of words the logical relations of formal originals. But this leaves inexplicable how we distinguish between a true and a false discursive copy. Presumably the false copy will misrepresent the logical relations of the original. But if an original is defined by a specific set of relations, then a copy of some other set of relations must be a copy of some other original. No explanation is offered of how we are able to distinguish between copies of originals and copies which "correspond" in some sense to originals, but are created by the copyist. We find throughout the dialogues the thesis that words are images of things.[8] Sometimes this thesis is regulated by reference to intellectual intuition of Ideas, and sometimes it is not. In the latter case, the Ideas are presumably replaced by logical forms, but this does not carry with it the advantage claimed by contemporary analytical scholars. It is scarcely an increase in clarity to be told that language is a copy of logical relations, without being told how we have access to logical relations. This suppression of intellectual intuition leads finally to the defects of contemporary analytical philosophy discussed in the first three chapters of this book. But it is crucial to notice that all difficulties are not resolved by the reinstitution of intellectual intuition. We still have to decide what to say about what we see. Good judgment may include the interpretation of forms, but it is not itself explicable as formal intuition.

The Stranger's not-so-tacit argument continues: human beings who lack technical expertise are forced to learn by suffering, and what they learn in this manner is limited in the same sense that nature must be completed by art. When young men grow older, they come closer to things and are forced by suffering to grasp them openly, i.e., to become disabused by bitter experience (234d4–6). Theaetetus is a promising mathematician, a student of Theodorus, as is young Socrates. It is no doubt his mathematical aptitude that makes it possible for his elders to try to bring him as close as possible to things "without the suffering" (234e3–6). This is the Cartesian aspect of the character of the Stranger. Mathematical analysis, *ordo et mensura*, is a substitute for growing old, or for experience in the ordinary sense of the term.[9] The study of mathematics is "youthful" because it does not require experience of life; thus it seems to be safer than philosophy because it frees us from the magic tricks of the sophist. This safety arises from the manner in which mathematics grasps originals. Numbers are not images.[10] On the other hand, there is no reason to assume, and the dialogues as a whole do nothing to support the assumption, that all originals are mathematical. Even if Ideas were numbers (which Aristotle denies), the task of judging their manifestations in everyday life, or of distinguishing sound from unsound, and fitting from irrelevant analyses, would still require age and suffering. In order to get closer to things without being blinded,[11] or to free oneself from the trickery of sophistical copies, it is necessary to learn how to see correctly. The branch of mathematical science that deals with vision is optics. But optics starts with appearances and then transforms these into mathematical structures. Even if these structures are in some sense "originals," they are not the originals of the appearances from which we began. In fact, the Stranger does not make use of optics or anything like it in refuting the sophist. Instead, he uses ridicule and metaphor or rhetoric: he brands the sophist a magician and a trickster.

However, at a deeper level, we have here the familiar problem of predication. In general terms, images are pictures of something else that can usually be identified in the course of experience. But we must distinguish between two kinds of image, and so two senses of "picture." The first kind of image is a picture of a physical thing, which is "painted" in the activity of sense-perception. The second kind of image is not a picture of a body, but an expression of its activity or nature. A not unrelated distinction is that between realism and expressionism or abstract art. In the first case, we do not normally say that the original (e.g., a tree) "looks like" something (our image of it). Unless we happen to be concerned with the image as an element in the process of knowing, we identify it *as* a "something" of a certain kind, whether or not we refer to the image in the process. Of course, instances arise in which we have difficulty in identifying the "something," and then we say: "That looks like such-and-such." But these cases are deviations from the norm, and we attempt to rectify them by discovering, not what the image looks like, but *what* it is (or *of what* it is an image). In the second case, of which an example is the reference to the sophist as a magician, the speaker means (whether or not this is evident to his audience) that the thing "looks like" such-and-such, or shares some property with something else in such a way as to establish an illuminating resemblance, yet one that is not sufficient to identify the thing *as* a such-and-such. An image of this second kind is a picture in the sense that it reflects a part of the meaning or definition of something other than the object to which the image primarily refers. The fact that meanings or epistemic characters are reflected from one thing to another is an essential cause of the recognizability and (partial) intelligibility of things. It is also an essential cause of error. In addition, whatever else it may be, to know is to classify, or to say that a given x is also a y. And error arises when we say that x is a y when it is not but only "seemed to be."

The problem is now evident. We cannot distinguish between icons and fantasms simply by spelling out the predicates. First we must know which predicates belong to which originals, and this requires us to see the originals independently of their copies. All the technical problems discussed in the first three chapters of this book are implicit in the passage of the *Sophist* that we are studying. But the passage remains invisible to those who concentrate upon the "arguments" of the dialogue, just as they are invisible to those who believe that visibility is a consequence of analysis. The problem of knowledge is then not one of logical analysis, which is an entirely subordinate aspect of the cognitive process. The central problem is that *the whole is itself a sophist*. The same reflectedness of things that makes knowledge possible, to say nothing of art, also guarantees error and confusion. The deepest philosophical problem is not how we verify propositions like "that is a tree," but what it means to compare the sophist to the magician, and how to distinguish between the sophist and the philosopher.[12]

To summarize: there is a relatively straightforward procedure for checking the original of an image in the first sense. We look at it. This is not as naive as it sounds. The senses correct each other. Even if it should be true that we have access to nothing but images, and hence must check one image by another, we proceed as indicated, and with rather good results. But the situation is quite different in the case of images of the second kind. In order to understand the comparison of the sophist to the magician, we need to make comprehensive judgments about the whole of experience. But if there is any "object" of this judgment, it is *the* whole, or a mirroring of mirror-images, reflections, partial similarities, and illusions. In judgments of this sort, we are not simply checking one visual pattern with another. Instead, we are comparing interpretations; and we will escape the hermeneutical relativity of the contemporary world only if we can *see the point* to the comparison. This is why philosophy, as opposed to the sleep-walking slogans of the schools, is an eternal dispute, not an argument leading to a conclusion. And that is why the sophist, whose method is disputation, is an image of the philosopher. It is thus a faulty resolution of the question to say that we distinguish between the sophist and the philosopher by replacing disputation with diaeresis.

Nature Modified by Work: Large and Small Copies

The sophist engages in childish tricks (234e7–235a7). As a maker of images (235a8), he belongs to the class of mimetic poets. If the sophist is himself an image of the philosopher, does it follow that the latter is also a poet? Is it possible, for example, that mimesis is a fantasm of genuine poetry? That this suggestion cannot be altogether wrong is apparent from the argument of the dialogue. The philosopher's method is diaeresis and this is a *technē*.[13] On the other hand, it is not a pure productive *technē*, but one which "perceives" and judges, not simply definitions or concepts, but the "greatest genera" constituting the web of intelligibility (253d1ff). Perhaps the clearest indication of the Stranger's meaning is to be found in the division of two kinds of distinguishing or judging (226c1ff). The model for the philosopher is the household servant who takes natural materials (wool, grain) and makes products necessary for life (clothing, bread). I suggest that the philosopher grasps natural kinds and "weaves" them into interpretations of the whole. Philosophy is thus a combination of making and acquiring, or of theory and production. And the root of the unity of theory and production is judgment, the capacity to distinguish, not just in a technical sense, but in a way that is expressed by the measurement of the fitting. Thus the Stranger is confident that now the "beast" they are hunting is almost trapped in a net of "tools" that are used in discussions about these matters (235b1–3). The philosopher is a hunter or fisherman, and his tools are those of technical analysis. But tools are products of art, unlike the animals that they are used to capture.

In one passage, the Stranger summarizes his divisions of the image-making art (235b5). If we review the various divisions (235a5–b10) the following general pattern emerges. The family of jokers was divided into sophists and unnamed others (probably philosophers). The sophists were called mimetic tricksters and then subsumed under wonder-workers and image-makers. If we assume that jokers, tricksters, and wonder-workers are synonyms here, this class must fall in turn under imitators, who are presumably equivalent to image-makers. If image-making is a branch of poetics, then according to the initial explanation of the diaereses, it is co-ordinate with therapy, i.e., with "farming and whatever takes care of the living body" (219a10f). And the sixth diaeresis, itself separate from the first five (in the string of seven exercises with which the dialogue opens), shows that the caring function is one of those fulfilled by the art of distinguishing, separating, or judging, via the household arts. It is therefore possible that a final understanding of the diaeresis section of the dialogue would require us to weave together poetry, acquisition, and discrimination in some new and subtler way, if we are to distinguish the sophist from the philosopher. Whatever may be the truth about Plato's own intentions, this is the suggestion I draw from his dialogue, and that I propose as the "method" for thinking the context of analysis.

So far as his explicit methodological remarks are concerned, the Stranger represents what I have called Plato's Cartesian experiment. This experiment is carried out by presenting a universal method within a rhetorical context. For example, the Stranger tells us that we are to divide the image-making art "as quickly as possible" (235b5–6). This is odd advice to give a young man with little experience of the world. Equally significant, the hunt for the sophist is accented by the rhetoric of politics:

> should the sophist stand his ground against us at first, we will seize him on the orders of reason, the king, to whom we will deliver the sophist and display the booty. But if he tries to sink away into any of the parts of mimesis, we will follow him, always

dividing the part that has received him, until he is captured. For certainly neither this nor any other genus will ever boast of having escaped from those who are able to pursue, in each and all points, the method. [235b8–c6]

In Aristotle, theory, production, and practice are distinguished and detached from each other. In Plato, the distinctions are suggested, but as strands within a web. Art and nature (production and theory) combine under the rule of reason (practice). Reflection on this passage helps us to understand the Platonic convictions held by the founders of the modern scientific revolution. When the Stranger attributes the art of dialectic to the philosopher who is marked by purity and righteousness (253e), he is making a political statement, however rare in this dialogue, not a methodological one.

In keeping with the rhetoric of poetry, politics, or contextual thinking, the Stranger "seems to see" two forms of image-making, but does not yet "believe [himself] to know" which of the two is characteristic of the sophist (235d2–3). The two kinds of image-making are the aforementioned eikastics and fantastics (235d6ff). The first kind occurs especially whenever someone produces the copy by preserving the proportions of the original in length, breadth, depth, and color. This is an extremely odd statement. In light of the initial example of the sketch artist, it would lead one to assume that the stranger is talking about the visual arts, and especially sculpture and architecture. However, as we shall see in a moment, the genuine artist makes his statues and buildings, at least when they are of a certain size, by means of fantasms rather than icons. One is tempted to take this image as a metaphor for mathematics. In other words, a veridical or *proportional* copy is a mathematical image of the numbers or ratios in the original; incidentally, the theory of proportions is central to the mathematical thought of both Plato and Descartes.

We are given two families of artists, who are to be distinguished by the size of the artworks they produce. Theaetetus, like a good geometrician, believes that all imitators aim at proportionally accurate copies. However, we are in for a surprise, at least if we are excessively mathematical. For the Stranger now turns to the fine arts and criticizes Theaetetus' ignorance in this area. In the case of large artworks, a proportionally accurate image would produce a distorted copy. Geometry must be modified by sense-perception and human perspective. Copies of "the beautiful things," if true to the original proportions, would make the upper parts smaller and the lower parts larger than is fitting (235e3–236a2). Arithmetical precision would thus violate the art of measuring the fitting or appropriate. It is not quite clear what the Stranger means by "the beautiful things." Take as an instance the case of a temple. This is large enough to require the use of fantasms rather than icons. But of what original is the temple a copy? To make a long story short, I suggest that it copies a state of the soul, whether of gods or mortals. In this case, however, it seems reasonable to insist that the truth of the original, namely, the soul, is visible only within disproportional images. Otherwise, one would have to deny that works of art contain any truth, or that the soul can be presented in any way other than by pure mathematical icons. But then the example of small copies, in which icons are employed to convey the true proportions of dimension and color, loses its meaning. Why should a temple be a less true representation of the divine than a statue or a vase? Even if we insist upon magnitude as appropriate to the expression of the divine, this is a non-mathematical judgment.

Craftsmen of the second kind, who employ fantasms, "say goodby to truth and work into their images, not the actual proportions, but those which seem to be beautiful" (236a4–6). So the distinction between small and large is co-ordinate to a distinction between truth and beauty. One ought perhaps to infer from this that the truth, understood as "rational" or proportional, is accessible in small things but not in large ones. However this may be, what we require is a tripartition of copies into small, normal, and large. But it is not at all clear what the standard is for such a tripartition. The language of the example suggests that the standard is the human body. If this has any bearing on our understanding of the cognitive processes, it can only be as a hint that knowledge is relative to human nature. Furthermore, the size of copies seems to be determined by the nature of the original. To take the decisive case, there can be no geometrically or arithmetically accurate copy of the whole. Again, the shift from truth to beauty raises a further difficulty. In the fine arts, a deviation from the original proportions is intended to represent perspectivally the original as it is in itself. An exact copy would result in perceptual distortion. So far as our perception of the original is concerned, the exact copy would produce a false impression and not merely an ugly one. This point is expressed by the Stranger in terms of his doctrine of mimetic art. According to this doctrine, a beautiful copy is one that is perceived as a true copy. But the mechanics of perception are such that in the case of large originals we can only perceive a "false" image as though it were a true copy. In this situation, false copies look like true copies, and true copies look like false copies. So far as knowledge goes, since we cannot know large bodies without perceiving them, *a false copy is superior to a true one*. And in fact, we must say that a false copy *is* true in this case, or that "truth" is a function of the relation between subject and object.

Now what about objects of "normal" size? In order to get to the heart of the problem, let us assume that the corporeal language is a necessary feature of the metaphor of painting, but does not serve to limit us to cognition of bodies. May we not interpret veridical copies as quasi-mathematical ratios which, regardless of the original "size" of the copied object, can be duplicated in the icon? Again, we assume that this is possible.[14] Nevertheless, difficulties remain.

First, the replication of ratios is not in itself sufficient to account for the specifically *phenomenal* nature of either original or copy. Second, "rational" copies, i.e., those which accurately reproduce the original ratios, may distort the originals in another way by representing them in isolation. These two difficulties lie at the heart of contemporary analytical philosophy, or the attempt to employ a mathematical method without concern for the context of analysis. Rational explanation is equated with the definition of ratios or the mathematical structure common to a class of phenomena. But in this way the phenomenal nature of the class, and so the specific differences, are ignored, except to the extent that they can be expressed formally, i.e., in *formulae*. Mathematics is, as we may call it, the structure of precision. The more we progress into the laying-bare of this structure, the more we regard ourselves as having laid bare the nature of the phenomena we are analyzing. But this is a false assumption and is closely connected to the ambivalent attitude toward immediate experience that I discussed in connection with Saul Kripke and his commentators.

"Appearance," as Hegel emphasized, is not just illusion (*Schein*) but also the genuine showing of the essence (*Erscheinung*). The dialectic of illusion and show cannot be expressed in mathematical logic. In other words, the significance of mathematical structure is a dialectical function of the appearances from which we extract it. The ironical aspect of contemporary scientism is that the insistence upon making the isolated proposition the bearer or unit of truth is contradicted by the dialectical nature of the scientific enterprise itself.[15] There is no true proposition except within a theory, and the truth of a theory cannot be established by the confirmation of a proposition. Current controversies in the philosophy of science often turn upon just this point, but because there is no clear conception among the disputants of a mode of rationality other than analysis, attention to the context of analysis dissolves into historicism and conventionalism. This in turn is an opening into which the "virus" of continental speculations has infiltrated the unself-conscious dogmatism of the "hardheaded" analysts.

The difficulty in distinguishing between icons and fantasms is then a paradigm of the problems that haunt the entire tradition of analytical philosophy. This distinction is rooted in the nature of the cognizing intellect. It can be made only if we possess an intuition of the original, one which combines its phenomenal and its mathematical properties. This is evident from the distinction itself, as the Stranger makes it. Accurate images of things may well be inaccurate when seen from a larger or more comprehensive perspective, whereas inaccurate images may *look accurate* and so provide us with the larger perspective needed to restore an accurate look to accurate images. In other words, precise analytical results may, and indeed must, be inaccurate or misleading when isolated from the larger context that gives them sense and value. I repeat:

an accurate image (say, of mathematical ratios) which, as image, looks like the original, may, in looking so, be inaccurate, and thus not look like the original. A clear recognition of this paradox should lead us to distinguish among mathematical, phenomenal, and political senses in which our copies, whether in symbols or "natural" languages, mirror originals. A confused recognition of this paradox leads to the misdirected attempt to reconstitute everyday experience in scientific or mathematical terms. The result is the deconstruction of experience. Hence we may understand the vulnerability of contemporary analytical philosophy to post-Heideggerean deconstructivism. The attack upon tradition is today united with fashionable political ideologies; the result, whatever its intrinsic value, is superior to analytical philosophy in that it provides some comprehensive account of human existence, and thus an account of the significance of analysis. Analysis itself can give no such account.

I pass now to a further aspect of this complex situation. Eikastics, says the Stranger, is the making of icons: of that which is "other but like" (236a8f). The Stranger obviously intends that the emphasis be placed upon the copy. However, we must ask whether "other but like" does not also characterize the original. In fact, this very point is made by the Stranger later in the dialogue, when he attempts to resolve the problem of nothingness and to explain rational discourse by introducing the hypothesis of a logical web of pure forms (250a4ff). Each thing is what it is by possessing, among others, the property of being other than all other things. This relation also obtains at the level of the logical genera themselves. Thus, for example, Rest is other than Change through the mediation of the logical form of Otherness. In this case, an original is obviously "other" than the remaining originals. But, in the Stranger's account, it is also the same as itself, by sharing in the form of Sameness. In contemporary language, everything is identical to itself. Does not this turn upon an implicit notion that each thing is "just like" itself, namely, that identity is established extensionally where x and y have the same properties (i.e., their properties are in one-to-one correspondence)? The logical originals to one side, when we turn to natural beings, is not the original other than, but like, its copy? As the basic examples of perceiving and making illustrate, what counts as an original is relative to the intention or context within which we draw the distinction. I can distinguish reflections of objects in pools or mirrors because, under ordinary circumstances, the objects are primary points of reference. Whereas the reflection of, say, a tree in water may have some kind of existence of its own, the solidity and utility of the tree in everyday life make me take it as the dominant member of the pair (that is, of the tree and its reflection). Under special circumstances, such as daydreaming or poetic meditation, the reflection may become more important to me than the tree itself. The reflection does not lose its status as image of a tree, but this status recedes into the background. I am now directly concerned with the reflection and *I can make copies of it* in various media, including that of thought. The reflection now assumes the status of an original. For the Platonist, the tree is itself a copy of the Idea or Form, Tree. By the doctrine of Ideas, the Idea "Tree" is itself a quasi-arithmetical compound of other Ideas, and so is both other than and like itself.

This very simple example suggests, among other things, that even when we can perceive both original and copy directly, the distinction between them is relative to an intention, a human judgment, which is itself neither an original nor a copy. However, the issue that concerns me here is whether the tree is other than but like its reflection in the pool. And I think that we answer this question with reference to the intention. "It all depends what you mean," we might say. A tree is not like its reflection in the sense that the reflection is not alive, has no sap, no trunk, no branches, and so on. We cannot build a table or a house out of the reflection of a tree. But there is something tree-like about the reflection which allows us to say: "This is in fact the reflection of a tree." And we can build remarkable mental structures from the shadows of trees as well as from their reflections. I am not trying to disregard our normal inclination to give preference to the tree over its reflection. The tree is alive, solid, stable, directly useful. The image flickers; it can be changed or obliterated by stirring the water; it is not alive and not directly useful in the normal sense. Nevertheless, if the tree were not like its image, the image would not be of the tree. The very existence of the image *qua* image depends upon the likeness of the tree to it. This is independent of the question which mode of existence is superior. That question can only be settled by our intentions. Do we wish to build a house or to produce a work of art? Granted that we cannot protect ourselves against the elements in a daydream house, how will it be refuted if someone claims that the value of real houses lies in their permitting us to engage in the higher activity of daydreaming?

The analytical philosopher might well become restless reading these lines. He may wish to protest that to call a tree "like" its reflection is to misuse language. He will want to say that the image is like the original, but not vice versa. However, this linguistic point depends once more upon the prior distinction between original and image. For it is also true that the tree and its reflection can exist independently of each other. The pool can be drained, but it can also be photographed or painted. And in this case, as I have noted, the image becomes an original in its own right, and quite independent of the tree, which might be chopped down and converted into lumber. Again, suppose that someone paints the tree and exhibits his painting in a distant gallery. I might see the painting before the tree, and then, on a subsequent voyage, perhaps to pay homage to my favorite artist, visit the tree and say, "Oh yes, this tree looks just like the painting by so-and-so." It then becomes a matter for debate whether the painting of the image, and hence the image itself, is more "substantial" than the tree. Of course, if the painter had not initially perceived this tree, or some other tree, he could presumably not have made his painting. We may insist on this ground that the tree is the original. And so it is, in one sense of the term. On the other hand, the painting can continue to exist when all trees have vanished. More important, it can tell the perceptive observer something about trees that trees themselves may fail to make clear, even to the painter.

The pedagogical function of paintings draws our attention now to the relation between the actual tree and its "essence" or Idea. If we assume that there is an Idea of trees, may we not also call the Idea the original? One is tempted to do so, but there are difficulties. The doctrine of Ideas holds that essences are eternally what they are, or that we discover, rather than make or contribute to, their being. Presumably the original (the Idea of the tree) is discovered by intellectual intuition together with perception and, let us say, the science of botany (to cover scientific versions of Platonism). However, even science makes use of images to acquire its knowledge of the essential tree. The distinction between the original and the images is again based upon the scientist's ability to compare the tree directly to its copies, and it depends also on the scientist's intentions. He wishes to understand trees, not images of trees. But this has no bearing upon the likeness of the tree to its copies. Nor does it decide the question whether an artist's representation of a tree reveals something essential about the tree that the science of botany does not. After all, science is as much a human activity as is art. The scientific "essence" or form of the tree is no more distinct from human cognition than is the artistic representation. And if we take our bearings by intellectual intuition, or even the doctrine of recollection, or return to the explicit teachings of the dialogues on these points, then in my opinion (and contrary to the explicit subordination of art to science in the dialogues) there is no reason why a painting should not give us more direct access to the original than a scientific analysis. It has to be seen that access to the original is by way of the presence or show of appearance; the "reconstruction" of science is posterior to this. We do not avoid relativism by turning to science, nor do we fall into subjectivism or psychologism by an orientation in terms of pre-scientific presence. Of course, one may quarrel about appearances and mistake their natures in the pre-scientific as well as in the scientific domain. But if it is not possible to arrive at a foundation of things as they show themselves to us, then it will be impossible to discover the scientific "structures" or "inner natures" of things. There will be nothing to identify as the *originals* of the discovered or constructed structures. This is exactly what has happened in contemporary philosophy of science.

According to the Stranger, then, the sophist makes fantasms whereas the philosopher makes icons. Thus the sophist is himself a fantasm of the philosopher.

However, it is also true that the philosopher resembles the sophist. In orthodox Platonic language, one might say this is because both are copies of the wise man. The Stranger assumes that the philosopher is the veridical image of the wise man. If, however, we move from definitions of terms to the actual attempt to distinguish which of two human beings is a philosopher and which is a sophist, we can do so only if we ourselves perceive the original. But the perception of the original is an affair of intuition, or as I have broadened the term in this chapter, of dreaming. The "hard-headed" students of nature (mentioned in the *Philebus*), the "demythologizers" (or physicists: see the *Phaedrus*), and the terrible materialists (mentioned in the *Sophist*) all oppose dreams of the whole in the name of their own dream: precision, clarity, and the axiom of Lucretius: "to be is to be touchable." The Cartesian descendents of these awesome ancestors revert to their pre-Cartesian heritage by forgetting the essential connection between mathematics and intuition. As I have argued, and as is clear from the views of contemporary mathematical Platonists, this connection is not dissolved by the shift from a metaphysics of substance to an ontology of functionalism or operationalism. The Platonic Idea is still visible in the domain of the function or the structure of the proposition. The Stranger, as the spokesman for diaeresis, persuades us to study both sophistry and philosophy on an exclusively technical model. He more than implies that both are techniques like angling, shoemaking, sailing, and so on. In a sense, this is true; but it is true because angling, shoemaking, sailing, and the rest are themselves more than constructing and analyzing. Each capacity or art is already an expression of the unity of theory and production expressed in the practical activity of judgment, discrimination, or sound, i.e., fitting measurement.

In the *Statesman* (277d1ff), the Stranger compares our knowledge to a dream that disappears when we are awake. Just as dreams are presumably images of actuality, so our knowledge, expressed in definitions, axioms, propositions, equations, and functions, is an image of an original. To say that the original is perceived or intuited, and thus made available to the copying powers of the discursive or analytical intelligence, is to say that the philosophical dream of grasping, and so of giving a rational account of, the whole, is not to be mistrusted, scorned, or rejected in favor of "tough-minded" analytical piecework. Without the dream we are working in the dark. On this point, popular rhetoric is much wiser than analytical scholasticism. The modern epoch of western European civilization is a *dream*, and is often referred to as a dream. Descartes gave this dream a motto: man will become master and possessor of nature thanks to the *mathesis universalis* of the one true method of *ordo et mensura*. But, as I have noted, Descartes remains a true Platonist by founding his method upon the faculty of intellectual intuition. This is the methodological counterpart to the famous series of dreams Descartes is reported to have experienced as a young man still in his twenties. These dreams, presumably stimulated by the work of Kepler, Clavius, and others, led him to give a philosophical formulation to what we now call modern science. The fundamental question of our own generation is this: why has this dream become a nightmare? Why is the confident and "hard-headed" assertion of mathematical rationality rapidly decaying into an advocacy of irrationalism, arationalism, absurdism, surrealism, and the outright celebration of madness? My reply to this question is that we are steadily forgetting how to dream; in historical terms, the mathematicist and technicist dimensions of Platonism have conquered the poetical, mythical, and rhetorical context of analysis. We are forgetting how to be reasonable in non-mathematical dialects, and so we are forgetting the rational basis of mathematics.

The meaning of the *Sophist* is far too rich and complex to be more than summarized here, even on the basis of what is a crucial passage, a transitional text in which the main themes are rather plain to those with eyes not deformed by the sclerotic rage induced by the "battle of the giants" to which the Stranger refers, and what is now called in some quarters the *Seinsfrage*. The relation between original and image must be understood poetically as well as mathematically. Without the poetical context, a mathematical distinction between original and image is impossible. Without the mathematical distinctions, poetry deteriorates into history. And without the dream of wholeness (an original condition of wisdom, to which we can only approximate by images), the vision that guides our images and by which we can distinguish between icons and fantasms, we shall never be able to distinguish between the sophist and the philosopher. Some may ask: why is it necessary to formulate this thesis in terms of original and images? But this is another way of showing that we have not yet grasped the sense of the metaphor of the dream. In the *Phaedo*, Socrates warns his friends against attempting to see things directly, just as it is blinding to look directly at the sun during an eclipse. Instead, he says, we must proceed through *logoi*. Without going into all the subtleties of this passage, one can say that, in principle, Socrates makes the same point as does the Stranger. We cannot see the originals except through images. This advice, of course, does not mean that we ought to turn away from the things of the everyday world toward scientific theories and hypotheses. The meaning is the reverse: the attempt to look directly at the beings, essences, or Ideas exceeds human capacity. If we look away from the things of our everyday life, what we shall see are only the fantasms of our imagination, however these are articulated into mathematical structures. A rational science fulfills the official rhetorical program of science: it begins from experience. The "originals" are mirrored in the images of the everyday, and this gives stability and substance to the images themselves. By starting from this image-world, we in fact start from an accurate and exact representation of the complexity, depth, and finally unconquerable extent of the original situation. We are then saved from the fatal temptation to simplify the "pre-scientific" situation by mathematizing it.

The unsympathetic reader may take these remarks as primitivism, or a literary attack upon science, mathematics, and rigorous reasoning. I am willing to run this risk because there is no other way in which to state the radical deficiencies of contemporary analytical philosophy. But I have also gone to great lengths to show, on the basis of a detailed study of certain crucial aspects of analytical thinking, why analytical philosophy is deficient. It is time to state that philosophy is neither analytical nor synthetic, but both, and more. Philosophy is the dream of the whole. This dream is known in the textbooks as metaphysics. I have been arguing that metaphysics is much more realistic, much truer to experience, than the decayed rhetoric justifying the ostensible refutation of traditional metaphysics. I am also aware that the term "metaphysics" has had something of a renaissance among analytical philosophers. But an analytical metaphysics is no more capable of leading us out of the limitations of excessive analysis than is an analytical history of philosophy. What is required is the capacity to see outside the limits of analysis, and this means to see, indeed, to dream, the context of analysis. In so doing, we must not reject analytical thinking. The turn to the pre-scientific is not a turn away from science but an act of obedience to the original intention of science, of which contemporary analytical philosophies of science are fantasms.

To conclude this section: sophistry is the dream of the whole expressed as the will to power. The will to power is a metaphor for the desire to satisfy desire. If there are no forms, essences, or original natures, but only a primordial flux, then we are free to construct technical devices by which to reshape this flux into the fulfillment of our dream. However, if the world is basically flux, then so are our technical devices. The technical fulfillment of the dream is thus transformed into the suppression of its technicist version, which brings us to the Nietzschean dream of the will to power. (See section 16.)

15. Transcendental Deconstruction

There are two main groups in contemporary analytical philosophy, corresponding approximately to the traditional difference between realism or Platonism and nominalism. This distinction is not the same as, but is also not unrelated to, the difference between the formalists and the ordinary-language analysts. In more or less contemporary terms, it is the distinction between the Fregeans and the followers of the later Wittgenstein. One of the main themes of this book has been the dependence of Fregean "Platonism" upon intellectual intuition. If, on the other hand, Frege is given a Kantian interpretation, then he must be supplemented with a doctrine of the transcendental ego. For without intellectual intuition or the transcendental ego, Fregean concepts inevitably become transformed into the "nominalist" linguistic constructions of the later Wittgenstein. Whether he admits this or not, then, the Fregean Platonist's propositional functions are copies of originals, namely, of the eternal concepts. The procedures by which we give values to the variables of these functions is thus analogous to the operation called "participation" in the Platonic dialogues, although it is by no means the same. Strictly speaking, a sensuous particular "participates" in an Idea in the way that an individual falls under a concept. The individual man falls under the Idea (concept) of man. However, the attempt to state the properties of man uncovers the problem of the "participation" or "combination" of Ideas themselves. To give values to variables is in effect to say that something exists. To say this is to identify it as a such-and-such; and this in turn is to raise the issue of the combination of concepts. We may restrict these eternal concepts to mathematical properties, or extend them to any agreed-upon ontological domain. The extent of our universe of discourse is obviously not determinable by the mechanism of propositional functions. These figure only with respect to the prejudices of the quasi-mathematical philosopher, although often such prejudices are expressed as stemming from the convenience with which the method of functionalism may be applied.[16]

The problem of the relation between originals and copies, then, lies at the very heart of contemporary Fregean Platonism. It is rarely made explicit because it is not susceptible to resolution by analytical devices. More sharply still, analysis conceals rather than uncovers the problem of the relation between originals and images, even when the problem manages to acquire an explicit "analytical" formulation. The phantom status of the problem is apparent from the pervasive and inconsistent use made of "intuition" by formalist analytical philosophers. Our "intuition" tells us that such-and-such is a mathematical structure, or that this procedure will lead to fruitful results, or that a given theory is counter-intuitive. On the other hand, if we follow our intuition in certain extreme cases, we arrive at antinomies, paradoxes, or self-contradictions. In my opinion, little or no attempt has been made to study carefully what is meant by "intuition" for two closely connected reasons. First, the great majority of contemporary academic philosophers accept, almost without question, Frege's (or Husserl's) critique of psychologism, and intuition is a cognitive faculty. Second, of course, analysts (and many phenomenologists) take it for granted that philosophy is a science, or that it must follow the scientific method, the paradigm of which (in the case of the analysts) is mathematics. Mathematics apart, and in terms common to analysts and (most) phenomenologists, whether we are explaining or describing, it is widely believed that the task of philosophy is to reconstruct scientifically (i.e., by means of a rigorous method) the pre-scientific or pre-analytical domain of everyday, ordinary experience. Since ordinary-language analysts share the basically technical conception of reason held by the formalists, their denial that ordinary experience is amenable to the suasions of mathematical logic does not serve to distinguish them from the formalists in the present context.

One interesting development among some formalists is the view that contradictions can be isolated, or that it is not necessary to reject an entire theory or calculus simply because, in certain unusual cases such as those involving self-reference, contradictions result. I suppose that the general motivation behind this development is empirical or pragmatic, and so in some sense nominalist or constructivist. However, we may be permitted to offer our own interpretation of this line of investigation. If intuition works in some cases but not in others (assuming that "to work" means "to obey the principle of non-contradiction"), it may be because different species of intuition are involved, along with different objects. For example, it would be extremely interesting to try to discover whether there is any connection between self-referentiality and the difficulty of referring to the unity of consciousness which Kant plausibly says is the precondition of all discursive connections. We can refer to the unity of consciousness as a logical precondition, but difficulties arise when we attempt to give a discursive analysis of what Kant would call the unity of the empirical ego. Curiously enough, it is self-consciousness, or the empirical ego, that is the original here, not the logical concept of the unity of the transcendental ego. Perhaps the distinction between the transcendental ego and empirical self-consciousness is a sign that it is a mistake to attempt to analyze empirical self-consciousness, as though we were analyzing a logical concept. In mathematics, as we have already seen, contradictions of self-reference are avoided by ordinal hierarchies, or the distinction between sets and their operations and classes and their operations. For example, once we reach a certain level in the hierarchy, the standard power-set operation of ZF set theory can no longer be employed. I am not suggesting that there is any direct application of the situation in set theory to that in the philosophy of self-consciousness or "mind" (as it is now called), but there may well be some interesting analogy. Our "prehension" of L, the constructible universe, is obviously not the same as our intuition of a set that is directly constructible by the standard axioms of set theory. However, the role of intuition in mathematics is not taken seriously by analytical philosophers; little wonder that they have nothing of interest to tell us about our intuition of the unity of the self. This unity disappears upon analysis. But that disappearance

177

he inappropriateness of the analysis than for the non-existence
= this is granted, the possibility immediately arises that there
the analytical for speaking reasonably about oneself. And as
.., well known to everyone. We call it common sense. Unfor-
, our obsession with science and scientific theories leads us to disregard
common sense by the very acts with which we claim to practice it.

It is a far cry from common sense to Fichte's transcendental and dialectical logic. Nevertheless, I believe that it will be illuminating to spend a few pages on this difficult topic at the present stage of our investigation. One could say that dialectical logic arises precisely because of the recognition that mathematical or non-dialectical logic is inadequate to the task of explaining consciousness, or more broadly, life. Common sense, not logic, tells me that it is I who am thinking, not just my thoughts, but me. We can employ the flexible term "intuition" at this point. I intuit what Descartes, for example, expressed in the notorious (and misused) formula, *cogito, ergo sum*. As soon as we attempt to "unpack" the conceptual sense or structure of this expression, difficulties, antinomies, and contradictions arise. At the risk of infuriating a whole tribe of scholars whose professional careers center upon the "analysis" of this expression, I have to say that neither thinking nor existing is a concept, but an activity of a living individual. As soon as we conceptualize this activity, we detach ourselves from it. We shift, as it were, from our intuitive to our discursive understanding. Whether there is any way in which to bridge this gap remains to be seen, if by "way" we mean some rational and hence articulate explanation or description. If there is such a way, however, it will not be found among the techniques of analytical philosophy. To analyze is to divide, and self-consciousness is a unity. Analysts analyze concepts, and self-consciousness is not a concept.

Dialectical logic was not conceived as an opponent to mathematical logic. Instead, it is intended to serve as the *logos* of what I have been calling the context of analysis. Dialectical logic is related to Platonism in the following way. In the Greek tradition, the term "dialectic" has two main senses. The first sense is criticized by Aristotle and refers to the exercise of disputation about broadly philosophical or speculative problems. The second sense is introduced by Plato and refers to the technical exercise of diaeresis, or the division and collection in accordance with kinds. Since this second or technical kind of dialectic is introduced in the form of dramas or *dialogues,* and since it is obvious to the unbiased reader that diaeretical dialectic breaks down at crucial points and must be supplemented by myths, hunches, intuitions, daydreams, and the art of writing dialogues, the question naturally arises whether the Platonic dialogue is not itself a third kind of dialectic, neither merely disputatious nor purely analytical. The question can be extended to *all* philosophical treatises, starting with Aristotle. Another way to phrase the question is this: what is the nature of philosophical rhetoric? Granted that Kant, Frege, and Quine all use arguments and more or less rigorous devices of analysis, what about the form of their essays and books? What about the context by which they introduce their arguments and attempt to persuade us that these and their associated analyses are pertinent to our deepest concerns? There is not even a vestige of an answer to this question in contemporary analytical philosophy; this is because the question has not even been noticed.[17] We can see this in the shocking case of analytical Plato scholarship, where the first rule of philology, to read and explain the entire text, is regularly violated on the basis of a distinction between "literary ornament" and argument, a distinction which Plato has *self-evidently* rejected. I want to be brutally candid here. Competent Plato scholarship has to explain each dialogue as a whole, and as a unity. To proceed by the now usual method of detaching "arguments" from their dramatic context is exactly like saying that Shakespeare preferred horses to political power because the sentence, "A horse, a horse; my kingdom for a horse!" appears in one of his most important plays.

There simply cannot be any question about the fact that, in cases like that of Plato scholarship, the model of mathematics is operating, at whatever level of consciousness, to dissolve the philosophical intelligence of the scholar. I am only tangentially interested in Plato scholarship. My point is that the dialogue-form is already a step toward dialectical logic. However, it preserves the distinction between mathematics and poetry or tries to display each in its separate identity as well as in its relation to the other. Dialectical logic crosses this bar; in the terminology of Hegel, the separate identity or *An Sich* is developed into its relations with the other, or its *Für Sich*. Kant, Frege, and Quine are on this point unconscious Platonists. They employ poetry, rhetoric, or Platonic dialectic without being aware of the fact, or without attaching any importance to it. No doubt they would reply to me that what I call Platonic dialectic is just a way of talking about the pre-scientific situation, something that must be transformed into scientific theory, or scientific formalism. My reply is that if we do this, the work of Kant, Frege, and Quine disappears, to say nothing of Kant, Frege, and Quine themselves, together with the pre-scientific world that nourishes them and their scientific reflections.

The acceptance of dialectical logic is presumably designed to explain the context of analytical logic, not to replace it. Nevertheless, this is an oversimplification of what actually occurs. The shift to dialectical logic carries with it a radical revision of the relation between originals and images. Not merely are the originals "woven together" among themselves, but they are also woven into their images. Stated somewhat more sharply, the distinction between original and image is overcome; the images are now said to be the presentation of the originals. The original motivation of a desire for a logic of unity requires a logical account of unity, and this in turn requires a unification of what were previously called originals and images. This is the logical version of the thesis known more popularly as the overcoming of alienation, or the rejection of the doctrine of two worlds, with the consequent depreciation of this (ostensibly the image world) in favor of the other (original) world. In the Hegelian version of dialectical logic, the "originals" are eternal in the sense that they are the structures of temporality. The speculative dialectician thus dwells in two dimensions of one world: as logician, he dwells in eternity; but as dialectician, he dwells in temporality. It should be obvious that the Hegelian solution is unstable; if not for him, certainly for his successors. Hegel is followed by two main developments. The first was marked by the slogan, "back to Kant." We may translate this slogan as the expression of a return to mathematical Platonism, with the consequent rejection or subordination of the problem of Platonic dialectic or philosophical rhetoric. The second development is that of existential and life-philosophy, the immediate ancestors of such twentieth-century movements as fundamental ontology or historicist and post-historicist structuralism and hermeneutics. I have not cited Marxism as a major development after Hegel because Marxism is a hybrid of the two lines of thought I have just mentioned. Marx resembles Neo-Kantian scientism in some ways and Nietzsche in others. To say this is to suggest that, in his philosophical dimension, Marx is a deteriorated version of Hegel himself. Since I am not concerned with Marxism in this book, I leave it at this suggestion. Marxism's ambiguous nature is also visible in the ease with which it is assimilated by distinct philosophical movements. Its power, which I am old-fashioned enough to believe comes from its Hegelian core, is obvious from the fact that Marxism soon digests the doctrines that attempt to assimilate it. If what emerges is a variation on the original Marx, the image is nevertheless sufficiently powerful to force analytical philosophy to its knees. Marxism is Hegel for the masses, and we live in an age of mass ideologies. After all, what could be more liberal, more progressive, and more egalitarian, than science plus Marxism?

But let us return to the problem of the whole as the relation between the original and its image. The Hegelian solution of this problem is to say that there is no split between original and image. The danger of this solution is explicit in Nietzsche: once the original is "dissolved" into the image, i.e., once the motivation and force of dialectico-speculative logic evaporate, then nothing remains but the image, which is consequently an image of nothing. (For a further discussion of this point, see section 16.) Fichte's solution, apparently not known to Hegel, but elaborated during Hegel's lifetime and dating to the period when the *Phenomenology of Spirit* was being prepared, is quite different. In the *Doctrine of Science* (1804), not to be confused with the

1794 version, Fichte develops a dialectical logic by which we move from a preliminary intellectual intuition of the Absolute (actually he calls this by various names) to a dialectical "deconstruction" (my term) of the image-world. This deconstruction is intended, not to dissolve the world of genesis, but to free us from its illusory nature. It is designed to take us from the image to the original, not in such a way that we cease to exist in this world, but in such a way as to complete us, or to give us access to the whole, and hence to the context of analysis or non-dialectical rationality. Fichte's doctrine is of special interest because it presents us with a conception of intuition quite different from the main Platonic senses of the term, yet it does so in a way that is intended to explain the possibility of logical analysis as well as to give access to the unity of the Absolute.

Like Plato, Fichte accepts the distinction between original and image. Unlike Plato, he claims that it is possible to move from the domain of images to the domain of originality. The method of the voyage is a logic rooted in intellectual intuition. But the intuition is not of pure logical structures; it is an intuition of pure consciousness. More accurately, it is an intuition of the Absolute (original) "concealed" as my self-consciousness by its very manifestation in the image-world. The original is the Absolute, or as we may call it, absolute consciousness: something like a spiritualized version of the Aristotelian god. This god is in one sense a "self" because it is the Christian deity. But, as the Absolute, it cannot adequately be captured by the limiting prefix "self," which suggests a finite determination. The Absolute, in thinking itself (as in Aristotle), "creates" the world as its own image (as in Christianity). The image-world is the "appearance" of the Absolute in two senses. First, it is indeed the Absolute that "presents" itself as the world. But second, the Absolute is concealed by its own image, namely, the world. We see here a not-so-distant ancestor of Heidegger's doctrine of Being. Another way in which to put the point is this: Fichte attempts by his dialectical logic to overcome the split between the transcendental and the immanent interpretations of the Cartesian *cogito*. Despite the peculiarity of Fichte's terminology, his conception of the Absolute makes his enterprise significant to our study of the context of analysis. I have already mentioned that Fichte introduces a new sense of "intuition" into the discussion. But he may also be regarded as a way station from Plato to Nietzsche. This is because the distinction between original and image is preserved, whereas the original is *emptied of all definite content*. To be definite is to be accessible to discursive or analytical thinking. As we have seen at some length, the accessibility of definite forms, structures, or beings, is itself rooted in a unity or being that is not analytically accessible. Fichte identifies this unity with that of self-consciousness; that is, the unity in both cases is that of the Absolute. In other words, Fichte understands the impossibility of making sense of the object except by way of a doctrine of the subject. His attempt to overcome the split between the object and the subject terminates in the triumph of absolute subjectivity. The Absolute is the activity by which subjects and objects are *produced*. We can, by a kind of negative dialectic, return to the intuition of the Absolute, but we cannot discuss it analytically. Fichte's Absolute is thus to all intents and purposes Wittgenstein's unspeakable form of life and language. Wittgenstein is then both in his early and late manifestations a kind of Fichtean.

In saying this, I am of course not suggesting that Wittgenstein ever read Fichte, or would have had the slightest interest in Fichte's logic of the Absolute. I am drawing an analogy between the silence that underlies all modes of discourse in Wittgenstein, and the Absolute. Wittgenstein advises us in the *Tractatus* to keep silent about that whereof we cannot speak. I am now suggesting that this advice is meant to hold good in the case of the later Wittgenstein as well. To abbreviate matters, I will employ the term "mystic" to describe Wittgenstein's ultimate orientation. A mystic is one who "sees" determinate intelligibility as a consequence or emanation of an unspeakable power that lies always just beyond the margin of discursivity. Fichte, however, is *not* a mystic. He attempts to speak about the Absolute in the sense of showing us how we can attain to it: through a discursive or analytical deconstruction of determinate intelligibility. One could therefore say that Wittgenstein is a Fichtean who warns us against taking Fichte's "transcendental turn." If, however, we follow Wittgenstein's advice, the result is much the same as if we disregard it. For if we follow Fichte, the world of determinate intelligibility is replaced as the object of intellectual cognition by a world which, as absolute, lacks all content. On the other hand, if we follow Wittgenstein, we arrive at a process of unending talk which is saved from decaying into nothingness only as long as our analytical enthusiasm keeps us from reflecting upon the nothingness our enthusiasm articulates. The "logical" conclusion to both versions of the thesis is Nietzsche. In an effort to save the image-world from nihilism, Fichte annihilates it; he does, however, arrive (or supposes himself to arrive) in an absolute domain or ultimate originality. The later Wittgenstein, in an effort to save the image-world from the ostensibly distorting effects of an imaginary original world of Platonic forms, plunges us into a multiplicity of language games and linguistic forms, where it is a mistake to seek the common structure. We see here the fundamental sameness of attempts to champion either the One or the Many in isolation from each other.

In sum: I regard Fichte as an essential step in the development of a dialectical logic, based upon a new form of intuition (or at least a new interpretation of Cartesian intuition) that is intended to render intelligible the accessibility of formal structure and thus overcome the split between the subject and the object, or to think the whole by overcoming the distinction between original and image. We can describe Fichte's intention as the purification, preservation, and completion of Platonism. The result, however, is curiously similar to those great anti-Platonist enterprises undertaken by Nietzsche and Wittgenstein. As I turn to my analysis of Fichte, let me remind the specialist that my intentions are not historical but theoretical. Conversely, if the analytical reader finds Fichte's doctrine odd, he should remember that the task of the philosopher is to learn what is novel, not to restrict himself to the familiar. This, after all, is the difference between the philosopher and the schoolman.

Kant begins his critical philosophy with the fact of scientific knowledge and asks: how is knowledge possible? Fichte begins his *Doctrine of Science* with the assertion that there is actual, eternal, immediately apodictic, and spontaneous truth, which must be generated from the individual who sees (intuits) it.[18] But Fichte does not mean the same by "truth" as does Kant. The first principle of his *Doctrine of Science* (hereafter DS) is that it is impossible to doubt the immediate certitude of thinking or "intelligizing" (FW, 196). Wherever one begins to think, the content of this thought is known, not, as we may say, objectively, but reflexively, namely, in the sense of knowing *that* we know. Fichte's point is reminiscent of the usual interpretation of the Cartesian *cogito*, from which, in earlier editions of the DS, he is careful to dissociate himself.[19] It is not the being of the individual (or empirical) ego that is Fichte's first principle, but the intellectual activity exhibited within the consciousness of individual egos. Although the analogy may not be apparent at first glance, I would nevertheless compare Fichte's principle with the linguistic capacity of human beings that is the explicit or implicit first principle, and indeed, Absolute, of most analytical philosophers, but especially of the Wittgensteinians. To say that the truth is generated "from" the individual is no more to say that each individual creates his own world than that it is a consequence of Wittgenstein's doctrine of linguistic horizon or *Lebensform* that each individual lives within, or is playing, his own language game. However, since Wittgenstein is unable to arrive by rational steps at the *origin* of linguistic activity, the various linguistic horizons of the empirical world achieve a *de facto* status of a relative absolute, as we may call it. These change, but we change with them, and so we cannot see beyond them. Hence the similarity between the later Wittgenstein and the early Heidegger: both are historicized Fichteans.

Each instance of thinking on the part of the individual ego can thus be factored into two dimensions. In addition to the insight into the activity of thinking or cognizing (the original), there is a determinate content (the image). Fichte's dialectical logic is the attempt to lead us from the image back to the original, but it could not begin if it did not start with our intuition of the original. Initially, then, our intuition is dispersed into the determinations of discursive thought and ordinary perception. The return to the origin is then a journey from each manifold (or dispersion) to absolute unity. Truth is "absolute unity and unchangeableness of *Ansicht*," which may be translated as intellectual intuition (FW, 92f). The manifold is the empirical world, or, as Fichte also entitles it, history (FW, 93). Fichte's dialectical logic is thus an anticipation of Hegel, in that the journey to the Absolute is a kind of completion of history, as well as its unfolding. However, Fichte's intention is not to "identify" eternity and temporality; this is clear from the outset. His goal is to reach eternity as unencumbered by temporal dispersion. The dialectical logic by which this goal is enacted is, as a resident of temporality or the image-world, itself a manifold. So the completion of the movement from the image to the original is also a completion, and thus a termination, of dialectical logic itself (as is not the case in Hegel). To interpolate a pertinent image from the early Wittgenstein, we draw up the ladder of language into silence. So long as we are ascending the ladder, the unity of subject and object, being and consciousness, or original and image, is available to us only in images (FW, 99).

According to Fichte, Kant also saw the unity of being and thinking, but in a dispersed form corresponding to the three critiques: sensuous experience, the moral world, and the totally unexaminable root of the sensuous and supersensuous worlds. Fichte symbolizes these three dimensions as X, Z and Y (FW, 102–4). In other words, Fichte interprets Kant's transcendental ego, not as a logical function, but as absolute intellectual activity. This activity, although superior to the pre-Kantian versions of the Absolute, is still defective because of the modifications to which it is subject. Fichte proposes to go beyond Kant by thinking the unthinkable, or by discharging the "hypothetical" premises of Kant's third critique. He proposes to begin the investigation of Y, the root of the phenomenal and noumenal worlds, to provide what Kant failed to give us, "the actual and conceivable deduction of both worlds from one principle" (FW, 104). It is therefore not quite right to call this root "unthinkable." First, we view it directly in (reflexive) intuition.[20] Second, we may think it conceptually in its dispersed form as the image-world. But we may call it "unthinkable" in the very real sense that it is not discursively accessible as a set of properties or predicates. Unity is not a sum of parts, but (to engage in a necessary circle) the unity of that sum. And this takes us to a crucial aspect of Fichte's doctrine. The unity of the image-world is the Absolute that shows itself in the activity of thinking that world. The activity is initially accessible to us as determination or formal structure. But the activity is itself not a formal structure. It is absolute spiritual being, that is, not a "being," but Absolute Spirit.

The contemporary reader, one may assume, is not sympathetic to doctrines of absolute spiritual activity. This is obvious from a hasty perusal of books and articles on Kant produced by members of the analytical school. One will look

in vain among these productions for a kind word about the transcen[...]
let alone about the Absolute. However, it could be argued that Ka[...]
the transcendental ego is virtually indistinguishable from Hume; no[...]
explains part of his attractiveness to the empirical school, in his trunc[...]
Unfortunately, the truncated version of Kant leaves the doctrine of the synthesis of concepts unintelligible, or rather, invisible; and this has disastrous consequences for analytical formalism itself. One could do worse than to characterize contemporary analytical philosophy as the attempt to preserve conceptual
synthesis without a coherent doctrine of synthesis. It is this which underlies my
analogy between Wittgenstein and Fichte. If Wittgenstein's thought had been
given a more complete formulation than he gave it, we would be faced with the
relation between synthesis and analysis as following from the structure of the
linguistic horizon or *Lebensform*. Wittgenstein in effect returns us to the
image-world of dispersion (multiplicity of language-games). Fichte propels us to
the inner dimension of the linguistic horizon, identifying it as absolute spiritual
activity. However, since this inner dimension has no determinate content, we
lose (and are intended to lose) dispersion in exchange for absolute unity. No
doubt the *echt* Fichtean would insist that the insight into the Absolute is the
understanding of the image-world, not its sacrifice. But it is an understanding
that gives as an explanation of each manifold or image the unspeakable unity
of its presentation, thereby withholding an explanation of the manifold *qua*
manifold. This amounts for all practical purposes to a loss of the image-world,
i.e., to an inability to offer an explanation of it in its own terms, and also to a
necessary depreciation of it as an *image*. In passing, this is why Hegel's attempt
is superior to that of Fichte's, regardless of whether Hegel was familiar with the
DS of 1804 and its "new" solution to the problems of German Idealism.

Fichte himself offers a reply to the analytical thesis that no doctrine of the
Absolute is necessary. In his view of the history of philosophy, there are two
poles: Realism and Idealism. The Realist begins from, and in a genuine sense
does justice to, things, or what is "opposite to" (*objectum*) the subject. The Realist takes account of the externality of *res*. But he cannot explain how we grasp
conceptually the *res extensa*, or more fundamentally, how we grasp *ourselves* as
so conceiving this or that thing. The Idealist, on the other hand, begins with
life, and reflection or thinking. But he makes impossible, or cannot explain,
the beings that are opposed to subjectivity or thinking. Equally serious is his
failure to give an account in genetic terms of reflection, his starting point (FW,
177–181). This last contention amounts to the accusation against Kant that he
failed to provide a transcendental deduction of the *ego cogitans* from what is for
Kant the unthinkable Absolute, represented in purely functional terms as the
transcendental ego. Fichte thus proposes to overcome the split between Realism and Idealism, or to provide the transcendental deduction omitted by Kant,

by thinking Y, the root of the sensuous and the supersensuous. (We also see here how important is Kant's third critique for the development of the next period of German thought: Schelling, Fichte, and Hegel). However, as I have regularly noted, in surpassing Kant, or thinking through the structure of the image, we think *through* it, think it away, and thus rise "up" (or perhaps "into") the Absolute. The DS thus ends, *as must we*, if we have understood it, in the transcendence of finitude, manyness, dispersion, and conceptual discourse.

One need not accept the spiritual or Christian nature of the Absolute in order to see that Fichte's critique of Realism (putting Idealism to one side for the moment) or what we now call analytical philosophy, is sound. Neither, I think, need we be disturbed by the fact that Fichte formulates the problem in terms of the subject-object distinction. Nothing is lost by shifting to the *noēsis/noēton* terminology preferred by partisans of pre-modern (or even in some cases of contemporary phenomenological) philosophy. As it happens, analytical philosophy itself continues to speak the language of subjects and objects, and so objectifies the subject, or overlooks the presence of the subject in the structure of the proposition, via the selection of the values for the variables of a function. This tendency is illustrated in the attempt by Kreisel and others to mathematize Brouwer's conception of the creative subject as expressing the force of mathematics, a force that cannot itself be expressed in mathematical terms.[21] In a significant sense, Fichte himself commits, perhaps inevitably, an analogous error (if that is the right term). If conceptual language is already an image of the Absolute, and if the original cannot be grasped in the manifold of discourse, how can Fichte even state its function as the unity of the articulated whole? The tripartite distinction symbolized by X, Z, and Y must be a structural characteristic of conceptual thinking. It is, as it were, more like Kreisel's $\sum$ than like Brouwer's creative subject. Y, presumably the root connecting the sensuous and the supersensuous worlds, is an image of the unity of the Absolute. Furthermore, $\langle X, Z, Y \rangle$, as we may mathematize Fichte's "ordered triple," is not the same as, but parallel to, another division between being and thinking.

These two lines of division are presented by Fichte in a schema as emanating from a point co-ordinated with, but not identical to, the Absolute (symbolized by the letter A [FW, 114]):

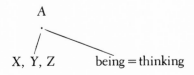

A

X, Y, Z   being = thinking

A represents unity; the point is the locus of the manifold, or in other words, a unity that is not the same as absolute unity. One cannot therefore formulate precisely the sense in which A stands to the Absolute, since A is an image. Fichte is trying to schematize (and hence, speaking broadly, to mathematize) his basic intuition of the unity of the basic structures of the image-world. But this is impossible. Representation is multiplication, and language is representation. On the other hand, the original, or the origin of the image-world, is not a representation, not a concept (which is already a discursive image), *but intuition itself*. Although not conceptualizable, the Absolute is "visible" or evident as evidence as "pure light" (FW, 117f) or, rephrased, as intelligibility.

Fichte's central image of the Absolute is Platonist: the light. In place of Ideas, however, Fichte attempts to articulate spiritual activity by means of his bipartition of structures or dimensions. Perhaps we could say that the light is the shining of the Absolute (somehow analogous to Plato's sun). The manifold of the image-world is then to be derived purely from "the reciprocal activity of the light with itself" (FW, 119). Fichte thereby imports diversity and self-dispersion into the unity of absolute light. *The very notion of activity is unintelligible except via diversity*. But this diversity cannot be genuinely captured within mathematical symbolism. The attempt to do this is very much like the contemporary effort to "analyze" intentional activity into types of modal propositions. The analyst deludes himself into supposing that his modal operators or "belief-verbs" capture spiritual activity. As a consequence, he studies residues of spiritual activity, not that activity itself. The important point to be made here concerns the relation between mathematics and philosophy. I have no intention of denying this relation. In the mathematics of each epoch, one sees the epistemological and ontological assumptions of the dominant philosophy of the time. But one cannot see these assumptions by *applying* or working within the mathematics, as for example by proving theorems, constructing calculi, or refining one's meta-mathematical conceptions. Mathematics is an image of original philosophical doctrines. The attempt to philosophize by engaging in mathematics results in the production of images of images. As a consequence, we come to forget the original.

I want to illustrate this with a brief summary of a difficult but crucial strand in Fichte's thought. The light, as Fichte in effect admits, is an image of the Absolute, or, as he puts it, of the interior living light, which is not only inaccessible to the concept, but is "absolutely not in insight" (FW, 163). We are therefore permitted to say that Fichte develops his complex light-imagery against the *darkness of the Absolute*. Our insight into the light must be genetic or constructive (FW, 157). If we are thinking (in whatever sense) the Absolute, then we must produce it or exemplify the process by which it manifests itself as the world. Unfortunately, the light, as the schematism depicts, externalizes as the concept; therefore, it is in itself invisible. It is present as absent, showing itself only indirectly "through" dispersion and dualism within the conceptual image-world. Fichte makes this "through" (*Durch*) into a technical term (FW, 168ff). As the infinitely divisible continuum of quantitativeness, it corresponds to the spatio-temporal continuum in the first part of Hegel's logic. However, Fichte says that the "through" is the whole content of the DS. In short, contrary to the situation in Hegel, we never arrive at a discursive grasp of the Absolute. Permit me the following metaphor: Fichte is a Platonist who claims to be conceptualizing or logicizing the process by which we attain to the original condition or to an account of the whole. But he formulates this process in such a way as to render it impossible. Hegel, on the other hand, actually invents a dialectical logic, or still more profoundly, a way of conceiving of the original and the image-world that enables him to produce a plausible account of the unity of the two. In this sense, Hegel is the paradigm-case of the conceptual analyst. In technical language, Hegel offers a plausible logicizing of being, unity, and nothingness. Fichte has not yet succeeded in this task. This is because, despite all appearances to the contrary, he is too analytical. Hegel completes the analytical enterprise because he recognizes its deficiencies and is able to compensate for them. Such at least is his intention, and one need not be a Hegelian to understand the degree to which he fulfilled it; but one must also see how he failed.

For Fichte the image-world that conceals the Absolute is the product of the finite or empirical subject. In order to attain to the Absolute, we must negate the self via the highest form of thinking: "the thinking of absolute, immanent life" (FW, 175). Even truth is an image of this absolute life (FW, 176). This exhibits the *Lebensphilosoph* in Fichte, or the sense in which he is an ancestor of existential philosophy. Fichte sees the impossibility of conceptualizing life. It often looks as though he is trying to overcome this impossibility by his dialectical *deconstruction* of the image-world. But the deconstructive process is itself an image of the genetic or creative process by which the Absolute produces the world. Whereas deconstruction reveals the negative dimension of finite or determinate existence, construction conceals the creative activity of the Absolute. Fichte's transcendental deconstruction thus leads in our own century to a deconstruction of the transcendental, or to a celebration of the *nihil* implied in the prefix. *de-*. Fichte's attempt to think the Kantian "ought" (*Sollende*), and to conceive the Absolute as absolute will, deconstructs itself into Nietzsche's will to power, the grandfather of contemporary nihilism. The Absolute, already in Fichte, is indistinguishable from the *nihil*. As he himself says, to see the world of finite determinations as an unreal condensation on the surface of thinking is at once to intuit the Absolute as "absolute pure nothing" (*Nichts*:

[FW, 184]). Our deconstructive intuition into the non-constructive nature of what endures, is itself the negation of the world of finitude. In analytical philosophy, the strikingly parallel process is that of attempting to deconstruct ordinary experience in order to reconstruct an ideal world of mathematical structures. The deep philosophical motivation underlying formalist analytical philosophy is the Enlightenment version of Platonism, or one-half of Platonism turned into the whole. It is a search for the original world as written in mathematical equations by God the mathematical physicist. Unfortunately, mathematical equations are dead.

I have presented only a few aspects of Fichte's complex thought. Nevertheless, these aspects are among the most important for him, and they illustrate the problematic of the whole in a way that shows the metaphysical interior of analytical philosophy. It is extremely important to remember that one motivation in the development of contemporary analytical philosophy was Russell's rejection of Absolute Idealism. Today it is no doubt taken for granted that this rejection is definitive, or somehow "proved" by the extraordinary proliferation of mathematical logic. All that is proved, of course, is that we have shifted from one justifying metaphysical doctrine to another. At least Russell was aware of this, and however inaccurate his grasp of Hegel may have been, he struggled honestly with one tradition in the process of contributing to the development of another. This vantage point between two images gave him a better perspective for intuiting the original than the great majority of his successors. Even Wittgenstein, who presumably had very little interest in the history of philosophy, was obviously deeply influenced by nineteenth-century German thought, and not simply by Kierkegaard and Schopenhauer. In my opinion, Wittgenstein was a deeper thinker than Russell, and we can perceive in what has aptly been called his "glory and misery" the struggle to come to terms with what Fichte calls the Absolute. The *Tractatus* is a more explicitly mathematical version of Fichte's *Doctrine of Science*. Wittgenstein came to see the defective character of this enterprise; but his return to ordinary language, however sensible in certain ways, is a falling away from the original into a world of images. I conclude this section with a conjecture. Wittgenstein's later philosophy shows his insight into the medicinal nature of ordinary language. His world of images is "politically" safer and saner than that of his predecessor and archrival in the celebration of constructivism, Nietzsche. I can therefore sympathize with Wittgenstein's anti-speculative tendencies on "political" grounds. Perhaps he practiced a kind of salutary esotericism from the conviction that human beings are too defective to engage in metaphysics. This is a religious thesis that dates back at least as far as the Middle Ages, to say nothing of still earlier manifestations.

16.   Nietzsche's Image of Chaos

Men have always dreamt of an original world of which this world is but an image. The western philosophical tradition has its decisive beginning in a rather ambiguous suggestion that we may awaken from the dream by the exercise of reason. In the Platonic dialogues, knowledge is compared both to dreams and to wakefulness. What we call the Enlightenment may thus be styled a dream of complete wakefulness. The rhetorical force of this dream is not as coherent as we sometimes think, but it seems to derive from the confidence in power, or the desire to become master and possessor of nature. Since man cannot become master without disinheriting the previous ruler, the Enlightenment is by its intrinsic character, not quite atheistic, but the dream that man shall become a god. Gods, however, create in their own image. The desire to become master of nature is thus at odds with the Platonic conception of original mathematical structure. The rejection of intellectual intuition, or of the view that we have either direct access to originals, or at least can see them reflected in their images, may itself be caused by what Nietzsche calls the will to power. From this standpoint, mathematical structure is an imposition on human creativity. In addition, if man is in the process of becoming a god, then he must be presently imperfect, in the process of transformation, or what Nietzsche called "the incomplete animal." The incompleteness of man, the will to power, and the inaccessibility of mathematical originals, leads eventually to the most radical revision of the paradigm of original and image. We saw in the previous section that, for Fichte, the world is a "construction" of the activity of the Absolute. Our own effort to return to the Absolute is thus a "transcendental" deconstruction of the world. We may give this deconstruction a specious appearance of positivity by saying that we, in thinking the Absolute, must construct the world just as does the Absolute we are thinking. But since the Absolute is empty of content, our construction is a creation *ex nihilo*. By a slight shift in our dream, or in the rhetorical economy of the psyche, the Absolute becomes nothingness, and creation is the shaping of chaos in one's own image.

Contemporary analytical philosophy combines elements of the Platonic and Fichtean paradigms in its more or less conscious ideology. I use this latter term because, strictly speaking, concern with the whole is not properly philosophical, given the criteria of the analysts themselves. The dream-like nature of analytical philosophy is easily inferred from the fact that, if the context of analysis is unphilosophical, then analysis loses its basis. I do not mean by this that philosophy must be completely rational in the sense of having no presuppositions. My point is rather that we need various senses of rationality. If the motivation to analyze is rational, then so too is reflection upon this motivation. We may of course attempt to analyze this motivation, but the result will be self-certification, or worse, structures of discourse. No structure is self-certifying. But this is merely a sober reformulation of Nietzsche's assertion that the world is valueless. We are now ready for our transition to Nietzsche.

The Platonic dream of the whole, expressed in terms of the distinction between original and image, turns upon mathematics and quasi-mathematical techniques of analytical thinking. But the turning point of mathematics is still embedded within a drama or poetic expression of the significance of mathematics. When the power of the mathematical techniques overcomes the charm of the poetry, when we succumb to the charm of competence, the desire to mathematize poetry becomes overwhelming. One form of this desire is transcendental logic. Broadly stated, the purpose of transcendental logic is to overcome the split between theory and practice. However, as we have seen in the case of Fichte, it proceeds by converting both theory and practice into production. If man is the divine constructor, then he must come to terms with nothingness or be dissolved by it. The religious doctrine of a creation *ex nihilo* is a miracle; we are thus warned not to attempt to grasp nothingness conceptually. In philosophy, however, such warnings cannot be obeyed, even when they are issued with the authority of a Father Parmenides.

Nietzsche presents us with the most powerful and profound attempt to reconcile creativity with nothingness of the past hundred years. Although this attempt is couched in poetry, prophecy, and epigram, it is altogether more lucid than the scientific rhetoric employed to justify the analytical philosopher's dream of the whole. I propose in this section to study this doctrine of reconciliation in some detail. Let me emphasize that, in so doing, we are also studying the deep implications of contemporary analytical philosophy. To utilize the metaphor of an earlier section, we are engaging in the psychoanalysis of analysis. The language of Nietzsche, or rather, our interpretation of this language, is the language of the art of psychoanalysis, designed to bring out the hidden sense of the language of analysis. I shall, then, organize my therapy in terms of Nietzsche's conception of the world as an image of chaos. In accordance with the guiding motif of this chapter, I shall be especially interested in Nietzsche's use of the metaphor of dreaming to stand for poetical, creative, or perspectival thinking. I have arranged my remarks that they may comply with a subordinate purpose: to show that there is no serious change in Nietzsche's thought concerning dreams and chaos during any of its major periods. I begin with a general statement based almost entirely upon the unpublished fragments of the period following *Thus Spoke Zarathustra*. I do this because of the widespread belief, due to Heidegger, that Nietzsche's later and unpublished writings contain the fullest and indeed a new version of his deepest thoughts. This belief is typical of the Heideggerean notion that the truth must conceal itself; and it leads to a preference for both archaism and the unpublished or suppressed as opposed to the published or revised. In the second part of this section I consider some passages from writings preceding *Zarathustra*. We shall see that, virtually from the beginning, the same treatment of dreaming and chaos is present throughout. The third part of this section deals with *Zarathustra*, and at its center is the analysis of a dream attributed to Nietzsche's great spokesman.

As a psychoanalyst rather than a philologist, I do not wish the systematic character of this section to be overemphasized. It is not a transcendental deduction, but perhaps a medicinal deconstruction of a revelation. One of the most serious difficulties facing any student of Nietzsche is how to bring out his author's teachings (or dreams) without distorting them by the exigencies of academic prose. There is a difference between the free associations pursued in the psychoanalyst's office and the rigorous scientific prose of a clinical report. This section is neither the one nor the other. Or to put the same point somewhat differently, since I am an admirer but not a disciple of Nietzsche, I shall not be regaling the reader with parables and revelations. My prose will be discursive rather than musical. As a deconstructor, I must keep my feet on the ground of my dream, so to speak, rather than leap or dance from mountain peak to mountain peak, as Nietzsche preferred. Nevertheless, I must dare to dance and leap a bit, if only to come within hearing distance of the extraordinary thinker who is in the process of conquering late twentieth-century thought in a variety of disguises.

The Late Fragments

In Nietzsche's mature teaching, the will to power functions as the *principium individuationis*. To put the point in the simplest way, men will the interpretations of beings, not beings themselves.[22] The most comprehensive or powerful will asserts itself as a perspective or world, a way of seeing that creates what it sees by defining the sense of the vision.[23] The centrality of interpretation, and so of sense, in Nietzsche shows that he too falls within the horizon of Kant, and is therefore related to Husserl and the contemporary analytical philosophers, as well as to Heidegger and his successors. The Nietzschean act of definition, of course, is not conceptual or discursive in the analytical sense. Those who are overly impressed by Nietzsche's "linguistic" doctrines overlook the core, namely, the will to power. "Making sense" is for Nietzsche, who anticipates Heidegger in this respect, an existential choice. More comprehensively, Nietzsche interprets the justifying doctrines of any philosophical epoch as such a choice, whatever explicit form the rhetorical formulation may take. It

is very easy to see the similarity between this view and much current speculation in the philosophy of science that is ostensibly motivated by the late
Wittgenstein. Whether scientific change occurs by way of existential choice or
a shift in the historical framework and linguistic horizon, the fashionable accounts of the history of science are in surprising conformity with the early or
the late Heidegger, and thus, with Nietzsche. Heidegger's first major work,
Being and Time, is still an academic or "scientific" attempt to express the revelations of Zarathustra systematically. Thus the interpretation of Being which is
opened or projected by man is common to all through their common *Dasein*
(mode of existence). My choice of my life is an individual attunement of a
comprehensive ontological structure that defines all men.

For Nietzsche, on the contrary, Being is "uncovered" only in the sense that
it is exposed as a fraudulent concealment of Becoming. To be sure, the falseness of the stability of the world is entirely compatible with the fact that lies are
required for life.[24] Art is worth more than the truth.[25] Nevertheless the structures of the public world are the crystallization, and often the detritus, of individual acts of will. I must choose, not simply my life in the world, but the
world in which I live. Submission to the public, reaction instead of action, is a
failure of will, a *failure of nerve* in a sense peculiar to Nietzsche's physiolo-
gizing of ontological processes.[26] In contrast to what one may call the official
pacifism of contemporary liberal intellectuals, it is interesting to note the regular conjunction of philosophy and war in the history of western thought. Between Plato's philosopher-soldier and Nietzsche's artist-warrior falls the war
against nature, symbolized by the scientific experiment, and made the basis of
philosophy by the ex-soldier, Descartes. What is today called "hard-headed-
ness" or "tough-mindedness" in analytical circles is a technologized version of
Cartesian "militarism." The line from Cartesian passion to Nietzschean will is
not only transmitted by the *Sollen* and *Streben* of the Kantian school, but has
its own antecedents in the political dimension of Platonism. Hence the connection between mental toughness among analysts and a good "digestion" in
Nietzsche is easy to see, if one knows how to look.

The failure of nerve is transformed into success to the extent that "I" adapt
public structures to a new and comprehensive interpretation. Furthermore, in
Nietzsche, the extent to which "I" am responsible for, or act as the agent of,
my world and life, is superficial. The act of will that opens the perspective of
my world is also the act by which "I" as self-conscious ego am created.[27] In
Plato and Aristotle, the empirical "I" seeks to lose itself in pure noetic activity.
Seventeenth-century thought in effect sublates the *ego cogitans* in the transcendental domain (of which Leibniz's monads are the first version). Nietzsche's
deconstruction of the ego is in this sense entirely traditional, as is the contemporary effort to "analyze" mind into the formal structure of its assertions, or the

classifications of its speech-acts. Once again, it is the political context of classical rationalism that prevents its mathematical core from dissolving the individual, or from transforming perfection into disappearance. Exactly the same is true in Nietzsche: his doctrine of nobility is strictly speaking incompatible with his doctrine of power, itself the existential version of seventeenth-century scientism. The ego is the public surface of the body; the body draws its sustenance from the earth, but the ego civilizes the earth by its "taste" (in both the physiological and aesthetic senses) for nobility. In Nietzsche, it is not logic or mathematics, but the love of the noble, that *articulates* the will to power. It is not necessary to do more than ask oneself what status the noble is given in contemporary analytical philosophy. Without the love of nobility, as that love is expressed by individual egos, the will to power is both the principle of individuation and a principle that always manifests itself as a unique perspective.[28] We should also note that, despite the finally superficial nature attributed by Nietzsche to the ego, every perspective is necessarily *my* perspective.[29] Nietzsche himself abolishes the possibility of an impersonal perspective in the scientific sense of that which is universally valid.[30] The perspective of a society or of an age is determined by the triumph of the original viewer over his contemporaries. The individual who opens an original perspective is thus Nietzsche's version of the founding prophet or political father. The traditional difference between the public and the private understanding of the founding revelation takes the form in Nietzsche of a paradox. Each manifestation of the principle of individuation, as unique, amounts to a new interpretation of the principle. Each originative perspective is an image of a principle having no original form or content.

The original perspective is an "origin" only in a derivative and contingent sense, as is evident from the fact that it imposes an order onto primal chaos.[31] To "impose an order onto," however, is not to impress a form via a higher, distinct paradigm, but rather to "open a perspective within." Perspectives are chaotic organizations of chaos: the order is itself the activity of chaos and not of a separate principle. We may say that chaos is continuous origination, but this is equivalent to the assertion that it is continuous negation. To create, as Nietzsche regularly insists, is to destroy. Order, at its interior, is chaos. The principle of the will to power must accordingly be understood in a dual sense. Genesis is both coming-to-be and passing-away. What is coming-to-be achieves visibility only by asserting itself over, and hence negating, what is, which thus passes away. The visibility of presence is thus the circle of past and future: genesis emerges into the open from the "not yet" of the future and is covered over by the "no more" of the past. (This line of thought, incidentally, was appropriated by Heidegger in his existential analysis of temporality.) Hence neither future nor past can be a *nihil absolutum;* each contains totality. In Nietzsche's interpretation, the circle of Becoming is the eternal return of the same. The future cannot be emptied of content or it would itself disappear into the past. If on the other hand it were infinite, the past would disappear into the future. That is: the significance of the present depends upon the finitude of past and future in the very specific sense of the comprehensiveness of a perspective or interpretation. In the fragments of the *Nachlass,* Nietzsche occasionally gives this thesis of eternal return a scientific format: it is required by the infinitude of time and the finitude of matter.[32] And in the last years of his productive life, Nietzsche was making plans to study physics in an effort to confirm his thesis of the eternal return. In my opinion, such a project goes counter to the strict sense of Nietzsche's own doctrine. For him, modern physics is itself a perspectival manifestation of the will to power and cannot serve as the basis for interpreting its deepest roots. The error is like that of the analytical thinker who uses mathematics in an attempt to lay bare the foundations of mathematics.

The basis of Nietzsche's teaching is neither scientific nor (in the vulgar sense of the term) metaphysical. Neither, despite points of resemblance to Kant, Fichte, Schelling, and even Hegel, is it marked by transcendental argument, whether actual or as an ideal. We may perhaps use "phenomenological," because of the fluidity of the term, to characterize Nietzsche's description of the temporality of existence. Human life is "always" a dialectical circle of coming-to-be and passing-away, which is to say that "always" is an image of "never," or less cryptically, that the permanent is an image of the transient. What endures is the circularity of temporal flow. The nature of temporality imposes limits upon the content that is able to manifest itself within the perimeter of that circle. It does not merely bring this content to a focus or impose principles of combination and separation onto it. Temporality allows content to acquire significance, but at the price of being emptied of significance. This thought is not as paradoxical as it may initially seem. Significance depends upon human activity. For Nietzsche (as for most of his successors) it is literally senseless to look for the meaning of human life in a source external to it.[33] This view is at least as old as Aristotle's criticism of Plato, however different Aristotle's solution may be from that of Nietzsche. The presence of significant form within human spiritual activity means for Nietzsche the temporality of that form. Aristotle's forms are preserved forever within time by thought thinking itself: the divinization of circularity. Nietzsche replaces the pure intellective god by Dionysus,[34] or pure thinking by the will to power.

In Aristotle, the prince of common sense, pure thinking binds together the world by thinking, not the world, but itself. Is this not a prefiguration of Nietzsche's doctrine of the will to power in which the creative genius thinks

195

and so produces the world, a process that is perpetually repeated in the circle of time? In defense of Nietzsche, it could be argued plausibly that the axiom of philosophy, from its serious formulation in the Platonic dialogues, is the intelligibility of the world. As Socrates admits in the *Philebus* (28c6ff), philosophers actually exalt themselves in agreeing that intellect (*nous*) is the king of heaven and earth. Nietzsche differs from the Greeks in his temporalizing of form, but it is not clear how the doctrine of the world as a focusing of temporalization is less "reasonable" than the doctrine of order as a pure thinking of eternal forms. That is, it is not clear so long as we define clarity in mathematical terms. For the issue is precisely the status of mathematical structures. Are these eternal or temporal? The self-exaltation of the classical philosopher is like the Nietzschean philosopher's perception of nobility. And this perception belongs to the "empirical" ego of the everyday world, even though the perception is "somehow" (to employ an appropriate technical term from Aristotle) of what surpasses empirical perspectives. So long as we stay at a more or less philological transcription of the surface of Nietzsche's thought, there can be in my opinion no reconciliation of the conflict between nobility and radical chaos. In order to preserve Nietzsche's deconstructive enterprise in a positive (but not positivist) form, it is necessary to think through the comprehensive implications of his *political* teaching, not just his ontology. In order to do so, of course, one must come to terms with the ontology, or more accurately, the mēontology, the doctrine of nothingness. But this in turn requires us to distinguish two kinds of rhetoric in Nietzsche, corresponding approximately, at least in their intended functions, to the distinction between analytical and contextual discourse.

Nietzsche's articulation of temporality into finite worlds is hierarchical. Finitude is required for intelligibility, and intelligence is evaluation. The intelligibility of each originative perspective depends upon the finite number of such perspectives; otherwise, we could not perceive their rank. This brings us to the fundamental difficulty in Nietzsche: the opposition between rank (or evaluation) and intrinsic chaos. But this difficulty does not become properly visible if we follow Heidegger in taking Nietzsche as an ontologist or as the last metaphysician.[35] To put it as simply as possible, Heidegger takes Nietzsche to absolutize time, or to transform it into eternity via the doctrine of the eternal return, hence into the traditional notion of being. Heidegger's error, I think, is to take Nietzsche's analysis of time as ultimate, whereas it is only the beginning of his philosophy. (An analogous error is made by those who try to understand Wittgenstein in terms of his doctrines of logic or mathematics.) I agree that the eternal return is the form of the manifestation of the will to power. But the temporalizing process is the presentational mode of originative perspectives. It is indeed ingredient in the perspective *qua* perspective. But for Nietzsche, what is common to every perspective cannot express the uniqueness of every perspective; and each perspective is unique. The essence of each perspective is its complete lack of essentiality; this is a more radical version of Wittgenstein's doctrine of "language games." *Uniqueness is an image, not of eternity, but of chaos.* There is no original corresponding to the image because the very possibility of uniqueness or creativity requires an absence of originals. An original perspective gives to chaos any significance it wills. In this very special sense, the manifestation of chaos is the concealment of chaos, just as for Heidegger the manifestation of Being is the concealment of Being. This is the core of contemporary analytical philosophy, whether in its secular or its crypto-religious species. Whether in the case of the doctrine of possibility held by contemporary modal logicians, or in "ontological" doctrines of difference, creativity, and historicity, nothingness is the Biblical chaos. In the new creation *ex nihilo*, man replaces God. The doctrine is then true to the extent that we can will it to be so. Nietzsche, who resigned his university professorship, is honest enough to say this explicitly; others confess their moral bankruptcy with an ironical wink that justifies the exercise of power. "True" is a meta-linguistic term only in the fantasies of the mathematically bemused. Nietzsche is more honest and more self-conscious: "true" means for him life-enhancing, powerful, or creative.[36] Truth is a fertile dream. If we refuse to dream or if we insist upon an "objective" eternity, then life is emptied of value and the image of chaos is replaced by a sterile fantasm of order.

This is the background for understanding Nietzsche's fundamental difficulty. He insists upon the typically Platonic distinction between high and low, noble and base, or esoteric and exoteric. He insists upon the hierarchical ranking of perspectives, human beings, deeds, and speeches. But he also insists that evaluating is rooted in finitude or temporality. If the intelligible is finite, then the standards must be finite. But for Nietzsche, finite means transient. To the extent that we may speak of forms, they are accessible to desire, not to the intellect, and finally they are accessible to the desire for desire or the will to power. Men value what they desire: this is Nietzsche's link to empiricism and twentieth century rationalism. If the highest activity were disinterested contemplation, the world and eternity itself would be worthless. Paradoxically enough, Nietzsche himself insists upon the worthlessness of the world, of Becoming or chaos, as the necessary condition for the possibility of value, or of a desire that poses its own goals. This is perhaps as close as Nietzsche comes to a transcendental argument; yet it cannot be called that since there are no deductions in Nietzsche but only acts of will. Nietzsche proceeds as a writer by rhetoric rather than by deductive argumentation, not because he is an inferior thinker but because he devotes himself completely to one comprehensive problem: that of the origin, and hence the dream of the finite whole.[37] He is too great a thinker to try to resolve this problem by inappropriate means.

The Early Dream

Nietzsche attempts to rethink negativity as the origin of creation. He is no Christian, but one might perhaps call him "god-intoxicated," in view of his regular association of the will to power with Dionysus. But the Apollo-Dionysus dualism, interesting though it may be, does not go to the heart of Nietzsche's thought. Dionysus and Apollo are images of images. What we want to understand in Nietzsche is the process of imaging an absent or chaotic model. Having looked at the sketch of this process which emerges from the late *Nachlass*, we turn now to some passages from Nietzsche's early publications.

Nietzsche claims to possess an intuition of eternity, but it is one that is only superficially the same as Fichte's. Nietzsche's intuition is of the *Augenblick* or instant of presence as the gateway between future and past. However, it is not the Absolute, but primeval chaos that presents itself in this instant. Perhaps one could say that Nietzsche's intuition recognizes the fate of the Fichtean Absolute. If this intuition is in any sense Platonic (as Heidegger in effect claims), it derives from the doctrine of eros, not of being or the Ideas. In fact, we might reconstitute the Platonic interpretation of the context of analysis by following up this affinity between Nietzsche and the connected themes of eros and divine madness in Plato. Suffice it to say that, in Nietzsche, the *Augenblick* is an image of the eternity of chaos as the source of continuous creation.[38] In Zarathustra's words, "what could one create if gods were present" (*da waren*).[39] In the Fichtean revision of Platonism, form is process. Nietzsche goes beyond this: process is chaos. Chaos is then not accessible in its own terms because it has no terms. Nietzsche's insight into the chaotic interior of order is based upon his refusal to accept what he regarded as the nihilistic consequences of the doctrine of a determinate origin; in that sense it is based upon his own will to power. The insight into chaos is a dream, a "wish-fulfillment" or insistence of conditions preventing significance or health in human life. Whereas the Freudian dreamer poses a nonexistent situation as actual or present and thereby maintains the balance between sickness and health, Nietzsche dreams away presence in favor of absence and thereby asserts the triumph of health over sickness. This is a regular theme in Nietzsche's writings.

We may take our bearings by a remark from *Human, All Too Human*: "we *exist* in prison; we can only dream, not make ourselves free."[40] The clearest commentary on this passage is to be found in *The Dawn*, published three years later (1881). In a paragraph titled "In Prison," Nietzsche says that we live within our horizon as in a prison: "in accordance with these horizons in which, as in prison walls, each of us encloses our senses, we now *measure* the world . . . these are all, all errors in themselves."[41] With the possible exception of the prison rhetoric and the remark about error, this passage could have been written by Wittgenstein. But Nietzsche's rhetoric serves at a minimum to make the human implication of the Wittgensteinian philosophy of language fully visible. Truth and measurement are not accessible to us outside the prison (as they are outside Plato's cave) but like freedom are themselves dreams. One might object that the image of prison makes sense only if Nietzsche knows what it means to be free. But the peculiar force of his doctrine derives from the contention, reminiscent of Spinoza, that to be free is just to know oneself to be a prisoner. The dream of freedom is possible only for a prisoner. The walls of our prison define us, preserve us from chaos, and allow us to enter it in our dreams. On the one hand, then, intelligibility is a consequence of finitude. On the other, finitude is a human project or creation. Again, the parallel with Wittgenstein is exact.

In another striking anticipation of Freud, Nietzsche surmises that "our *dreams* have just the value and significance of *compensating*, up to a certain degree, for that accidental absence of 'nourishment' during the day."[42] Dreams are free interpretations of "the irritation of our nerves during sleep." It would be a mistake to take passages like these too literally as evidence of Nietzsche's "positivist" period. All measures, including those of physiology, are, if we consider them *an sich*, errors. Physiology is itself a dream or an episode in the dream by which the natural scientist frees himself from a metaphysical interpretation of the whole. As Nietzsche says, the interpreter of the irritations of the nervous system himself changes each night. The scientist is as insubstantial as any other image of the dream process by which we make articulate the will to power. The "day" in this passage stands for our perception or feeling (a favorite Nietzschean term) that life is a prison. But such a perception lacks nourishment. One could say that even if true, it arises from a loss of will power and the consequent deterioration of the dreams or perceptions that disguise and make bearable our prison existence.

Because Nietzsche makes every allowance for fertile contradiction, we can discern a threat to the inner coherence of his revelation. It is one thing to prophesy the fecundity of chaos, but something else again to prophesy chaotically. Nietzsche both denies and asserts the accessibility of truth. Taking this even further, he claims that the assertion of the truth is both exhilarating and enervating. To know that one is a prisoner is to enter the bright midnight of global nihilism that is the ostensible precursor, or even shadow, of the high noon in which Nietzsche's doctrine is accepted. We may attempt to resolve this difficulty as follows. The gradual enervation or decadence of European man produces both the base nihilist and Nietzsche's version of the noble implications of nihilism. Both Nietzsche and the base nihilist perceive or feel the inner chaos. For Nietzsche, however, this feeling allows the exercise of will, or the dream by which chaos is transformed into a doctrine of creativity. The truth is a prison in more than one sense. First, all conceptions of truth are, as we have seen, horizons or perspectives. In the terminology of contemporary analytical philosophy, truth is a semantic property of a meta-language, or an interpretation of a language with a finite, well-defined scope of application.[43] Second, the insight into the chaotic interior of perspectives is accessible only to one who dwells within a prison, who is given consciousness and intensity by the bounds or measures of a dream, albeit of what one knows to be a dream. This is the conscious formulation of the claim by the analytical philosopher to possess an insight into the restricted nature of the truth-predicate. The analyst, however, pays no attention to the "dream" by which he sees that truth is a predicate. Is this dream true? Third, the vision of chaos itself binds us to necessity or *amor fati* (as in Spinoza). In contemporary terms, necessity is a formal trick, the essence of which is chance, contingency, or possibility. It is at this stage that Nietzsche's solution seems to break down. If health, creativity, and nobility all depend upon the imposition of an intense perspective upon oneself as well as upon others, then, as Nietzsche says, art is worth more than truth. Must we not then *forget* or cover over the truth as soon as we have perceived it? Is not such a covering-over affected by the charm of mathematical creativity?

Whereas Plato teaches recollection, Nietzsche (and *a fortiori*, contemporary analytical philosophy) advocates forgetfulness. It is not mere logic-chopping on our part to refer to this as Nietzsche's inconsistency. This inconsistency expresses, and is intended to express, the chaotic interior or ultimate origin. The origin, as chaos, is self-contradictory in its "utterances." By analogy, if logic is a free creation of the human spirit, why can there not be alternate and conflicting axioms of contradiction? If we insist that Nietzsche's doctrine is either true or false, he replies that its truth lies in its persuasiveness or the power of his will and so in its very falseness. This is a poetical version of the thesis that our choice of two-valued, three-valued, or n-valued logics depends upon our intention. Some will regard this as the deepest rehabilitation of sophistry. Others will be exhilarated by it. What to one man is courage is to another enervated self-deception. We must grant to Nietzsche, however, that this very difference is couched in terms of intuition, evaluation, and *passion*, not of logical deduction. Only the noble soul will perceive the nobility of a noble life; and Nietzsche identifies truth in the best sense, not with a predicate, but with a perception of nobility. As is shown by his defense of courage in the face of our insight into chaos, Nietzsche never reduces nobility to an image of chaos. Rather he insists upon the truth of chaos in order to sustain nobility.

Hence the assertion in *The Dawn* that ours is a dreamt or phantom world; that although the dream life possesses a freedom of interpretation not available to the waking life, the nervous irritations are similarly interpreted in both worlds. There is no essential difference between dreaming and waking.[44] This is neither cynicism nor positivism but a testing of our courage. Waking is on the one hand an inferior version of dreaming. On the other hand, it is wakefulness that provides us with our comprehension of dreaming. We are not asleep when we recognize that our moral judgments and evaluations are only "images and fantasies about a to us unknown physiological process."[45] Again, "physiological process" is a mediated image of chaos. But Nietzsche wills us not to dissolve into chaos: "nothing is *more* your own than your dreams."[46] I become myself by dreaming, and this is something deeper than to imagine the significance of my life in accord with the paradigm of physiology. Nietzsche advocates, not quite that we forget ourselves in our dreams, but that we awaken to ourselves within the dream that most fully expresses the will to power.

The Dreams of Zarathustra

Thus Spoke Zarathustra is the most mature and hence the most difficult presentation of Nietzsche's thought. Since the book is a revelation rather than a treatise or the conscious dreaming of a dream, we may expect a certain oddity of language with concomitant problems of interpretation. I want first to consider a selection of passages that are crucial to the theme of original and image. In Part One, in a section called "Of the Afterworldly," we are told that "at one time Zarathustra too cast his delusion beyond man, like all the afterworldly."[47] That is, he once attempted to imagine a creator-god. But even then Zarathustra was closer to Freud than to Christ: "the world of a suffering and tortured god, the world then seemed to me" (II, 297). In keeping with the views expressed in *The Dawn*, this suffering (or alienated) god is taken to be a divine poet, exactly like the mortal dreaming in his prison cell. "A dream the world then seemed to me, and the poem of a god; colored smoke before the eyes of a divine malcontent." This god is evidently somewhere between the base nihilism consequent upon the insight into chaos that sickness or decadence vouchsafes, and the creativity of health. Zarathustra does not explain why he is dissatisfied ("the creator wanted to look away from himself—hence he created the world"). Obviously, however, this god is unfinished (like the animal "man")[48] and dreams in order to produce the illusion of wholeness.

"Drunken joy is for the sufferer to look away from his suffering and to lose himself. Drunken joy and loss of self the world once seemed to me" (II, 297). Since the suffering god is a product of Zarathustra's imagination, we may assume that he represents a stage on Zarathustra's own path toward health or return to the earth. When Zarathustra comes to recognize that this god is an image of himself, he does not reject the significance of the image. The creator is indeed driven by suffering to complete himself in a comprehensive expression of the will to power. But he then grasps the central insight into the interior nature of every comprehensive perspective: "This world, the eternally incomplete, image of an eternal contradiction and an incomplete image—a drunken joy for its incomplete creator—thus seemed to me once the world." The world is an incomplete image of the eternal contradiction of chaos, and it is incomplete because contradiction is self-canceling. There is no speculative logic of negativity in Nietzsche. The inner temporality of the world exemplifies the perpetual flux of chaos. We note in passing that if it is true to say that eternity is temporal, the copula in the expression collapses as it is asserted: the defining bounds are actually complementary arcs of a single circle, the eternal return of the same. Each life is an incomplete image of the circle that it conceals by the intensity of the will and reveals by the dynamics of its own shifting desires, viewpoints, or anticipations of chaos.

Zarathustra came to see that he had created this god "out of my own ashes and fire" (II, 297), the tangible symbols of the dialectic of creation and destruction represented by the image of the phoenix. All gods and hence all worlds are man-made. It would be suffering and torment, now that we are healed of our belief in gods, to return to a belief in ghosts. More important, it would be a degradation or "bowing down" (*Erniedrigung*) of man before his own creation (II, 298). This is a delicate point in Nietzsche since, as we have already seen, health requires us to be assimilated into the world or perspective we have ourselves willed into being. Strictly speaking, there is no reason to exclude *all* worship of gods, as Nietzsche's approving attitude toward Dionysus suggests. Presumably the difficulty is overcome by distinguishing between debasing and exalting worship. Here Zarathustra is more categorical, and more careless. He says that the cause of "all gods and afterworlds" is "a weariness that wants to reach the last stage with one leap, with a leap of death, a poor unknowing weariness that no longer wills to will." Man, as in the Platonic doctrine of eros, is *permanently unfinished*. This is another expression of "the eternal contradiction." Completeness is death, whereas life is the desire for desire, or discontinuous negativity. To employ an appropriate metaphor, a "completeness proof" would be proof of our loss of humanity. The inconsistency of existence is thus a consequence of discontinuity; and this in turn emerges from the ambiguous nature of the insight into originative chaos. A refusal to bow down before one's own creation is equivalent to knowledge of the emptiness of one's own dreams, and so of health, life, the will itself.

Zarathustra does not refer to this aspect of the problem. Weariness, he indicates, comes from the body's despair of the earth or from the inability to preserve the intensity of creation *ex nihilo*. It leads man "to that dehumanized, inhuman world, that is a heavenly nothingness" (II, 298). The implication is that the strength to create is also sufficient to preserve us against the enervating effects of total lucidity concerning the emptiness of heaven. The "belly of Being" speaks only to the man of strong digestion. Nevertheless this is an intermediate stage in Zarathustra's revelation, as becomes clear from his next series of assertions concerning the ego, "this creating, willing, evaluating I, which is the measure and the value of things." The turn to the "I" is intermediate between the turn away from gods and the expression of the roots of the will to power or (in Nietzsche's usual formulation) the self. "A new pride my I taught me," namely, "I teach men a new will: to will this way which men have blindly taken" (II, 299). But this is ambiguous. How can we will the way we have taken without subordinating it to the deepest pride of the I, a pride springing from the knowledge that man creates *ex nihilo*? Does not Nietzsche teach that all lives are lies because the truth is chaos, and that in order to inoculate ourselves against the base nihilism we must forget our knowledge as soon as we have acquired it, and hence too the pride of the I, via assimilation into a dynamic and comprehensive dream?

The invocation to return to the earth, or the claim that the healthy body speaks honestly and purely "of the meaning of the earth" (II, 300) is usually couched in terms of creativity. However, death, too, is a return to the earth. In the next paragraph, "On the Despisers of the Body," we learn that the waking knower identifies the I, the soul, and the spirit, as images of the body (II, 300f). But the body itself is the image of the earth. Fidelity to the earth, here called wakefulness, is in fact immersion within a dream, serving to conceal the true wakefulness or knowledge of the ultimate significance of the earth as an image of chaos. To say that man creates values is to state the inverse of the doctrine of the meaninglessness of the world. Yet, as in the crucial paragraph, "On the Thousand and One Goals," where tablets of laws or ends are implicitly compared to fairy tales, Zarathustra, when told to prevent man from succumbing to boredom, again camouflages the inner meaning with the rhetoric of creative warriors. The creator destroys; the still missing thousand-and-first goal is the yoke for the neck of the thousand peoples, namely, creation as both will to power and the eternal return, which yokes man to fate. So creativity and freedom are also slavery (II, 323). Chaos, the origin of creation, also negates the value of creation. We must therefore lie to ourselves, or will that our creation be meaningful.

We turn now to Part Two, which begins with the awakening of Zarathustra from a dream in which his own innocence shows him the error of the gift-giving prophet of Part One. Zarathustra spoke too soon (II, 341: "The Child with the Mirror"). It is significant that this enlightenment comes to Zarathustra in a dream. But one must be awake in order to interpret a dream. The interpretation is developed in the next paragraph: "Upon the Blessed Isles." If a comprehensive perspective is a dream, then the first part of *Zarathustra* was the dream of a dream. In the second part, Zarathustra alternates between dreaming and awakening. Here, Zarathustra is awake. The time is autumn: "pure sky and afternoon" (II, 343). We are between noon and evening, and the teachings of this paragraph are autumn fruit. Zarathustra has seen the great noon, but his revelation was not understood. If his disciples could not assimilate the summer fruit, then Zarathustra must offer them something riper. The afternoon fruit is easier to digest because it is more decadent than the fruit of noon.

Zarathustra shifts from the fullness or ripeness of the figs to the fullness of the sky and afternoon. The horizon of this afternoon world is his accommodation to his disciples. The horizon opens out into distant seas (just as God looked down on the waters of chaos). Man replaces God, who is exposed as a "conjurer" (II, 344). Our conjectures must not reach further than our creative will. That is, we cannot *create* a God who is an origin distinct from ourselves. We cannot will anything distinct from ourselves because "I" am my will. I am the origin; in willing myself, I become the superman. The superman is also a conjecture or a lie, but one that man can accept. The disciples can be the fathers and the forefathers of the creators of the superman. They can dream of the dream of creative self-overcoming. The will to truth is "that everything be transformed into the thinkable for man, the visible for man, the feelable by man" (II, 344). It is in fact the dream of man as *measure*: the prison walls of *The Dawn* are transformed into the measure of one's perspective or world. Thus the great series of dreams of Descartes, which led to the production of the universal method of order and measure, terminate in Zarathustra's dream of measure as the will to power.[49]

What is the fundamental difference between the afternoon teaching and the morning teaching of Part One? Part One takes place in the city of the motley cow, or in nineteenth-century bourgeois Europe. Zarathustra is not understood because he addresses the enlightened intellectuals who have mistaken decadence for progress. In this light, the "tricks" of the circus performers, and especially perhaps of the tightrope walker, awaited eagerly by the intellectuals as Zarathustra arrives in the city, correspond to the contemporary intellectual's fascination with technique. Part Two takes place on the mountain top from which Zarathustra originally descended. Whereas he was previously alone, he is now accompanied by disciples, who must therefore have returned with him from the city of the motley cow. Zarathustra asserts at the beginning of Part Two (II, 342) that he requires new ways and new speeches that will take him across distances and wide seas, driven by the whip of wickedness. I note in passing here a Machiavellian revision of the Mosaic theme that figures regularly in the major works of modern philosophy. Zarathustra says that he is going, not to Jerusalem, but down again to his friends and enemies. However, there is no indication in the second part of such a descent. Instead, the mountain top blends seamlessly into the blessed isles or a dream-like revision of Zarathustra's original solitude, now peopled with his disciples. There is no essential difference between these disciples and the residents of the city of the motley cow. The name "blessed isles" conveys the insubstantial nature of the synthesis of Zarathustra's solitude with even the best of his own generation. We are still very far from a genuine grasp and enactment of his real teaching.

The inadequacy of Zarathustra's disciples is an enduring theme of the book. One may consult in particular the paragraphs of Part Four entitled "The Welcome," "On the Higher Men," "The Song of Melancholy," and "The Sign." Accordingly, I suggest that there is no essential difference between the teachings of the first and the second parts. To employ new ways of speech is not the same as to assert new teachings. The rhetorical differences do perhaps accent the role of dreams in *Zarathustra*. In other words, Part Two contains a more affirmative version of Zarathustra's teaching than does Part One. The emphasis is largely upon the joyous consequence of willing: "And how would you bear life without this hope, you lovers of knowledge?" Or again: "But let me reveal my heart to you entirely, you friends: *if* there were gods, how could I endure not to be a god! *Hence* there are no gods" (II, 344). If Zarathustra is a deity, his disciples must worship him—scarcely the mark of supermen. And so the positive aspect of Zarathustra's doctrine becomes a revelation accommodated to the intelligence of natural disciples. "God is a conjecture"; hence we too may conjecture of our own divinity. Of course, "God is a thought that makes crooked all that is straight," but this means that the eternal return is the chaotic "essence" of each conjectural creation. "All the permanent—that is only an image. And the poets lie too much" (II, 345). In sum, Zarathustra gives hints of the dark side of his teaching, but covers these over with the affirmative language of the prophet and physician: "Creation—that is the great redemption from suffering, and life's growing light" (II, 345). In order to create, we require suffering. Nevertheless, the rhetorical context implies the triumph of the suffering of birth over the suffering of death.

We can now connect the positive statement of Zarathustra's afternoon teaching to our initial formulation of Nietzsche's central doctrine. Eternity and temporality are images of each other or of the origin as chaos. *The origin is whatever we will it to be.* This is the climax of the Cartesian innovation, by which human will determines the origin *qua* presence of clear and distinct ideas.[50] The penultimate question, also to be found in Descartes's formulation of the context of analysis, is whether we will to be sick or healthy. In Descartes, there is no surface ambiguity associated with the desire for health, since Descartes begins with the conception of man as the desire for power.[51] In Nietzsche, however, "health" is an exoteric name for a contingent disguise of chaos. Nietzsche is a decadent Descartes. There is, then, an ultimate question in Nietzsche, not fully faced by him but implicit in his writings. *Why is health better than sickness?* This is either the same question as, or a variant of, the question concerning the distinction between the noble and the base. It also casts light upon the relative rank of Nietzsche's own doctrine as a product of decadence, in comparison with what may be called unconscious creations. Zarathustra claims both that "willing frees" and also that "to say it more honestly: this very destiny—my will wills." The honest doctrine of destiny or chaos as the will to power is that *I will it to be so.* As a creator, and therefore healthy, I do this in a higher sense than does Nietzsche (or Zarathustra), who is sick but striving for health. The doctrine of human projects is itself a human project. If, however, art is worth more than truth, what is the value of the truth of the doctrine of art? If truth is a work of art, why not some other truth, say, the truth of decadence?

We turn now to the evening and the darkness of night. Zarathustra first gives an affirmative interpretation to the night. It is the source of his soul and the songs of love or creativity ("The Night Song," II, 362ff). There is, however, a darker side to nightlight. The world we create is "the mirror and image" of ourselves (II, 351). If our values are passengers in the bark of the will, adrift on the river of Becoming (II, 369), then nightlight is of course moonlight, the phosphorescent afterglow of fireworks, and thereafter the same as the light that illuminates the mirrors of traditional and sterile metaphysicians who touch "with the eye alone" ("On Immaculate Perception," II, 378). The night teaching is thus the darker side of what is affirmatively presented as the afternoon teaching, itself in turn an accommodated version of the initial revelation. In "On the Poets," a disciple asks Zarathustra why he previously said that the poets lie too much. The master replies: "I am not one of those whom one may ask about their why . . . But what was it that Zarathustra once said to you? That the poets lie too much? But Zarathustra too is a poet. Do you now believe that he spoke the truth here? Why do you believe that?" To this the disciple naively replies: " 'I believe in Zarathustra.' But Zarathustra shook his head and smiled" (II, 382). This passage scarcely requires commentary. Zarathustra partly covers his tracks by next repudiating the poets as "shallow seas." But how can we fail to infer that this is a noble lie, *ad captum vulgi*, to employ an appropriate phrase from Spinoza?

The puzzle of Zarathustra's ultimate teaching is treated most extensively in "The Soothsayer." Again, it is presented as an extraordinarily difficult dream. Also present is the enthusiastic disciple who offers an affirmative interpretation of the dream. The paragraph opens with the speech of a soothsayer who envisions the coming of "a doctrine, accompanied by a faith: 'All is empty, all is the same, all has been' " (II, 388). This doctrine seems to have fallen down "from the evil moon"; it destroys the fruit of fields and heart (II, 389). It dries mankind into tinder; a fire would produce ashes but no phoenix. Mankind longs for a sea in which to drown itself: even death is inaccessible to the last men or nihilists. "Verily, we have become too weary even to die. We are still waking and living on—in tombs" (II, 389). Thus the soothsayer. Is he warning Zarathustra of the disastrous consequences of the doctrine of the will to power? The prophecy touches Zarathustra's heart and changes him. "He walked about sad and weary" and spoke to his disciples of the coming of the long twilight. "Alas, how shall I save my light through it?" (II, 389). This is the dilemma of the previous versions of Nietzsche's teachings. Nietzsche's affirmations are virtually indistinguishable from the nihilism he condemns. And what if the will to endure in the heart of darkness is lacking? What if the force of the rhetoric of creativity is sterilized by the routine of technique?

If man can neither live nor die, his condition is like that of a shade: a tombdweller, or evil image (lit by an "evil moon") of the living and the dead. After three days of fasting and silence, Zarathustra falls into a deep sleep, watched by his disciples throughout the long night. When he awakens he tells them a dream that is obviously inspired by the prophecy of the soothsayer. Zarathustra has interpreted the prophecy in a dream, and the result is indeed a riddle wrapped in an enigma. One thinks here of the central dilemma of Marxism concerning the future; necessity is diluted by the requirement of the will to revolution. In both cases the future is defined by dreams. Zarathustra states at the outset that his dream is still a riddle: its meaning is imprisoned like a shade in a tomb. In the dream, Zarathustra had turned his back on life and become a nightwatchman of graves, "a guardian of tombs upon the lonely mountaincastle of death" (II, 389). We have moved from the afternoon to the long twilight, and thence via the long night into the kingdom of death. Zarathustra has turned away from life but he is not himself dead. "Life that had been overcome looked at me out of glass coffins. I breathed the odor of dusty eternities" (II, 390).

Zarathustra is intermediate, the link between life and death. Since life is in a coffin, Zarathustra is more alive than life itself. As the watchman, he has presumably been employed by death; yet the need for his services implies the possibility of disturbances or of a resurrection of life. Is such a possibility contrary to the interests of death, or is it not rather the case that death depends upon life as the origin of its subjects? The doctrine of the eternal return ("dusty eternities") thus guarantees the perpetual replenishment of the kingdom of death. Zarathustra in this dream is an ambiguous anticipatory image of the *Augenblick*, of the present instant as the gateway between future and past. The watchman is the presence before the ambiguous overcoming of life by death, or the circle of temporality.

The crucial question of Nietzsche's thought is in my opinion visible at this point. Can the doctrine of creativity master death, or is the "nightwatchman" condemned to the role of perpetual servant? Does the possibility of resurrection contain a source of meaning and value for life, or does the cycle of resurrections occur throughout eternity *within* the kingdom of death? "The brightness of midnight was always about me; loneliness crouched next to it; and as a third, death-rattle silence, the worst of my friends" (II, 390). These three replace Zarathustra's animals in the dark side of the image of high noon. Throughout the last three books of *Zarathustra*, the opening revelation is interpreted via dreams (cf. "on the Vision and the Riddle" in Part Three and "At Noon" in Part Four). The will to power and the eternal return are dreams or creations, hence images of chaos, just as the sun is an image of night and Zarathustra's animals are symbols of death as well as of nature. To overcome nihilism is thus also to be reconciled with the world as it is, or *amor fati*. Creativity is invoked as an image of the meaning of destruction. However, the converse interpretation is also possible. Which one we choose is a matter, not of logic, but of mood or will. Life is a riddle: it either contains or is contained by death. Nietzsche is honest enough to state the riddle, even if he does so in the form of a riddle. Analytical philosophy, the ostensible "bright side" of contemporary thought, banishes the riddle to the extra-philosophical suburbs of the soul, just as it had earlier banished the soul itself. Unfortunately, the emptiness remains.

To return to the dream, "thus time passed and crawled, if time still existed: what do I know of that?" (II, 390). This is an apt description of the present, which both is and is not a part of time. "But eventually that happened which awakened me." The watchman's keys cannot open the gates for an approaching black coffin, which is deposited before him by a raging wind:

> And amid the roaring and whistling and shrilling the coffin burst and spewed out a thousand-fold laughter. And from a thousand grimaces of children, angels, owls, fools, and butterflies as big as children, it laughed and mocked and roared at me. Then I was terribly frightened; it threw me to the ground. And I cried in horror as I have never cried. And my own cry awakened me—and I came to my senses. (II, 390)

Perhaps we are meant to remember the thousand peoples of the thousand goals. This apart, I suggest that the black coffin is the meaninglessness of death. Zarathustra's "keys" cannot open the gates for it. *It comes from beyond his doctrines*, if not quite from beyond his dreams, and on the winds of chaos, which are not quite a creation but an image of the absent origin of creativity. The contents of the coffin are described in a marvelous mixture of randomness and design: innocent laughter (children, angels, fools, butterflies) and the nocturnal symbol of wisdom, the owl, that does not speak but hoots. The wisdom of death is that it flattens the contradictory discourse of life into a single tone. Its innocence is its meaninglessness or laughter at the pretensions of the living. Death both mocks and terrifies Zarathustra because *it is impervious to his will*. This is not the free death of Zarathustra's courageous choice. He dreams it as the negative origin of his own awakening. Since the origin is "present" only as absent or as devoid of meaning, we cannot return to it except via dream-images, and then only to be repelled or awakened: that is, thrust back into life. It is this "thrownness" (Heidegger's *Geworfenheit*) that Nietzsche chooses to interpret as the will to power. However, as the present dream indicates, death, night, and nihilism are all closer to chaos than are life, day, and creativity. Death brings us into the absent origin, into nothingness. Death is the reality, whereas life is only the dream.

Nietzsche's dilemma, as I have been regularly asserting, is the explicit form of the dilemma intrinsic to contemporary analytical philosophy. This is because Nietzsche, very far from being an irrational mystic or pseudo-philosopher, is as direct a consequence of the modern scientific Enlightenment as are the logical analysts and specialists in recursive functions. If we take Descartes as the useful symbol of the philosophical beginnings of modernity, the analysts stem from Cartesian method, whereas Nietzsche is the last conscious representative of Cartesian rhetoric, or perhaps more accurately, of Descartes's doctrine of the passions and so of the will. In the analytical community, in keeping with the loss of consciousness characteristic of rules and routines, Descartes's doctrine of the passions is not studied, or if it is, never with the "passion" invested in his "arguments." Despite all attempts to overcome the classical empiricist split between theory and practice, despite increasing recognition that this split is itself a practical act of the will (thus transforming theory into practice), the split continues to dominate the practices of analytical philosophers. Nietzsche's fundamental question remains that of Plato and of every great thinker: what is the good life? Nietzsche's anti-Platonism stems from the belief that this question cannot be meaningfully posed in the Platonic context. We ought to take seriously Nietzsche's anti-Christianism as well, something that is not done as frequently. Christianity, or more generally, revealed religion, is a rival to the classical philosophical desire to think, and thus to assume responsibility for, *the whole*. Christianity and modern science, far from being rivals, are in accord on two basic premises. The first is the radical contingency of the spatio-temporal world. And the second is that the question of the good life cannot be answered by philosophy. The conceptual analyst clears up logical or syntactical muddles; at the most, he checks the validity of arguments purporting to establish that one life is better than another. But the actual choice of the life is a *value*, precisely Nietzsche's term. And values are neither valid nor invalid.

Nietzsche does not quite make it explicit, but he at least provides us with the evidence to formulate the following dilemma. Because there is no origin, we can make the origin whatever we will. Each finite will is the source of its own uniqueness: hence the indistinguishability of value and valuelessness. The final justification of the central importance of courage is that we must insist upon value where none exists. Zarathustra's most beloved disciple "quickly" offers an affirmative interpretation of the dream. "Your life itself interprets this dream for us, O Zarathustra. Are you not yourself the wind . . . Are you not yourself the coffin . . . ?" On this account, Zarathustra is himself the children's laughter that overcomes his enemies, represented here as the death over which life triumphs (II, 391). But this is not a satisfactory interpretation, as is clear from its failure to take into account all the symbols in the dream. And Zarathustra himself plainly does not accept the interpretation. After a silent period of detachment during which he becomes a stranger to his disciples, they lift him up and put him back on his feet. The support of the disciples once more awakens Zarathustra, and he supports them in turn by requesting a good meal to atone for bad dreams. "Thus spoke Zarathustra. But then he looked a long time into the face of the disciple who had played the dream-interpreter, and he shook his head" (II, 392). The gesture speaks for itself.

The doctrine of the eternal return is represented by other symbols in Part Two of *Zarathustra*: a bridge, a precipice, the "stillest hour" (corresponding to midday). In order to give substance to these symbols, Nietzsche has Zarathustra in dramatic locations other than on his mountain top. But the comprehensive structure of Part Two is that of an afternoon spent with his disciples from the city of the motley cow. At the end of Part Two, Zarathustra announces that he must depart for the second time. Initially, Zarathustra gave up his solitude to preach to his enemies. Now, having preached to his friends, he must return to his solitude, compelled by his mistress, "The Stillest Hour" (II, 399ff). In Part Three, Zarathustra turns from his friends into himself. The episodes of this part dramatize the maxim, uttered by Zarathustra in the opening paragraph "The Wanderer," that "in the end, one must experience only oneself" (II, 403). The key to this part lies in the following remarks: "What returns, what finally comes home to me, is my own self" and "I stand before my final peak now and before that which has been saved up for me the longest. Alas, now I must face my hardest path! Alas, I have begun my loneliest walk!" In this part, "peak and abyss—this is now joined together" (II, 404). The stillest hour condemned Zarathustra as not yet hard enough to rule. As he himself puts it, "I lack the lion's voice for commanding" (II, 400). The initial solitude of ten years was a preparation for still deeper solitude; in this sense the sojourn with enemies and friends was a detour. The unity of peak and abyss, or the overcoming of the distinction between enemies and friends represents Zarathustra's surrender of mankind as the necessary condition of final acceptance of the eternal return. Whereas previously Zarathustra was nightwatchman in the kingdom of the dead, he must now himself assume the regal role. The final acceptance of the eternal return is also the ultimate expression of the will to power. Having accomplished this, Zarathustra recalls his friends. But this does not contradict the essential solitude of the third part, any more than the change of scene in the second part alters the essential community of Zarathustra and his friends, whether on the mountain top or on the flatland of the blessed isles.

We turn now to paragraph two in Part Three, "On the Vision and the Riddle." Zarathustra is on a ship bound for a long voyage, far from the blessed isles. As is clear from paragraph three ("On Involuntary Bliss," II, 411), the ship and all aboard it symbolize Zarathustra's conscience. The voyage of conscience is in response to the criticism of his mistress, the stillest hour, that he is not yet ready for commanding the greatest deeds. Zarathustra speaks in sympathy with those who wish to live dangerously and, drunk with riddles, hate to deduce where guessing is possible (II, 406). "To you alone I tell the riddle that I *saw*, the vision of the loneliest." The account begins with the description of a gloomy walk Zarathustra took not long ago "through the deadly pallor of dusk." We are between afternoon and night. Zarathustra will be given another chance to assume mastery over death.

Zarathustra is walking upward with great difficulty on a stony mountain path. At each step he must defy the spirit of gravity, "my devil and archenemy," who sits on his back, pulling him downward, "half dwarf, half mole, lame, making lame, dripping lead into my ear, leaden thoughts into my brain" (II, 407). We see again that the advice to return to the earth is ambiguous. In exoteric language, the creator draws sustenance from his instincts, blood, or body, all symbols of genesis as the will to power. More fundamentally, however, the vision of the roots of creativity comes only from above, to the dancer or eagle.[52] The way up is not the same as the way down. We note a difficulty in the image of the "circle" of the eternal return, which is the same as the earlier difficulty of reconciling nobility and the worthlessness of the world.

The spirit of gravity is the heaviness that prevents dancing on mountain peaks (cf. II, 419ff). It is the dizziness that accompanies us to the edge of the abyss and threatens to send us plunging down into what Zarathustra calls "pity." Gravity may more simply be called piety toward tradition. There is also a reference to the lack of hardness, noted earlier, in the face of man's solitary condition at the edge of chaos. Self-pity is a sickness that generates wicked dreams. It can be vanquished only by the "best slayer, courage that *attacks*," that is, not simply by resolution or *Gelassenheit* but by the creation of meaning

(II, 407). We require a good dream (like good digestion), or health rather than sickness; but we become healthy through an act of will. We must will the *amor fati*, not fall into it as into an abyss. The active rather than the reactive courage "slays even death itself, for it says, 'Was that life? Well then! Once more!' " (II, 408). The Christian compassion that initiates the choice of immortality in Christ is rejected in favor of the courageous choice of the eternal recurrence of the self. This is the deeper corollary to the free choice of an appropriate death (a theme again borrowed from Nietzsche by Heidegger).

The dwarf or spirit of gravity responds to Zarathustra's challenge by jumping from his shoulder onto a nearby stone. He does this, not because he is frightened of Zarathustra, but out of curiosity, presumably directed toward a gateway on the spot they have just reached. The word "curious" (*der Neugierige*; again cf. Heidegger) designates the dwarf's lack of emotional resonance or depth. It is Zarathustra who explains the situation to the dwarf. The gateway is the eternal present, connecting the two infinite and mutually contradictory paths of past and future eternity. The name of the gateway, written above it, is "instant" (*Augenblick*). No one, says Zarathustra, has yet followed either path to the end. This is because no one has yet grasped the significance of the gateway or the structure of temporality. The paths are contradictory because the past negates the future. Yet whoever stands in the gateway or correctly grasps the present must be on both paths at once.

The dwarf murmurs contemptuously: "All that is straight lies. All truth is crooked; time itself is a circle" (II, 408). But the dwarf has trivialized the nature of time; his contempt is the wrong mood. Zarathustra angrily replies: "do not make things too easy for yourself! Or I shall let you crouch where you are crouching, lamefoot; and it was I who carried you to this *height*." Nietzsche in effect does not claim to have created the gateway or the doctrine of eternal return. His originality lies in the creation of the *sense or significance* of the gateway. This is Nietzsche's version of the Kantian doctrine of the conceptualization of temporality as the essence of the human world. It is his version of semantics, and thus his solution to the problem of the relation between theory and practice. In the doctrine of the will to power, Nietzsche teaches us to appropriate the eternal Becoming as *my* project. I must stand in the gateway; no one else can do it for me. And I do so, not by a transcendental deduction or even an existential analysis, but by an act of will, by the spiritual attunement of courage. The result is a paradox, even a contradiction. The gateway is empty until I actively step into it. It must therefore be *an sich*, independent of my action precisely in order for me to be able actively to appropriate it. But since this act of appropriation produces the meaning of the gateway, it must be meaningless *an sich*. The empty and meaningless gateway is the necessary precondition to the activity by which I step into it and thereby create meaning for it and myself. So the gateway, and temporality, are not just chaos, but the *presence of absence*. The gateway is the origin understood as nothingness; it is the *nihil* from which I shape my image.

Meaning is willed, created, the result of action. This is basically the doctrine of intuitionism as applied to philosophical semantics. We cannot will literally anything we please, but we will the structure of significance of a world.[53] The line from Nietzsche to Nelson Goodman is considerably straighter than is generally recognized. We note that it is not possible to say that man *always* stands in the gateway and needs only to become fully self-conscious. This, after all, is the traditional doctrine of Being or eternity, and of the reactive or contemplative man rejected by Nietzsche. Even the German speculative tradition teaches a mode of production that culminates in arrival at an eternal absolute. Furthermore, since there is no genuine meaning until I step into the gateway, since both I and the gateway are meaningless until this conjunction via the will to power occurs, how can one explain the creation of meaning from the union of two sources of meaninglessness, two apertures into nothingness? From what source does the will to power derive its energy? Is not the will to power or the pulsebeat of genesis simply another image of the gateway? If I explain my activity as an exemplification of the will to power, then I am accounting for my capacity to step into the gateway by the fact that the gateway is empty. Such a choice is indeed empty. Such a willing lacks volition.

This paradox is not stated by Zarathustra. Instead he asks whether it is not the case that whatever walks *must* have walked this path, i.e., stepped into or passed through the gateway before (II, 409). "Must we not eternally return?" To this question one may respond with another. If we are eternally passing through the gate, in what sense can we genuinely will, or choose to step into the gateway? The doctrine of the eternal return requires that we are eternally choosing. But the eternal act of choosing is altogether different from, and indeed cancels, the doctrine of the unique choice of eternal return. Perhaps the most that can be said is this: reconciliation with the world as it is, or *amor fati*, amounts to an acceptance of the identity of eternal choosing with the will to choose at this unique moment. We may grant Nietzsche the impossibility of stating fully a doctrine of uniqueness, or one that requires to be uniquely fulfilled by each individual who accepts it. Nevertheless, it cannot be overlooked that the circumstances required by human creativity, in the radical sense of creation *ex nihilo*, also serve to empty the creative act of its substance. Spinoza's definition of freedom as knowledge of bondage is perhaps defensible. Nietzsche's definition of creativity as chaos is perhaps indefensible.

Little wonder that Zarathustra experiences a growing fear as he speaks of the eternal return, and again experiences pity: the dwarf, the gateway, a spider crawling in the moonlight (whose web represents the eternal return), all have disappeared. In their place is a man lying in the moonlight before Zarathustra, and a dog howling for help (II, 410). The man is a shepherd, gagging on a black snake that hangs out of his mouth, having bitten fast while he slept. The snake appears at the end of the preface to Part One, coiled round the neck of an eagle that soars through the sky in wide circles. There the snake is the eternal return, supported in flight by the eagle's courage and strength. Here the eagle is a shepherd, or pre-Nietzschean man. The guardian of sheep may be the Platonic king or Christ. Zarathustra cannot tear the snake out of the shepherd's throat. At last he cries out: "Bite! Bite its head off! Bite!"

Before revealing the climax to this vision, Zarathustra interrogates his audience as to the identity of the shepherd, the "loneliest one." He gives no answer here. The language of "The Convalescent" (II, 464) strongly implies that the shepherd is Zarathustra himself and that the snake is the disgust with mankind that must be overcome in order to free Zarathustra for his final ascent. If so, this seems to be inconsistent with Zarathustra's regular denial that he is himself, or can become, a superman. The markedly rhapsodic character of "The Convalescent" makes it hard to cite as clear evidence for the identification in question, but the implication is nonetheless visible. In my reading, the human spirit that created the Christian perspective is now in the death throes of nihilism. To the extent that Zarathustra represents the human spirit in its (almost) full range of possibilities, these two identifications of the shepherd may be connected together. The snake, symbol of nihilism, is also the symbol of the eternal return. Zarathustra concludes his account of the vision in an affirmative, exhilarated sense. The shepherd bites off the snake's head as Zarathustra advises, spits it far away, and leaps up transformed: "No longer shepherd, no longer human—one changed, radiant, *laughing!*"

The problematic nature of the shepherd inspires a continuous longing in Zarathustra that makes it hard for him to live or die. This again leaves it unclear whether the shepherd is the superman. Another interpretation is possible. If the snake is the doctrine of the eternal return, may not the restoration of mankind to health depend upon the *rejection* of Zarathustra's most fundamental teaching? As always, one finds in the speeches of Zarathustra's solitude a radical ambiguity concerning the meaning of his own doctrines. Of course, Zarathustra's new tablets are only "half-covered by writing" (II, 443). A doctrine of uniqueness and radical creativity, of philosophers of the future who give themselves their own laws,[54] cannot be stated fully without suppressing what it teaches. But more important, the condition of uniqueness and radical creativity is itself unthinkable. Nietzsche, as it were, inverts the doctrine of Parmenides; he cancels Being by the "altogether not."[55] In my opinion, this inversion empties of all meaning Nietzsche's revelation of the superman as a bridge for the overcoming of man, and a great noon (II, 445).

To say, as Zarathustra's animals attribute to him, that "I myself belong to the causes of the eternal return," is then finally unsatisfactory (II, 446). The emphasis here upon the uniqueness of the discovery of the eternal return is, as I have tried to show, misplaced. If the doctrine is unique, then it is a poem and is itself subject to decay. We are free to accept it or not, as we see fit. If it is the eternally recurrent truth of eternally recurring uniqueness, then not only are the tablets of Zarathustra completed, but their completion transforms uniqueness into the empty gateway of the present, understood as the mutual cancellation of past and future. These criticisms might be further exemplified by an analysis of Part Four, but nothing substantially new would emerge. The main theme of Part Four is Zarathustra's pity for and renunciation of his disciples, the "higher men" of the present age (cf. especially "The Sign," II, 561). This is connected to a final affirmation of joy in the eternal return; the crucial paragraphs are "At Noon" and "The Drunken Song." The titles suggest a synthesis of Apollo and Dionysus. Zarathustra chants the coming of the deep midnight, the hour when the question is asked: "who shall be the lord of the earth?" (II, 554). The rejection of his disciples, and so of pity, is now expressed as the rejection of the day: "Leave me, you stupid, boorish, dumb day! Is not the midnight brighter?" (II, 555). In the synthesis of the two, Dionysus assimilates Apollo.

The "midnight souls" will be lords of the earth. They are the most unknown and the strongest, "brighter and deeper than any day." At high noon we see the doctrine of the will to power and the eternal return, but midnight is the hour at which we either conquer death or are conquered by it. Midnight is the hour for action, and so for stepping into the gateway of the present, for beginning a new day, a new epoch. And so, at this moment, the peak and the abyss are united: "Just now my world became perfect; midnight too is noon; pain too is a joy; curses too are a blessing; night too is a sun—go away or you will learn: a sage too is a fool" (II, 556f). To this we may add: enemies too are friends; community is also a solitude. And we may close our study of Zarathustra with a question. What becomes of the orienting distinction between the high and the low in the final reconciliation of opposites? Obscured by the darkness of midnight, has Zarathustra not repeated inadvertantly the conditions set by Saint Paul for the completion of time within eternity? "There is neither Jew nor Greek, there is neither bond nor free, there is neither male nor female: for ye are all one in Christ Jesus" (*Galatians*, 3, 28).

CHAPTER FIVE

The World as
a Concept

17. The Copernican Revolution

ANALYTICAL PHILOSOPHY belongs to the great western tradition of rational thought, which is in turn based upon the assumption of the intelligibility of the world. This assumption is given a more or less technical formulation in principles governing the definiteness and countability of beings, as well as their obedience to what we now call the principle of non-contradiction. To be is to be something definite, this rather than that; consequently, to know is to say something about something, and to say this rather than that. That we do in fact know something, and this rather than that, is in one sense obvious and in another, puzzling. Philosophy may be said to originate in the attempt to remove the puzzle in terms of the obvious. What is obvious, we call *given*; what we call given, varies. For one thinker, it is sense-perception, for another, the truths of arithmetic and geometry. But the variation in our choice of the given is rooted in the invariance of givenness. We are provided initially with the compatibility between our environment and our sensuous and cognitive faculties. This compatibility is not the same as total lucidity, nor does it (at least in our initial consideration) lend itself to rigorous axiomatization. But it permits us to find our way about, to distinguish between this and that, between pain and pleasure, between the useful and the dangerous. We recognize the beings in our world, and our own concern with them, and consequently our concern with ourselves. If I may summarize the processes that my examples are meant to suggest, the whole of experience, or "the world," is intelligible in a sense that both precedes and is the ground of the special senses of intelligibility designated by one philosopher or another. To be rational, then, is not simply to pursue the technical implications of definiteness, countability, and logic. It is also to reflect upon the indefinite but intelligible context of the definite.

The desire to explain puzzles in terms of the obvious is part of human nature, and thus is an ingredient in the context of analysis. One could of course offer a physiological explanation of this desire, or demote the love of truth to the desire for self-preservation, pleasure, power, or satisfaction. Even if any of these explanations should be true, the explanation of desire does not on that account itself become a desire. The desire for truth is not yet the desire for desire. The capacity to satisfy our desires is still rooted in the accessibility of the world to sensation and cognition; more comprehensively, the world is accessible, not simply to our use and enjoyment, but to our *judgment*. According to the Hebrew Scripture, when God had created the world, He looked at it, and found it good. The judgment of the goodness of the world (or for that matter, of its badness) is thus distinct from the technical processes of its construction. But the same can be said of the judgment that the world is neither good nor bad, as for example, in Nietzsche's judgment that the world is "worthless." The rationalist distinction between theory and practice was initially part of a judgment that truth is the highest good. Philosophers who reject this judgment as extra-theoretical are not in a strong position to defend their desire for the truth. If the world is worthless, then I am free to follow my own desires. The strength of the theoretician's desire for truth is then at the mercy of my will to power. If my desire is more powerful than his, then *the truth changes accordingly*. In the previous chapter, I argued that this Nietzschean doctrine is already implicit in the Enlightenment rationalism by which reason is separated from goodness, or differently stated, by which the good is equated with the desirable.[1] I have been arguing that the judgment of the worthlessness of the world is a consequence of the rationalist's excessive shift in attention from the world as context of definiteness to the definite as rationally manipulable. I have *not* been arguing that we should reject reason, but rather that we must appreciate its diversity.

The capacity to analyze is cognitive or spiritual, a term no longer in good repute among academic philosophers. I use the term "spirit" for a number of reasons, none of them theologically motivated (although I am not necessarily excluding theological senses of the term from my purview). Suffice it to say that I wish to correct the view, at least as old as Descartes, that what was traditionally called "soul" is nothing other than the "mind" or *res cogitans*. It is essential to the success of the analytical enterprise that we not forget our spiritual function in the pursuit of definiteness. However, the replacement of the soul by the mind is not satisfactory, as is already evident in Descartes, for whom rationality is equivalent to mathematical analysis. It is true, and should never be forgotten, that Descartes grounds mathematical analysis in intuition. But if to be rational is to analyze (and synthesis is just analysis in reverse), then nothing rational can be said about intellectual intuition. In the very act of asserting the accessibility of mathematical order to intellectual intuition, Descartes set the stage for the rejection by later thinkers of intellectual intuition as a cognitively empty, analytically superfluous hypothesis. Whether Descartes was fundamentally a mathematical physicist or a metaphysician, the historical fact remains that the consequence of his ostensible dualism, as perceived by the analytical branch of his progeny, has been to transform the "philosophy of mind" into the logical analysis of propositions about the mind. This is doubly defective. In the first place, the mind is not a proposition or a logical structure. More fundamentally, the mind is an aspect of the soul (or spirit); it is not just a geometer or algebraist. In saying this I have summarized a more complex issue: the link between desire or passion and the analytical structures intuited by the *res cogitans* is one of judgment, and hence neither one of desire nor analytical structure. Descartes has nothing rational to tell us about judgment, and neither do his analytical progeny.

In the first three chapters of this study, I concentrated my attention on the theme of definiteness. It was my intention to show how the context of definiteness is visible within the technical analyses of definite structures, and that these analyses fail *on technical grounds*, not altogether and everywhere, but in those cases in which they are designed to remove, or to resolve, the problem of the context of analysis. To take what is perhaps the main point in these three chapters, the problems of unity, being, and nothingness are inseparable from the problem of (what I have called) intuition, or the visibility of the given units and structures of definiteness. I also put this point as follows: if the doctrine of meaning is the foundation of philosophy, then the arguments against psychologism, made popular by Frege and Husserl, require re-examination, and to a considerable extent, rejection. To speak of the "concept" of meaning is already to speak of the intellect to which the concept *means*. But the attempt to do justice to the intellect (more comprehensively, to the human spirit) requires an extension of the senses in which we permit the concept (if that is the right term) of meaning to "mean." In Chapter Four, I accordingly introduced the theme of the whole, an imprecise but nevertheless in many ways more satisfactory expression of "the context of analysis." My intention in this chapter was twofold. First: I wanted to illustrate the rhetorical and dreamlike nature of the genuinely philosophical attempt, suppressed but still just visible in contemporary analytical philosophy, to think the whole. My intention, let me repeat, was not to attack rationalism, nor to reject mathematics in favor of poetry. On the contrary, I wished to show how mathematics is itself the expression of a dream of wholeness or unity, as well as the non-mathematical yet rational sense (or "meaning") of this dream. Second: I wished to show how the original formulation of this dream by Plato, in terms of a quasi-mathematical original order of which this world is an image, leads us astray if we attend exclusively to the analytical elements within the dream, or as one could also say, to the originals but not to the images. The ultimate consequence of this error is that the originals are themselves transformed into images. Analytical philosophy, ostensibly opposed to the speculative dreams of continental metaphysics and post-metaphysical dialectics, gradually and at first imperceptibly erodes into the very speculations it scorns.

Permit me to overstate my thesis for the sake of initial clarity. Philosophy begins in a dream of the whole. This dream is eventually transformed into a concept. But the mode of intelligibility of a concept is such that no light is cast upon the nature of the conceiver, who thus becomes once again a dreamer. The concept therefore is transformed into a poem. If clarity and distinctness, or for that matter, precision, are properties of conceptual structure, then the conceiver is reduced to the status of an analytically superfluous phantom, a shadow hovering over the logical structures of belief, disposition, and other such propositions. In previous chapters we have studied the relation of the concept to the conceiver with respect both to the unity and definiteness of the concept, and the indefinite context of conceptual clarity and precision. In the present chapter, I turn to a different aspect of the problem. I have already argued that it is not possible for philosophy to be equivalent to conceptual analysis. I want now to look briefly at the crucial steps by which the context, whole, or world has itself been conceptualized. In this case, my historical paradigms are Kant and Hegel. In conceptualizing the world, Kant removes the conceiver from its structures, or from rational explanation. Hegel goes one step further; he reconceptualizes the conceiver, or attempts to carry through the definition of philosophy as conceptual analysis. The failure of Hegel's attempt had, as I have already suggested, two main consequences. The first was an attempt to do justice to the conceiver, or to the soul, now called the existing individual, by extra-rational modes of thinking. The second was simply a return to the Kantian conception of rationality, and so, to the procedures of the Enlightenment.

In the twentieth century, we therefore find ourselves in the following situation. On the one hand, there is a widespread conviction that philosophy begins from ordinary experience, everyday language, or the pre-philosophical life-world. On the other hand, the conviction is itself articulated in the language of concepts. The return to the life-world by the phenomenologist is as much a conceptual reconstruction of that world as is the theoretical world of the conceptual analyst. It is true that the contemporary progeny of Nietzsche and Heidegger speak of deconstruction and creation rather than of conceptual reconstruction. In both cases, however, the "natural" world of the prephilosophical individual is understood as a conceptual construction requiring transformation. It is important to emphasize that even the phenomenological description of the life-world is a conceptual analysis of structure, and not a presentation of the world as we live in it. I do not mean to imply by this that conceptual theorization is entirely superfluous, or that it is possible to give any reflective account of human experience without some kind of structural analysis. But the difference I have in mind is immediately illustrated by comparing a Platonic dialogue with a Husserlian analysis of everyday existence. It is often said, or taken for granted, that the difference between Plato and Husserl is that of modern science. The Platonic presentation of the context of analysis is presumably rendered obsolete by the "Copernican Revolution" (as we may abbreviate a long and complex process). However, the Husserlian himself insists that the conceptual schematism of modern mathematical science has functioned at least since Galileo to *cover over* the original structures of everyday life. There is at least some ambiguity in the enterprise of uncovering that original structure with a methodological procedure which is itself rooted in modern science and mathematics. It is true that phenomenologists claim to begin with the *evidence* of common experience. But the meaning of that evidence is rooted in, and derived from, a conceptual schema that mixes together formal logic and a quasi-Kantian doctrine of transcendental subjectivity.

I am not advocating the rejection of phenomenology any more than I previously advocated the rejection of mathematical logic. What I am attempting to do is to clarify a problem. The problem is that the distinction between philosophy and poetry turns upon our ability to distinguish between conceptual construction and the natural or pre-analytical world of the conceiver. We do not make the distinction between philosophy and poetry, or between hardheadedness and soft-headed speculation, by total reliance upon mathematics and the "scientific method" (if there is such a thing). Even if we possessed a complete mathematical reconstruction of everyday experience, we could not certify it as true unless it were possible for us to compare the reconstruction with the original everyday experience. We might, of course, redefine truth in operational or pragmatic terms. But to do this is to grant that there is no fundamental difference between philosophy understood as science or poetry. The scientist may regard himself as more powerful than the poet, but the interpretation of science as power is poetic, as our study of Nietzsche was intended to make clear. I am tempted to say that it is the problem itself that gives us our bond with nature or truth, not the solutions that have been proposed to the problem. In this light, I have been arguing that fundamental problems like those of intuition or evidence, unity, being, and nothingness provide us with non-trivial access to the pre-analytical context of technical philosophical analysis. My objection to analytical philosophy is thus centered upon the belief that it has succeeded in eliminating these problems, or in restating them in a more precise, technical manner, and hence in a "scientific" way that permits our making steady progress toward their resolution.

I therefore do not intend the following discussion of Kant as a "refutation" of Kantianism. I take my cue from the obvious: contemporary man is in immediate danger of losing all capacity to understand himself, and this, as it were, in the midst of scientific plenty. I do not propose to engage in banal discussions of "the human condition." It will suffice to make two brief comments. The first is that to speak of the human "condition" is already to grant that human nature is inaccessible. Our condition today is how we happen to find ourselves, the "way we live now" rather than the way in which we have deviated from how we ought to be living. My second comment is closely related to this. Since everyday or "natural" existence has long since been dissolved by scientific progress, we require elaborate, highly technical modes of *hermeneutics* in order to understand any human production, ranging from a conversation to a work of art or science. Technical guides are now easily available on every aspect of everyday life, from interpreting facial gestures to making love. One might use these guides in the way that an engineer uses his manuals, blueprints, and equipment, to construct a life that is in conceptual agreement with "the latest discoveries" of science and technology. It does no good to protest that these manuals are vulgarizations of science and technology. The serious question is why they have become necessary to the *vulgus*. How can the philosopher of science assume that the equation of philosophy with scientific methodology will not have the most extensive social and political consequences? If we put to one side the childish Marxism that seems to underlie much political opinion among contemporary intellectuals and academic philosophers, or indeed if we take it into account, the question immediately arises: what is the scientific basis for the ethical value of Marxism, or human progress, or perfect justice? How can we reconcile the rhetorical presentation of the excellence of science, or of the connection between science and justice, with the scientific equation of rationality and mathematical analysis?

These are not the questions with which I am presently concerned. They are, however, the pervasive questions of our epoch: no doubt "banal" or "unsophisticated" when contrasted with the conceptual schemes of analytical philosophers or theorists of any persuasion, and yet they are as much a consequence of those conceptual schemata as are the popular manuals on the art of interpreting body language or attaining complete satisfaction in the act of love. What I shall take the liberty of summarizing as *the hermeneutical problem* has its roots in the process by which the world is transformed into a concept. Our need to "decode" the sense of everyday life in accordance with technical rules of a theory of sense or meaning is a consequence of this transformation. Let me restate the problem: the very attempt to understand the world leads to a conceptual reconstruction that separates us, by having acquired theoretical understanding, from the world we set out to understand. There is no solution to this problem compatible with our humanity. But it may be possible to retain our grip on the problem and hence avoid dissolution by its ostensible solutions. It is in this spirit that I wish to consider Kant's Copernican Revolution, the most profound and influential step in the process of interposition of scientific concepts between man and his experience.

I begin with a quotation from Hegel's *Phenomenology of Spirit:*

> The manner of study in antiquity is different in this respect from the modern manner: the former was the genuine education of the natural consciousness. Examining separately each part of its existence and philosophizing on each occurrence, natural consciousness constructed itself into a thoroughly active universality. In modern times, on the other hand, the individual finds the abstract form already prepared. The exertion of grasping it and making it one's own, is more the unmediated setting-to-work of the interior, rather the abbreviated formation of the universal than its process out of the concrete and the multiplicity of existence. Our task today is not so much to purify the individual from the mode of immediate sensuousness and to make it into a thought and thinking substance, as rather the opposite: to actualize and infuse with spirit the universal by the suppression of its fixed, determinate thoughts.[2]

Hegel anticipates Husserl's observation that the pre-moderns, and especially the Greeks, philosophized from the direct sources of everyday experience. He does not say it explicitly, but the crucial point is that, for both Plato and Aristotle, beings are directly accessible to the intellect, which, as pure noetic receptivity, possesses no structure, and hence does not construct concepts. The constructive aspect of philosophy, to which Hegel does refer, is the consequence of *dianoia* or the discursive appropriation of direct intuition. We have seen something of this constructive activity in our brief inspection of *diaeresis*, or dividing and collecting in accordance with kinds. *Diaeresis* is a *technē* and therefore expresses human intention: it shapes natural beings or "stamps" them with a constructed form. The problem of the conceptualization of the world is thus already implicit in the philosophizing of the natural consciousness. A failure to understand the implications of *diaeresis* as *technē* leads to an oversimplification of Greek philosophy, and thus to an exaggeration of the difference between classical and modern thought. Hegel at least alludes to this in his remark that the result of Greek natural consciousness is a more or less fixed conceptualization of experience. The Hegelian phenomenology will not destroy this conceptualization, but set it into motion, develop it, and so reappropriate it at a deeper level.

In other words, the Hegelian phenomenologist does not return to natural consciousness (what is today called the *Lebenswelt*) in order to uncover the original senses of his scientific concepts. Such a return is impossible because of the historical transformation of the natural situation. For Hegel, "nature," as accessible within human experience, is itself historical. However, Hegel is spared from historical relativism by his conception of fulfillment or the "end of history." The beginning, as well as its intermediate stages, is rendered fully intelligible, and in this sense "absolute," by the completion of development. Hegel thus retains, if in a historicized form, the classical conception of the whole. More accurately, Hegel transforms the classical daydream of the whole into *the* concept. One may also say that the Hegelian equivalent of *physis* is logical, i.e., the structure of the concept. This already enables us to understand the sense in which Hegel is the complete logical or conceptual analyst. In the language of phenomenology, the force of history may be expressed as human desire, or as desire translated into work, and so into the power of negative (productive, transformative) activity. But the sense of work is to be found only in the Hegelian logic. Thus Hegel's "phenomenological description" is in fact a logical interpretation of human history. In this fundamental sense, Hegel's procedure is like that of Husserl. The scientific thinker cannot "unthink" the scientific conceptualization of ordinary experience. To do so would be to subvert science, not to uncover the authentic sense of the origin.

Hegel thus accepts the basic thesis of Kant's Copernican Revolution, which he sometimes expresses in the antiquated formula of the identity of being and thinking. This formula is the essence of conceptualism; whether stated or unstated, it expresses the essence of contemporary analytical philosophy. And the pivotal figure here is Kant. Kant articulates the major discovery of the modern epoch (as dramatized by the Cartesian *cogito*) that the most certain sense of "to be" is "to think." Modern philosophy is then, at least since Descartes, a recapitulation, at a higher level of logical explicitness, of Eleaticism, as we have already seen in the crucial case of non-being or nothingness. Philosophy is the conceptualization of the world.

I turn now to a concise analysis of three points in the Kantian teaching, corresponding to his three critiques. My purpose, as usual, is not philological completeness; I want to make visible a theoretical paradigm. In so doing, I shall represent Kant's three critiques by three words: synthesis, duty, and purposiveness. Very generally, I want to sketch the role of Kant as mediator between the Platonic tradition and twentieth-century thought. The contemporary attempt to find the sense or meaning of science in the pre-theoretical or pre-analytical situation is Platonic in spirit. However, the attempt to capture and express this meaning in technical concepts, or in a scientific theory, is decisively modern. It is not our main concern, but we may note in passing that, in a crucial sense, Plato, although he originates the history of philosophy, also stands outside it. Aristotle is the first professor (despite the fact that Plato is the first university president). The absence of a conceptual theory in the Platonic dialogues is relatively clear from the fact that these dialogues soon produced the opposed schools of dogmatism *and* skepticism. There is an indeterminateness in the Platonic daydreams which the conceptualizing intelligence finds repugnant. As Kant himself remarks, Plato is the father of *Schwärmerei*; the philosophy of Aristotle "is on the contrary *work*." [3]

In the First Critique, the synthetic activity of the transcendental ego is intended to exclude the intellectual intuition of structured unities or Ideas of the Platonic variety, and to replace these Ideas in an analytical context by the categories and objects of understanding. Beings and natures are thus replaced by concepts and objects (and objects, of course, are the conceptual products of subjects). This is the precondition for the transformation of philosophy into conceptual analysis. However, Kantian analysis cannot occur without a prior synthesis. [4] If Ideas are understood as originals of generated copies (or of phenomena), there is in this case no direct access, no return via "recollection" to the original (or noumenal). The logical relations of the phenomenal objects of understanding are "original" in the sense that they are constituted by the synthetic activity of the transcendental ego. They are not intuitions of eternal archetypes. But it would be going too far to call them "works of art." Instead, they are the structures engaged by the activity of thinking in a being that thinks through categories or concepts, and sensation, but that lacks intellectual intuition. We have no way of knowing whether these structures correspond to analogous forms in the originals understood as things in themselves. Even if we press the analogy between the categories of understanding and the specifically logical Ideas of Plato, the resultant structure remains empty of content. However, Kant is not a linguistic constructivist. The analysis of the transcendental ego provides us with the comprehensive categories of analytical thinking. These categories are timeless. But the discovery of timeless categories is not the same as scientific understanding of the world of space and time. The question arises as to the exact status of Kant's methodology of critique. We are, as it were, analyzing synthesis, but not in the same sense as we analyze the products of synthesis. The author of the First Critique is thus "doing metaphysics" in the sense of explaining the activity of concept-construction. He is not giving us a phenomenological description of beings as they show themselves to pure cognition. But he is implicitly showing us that beings *are* pure cognition, or alternatively, that pure being is cognition. However, he does not show us what the "is" in this formulation signifies.

If there is no room for intellectual intuition of structured paradigms in Kant, what about practical intuition? I do not mean by this term the intuition of the categorical imperative, but the procedures by which we see structured wholes within the categorially structured world, and perform various appropriate operations on these structures. In Kant, the world of genesis is the consequence of the synthetic activity of transcendental subjectivity. This is the world of exact science, or what might be called the "interior" of synthesis. The subject dwells *within* the synthetic world, and it is this dwelling-within that enables it to perform its analyses with precision and reliability. The Kantian world of genesis, then, even though it is phenomenal, is not an image-world. Is it a dream? We can answer in the affirmative to the extent that the world is forever subject to the illusions of dialectic. Our knowledge of the transcendental domain serves only to reinforce the fact that, as alive, we are residents within a radically finite world, the ancestor of Nietzsche's prison. We dream of emerging (escaping) from this finite world, and hence we engage in self-contradictory or dialectical fantasies concerning the first and last things, or (in the classical sense) the whole. Nevertheless, these dialectical fantasies do not play a regulative role in Kant's philosophy, in the way that myth, poetry, or daydream does in Plato.

One could say that for Kant, the idea of the sublime provides the basis for a poetic account of the whole, but not for a cognitive account. As for dialectic, Kant interprets Platonic Ideas as regulative Ideals of the unconditioned, or as the totality of conditions valid within understanding. These Ideals are the concepts or rules of reason that serve to unify, and thus to regulate, understanding. A constitutive or epistemic use of the Ideals, or an effort to know the whole discursively, produces the dialectical antinomies rather than genuine knowledge. And there is no "poetic" knowledge akin to dialectic. So Kant transfers the classical *aporiai* of discursive thinking to the attempts by understanding to define the whole. His position is thus part-way between Greek thought and twentieth-century doctrines based upon logic and set theory. An opinion about the whole is not the context within which understanding functions; it is illusion. One cannot extirpate the inclination toward dialectic, but it can be regulated or limited in its power to confuse us by the exercise of critical rationalism. When our confidence in critical rationalism wanes, the result, so to speak, is Nietzsche. When we become frightened by Nietzschean excess, the result is a return to critical rationalism. But this fluctuation itself looks like dialectic rather than analytical explanation or historical progress. The fluctuation can be expressed as a consequence of Kant's failure to overcome dualism. Hegel attempts to conceptualize dualism as dialectic, and thus to establish the unity of the whole, or to overcome alienation. Unfortunately, to the non-Hegelian, dialectic is indistinguishable from poetry. And so the fluctuation arises again.

Kant's world of genesis is meant to stand in its own right; yet it necessarily divides into two dimensions, corresponding to knowledge and to what may be called opinion, dialectically conditioned feeling, or finally, despite Kant's intention, illusion. The opinion about the whole, or the illusory consequence of dialectical thinking, cannot be separated from the extra-scientific experience within genesis. As was pointed out by Husserl, Kant has no satisfactory analysis of extra-scientific experience within the phenomenal domain. Since this is the origin of scientific experience, the latter seems to be compromised by the problematic status of the former. The categories of the transcendental ego, taken in themselves as empty of intuition or sensation, are not able to remove this compromising shadow. In Plato, the world of opinion (doxa) is like a dream, but it is not an illusion. It does exhibit "dialectical" properties that arise from the absence of a definite logico-mathematical structure for such a world as a whole. For even if the Ideas exhibit a structure analogous to those of numbers, this structure cannot encompass dreams and opinions, and so is not the same as, or the structure of, the whole. We may therefore call the Platonic whole an image-world in two senses. First, an act of imagination is necessary to constitute it. Second, since there is no epistemic account of such a world, and since the imagination generates *poetic* rather than mathematical universals (which must always be actualized as thus-and-so, and in such-and-such a way), the world is a concatenation of images reflecting universals that are not their paradigms but their origin. The whole originates in human thinking, but it is a product of natural materials. And these natural materials are directly grasped; they are not mediated by concepts. In Kant, the whole is a synthetic construction of conceptual thinking; and "natural" materials (sensations, for the decisive instance) are not directly accessible, but are perceived only through the mediation of concepts. Conversely, concepts lack sense or reference independently of sensations. Whereas Kant's whole seems at first glance altogether more rational, more conceptualized and rule-governed than the Platonic whole, the fact is that Plato's poetic or dream-like sense of the whole is based upon a direct contact with nature or the original condition. It is precisely the fact that we are "dreaming" rather than conceptualizing that permits us to come into contact with original nature. The Kantian suppression of dreams is also a suppression of nature, except in the sense of Newton's system of the world. But this is totally featureless, except as it is articulated by scientific concepts.

Let me restate this last point. In Plato, the natural consciousness begins with unmediated materials which are not yet modified by *technē*. The dream of natural consciousness is not of the materials, but of the ultimate transformation of these materials into a conceptual whole. This dream is also dialectical in the sense that the dreamer realizes it will never be fulfilled. He realizes that he will never awaken. In Kant, on the other hand, the world is constituted from the outset by categories, understood as a set of rules, that define a structure. There is no room for dreaming; yet, as dialectic shows, dreams slip in through the cracks in the walls of the edifice. We remain on guard against these dreams by a kind of rigorous obsessiveness with respect to our rules: this is the psychoanalytical paradigm of so much contemporary analytical philosophy. The result is a bifurcation between the world as conceived and the world as lived. Our experience of the lived world, of pre-scientific understanding, is thus compromised from the outset. It is treated as an illicit (or primitive) consequence of the misuse of the understanding. To be reasonable is to be scientific. Science then becomes an unending analysis undertaken by what is itself discursively inaccessible. This is an incoherence in Kant's doctrine which he attempts to repair in his critiques of practical reason and of judgment.

In the case of duty, the term characterizing for our purposes the Second Critique, we are at first glance much further from the twentieth century than in the case of the regulative-conceptual dimension of the First Critique. However, it is possible to understand the contemporary manifestation of Kant's ethical teaching as *the duty to obey rules*. If God is a geometer, or more generally, if the scientific enlightenment has persuaded us that reason is fundamentally mathematical, then human welfare and security depend upon our obedience to the rule-like or axiomatic nature of mathematical thinking. In this light, Kant's God is not radically different from Spinoza's natural order, at least insofar as He is accessible to us in this world. Spinoza's *deus sive natura* is a kind of quasi-geometrical articulation of the Cartesian *res cogitans*, or a mathematized version of the classical equation of thinking and being. Let us put to one side the question of the spiritual dimension of the Kantian God, as we are entitled to do when thinking of the twentieth-century consequences of Kantianism. If God is order and measure, then piety is obedience to the rules governing order and measure. The religious roots of the scientific enlightenment thus become visible, irregardless of whether the key figures in the progress of enlightenment believed in a personal or Christian God. *We dare not break the rules, or chaos will ensue.* In this version of eschatology, Nietzsche plays Satan to Frege's savior.

It is important to observe the unplatonic nature of Kant's doctrine of duty. This doctrine arises largely in opposition to the classical doctrine of *eudaimonia* or, as Kant interprets it, concern with one's own happiness. Kant's depreciation of happiness is connected to his denunciation of dreaming (*Schwärmerei*) by the fact that neither is or can be rule-governed. In addition, Kant misunderstands the classical notion of *eudaimonia*, or literally, of being possessed by a good daimon. He thereby assimilates it into the modern doctrine of happiness as the satisfaction of desire or the pursuit of pleasure. The concept of duty stands in opposition to both blessedness and the pursuit of pleasure. Kant starts from the fact of the moral law (4, 34, 37, 106).[5] Everyone knows his duty, or is governed in his feelings (if not in his acts) by conscience (43f, 84–87, 99). In spelling out the two components of duty, it is easy to see their origin in Cartesian apologetics. They must first be expressed in moral laws, understood as manifestations of the categorical imperative (38); and second, in order to be obedient, one must possess an autonomous will, the sole principle of all moral laws (39). It is true that Kant replaces the desire to increase one's power by moral laws.[6] But this amounts only to a more successful geometricizing of morality than Descartes was able to achieve. Despite Descartes's ostensible piety, the dualism between his Christian protestations and his materialist hedonism is all too visible (or it is if one reads the physical and physiological writings as well as the *Meditations*). In any event, pleasure for Descartes is a side-effect of one's recognition of one's power; and power accrues from our mastery of nature via the *mathesis universalis*. All other formulations of "virtue" and "piety" in Descartes are explicitly called accommodations to one's time, country, and public circumstances. From this standpoint, Descartes is altogether closer to Nietzsche, in his virtually public celebration of the will to power, than to his successors from Leibniz through Hegel. And with respect to the second feature of Kant's conception of duty, Descartes explicitly states that the good for man is the free exercise of his will.[7]

To return to Kant, the fact of the moral law, or the accommodation of the principles of morality to imperfectly rational beings who require commands, is then the basis for the deduction of the faculty of autonomy or freedom, the principle of moral laws (55f). The universality of the law expresses its independence from differences of taste. The autonomy of the will expresses our actual capacity to act responsibly, independent of objects or external circumstances. One could therefore say that the free man respects the moral law (87, 92) because he recognizes in it the "image" (my term) of his residency in the world of corporeal necessity (102, 113).[8] Here, in contrast to the case of knowledge, it seems inevitable to refer to two worlds rather than to one world with two dimensions. In any event, virtue is the supreme but not the complete good; it becomes this only with the acquisition of happiness (127f). And happiness in turn rests upon the possibility of the connection between morality and my reward, as guaranteed by God to members of the kingdom of ends or rational beings (137, 140–45). What one might call the dangerous allusion to happiness is securely regulated by binding it to the moral law, which we obey from duty, not from hope for eternal reward (149, 180). This is Kant's safeguard against eudaimonism. He goes so far as to say that it is better for us not to have knowledge of God and immortality since, if we did, hope or fear would almost certainly triumph over duty (168). Nevertheless, my duty to the moral law requires me to make the *summum bonum*, and hence my happiness as well, the object of my will. I have a duty to believe in God and immortality (164) as the seal on the harmony between nature and the human will. Hence I am obligated to believe in the possibility of my infinite progress toward holiness and in the effectiveness of my moral freedom (135, 140f, 143).

The Kantian pursues his happiness out of an obligation toward the rationality, which is to say, the conceptual coherence of the world. The "infinite progress toward holiness" is the practical version of the infinite progress toward complete scientific truth. The concept of duty, which I am suggesting functions in the theoretical as well as the practical domain, is the basis for what Vaihinger called the "as if" character of Kant's thought. We must live as if the world were a whole: at this point, the role of the dream in Kantianism is unmistakable. The dream is expressed mathematically, in the form of a hypothetical deduction from certain facts: the facts of scientific knowledge, or of the moral law. But the deduction goes altogether beyond the facts; this is especially evident in the case of the moral law, which Kant interprets on the basis of the Christian doctrine of conscience. In Kant's rigorous interpretation, I can never actually know whether I am acting out of selfish inclination or a pure respect for the law. Hence Kant gives preference to those actions that we perform against our inclinations, for the sake of virtue. This preference suggests that happiness is impossible on Kantian grounds. Instead, I must find contentment in my obedience to rationally formulated laws and rules. The counterpart to intellectual chaos is gross immorality; in both cases, the remedy is the same: *ordo et mensura*. We see here a modern, post-Christian version of the Platonic attempt to unite mathematical theory and prudence in the form of what I should like to call *arithmetical decency*. Once we have made the fundamental assumption that the world is intelligible, all human activity, whether theoretical or practico-productive, falls under the sovereignty of counting and measuring. The "as if" character of Platonism lies in the initial assumption of the intelligibility of the world, or in the notion of *cosmos*. But the world assumed by the Platonist to be intelligible is nature; in other words, the noumenal world. Kant's elaborate structure of concepts provides us with an intelligible world that is a subjective construction cutting us off from the noumenal world, so far as cognition is concerned. Kant starts from the typical modern axiom: we know only what we make. The certitude of this world, its intelligibility, lies in its subjectivity (albeit in a transcendental sense). The categorial structure of the intelligible world expresses the sameness of being and thinking. However, the disjunction between the noumenal and the phenomenal formalizes Cartesian universal doubt into a doctrine of two worlds, or rather, two dimensions. Human conceptual construction transpires within an unknowable dimension; it is our duty to believe that this dimension is benign and the kingdom of God, rather than of a malign intelligence who has created our world to deceive us.

The *summum bonum*, in the words of an eminent Kant scholar, is "a dialectical Ideal of reason. . . . It is important for the architectonic purpose of reason in uniting under one Idea the two legislations of reason, the theoretical and the practical."[9] In other words, it is the analogue to the Platonic Idea of the Good.[10] We can thus draw the following comparison. Both the Platonist and the Kantian have the "duty" to interpret the direction of their striving as a mark of the goodness of the world, which is governed by a just deity, and hence is intelligible.[11] Whereas Plato expresses this doctrine of wholeness and goodness in the form of myths (including the myth of a perfect analytical deduction), Kant attempts to systematize the Platonic myths in the form of transcendental deductions. The final version of this attempt is contained in the Third Critique. As we have seen, epistemic understanding is for Kant the result of our capacity to make judgments by acquiring knowledge through concepts.[12] This is the capacity of rules.[13] With this capacity, we are able to subsume individuals under the appropriate rule. In other words, there is a difference between rule-formation and rule-application. This leaves room for the distinction, developed in the Third Critique (15ff), between reflecting and determining judgment.[14] In the latter case, the universal is presented by the understanding as a rule, principle, or law. When the particular alone is given, for which the universal must be found, the judgment is merely reflecting or reflective. Reflective judgment does not determine the object either sensuously or logically. Its function is to classify the existing object under the appropriate rule, principle, or law. The capacity to do this is rooted in the assumption of the purposiveness of nature. We assume that the forms of objects are suited to classification under a unified system of rules, principles, or laws. This is the assumption of the intelligibility of the world. In Plato, however, this takes the form of intellectual intuition of the form as the basis for the construction of a classificatory system. In Kant, the form is constructed as well. The intelligible world is a concept. In this sense, one could claim that the Cartesian doctrine of subjective certitude is the actual foundation of Kant's assumption of the intelligibility of the world. It is not simply the case that I can classify, count, or measure; what is crucial here is that *I* can do this, or that what I do is fully visible to me in the very fact of my doing it. Just as there is no deduction in the famous *cogito, ergo sum*, so transcendental deduction is a consequence of the immediacy of self-certitude. The crucial step then in Kant's philosophy is his resolution of Hume's denial of the knowledge of self-identity. He resolves this by transforming the problem from one of perception to the conditions for the possibility of perception and cognition. But this transcendental argument continues to be rooted by subjectivity in the immediate experience of itself. What the transcendental arguments justify or explain is immediate subjective experience. It would, I think, be possible to raise the question whether a transcendental argument is capable of justifying immediate subjective experience, and hence whether this immediacy is not itself already certitude. The question would take the form of reopening Descartes's doctrine of intellectual intuition, or alternatively, of rejecting Humean skepticism, not on the grounds that we have conceptual or discursive knowledge of self-identity, but because the intelligibility of all arguments, skeptical or dogmatic, assumes, not the transcendental ego, but immediate unity and self-certitude in the finite, individual consciousness. However, this is not the place for such an investigation.

We remain within the Kantian perspective: the conformity of (phenomenal) nature to our intelligence raises the assumption that nature has been designed by an intelligence. How fragile is this assumption may be readily inferred from the implicit circularity of Kant's argument. Since the world of nature is a projection or conceptual construction of the thinking ego, it is scarcely surprising to find that this construction conforms to the operations of the ego's intelligence. For Kant, judgment is possible if nature is purposive. For the contemporary descendant of Kant, who has lost his faith or sense of moral duty, it is the purposiveness of the human intelligence that accounts for the accessibility of nature to rules and laws. In other words, the rejection of the transcendental dimension of Kant's doctrine reduces "purposiveness" to the assertion that we know what we make because we have made it and not because there is a divine purposiveness directing our constructive activity. What remains true for the contemporary Kantian is that the world is a concept. In other words, both Kant and his descendants require a hypothesis on the basis of which the pursuit of scientific knowledge is possible. Kant derives his hypothesis from the suitability of nature to be grasped by rules, laws, and principles (20). His descendant interprets this as an extension of the conceptualizing process: the underlying assumption of the contemporary Kantian is thus Nietzschean, whether this is explicit or not.

Knowledge, like morality (113), is for Kant rule-governed in a determining way. Reflection upon purposiveness proceeds by analogy with causal or analytical thinking (222). The absence of analogical thinking in contemporary subjectivism is a strength for those who prefer deductive argumentation, but it is a weakness because it signals an incapacity to make cognitive contact with anything beyond the powers of the thinking ego. Thus Kant retains the classical doctrine of a natural end, albeit now in the form of a concept that regulates the reflective judgment. It is an idealization of the limit-case, as it were; hence it is not constitutive of the world of scientific knowledge but acts as its defining boundary (239). The reflective judgment is critical: it refers to the subjective conditions for thinking a concept, with no reference to the nature of the objects falling under that concept (260). In its general form as teleological judgment, reflection leads us beyond rules and laws to the hypothesis of the unity of the

231

whole as a creation of a divine and benevolent intelligence. This condition for the possibility of rules is not itself a rule. But it is a hypothesis of a divine ruler who exercises his rationality through rules. I note again that, once we perceive and reject the implicit circularity of Kant's argument, we have no further requirement for the transcendental domain. The regularity of nature is then simply the way in which our intellect functions. Man is thus emancipated from servitude to a transcendent (and transcendentally accessible) deity: he becomes his own master and his own deity. The transformation of the world into a concept is thus apparently the highest expression of human freedom. Unfortunately, freedom, understood as the power to conceptualize, carries with it no limits that are meaningful for the conceiver as an individual existing within his own dreams. If we can do whatever we are able to do, this platitude does not succeed in making anything worth doing.

18. Grounds for Reason

The Kantian project to conceptualize the world is incomplete in at least three distinguishable senses. First, there is a split between the conceptual world of phenomena, and the unknowable or noumenal world. The categorial structure of the transcendental ego functions as the context of analysis, but it is itself situated within a transcendental dimension that, despite its immunity to conceptualization, plays an indispensable role in regulating the "shape" of the context. Second, there is a split between empirical self-consciousness and the logical operations of the transcendental ego. Kant's intention of conceptualizing the whole is checkmated, as Hume had already shown, by the phenomenon of self-consciousness. Kant resolved this problem by transforming the ego into a logical concept. In so doing, however, he tacitly admitted the impossibility of conceptualizing empirical experience. This is the third sense in which his project is incomplete. Whereas the incompleteness of scientific knowledge is the precondition for unending scientific progress, the non-conceptual nature of pre-scientific experience, noted by Husserl, leaves everyday life at a pre-rational level. This raises problems with respect to politics and history that Kant attempts to resolve by "daydreams" concerning the infinitely distant merging of intellectual cunning and the passions of the soul.

Hegel sets himself the task of resolving the three forms of incompleteness in Kant's world-conceptualization. First, the phenomenal world is reconceived as the self-presentation of the noumenal world. In other words, the difference between the two "worlds" is overcome within a dialectical explanation of appearance. Hegel argues in effect that it is impossible for the essence or interior of things to conceal itself. In this sense, Hegel's logic is the logic of Enlightenment: the truth necessarily manifests itself. Second, the split between the empirical and the transcendental ego is reformulated as a dialectical relation between the empirical and the absolute Spirit (*Geist*). Stated as simply as possible, Hegel transforms Kant's logical concept into the *activity* of concept-formation. He refers to this activity as the Concept, but in its comprehensive identity, the Concept is the fullest expression of the unity of thinking and being. The intelligibility of logical categories cannot be explained apart from intelligence (compare Descartes's doctrine of intellectual intuition as expressed in mathematical structure), and intelligence cannot be deduced from abstract logical concepts. The attempt to preserve a dualism between logical forms and the cognizing intelligence leaves the process of meaning itself unintelligible. The actual paradigm for Hegel's dialectical logic, and for his attempt to overcome the dualism of form and intellect, is the thinking (living) individual. The unity of thinking and being is already prefigured in everyday life; it is not a mystical intuition or a "metaphysical" speculation in the pejorative sense. Third, whereas Hegel makes no attempt to disregard the contingency of everyday life, he does make contingency a category in his logic. Since that logic is the expression or "pulse beat" of life itself, Hegel is prepared at least to attempt to reconcile scientific knowledge and political history within the development of the Concept. Kant, however, had to leave this possibility of reconciliation to hope or (at best) to a duty of the rational conscience to believe in and accept as a justification of God's ways in the human world.

Let us begin by formulating the senses in which Hegel's tripartite enterprise is a paradigm of contemporary analytical philosophy. We grant at once that the notions of Absolute Spirit and the conceptual unity of life or intelligence with its logical categories are alien to the analytical program. But this is not the point. Hegel's dialectical logic and his doctrine of the Absolute are consequences of his attempt to spell out the implications of conceptual analysis. If our goal is scientific knowledge of the whole, or the completion of the Greek attempt to give a rational account of all aspects of human experience, then the exigencies of rationalism lead us to the doctrine of Absolute Spirit. This point has to be doubly underlined in order to make clear Hegel's relevance to the contemporary philosophical situation. Speaking very generally, there are two ways of studying and discussing Hegel that, whatever their merits, will fail to bring out his importance for the analytical reader. The first is the purely philological-historical, in which Hegel is explained altogether, or primarily, in his own technical language and with respect to his historical context. This method has at least the merits that it is indispensable to a genuine understanding of Hegel's doctrine. Nevertheless, it is useless for our present purposes, since we are addressing, not a congress of Hegel scholars, but the analytical philosopher or the potential philosopher who is either tempted by the dominant analytical style or has never been shown a sensible alternative. The second way is becoming increasingly popular and is motivated by the contemporary fashions in politics and historical interpretation. Proponents of this method present Hegel as primarily a political thinker, whether as the precursor of Marx or somehow as a model for contemporary "progressive" aspirations. Once the initial enthusiasm of ideological motivations evaporates, it becomes plain that Hegel is neither a Marxist nor a liberal in the contemporary sense. Even worse, his advocacy of the Absolute Spirit, when presented without any grasp of his logical or rationalist motivation, poses an insuperable obstacle to our taking him seriously. Hegel's political views are unintelligible apart from his doctrine of the Absolute. But the doctrine of the Absolute is unintelligible except as a *consequence*, however odd, of the Enlightenment goal of total conceptualization of the world. The best way to grasp Hegel's "relevance" is neither through a falsification of his political views nor a popularization of his logic, but by a self-reflection on the nature of conceptual thinking. In a sense, this has been my program in writing this book. I am not a Hegelian, but I want to show how the failure of analytical philosophy (and regardless of its temporary popularity, it is a failure) may be understood as the inability to carry through to its full consequences the implications of its own assumptions. At the same time, I am not recommending that this be done, except for the purpose of philosophical understanding. I myself never understood contemporary analytical philosophy until I had spent ten years studying Hegel.

Analytical philosophy prides itself on its radical innovativeness, and in an important sense (via Russell), upon its birth in the rejection of Hegel and all forms of Idealism. In fact, analytical philosophy breaks down, upon close inspection, into two parts: the techniques of mathematics, or their adaptations to the exigencies of natural language, and a hodgepodge of unexamined presuppositions, many of which are derived from the modern Idealist tradition, and especially from Kant and Hegel. It is true that most analysts would reject the unity of thinking and being, as is clear from the importance they attach to the anti-psychologism of Frege. In most cases, however, this whole issue is misunderstood; the analysts are in fact rejecting phenomenalism when they suppose themselves to be rejecting Idealism. Differently stated, what one makes of the empiricist infrastructure of analytical philosophy depends upon what one makes of empiricism. But in itself, empiricism is nothing but a platitude. What sober thinker would look elsewhere than to his experience in an effort to understand himself and the world? I am *not*, incidentally, saying that empiricism, like mathematics, is a "metaphysically neutral" method that may be attached to any theoretical foundation. The nature of mathematics is a metaphysical question of the very highest importance. Everything turns upon our ability to grasp this question, and to decide the scope of mathematics. The uniform application of mathematics in analytical philosophy is an expression of the principle, stated or unstated, that *being is homogeneous*. The most powerful impetus to this view in modern history is undoubtedly the success of Galileo and others to mathematize the cosmos, or to show the falseness of the Aristotelian distinction between the heavens and the earth, at least so far as the phenomenon of motion is concerned. Yet at the same time, many analytical philosophers begin from another, quite Aristotelian principle, namely, that the verb "to be" has many distinct senses, or in other words that *being is heterogeneous*. These two principles are in clear-cut conflict, and in a way that goes deeper than the controversies between the ordinary-language analysts and their formalist rivals.

As I have tried to show, the conflict goes deeper because ordinary-language analysts share the view championed more powerfully and consistently by the formalists that to be reasonable is to be understood by the paradigm of mathematics. Ordinary-language analyses of sense, reference, types of proposition, existence, identity-criteria, and so on, exhibit the same paradigm of explanation that the formalists employ. The denial that ordinary language can, or ought to be, completely formalized, is undercut by the affirmation of the same axioms of rationality that underlie formalism. To be is to be nameable or countable; to exist is the same as to be, unless explicit and clearly-defined criteria for defining the speech-context can be presented; to explain is to provide a theory; to understand is to analyze concepts; the only appropriate mode of philosophical presentation is by arguments, and in fact, by deductive arguments. The list goes on. The major manifestation of this lack of self-consciousness on the part of ordinary-language analysts is that their entire procedure is rooted in intellectual intuition, prudential judgment, empathy, and introspection, all of which they deny or exclude from acceptable philosophical procedures. This lack of self-consciousness, together with the aforementioned acceptance of the principles of formalism, has led to the quite noticeable decay of ordinary-language analysis and to the corresponding triumph of formalist analysis. However, thanks to what Hegel calls "the cunning of reason," the triumph of formalism is the penultimate step in the total failure of analytical philosophy as a dominant movement. The reason for this is extremely simple. Formalist or mathematically-dominated analysis is even less self-conscious than ordinary-language analysis. Being is in fact heterogeneous, not homogeneous. And this brings us back to Hegel. The metaphysical or ontological defect of analytical philosophy (disregarding now differences within the movement) is that the attempt to transform the world into a concept cannot succeed with a purely mathematical logic. And the reason is obvious to every non-philosopher. The soul, spirit, or intellect is not a mathematical relation.

Having said all this, it is essential to emphasize that I am in no sense mounting an attack upon rationality or analytical thinking. My strictures on analytical philosophy as an academic movement are something quite different from this. As a lover of mathematics and an admirer of detailed, comprehensive conceptual analyses, I share many of the interests and goals of the analytical movement. My criticism arises from a refusal to accept the irrational context of contemporary analytical philosophy. I derive no great joy, however, from the imminent demise of analytical philosophy. Its own excesses have already guaranteed, in my opinion, the succession to power of even more irrational doctrines. Man is the excessive animal; he swings erratically from one extreme thesis to another. Rather than despair over this, let us learn from it, for it is already evidence of the plausibility of a dialectical logic. I say "plausibility" because, again, my purpose is not to preach Hegelianism. I want rather to suggest that analytical philosophy is an unself-conscious striving toward Hegelianism. I advocate neither the conscious nor the unconscious versions of this doctrine. If I advocate anything, it is self-consciousness. There is a time for sobriety and a time for madness. But there are no rules to tell us what time it is, no ontological clock we can consult in place of imprecise and pre-analytical good sense.

My presentation of the Hegelian paradigm takes its bearings with everyday experience. As I am claiming, this is how Hegel himself begins. I cannot provide an elaborate textual justification for this claim, but then it is unnecessary to do so, since here again, my intention is theoretical rather than philological. The reader who doubts the accuracy of my reconstruction of Hegel is invited to journey with me to a possible world in which a philosopher named Hegel holds the views that I am about to attribute to him. Once the scene is set, I will study a short but central text from Hegel's *Science of Logic*. Even then, I shall be concerned with the theme of the conceptualization of the world rather than with hermeneutical completeness.

The truism that philosophy takes place within the world is transformed, after a moment's reflection, into the extremely puzzling question of how to think the world as the origin or ground of philosophy. The question arises: what are the grounds for being reasonable? This is not quite the same as asking: what does it mean to be reasonable? We have to start where we are, and our very puzzlement about how to be reasonable is in a non-scientific but altogether convincing way evidence that we know what it means to be reasonable. We do not learn how to exercise our reason in the fundamental way required for the development of logic, epistemology, and ontology by taking graduate seminars in logic, epistemology, and ontology. We start by demanding evidence, and this is the demand of a rational animal. The real difficulty is that the evidence we demand is not always or unambiguously forthcoming. Philosophy, from Plato to Frege, traditionally begins when we assume that, despite its excesses and ambiguities, the world is basically intelligible. The original philosophical problem is then how to discharge this assumption. If the assumption is not discharged, then despite all technical progress, philosophy remains a hypothetical doctrine, or what I have called a dream of the whole. In my opinion, Hegel is unique in the history of philosophy in that he attempts to waken man from his metaphysical slumbers, not by plunging him into another dream, but by revealing the rationality of the world.

Hegel's intention is to show that there is no conflict between human existence and conceptual knowledge. He wants to show that the world is itself the principle of sufficient reason or ground for being reasonable. The sense of "ground" in everyday language must therefore be essentially the same as in conceptual explanation. For the sake of simplicity, let us restrict ourselves to a playful inspection of the English term "ground." (As it happens, the same inspection could be carried out in German.) As we normally use it, the term "ground" has two principal meanings: support and origin. These two meanings are expressed at the beginning of western philosophy in Aristotle's terminology as *aition* and *archē*. No doubt the literal equivalent of "support" in Greek is *hypokeimenon*; but we support what we do or say by "giving grounds," and this in turn requires us to supply a reason: "I stand on the reasons just given." For Aristotle, "reasons" are either principles, causes, or what we now call "arguments," but these are themselves grounded upon principles or the perception of causal connections. Arguments may be rhetorical or dialectical as well as deductive. But the basis for argumentation is the possession of grounds in the primary sense of principles and causes. The terms "ground," "principle," "cause," "reason," and "origin" are by no means synonymous, but they are so closely connected that it is difficult to neatly distinguish their meanings. For our purposes, the main point is this: we normally accept without question the need for grounds, whether in the sense of principles, causes, reasons, or arguments, whenever we ask ourselves what we ought to do or say. And whenever we believe that we are in a position to decide this question, it is because the world is intelligible or supplies us with grounds for self-justification.

In sum, we normally call a man reasonable if he believes that he must have and give grounds. The content of these grounds may be unacceptable to us. But we would condemn as unreasonable someone who called the grounds-giver unreasonable simply because of a disagreement over content. It is impossible to define precisely the line separating the giving of grounds from groundless self-justification. But even the latter, as in the case of the madman, is evidence that the human animal is constrained by his very nature to justify himself by the giving of grounds. We stand upon our grounds, and we are able to stand, rather than fall or stumble, because (as we normally believe) the ground(s) upon which we stand itself stands still. This is the belief that motivates Aristotle's defense of what we now call the principle of non-contradiction. Aristotle varies in his terminology, but we must not overlook the fact that he refers to the principle as "the most stable belief." We can therefore justify the belief, not so much by giving grounds, since the principle is itself the "ground of grounds," as by presenting rhetorical arguments on behalf of stability. So the principle or belief is capable of being defended to men who value, or acknowledge that they value, stability. If to be reasonable is to honor stability, and if the principle of non-contradiction is the ground of reason, then the defense of the principle of non-contradiction is indeed circular. The circle is by its own account reasonable; but it is so by an implicit assertion that it is unreasonable to stand outside the perimeter of the circle. The man who tries to square the circle is not open to objections based upon grounds that he rejects. For example, a putative Hegelian (say, Heraclitus) who interprets stability in terms of instability (kinesis or *Bewegtheit*) has his own grounds for attempting to supplement the principle of non-contradiction, or, as in the case of Hegel himself, not to reject it within its own sphere but to "ground" it in a deeper and more comprehensive stratum of experience and conceptual reflection.

Aristotle apparently denies the possibility of reaching deeper ground than the principle of non-contradiction. Perhaps this is why he was unable to give a coherent conceptual analysis of kinesis. In any case, Aristotle opts for stability and proceeds to give rhetorical warnings against instability. For example, he records instances purporting to prove that even those who verbally reject the principle must accept it in their deeds. But he does not show the impossibility of an alternative account of speeches or deeds, an account that, for example, would begin from the simultaneous cognitive grasp of p and non-p in the very formulation of the principle of non-contradiction. The Hegelian asks: how can I think p except in terms of non-p, and how can I distinguish them except by uniting them in my own intellect, which is then the subject or *hypokeimenon* of contraries? We do not need to enter into this debate. My point is simply that Aristotle's conclusion to the excellence of stability is a generalization from pre-theoretical experience, not a deductive argument. The quarrel between Aristotle and Hegel ought at least to begin from, and be largely carried out upon, the grounds of making sense out of everyday affairs. They would have to do so even if there were grounds for rejecting everyday affairs or everyday conceptions of being reasonable.

The sensible man has and gives grounds. The Hegelian is no less sensible than the Aristotelian because he gives, and so believes himself to have, additional or extra-Aristotelian grounds. Perhaps "being sensible" in the Aristotelian sense is not an adequate basis for philosophy, just as it is not a sufficient basis for grasping all of human experience. Are we actually able to make sense out of our lives without access to what Plato called "divine madness"? If "to be" has many heterogeneous senses, then it may be senseless to attempt to give the same kind of grounds in all cases. Furthermore, Aristotelian logic, and for that matter, mathematical logic, expresses the concept of the homogeneity of being. If the having and giving of grounds requires us to develop a logical analysis of the having and giving of grounds, then what we require is a logic of heterogeneous beings. We require a dialectical logic, a logic of change and development. Suppose that we ask a man why he did or said something, and are told that he was moved by God. Why is this rejected as an insufficient ground by the rationalist? To say that we wish to explain everything on the basis of our unassisted reason is to deprive ourselves of the world as grounds for being reasonable, unless we believe that we have created the world. But this belief is not normally regarded as reasonable. The world as grounds for reason may or may not be noncommittal with respect to its own origin. But ostensibly naive "proofs" for the existence of God, based upon the world as itself requiring a ground, are not so much unreasonable as in violation of the principle that the world is its own ground. It is not the case that the world clearly shows us its eternity, or that it was not created by God, or that there is no God. The world, eternal or created, shows us nothing but itself. The man to whom God has spoken, or who draws an inference from the world to God, is taking a step beyond the world, and this is in violation of the principle of rationality underlying western philosophy (at least before its corruption by revealed religion). Hegel does not take this step; instead, he claims to be able to show that God is revealed in and as the world. Whether this is atheism or "acosmism" (to borrow a term used by Hegel in criticism of Spinoza) is here irrelevant. The relevant point is that Hegel, while staying "within" the world, attempts to provide grounds for the Aristotelian principle of non-contradiction, and this requires him to conceptualize the grounds of the principle, or to give an account of the world as the ground of stability. But this account in turn requires him to explain instability since the world is both stable and unstable, at rest and in motion, definite and indefinite. Hegel, as it were, accepts the possible rationality of the assertion that one was moved by God. The assertion becomes rational provided one can explain this motion in conceptual terms derived from the motion and the rest of God's world. This same point could be restated without any reference to God, in the traditional sense of that term. Aristotle was wrong to say that thinking is more like standing still than like moving. To think is to move or undergo change, and change is a synthesis of being and nothing. An explanation of the "structure" of thought requires an explanation of the motion of thought, and such an explanation must itself be moving. It must move in the sense that genesis moves continuously through its cycle of coming-to-be and passing-away, or back and forth between being and nothing. The movement of thought, and so of a rational logic, must be the same as the movement or internal excitation of the whole.

Is this approach irrational—as many analytical philosophers would have us believe? I cannot see any grounds for accepting such a criticism. Reason is rooted in evidence, in the having and giving of grounds, and the world is neither entirely stable nor obedient to the principle of non-contradiction. Hegel, like the analyst, is attempting to conceptualize the world. The analyst's attempt, thanks to his doctrine of logic and concepts, requires him to dismantle the world, or to extract the stable skeleton from the living flesh and blood, which are then discarded. Hegel's attempt is based upon a different logic, and hence a different doctrine of the concept, but one that leads him to take his bearings by the world as it is, and primarily by the phenomenon of life. Since logical form is meaningful or intelligible only to an intelligence, and since intelligence cannot be deduced from form in the mathematical sense, it is more reasonable to begin the other way around, or to try to deduce logical form from intelligence. This can be done without destroying or restricting in any way whatsoever mathematics in the traditional or non-dialectical sense. All that is required is a recognition of the difference between mathematical and philosophical logic. And this difference follows reasonably and directly from the perceived fact of oneself as thinking. It is irrational blindness, not an attack against psychologism, to define the beginning of philosophy by a rejection of the fact of self-consciousness.

The problem intrinsic to Hegel's approach is in my opinion not due to his being illogical, but to an excess of logicism. To start again from the everyday, whatever we do or say may be justified on various grounds depending upon the circumstances. Whereas it is true to say that we stand upon one patch of ground or another, it is false to say that we move continuously on the ground. We also leap from patch to patch, and sometimes even, in Nietzsche's phrase, from mountain peak to mountain peak. This leaping is done within the world, and in some vague manner it can be justified with respect to the world. But such justifications are mythical, poetic, or rhetorical, not logical. In slightly different terms, when we are asked for the grounds of our deeds and speeches, sometimes it is reasonable to reply, and sometimes not. Sometimes we are justified in keeping silent or in walking away from our interrogator. And sometimes there is just nothing more to say; the grounds have been given. Either they are seen or they are not seen. Needless to say, there are no rules to guide us in these situations. The man who cannot see *this* either has no sense, or he has nothing but sense, which is not enough. The situation in human affairs is thus quite different from that in mathematics where the goal at least is to develop procedures for defining effectively when we have said enough. Putting to one side the more difficult case of meta-mathematics (wherein the goal is substantially the same), we say that a theorem is proved when, on the basis of a finite number of rule-governed steps, the conclusion is produced from the premises. But neither life nor philosophy can function in this manner. Hegel, of course, recognizes contingency, prudence, and insight. But the fact remains that his teaching is fundamentally a logical system: a conceptualization of the whole.

It is true that Hegel's logic is not deductive in the usual sense. Nevertheless he has an answer to the question: when have we said enough? His answer will sound unpersuasive, not to say absurd, at first hearing: we have said enough when, without essentially repeating ourselves, we have said everything. We object almost instinctively: if it is necessary to explain the whole in order to explain each individual, how can we ever come to understand any individual as that individual? And what is the meaning of the term "essentially"? What is to count as essential repetition? However, let us reconsider. As scientific knowledge progresses, the thesis of the interconnectedness of things becomes more and more plausible. It is true that science does not offer an assertion of the general thesis of interconnectedness as an explanation of this or that individual. But then, neither does Hegel. In accordance with Hegel's and our own sense of "ground," we are not explaining this or that individual (a task left to the appropriate science), but *the process by which there is this or that individual to explain.* Despite the initial peculiarities arising from the empiricist or "positivist" standpoint, Hegel's procedure is exactly the same as that of the experimental sciences in the following crucial respect. He attempts to construct a comprehensive conceptual theory of the whole, in which one aspect "follows" from another, not quite in the deductive sense of formal logic, but as a moment of development. Thus we have said enough when we succeed in articulating the whole as concept or as the Concept. The serious difficulty faced by Hegel is not that he is unscientific, but that he is, as it were, too scientific. He believes himself to have said enough about what it means to have said enough. If Hegel's logic, methodology, and confidence in his own triumph differ from those of the scientific analyst, the goals of the two are the same. Both are connected by a kind of grounding mathematism or attempt to conceptualize the whole. Nevertheless, let us bear in mind that Hegel's concept is self-conscious; it is the unity of being and thinking. In this sense, Hegel's enterprise is more reasonable than that of analytical philosophy. It is a more reasonable version of the same enterprise. And it is more reasonable because Hegel discovers, or claims to have discovered, a way of doing conceptual justice to conceptualizing, or to resolving the problem of the way in which concepts "mean" to intelligences.

Grounds become visible only when *this* happens because of, or arises from, *that*. In the case of man, the happening is the ground for the giving of grounds. And there is no logic of happening, no structure accessible to a precise conceptualization, whether deductive or developmental. Of course, we can make general observations and even theories about the kinds of things that happen to us. But there are no rules for determining what precisely will happen or the meaning of what happens. There are no rules to tell us how to respond to what happens. And this is altogether compatible with a belief in human nature or a hierarchy of natural ends. I myself, for example, believe that the noble is higher than the base, and I regard as base all "arguments" presented to demonstrate the non-rational nature of such a distinction. But whereas arguments designed to support the noble may themselves be noble, it does not follow that they are valid to anyone but the lover of the noble. Nor does it follow that there are rules to determine in each case what is noble and what is base. Once one sees this distinction, one may present *a posteriori* justifications for the distinction. But if the noble could be established by argument, then there would indeed be no difference between the true and the beautiful. To one degree or another, there is a tacit assumption that the true and the beautiful are the same in the unstated premises of the great philosophers. But this amounts to the unstated premise that only beautiful souls will perceive the highest and the deepest truths. This may be true, but it certainly cannot be demonstrated by logical argumentation.

Hegel's mathematizing of the ground, or his conceptualization of the whole, amounts to the thesis that the true is self-evidently the beautiful and the good. At the end of Hegel's system, we are, if we have understood it, in the position of God who has both created the world and looked upon it as good. But now the goodness of its look must be the same as the principles of its creation. If this were not so, then there would be a dualism: the good would be external to the Concept; that is, external to discursive intelligibility. With every allowance for the category of contingency, Hegel claims to provide us with a logic of happening. His conceptual calculus claims to provide us with all essential states of the future and past, in the way that some mathematicians claimed they could calculate the past and future conditions of the physical world from an exact mathematical description of its present state. Since what happens is rational, provided that we can express it in conceptual terms, it is a tautology to say that what happens, happens reasonably. Hegel's logic is a conceptual demonstration of the Leibnizian thesis that this is the best of all possible worlds, except that, for Hegel, no other world but this is possible. The difficulty here is characteristic of scientific explanation and is peculiar to Hegel only in the sense that he claims to extend scientific explanation to encompass the whole. The difficulty, to repeat, is that we are forced to turn away from commonsensical judgments and to accept theoretical explanations that follow from a system or set of axioms, but not from our direct understanding of our own experience. In some cases, this may be reasonable. For example, our commonsense view of the properties of matter is obviously quite limited by any scientific criterion. Nevertheless, even here, there are occasions when the scientific analysis of matter is irrelevant or even wrong. Everything depends upon human intentions. These intentions may be noble or base, but their nobility or baseness will not be demonstrated by showing them to be inevitable. The human deficiency of Hegel's logic is a characteristic of every scientific theory of the world. The nobility of science is not itself scientific.

Hegel brings to fulfillment the long tradition of philosophy that takes its bearings by man's desire to have and give grounds. This desire leads in turn to reflexivity or self-consciousness: the desire to ground desire, or to give a ground to the ground. It is our desire to demonstrate the initial assumption that the world is reasonable. At the beginning of this tradition, in Plato and Aristotle, there is no meta-science or rigorous formulation of the principles and grounds of scientific demonstration. The Ideal of a rigorous or exact science is itself presented within a rhetorical and dialectical context, and this is as true for Aristotle as it is for Plato.[15] Hegel's dialectical logic has as its goal the transformation of traditional rhetoric and dialectic into scientific knowledge. This knowledge must not merely explain, but must also be the same as, the world, and hence the same as God. What looks like an absurd or mystical requirement is in fact the last consequence of a rigorous empiricism or attempt to define the world as a concept or linguistic framework. The Hegelian thesis is the result of spelling out the implications of the definition of philosophy as conceptual analysis. The contemporary conceptual analyst may reject this interpretation on the grounds that he does not carry out the rigorous Hegelian deduction or attempt to enforce philosophy onto the whole. Unfortunately, the result is to leave philosophy isolated within an irrational context, thereby keeping it at the mercy of the forces of unreason. Hegel's apparent unreasonableness is in fact a rigorous defense of reason. If it, too, terminates in unreason, then the moral may be that we require new senses of reason, and not an application of a monotonous reason that either falls short or goes too far, or a rejection of reason in favor of radical deconstruction.

I turn now to the section of Hegel's *Logic* entitled "With What Must The Beginning of Science Be Made?"[16] The title of this section deserves a general comment. Hegel regularly insists that there can be no introduction to philosophy from outside itself. However, he provides us with a variety of prefaces and introductions to his own scientific logic. We cannot account for his procedure as simply a pedagogical or expository device. Such an explanation directly contradicts the claims that there are no pedagogical devices for introducing us to philosophy. The literary structure of the *Logic* thus faithfully mirrors a difficulty within scientific philosophy itself. The goal of scientific thought is to explain experience by reconstituting it within a conceptual theory. As we saw in the case of Saul Kripke and other contemporary philosophers, the problem is one of the status of what I have called *presence*. The analytical thinker combines two incompatible desires. His empirical bent directs him to the given as given, but his conceptual intention requires a transformation of the given. The conflict within the analyst amounts to a self-contradictory attempt to reconcile Hume and Kant, without reducing the one to the other. Everyday experience is then both regulative and unreliable. Differently stated, scientific philosophy has everyday experience as its presupposition, but philosophy cannot be scientific unless everyday experience is "axiomatized" and thus replaced by a deductive conceptual schematism. As a consequence of these conflicting desires, experience is treated as both the presentation of essence and as illusory appearance. In Hegel, this dialectical conception of experience becomes an explicit stage of the logic or unfolding of the Concept. Stated simply, everyday experience is indeed the self-presentation of the essence of things, but it remains in an illusory form or as appearance (*Schein*) until that self-presenting process has fulfilled itself. In other words, appearance shows itself to a completed conceptualization of the whole as actuality (*Wirklichkeit*). The distinction between appearance and essence is overcome by complete scientific knowledge. And by "scientific knowledge," Hegel means the possession of the comprehensive conceptual scheme for the explanation of every aspect of experience. He does not mean the specific consequences of the correct application of this conceptual scheme, which we traditionally call "scientific progress." In somewhat Kantian terms, the Concept is the condition for the possibility of experimental and mathematical science; in contemporary language, it is meta-science.

The problem for every scientific philosopher, whether of the empiricist or Hegelian variety, lies in shifting from everyday experience to the principles and deductive procedures of scientific theory itself. This problem is expressed in the Platonic dialogues as the relation between making and acquiring.[17] In order to acquire a conceptual grasp of nature (or of the given as given), we need to construct technical tools of acquisition. In this case, however, what we acquire is already shaped by the nature of the tools with which we grasp it. Kant's Copernican Revolution amounts to the ingenious suggestion that we regard this apparent dilemma as the foundation of conceptual knowledge. Unfortunately, it also institutionalizes dualism; it guarantees that the conceptual construction of science is built within an unknowable context that is also the *condition* of the intelligibility of the conceptual construction. It is almost as though we are engaged in the process of shaping the dark into light, an enterprise normally reserved for gods. In his effort to resolve this fundamental problem, Hegel reformulated it as follows. A complete science must be presuppositionless; it cannot depend upon axioms or principles that are not themselves grounded within conceptual demonstration. If science is not complete in this sense, then it cannot be distinguished from poetry or daydreaming. As I have already noted, the attempt to distinguish science from poetry then turns upon a quarrel over power. Since the quarrel is itself not part of science, poetry necessarily wins. In order to invert this poetic triumph, science must be circular. The principles cannot be demonstrated in the usual sense since all demonstrations require principles in turn. But *demonstrare* means "to point out," not just "to deduce." The principles must then point out their own truth in terms of their consequences. Hegel is not saying simply that we choose axioms on the basis of their fertility. Such a remark is again poetic rather than veridical. Principles show themselves to be true if and only if *all* the consequences follow from them. We know this to be accomplished if every attempt to state and develop new principles turns inevitably into the restating of the original principles. In terms of the quarrel over power, Hegelian science is validated in human terms because it *satisfies* our desires. As is manifest in the bond between logic and political history, the desires of all men, not just of sages or scientists (in the literal sense of "knowers"), are satisfied.

This teaching is of interest to us because it carries through with great consistency the implications of conceptual thinking. It therefore teaches us an essential lesson with respect to the context of analysis. The lesson, to repeat, is that if philosophy is defined as conceptual analysis, the definition entails the thesis that acquiring, in order to be rational, must be making. We cannot stop partway in the application of this doctrine. To do so is to leave philosophy at the mercy of poetry, as I may call those powerful attempts to make sense of the extra-conceptual context from which philosophy necessarily draws its sustenance. The traditional heroic figures of the history of western philosophy have all attempted to protect philosophy against poetry by assimilating poetry into philosophical rhetoric or dreaming. Those who take too literally the dream of the Enlightenment, and insist that the philosopher awaken from his dogmatic slumbers, have taken the first step toward an inevitable dilemma. Either they must become Hegelians, in the broad sense of the term, i.e., by presenting a total conceptualization of the world. Or else they must admit that such a total conceptualization is impossible, an admission that has two temporarily different results. The first result is an obsession with technical progress or the mathematizing of philosophy in the effort to avoid as "nonsensical" the situation I have just described. However, as is obvious from the need to engage in epithets, e.g., denouncing those who are awake as dreamers of nonsense, this obsessiveness eventually deteriorates into its own daydream. Science comes (initially with a barrage of mathematical weapons) to seek its meaning in science fiction. But sooner rather than later it becomes evident that the ontological implication of a fictive mathematics is fiction: poetry triumphs again. We are now witnessing the first stages of this process. Side by side with an outburst of progress in mathematical logic that borders on the frenzied is a progressive politicizing of the content and context of philosophical discussion. But the polis that now provides philosophy with its motivation is itself a consequence of the impasse within professional philosophy, or is its mirror-image. In simple terms: the desire for equality is at odds with the dependence upon a scientific and technical elite. The very science and technology, or dream of universal enlightenment, that produced the desire for equality is a fundamental obstacle to its achievement. As a consequence, the traditional metaphysical dream has taken a slightly different form: cybernetics, genetics, and bio-engineering are the saviors of the future.

It is not my intention to study this phenomenon more closely. I mention it only as the contemporary form of the effort to avoid the Hegelian option, while preserving our march upon the Hegelian highway. To return to our exposition of Hegel, a presuppositionless science nevertheless requires a pre-scientific introduction. We cannot do without our ladder to the Absolute. But this is a metaphorical expression of a comprehensive problem. If we can neither allow philosophy to be dependent upon the pre-philosophical situation nor deduce it from principles and axioms that themselves float in the void, then it must be shown that the beginning does not remain a presupposition nor does it "discharge" itself in the conclusion of the enterprise it initiates. According to Hegel, the problem of a beginning in philosophy first arose to the level of consciousness in modern times (51). For Hegel, the beginning is historical, not merely empirical. We cannot begin properly with our own experience because it is already a conceptual construction. It is the human race that begins, and the beginning was made by the Greeks. If I am not mistaken, this point is overlooked by contemporary empiricists. Hegel continues: the beginning of philosophy must be either mediated or immediate, and neither of these, taken without the other, is possible. A mediated beginning rests upon non-scientific presuppositions, to which the science is in perpetual bondage. But an immediate beginning is equally irrational, since to begin is to conceptualize, and to conceptualize is to mediate (in classical terms, to acquire by making). Hegel's own formulation is somewhat different here. As he puts it, all of his philosophical predecessors begin either objectively (with a natural substance like water, with intellect, with Ideas, and so on) or subjectively (with thought, with intellectual intuition, and so on). This observation was already made by Fichte and Schelling. Materialists begin with the objective world but then cannot find intelligence, life, or spirit within it. Idealists begin with the *ego cogitans* but then cannot derive nature or the external world. (I need not emphasize that exactly the same situation pertains today in academic philosophy.) Both Fichte and Schelling, in various ways, require that philosophy begin with the synthesis of these two procedures, or in the subject-object relation. Hegel agrees, but denies that either of his immediate predecessors has adequately explained the relation. And this is because they lack a dialectical logic adequate to describe the relation as a process that combines mediation and immediacy. Let me restate this obscure formulation. Philosophy begins as cognition, which is both immediate awareness *and* the interaction between knower and known. (This is a point that is both granted and overlooked by contemporary analytical philosophers.) A comprehensive analysis of the cognitive situation must bring together the principles of awareness and interaction between knower and known. In other words, Hegel denies that the empiricist division of labor between psychology and semantics is a valid paradigm for philosophy. The principles of philosophy are subjective as well as objective. Hence both must be grounded at some more fundamental level. This is the level of Hegel's logic.

According to Hegel, his predecessors, whether they begin with a principle of objectivity or of subjectivity, neglect the mode of presentation, the "way of introducing philosophical discourse" (51). Again, I believe that this continues to be true in our own time. The reason is that philosophers take for granted the validity of an "objective" or "scientific" mode of presentation of their theories and arguments. However, since the mode of presentation is related to the arguments and theories exactly as is the context of philosophy to philosophy *qua* analysis, we see here a question-begging lack of consciousness. For Hegel, since philosophy cannot be introduced or presented to the reader by an unphilosophical mode of discourse, the "introduction" must already be part of the scientific development. To this extent, Hegel shares the contemporary preference for scientific writing. Needless to say, since he begins with the subject-object relation, his conception of science, and so of writing, is not identical with that of our contemporaries. But the underlying thesis is the same. In the modern age, the ground of science is scientifically accessible; therefore, a direct presentation of philosophy is possible, as it was not, for example, in Plato's day.[18] For Hegel, as for certain contemporary students of Plato, the literary presentation of science is not itself a dimension of the doctrine.

What Hegel means by the mode of presentation is not literary style but the behavior of the cognitive process or the subjective act. This of course affects the literary style, which must be as transparent as possible in order to allow conceptual thought to show itself fully. The difference between Hegel's style and that of the contemporary analyst is one of logic, not of rhetoric. Literary style as an expression of subjectivity must be determined by the objective content of science. The Platonic dialogue-form becomes for Hegel an expression of the non-objective status of Greek subjectivity. We see here Hegel's "scientism." Like all extreme conceptualists, Hegel requires the assimilation of the subject into the object. It is true that he retains self-consciousness as a property of objectivity. But to the extent that self-consciousness is other than the objective structures of the concept, Hegel's system is incomplete. The conceptualization of the world requires the development of the self into a self-conscious concept. To use a very simple terminological distinction, there cannot be any difference, or any rational difference, between looking at and what one looks at. It is in this sense that the "existentialist" criticism of Hegel, namely, that he conceptualizes individual existence, is sound. The same criticism also holds good for contemporary analytical philosophy.

The problem of the relation between the mediated and the immediate, or between the pre-philosophical and the philosophical beginning, resurfaces for Hegel in the relation between subject and object. In a way that cannot be captured in language, which already reflects mediation, the ego is directly conscious of itself. The attempt to express this direct self-consciousness in discursive or conceptual terms leads at once to a mediation, which takes the form of the paradox of reflection. How can I come to be conscious of myself, or recognize that it is I of whom I am conscious, unless I already know myself in advance of attaining self-consciousness? We have to make a choice here. Either we deny that self-consciousness "comes to be" in the usual temporal sense, or we admit that it is an extra-conceptual condition of the conceptualizing, mediating process. In the former case, we are led to the doctrine of the Absolute; in the latter, the goal of the conceptualization of the world is surrendered. Hegel, of course, chooses the first alternative. "What is the first for thought ought also to be the first in the process of thinking" (52). Thinking is conceptualizing or objectifying. The subject must be present within this process, but the process is that of objectification. And it is I who am first for thought. However, Hegel is not simply repeating the *cogito* of the Cartesian *Meditations*. For Hegel, the Cartesian *ego cogitans* is the subject; at the level of logic, the subject must be identical with the object. Therefore, what is first for logical thinking is pure thought: not the transcendental ego in the sense of a set of logical conditions, but the pure thinking of the Absolute. The beginning is presuppositionless in the sense that it is already the end. Of course, this needs to be shown (not "deduced") by developing the beginning into the end. The logic proper begins, then, with an "analysis" of pure thought, and so with Being and Nothing. But this is the same as the problem of presuppositions. We cannot begin with pure thought because this is the end, or else it is a new beginning at the level of complete conceptualization. At the present beginning, Being and Nothing are empty abstractions; the Absolute is already and always their identity-within-difference. The need to begin analytically amounts to the need to present the process of development from beginning to end. And this in turn requires an introduction to bring the reader up to the level of analysis, to say nothing of the "absolute standpoint."

We return to the question: is the introduction part of the science or not? Hegel's answer is that it is a part, in the sense that the end grows out of the beginning, thereby raising up the beginning to its heights. However, what does this tell those of us who are still within the perspective, if not quite of the natural consciousness, at least of the pre-scientific? We are in effect told that the step up into Hegelian science will be justified by its ultimate success. At the level of the beginning, this is the same as the claim of contemporary analytical philosophy. What look like genuine problems from the standpoint of the pre-analytical, will be shown to be pseudoproblems or nonsense from within the bosom of the Lord. Unfortunately, analytical philosophy, like empirical science, cannot hold out the prospect of completion or wisdom. The first step toward salvation must therefore be certified by faith. To those who lack this faith, the "illusory" problems may be more substantial and significant than the purported solutions. To those who possess it, faith is a fragile commodity that may be lost as easily as it is gained. What evidence has the analyst that he has not been seduced by a false prophet? He cannot point to the explanatory powers of his doctrines in the domain of the pre-analytical or everyday, because the nature of the doctrine is to restructure the everyday in its own terms. Instead of being given solutions to everyday problems, we are told that the problems are unreal, meaningless, or naive. The conceptual analyst is then in a worse version of the Hegelian quandary. Philosophy needs to be presuppositionless for him as well, just as he must begin with the presupposition of ultimate success. But in his case, the presupposition remains, and on principle. As analytical philosophers, therefore, we never emerge from the ambit of the introduction to the true science. We are both within and outside of ordinary or pre-scientific experience. And this is to say that we are in a condition of dissolution, or *nowhere*.

One cannot clarify the nature of cognition from outside the domain of science (52f). Yet the only way into the domain of science is from the outside. However, the outside is the domain of *doxa*, not *epistēmē*. So we cannot begin at all, except in the non-dialectical circle of beginning with a conceptualized version of preconceptual experience. At this point, Hegel's philosophy of history, which is not in principle different from scientific philosophies of historical (i.e., scientific) progress, comes together with his logic. History or the development of the Concept has transformed natural consciousness into a conceptually appropriate beginning of the science of conceptualizing the world. To be outside is therefore actually to be inside the domain of science. In contemporary terms, pre-analytical experience is an illusory presentation of analytical truth.

In order to transform illusion into truth, we need only apply the correct techniques. But the selection of the correct techniques depends upon the pre-technical capacity to distinguish between the illusory and the veridical dimensions of pre-analytical experience. This is the analytical version of the situation described by Hegel in terms of the relation between the *Phenomenology of Spirit* and the *Science of Logic*. The *Logic* presupposes what the *Phenomenology* proves: "the Idea as pure knowledge" (53). But the fact of the proof itself presupposes its validation by the *Logic*.

When preparing to engage in logic, we start with simple immediacy or "what is there before us?" However, this is no more simple immediacy than its counterpart in the *Phenomenology*. It is a conceptual preparation of simple immediacy. "Simple immediacy is itself an expression of reflection and contains a reference to its distinction from what is mediated" (54). Put in plain language: the attempt to begin with simple immediacy is already to begin with a mediation of immediacy and mediation. If this were not so, we could never emerge from our ostensible beginning in pure thought; we would never think. We grant that the beginning is not the same as the process of development of the categories constituting Hegel's logic. If, however, this beginning is, as Hegel claims, pure thought or pure Being, then how are we to rise to this level of pure thoughtlessness, or at least the thoughtlessness for any pre-scientific thinker who is accustomed to think in terms of finite determinations?

> All that is present is simply the resolve, which can also be regarded as arbitrary, that we propose to consider thought as such. Thus the beginning must be an *absolute*, or what is synonymous here, an *abstract* beginning, and so it *may not presuppose anything*, must not be mediated by anything nor have a ground. . . . [54]

This is one of the most ambiguous passages in all of Hegel. And yet, it is quite revealing. Either we come to our resolution (a curiously Heideggerean term) within pre-scientific thinking and experience, or else we decide spontaneously to "leap" beyond that experience. We recall that, as a matter of fact, it was the *Phenomenology* that brought us to the point of resolution. But the *Phenomenology* is the story of the progressive conceptualization of the world. It is the *Logic* that transforms the story from a poem or dream into the Concept. One sees in the twentieth century an attempt to wed Hegel's *Phenomenology* with mathematical logic and empirical science. The cement of this union is not so much Marxism as a rather dilute form of progressive liberalism. But the weakness of the cement is merely a consequence of the inappropriateness of the union. In part, the present situation is due to a failure to grasp the nature of Hegel's speculative logic, despite some sympathy for its dialectical preliminaries. However, I believe that there is a deeper, and entirely Hegelian, reason for this error. According to Hegel himself, the comprehensive development of the Concept up to the stage represented by Hegel results in a suspension of content within the negative dimension of historical activity. The penultimate stage of the conceptualization of the world is Schelling, or the night in which all cows are black. This can be restated in everyday terms. In order to arrive at the logical validation of history, history must itself be complete. This means that all fundamental philosophical positions must have manifested themselves. The *Phenomenology* is not intended as a new philosophical position, but as the scientific description of the process of development of philosophical positions. However, when all the positions have presented themselves, the result is mutual cancellation. The history of philosophy prior to Hegel is just a working-out of the implications of the pre-philosophical or doxic situation. The pieces of the puzzle are all on the table, but the pattern of the puzzle remains to be identified. As an analytical philosopher might put it, the pre-analytical situation is self-contradictory; analysis is required to remove the puzzles and paradoxes caused by pre-technical discourse. In either case, prior to technical speech (whether that of Hegel or Frege), the practical situation is that of nihilism. From a contradiction, everything follows, and consequently there is no distinction between validity and invalidity.

The transition from the *Phenomenology* to the *Logic* is then one from nihilism to science (but not, presumably, to positivism). The negative condition of the penultimate or launching stage serves to purge thinking of all content. Nevertheless, negation is for Hegel suspension, not annihilation. The content must still be present, in latent form, waiting logical rehabilitation, in the way that, for the Marxist, the universal proletariat, although negated by capitalist history, remains present, waiting for the revolution to transform it into universal humanity. The lesson to be drawn from the phenomenology of human history is that pre-scientific experience is self-cancelling or self-suspending. But this is not the same as to say that it must be rejected. If the Marxist rejects pre-Utopian history, the Hegelian validates it, thereby justifying the ways of God to man. However, the method of validation is implicitly present within the phenomenological history itself. Seen through the prism of another logic, this history would look quite different to its participants. In order to avoid the charge of circularity, Hegel must therefore make the following contention. Not only is the *Phenomenology* an accurate account of the sense of history, but the sense of history is a comprehensive *reductio ad absurdum*. We are prepared for Hegel's logic by having proved to ourselves that pre-Hegelian logic makes no sense, or terminates in contradiction. Unfortunately, since the sense of pre-Hegelian logic is prepared by Hegelian logic, this is the same as saying that Hegelian logic contradicts itself. In that sense, one must indeed resolve to leap up to the level of pure thought, or to begin the study of Hegel's logic. And the motivation for this resolution cannot be furnished by the logic itself. Hence the need for connective tissue, such as the last chapter of the *Phenomenology* and the various introductory sections of the *Logic*. What this comes down to is that the explanation or justification of the transition from phenomenology to logic can lie in neither the one nor the other, since each is the image of the other. In order to decipher the image, or to recognize that we are not merely looking into, but actually are ourselves within, the mirror, we need to return to the pre-scientific or everyday situation. And this, strictly speaking, is on Hegelian grounds impossible.

The attempt to conceptualize the world requires as a crucial moment our existence at a self-conscious but extra-conceptual level. The ambiguity of the moment is evident from the fact that Hegel calls it both a presuppositionless beginning within science, and a pre-scientific resolve to rise to the level of pure thought. The Absolute is both an origin and a result. We begin with pure thinking or simple immediacy, and so, with the Absolute. But we proceed from this beginning back into the recesses of the origin, into the mediated interior of the immediate: back into history or pre-scientific experience. "Thus consciousness on its onward path from the immediacy with which it began is led back to absolute knowledge as its innermost *truth*" (55). What I am claiming is that, at the moment of transition from the *Phenomenology* to the *Logic*, the conceptualization of the world breaks down, and we are returned to ordinary experience. We must now judge, on the basis of the heretofore contradictory results of human experience, *what to do next*. This is the deeper Hegelian basis for the contemporary attempt to separate the *Phenomenology* from the *Logic*. But it is also the paradigm for the dilemma of contemporary analytical philosophy. Science tells us that the pre-scientific world is an illusion. Yet it is from within that illusion that we are asked to repudiate ourselves, with the promise that the repudiation is temporary, or that we will re-emerge scientifically reconstructed on the other side of the dream. At the same time, we are told that the dream will have no end, or that science cannot achieve its goal. The goal is the journey; in other words, it is the dream of science. But science denies its own nature, or repudiates dreaming, and assures us that to follow it is to leave dreaming for wakefulness. This denial is equivalent to a rejection of the rationality of the context of analysis. It is the rejection of the basis of science, and so it is the denial of the sense of science as the sense-seeking enterprise.

"The essential requirement for the science of logic is not so much that the beginning be a pure immediacy, but rather that the whole of the science be within itself a circle in which the first is also the last and the last is also the first" (56). This is the actual content of the dream of conceptual analysis. A perfect and comprehensive deductive system must produce its first principles as its conclusions. But the first principle of conceptual analysis is the conceiver, or self-consciousness. The first principle of the dream is the dreamer. In order to make sense of the context of analysis, we require a philosophical psychoanalysis. To mistake this for psychologism is the fundamental error of contemporary analytical philosophy. By way of a conclusion to this study, I want to make a final observation about a point of contact between Hegelian logic and contemporary philosophy of mathematics. In the language of philosophical psychoanalysis, this point also illustrates the sublimation of psychologism within mathematical theory. As an introduction to this final point, I note that the terms "truth" and "satisfaction" play central roles in both Hegelian and mathematical logic. In good Hegelian fashion, there is both an identity and a difference between these two roles, but the difference is not great enough to obliterate the common spirit.

Hegel attempts to unite the subject and the object, or to awaken the dreamer of western rationalism by the doctrine of truth as satisfaction. This dream begins with the posing of two questions by the Platonic Socrates: "Who am I?" and "What is X?" These questions are the properly human inflection of eros, and of desire, will, or striving—to give some of the pseudonyms of eros in the subsequent history of philosophy. In Plato at least, these two questions, despite their common source in eros, cannot be unified discursively or "conceptually." There is no concept of eros; or what comes perhaps to the same thing, there is a radical difference between *who* and *what*. The soul is neither an Idea nor is it deducible from the Ideas, in any sense that explains thinking and, more comprehensively, what Hegel calls "self-consciousness." One detects in Plato an impediment to erotic satisfaction that is expressed, both directly and indirectly within the dialogues, as a conflict between madness and sobriety. What is obvious is that the desire for wisdom is a kind of madness when measured against the sobriety of practical intelligence. It is of greater relevance here to see that the question "Who am I?" expresses a self-love that, although regulated by love of the Ideas, is nevertheless distinct from and at odds with its regulative manifestation. The paradigmatic role of mathematics is metaphorically visible within everyday life as "arithmetical decency." I use this phrase to express the Platonic conviction that the two kinds of measure characteristic of rational thought, the arithmetical and the fitting, weave together the ostensibly disparate dimensions of what we now call facts and values, or the "is" and the "ought." This is the defining characteristic of mathematical rationalism from Plato through the Enlightenment to Husserl. It is, however, a characteristic of hope rather than one of mathematics as a technical activity. From the standpoint of the classical version of mathematical rationalism, despair begins to erode hope when the web of measure transforms facts into values. In the typically modern version of mathematical rationalism, hope is a reflex of technical facility, or the bravado of power rather than the confidence of reason in its ends. This problem is already visible in Plato. The phrase "arithmetical decency" invokes a delicate balance of heterogeneous elements. The successful human life is the right ratio of madness and sobriety. But a mathematical expression of the ratio or proportion transforms these ingredients into a formal structure, or the *who* into *what*.

In contemporary terms, Plato avoids the *reification* of the soul by tact or the *esprit de finesse*, certainly not by the *esprit de géométrie*. This is to say that, in the Platonic account, human desire is intrinsically unsatisfiable. It is only partly true that we are what we desire. Desire, or eros, is reflexive as well as directed toward the Ideas. But the Ideas are unattainable, and reflexivity renders desire permanently unstable. To the extent that we can define the desire for desire, we transcend or extinguish it. For reasons like these, Plato presents us with the mathematical paradigm of reason within a poetical context: the dialogue or drama of questions. There is no answer to the question of the relation between context and paradigm, except in the sense that the answer is the continuous posing of the question. Let me restate the entire situation as follows. Satisfaction depends upon its identity with, and difference from, truth. I cannot be satisfied unless I possess the truth (*the* truth, not *my* truth); but possession of the truth is equivalent to the annihilation of satisfaction. If man is desire, whereas truth is mathematical proportion, then in the strict sense there can be no truth in human life, no truly human life. Human life is "true" to the extent that it ceases to be human and becomes divine. We achieve divinity in the pure intellectual intuition of the perfect forms or Ideas. But pure intuition is also the suppression of the *who*, or in the modern phrase, of self-consciousness. Man's desire leads him to employ mathematics to transform himself into a god, thereby extinguishing his desire. If, however, we are not transformed into a god, then desire is not extinguished but concealed within our instrument. The instrument then regulates the man. Human desire is transformed, as I have already suggested, into technical enthusiasm. But the initial motivation has been replaced by the exercise of technique for its own sake.

We are, however, already looking ahead of ourselves. I leave it an open question whether Plato regarded the situation he himself described as comic, tragic, or something else. For modern philosophy generally, and above all for Hegel, the Platonic harmony of opposites is too fragile to be preserved. Tact must be replaced by Hegel's cunning of reason. Hegel's attempt to transform the world into a concept is predicated upon his ostensible ability to preserve the distinction between the *who* and the *what* within the moments of the concept itself. As the unity of subject and object, Hegel's concept is the identity within difference of truth and satisfaction. In plain language, it is for Hegel part of the truth that human desire be satisfied. To this important degree, Hegel accepts and intends to fulfill the Enlightenment. Overcoming the alienation of the human from the divine within the fulfillment of the historical present is the truth that man desires as his birthright. It is a point of some delicacy whether one is to say that Hegel "gives" man satisfaction or "shows" man that he has already satisfied himself. For our purposes, the following remark suffices. In Plato, "theory" is not just a passive gazing upon mathematical structure but (whatever its active or even productive role) an interrogation of the paradoxical relation between truth and satisfaction; it is not a conceptualizing of that relation. It is not a conceptualizing because Platonic dialectic is not dialectico-speculative logic. There is no *logos* of the whole (and hence no mathematical physics, except in a dream). There is no mathematical model that synthesizes truth and satisfaction. Hegel, on the other hand, provides us with a *logos* of the whole just because his logic is dialectical rather than mathematical. The *Science of Logic* is thus Hegel's analogue to a mathematical model of totality. It is as though Gödel's constructible universe were shown, in a completely logical but non-formalized way, to be identical with the actual universe of human experience. Hegel's "constructible universe" is the total construction of the Absolute, which thus totally satisfies the desire of the human logician. Since the Absolute is the constructive activity of the logician, self-knowledge and knowledge of the Absolute are united within knowledge of the universe.

In the sense just sketched, "theory" is for Hegel constructive activity. But despite my analogy between the *Science of Logic* and a mathematical model, there is no distinction in Hegel (if we take his system as a totality) analogous to that between mathematics and meta-mathematics. The contemporary conception of theory as constructive activity is based upon the actual replacement of the concept of truth by that of satisfaction. This is not a merely verbal echo of the broader philosophical situation. As a meta-mathematical property, truth is no longer absolute but *relativized* to a specific model. (The term "absolute" has a technical sense in model theory; it refers to a formula that is true in more than one model, with the models themselves relative to the context.) To say that a formula in a given theory is "true" is to say that it is "satisfied" by a given model. The model is not itself a part of the theory; it is a meta-theory. The ground or sense of "truth" in the meta-theory or meta-mathematical model is itself relative to the mathematics we apply to construct that model. Since that mathematics has not itself been "satisfied" by a model, there is an inevitable circularity about the entire enterprise. For example, models of Zermelo-Fraenkel set theory are themselves constructed from set-theoretical elements. As we saw in the case of Kripke's "possible worlds" semantics, the interpretation of the mathematical model cannot itself be mathematical if the enterprise is to make philosophical sense. This should lead to the plain recognition of the relativity of mathematical modeling, and so of satisfaction, to pre-mathematical theory, in the classical sense of what I called previously phenomenology. If, however, phenomenology is itself a scientific theory, or if the phenomenological domain is regarded as inadequate and misleading unless it is scientifically reconstructed, then the circularity of modeling becomes an infinite regress, lightly concealed by the salubrious title of technical progress. There is an unending hierarchy of *possible* models: the replacement of absolute by relative truth, or of truth by satisfaction, is the same as, or co-ordinate to, the priority of possibility to actuality. Logic is detached from physics and identified with metaphysics, which is thus transformed into meta-mathematics.

We construct models to satisfy specific intentions. The apparent technical anonymity of model theory is in fact its utilization of mathematics as an instrument in the satisfaction of human desire. If the sense of desire is to be expressed in a mathematical model, then the truth of our intentions must be represented directly by the technical concept of satisfaction. But what of the relativity of the model to the desire or intention of its constructor? If mathematics is reason, then desire is unreason, and the desire for satisfaction is unreasonable, except as it lends itself to mathematical representation. The net result is that the ostensibly rational representation, since it is a model of unreason, is itself unreasonable. I am not a Hegelian absolutist. One must, however, say that Hegel's conceptualization of the world is philosophically self-conscious, and in that sense (since self-consciousness cannot be conceptualized) it is self-contradictory in a way that limits the dangers of Hegel's teaching. Contemporary analytical philosophy continues to pursue, in a thoroughly unself-conscious manner, the Hegelian goal of comprehensive conceptualization. As unconscious, or perhaps hypnotized by his own technical power, the analyst dreams that he is awake, but this is a contradiction leading to the intolerant suppression of one's opponents as "dreamers." The cunning of reason leads inevitably to the suppression of suppression. So long as analytical philosophers fail to address themselves to questions of the kind I have just sketched, while attempting to satisfy their human desires entirely within the divine activity of mathematics, they will finally transform themselves into symbols within their formulae. Or else their enthusiasm will surrender directly to the insatiable, and by their own reckoning, to the irrational desire of the human, all too human.

19. Postscript

I have now completed my demonstration of the radical deficiencies in the attempt to conceptualize the world. By a slight shift in focus, the negative aspect of my argument has been transformed into a positive one. What we require in philosophy is not a new system, or solutions to puzzles, but a deeper and more comprehensive grasp of the problems. This "grasp" is not a concept or system of concepts, but a dream, albeit a reasonable and lucid dream. The dream loses its reasonableness and lucidity if we attempt to analyze it with the instruments of modern science, or still more fundamentally, if we forget that analysis is itself a dream. We are often told that modern philosophy is a consequence of the scientific revolution that marks the sixteenth and seventeenth centuries. Even so, it must never be forgotten that the scientific revolution is a consequence of philosophy. The attempt to answer the question "Who am I?" leads one sooner or later, and rightly so, to define oneself in terms of who I am not. We go wrong, however, when we forget the initial distinction. The Platonic Socrates is the first to elaborate this distinction as one between human and divine or cosmic nature. What is called "Pre-Socratic" philosophy shares with modern scientific thought the failure to distinguish at a conceptual or epistemological level between these two dimensions. As a result, human life is conceived as an epiphenomenon of essentially homogeneous cosmic processes, regardless of how poetically the conception may be expressed. This oversimplification results inevitably in a powerful but crude doctrine of reason. Pre-Socratic and post-Socratic cosmology, one could say, forgets its poetic or dreamlike origins, and rhetoric hardens into technology. As a consequence, increasing technical mastery is accompanied by a corresponding vulgarization of the human spirit. To be sure, I am not advocating the abolition of science on behalf of a reactionary aestheticism. To do so would be as absurd as to offer definitive technical solutions to metaphysical problems. Rather, I am advocating consciousness of a dilemma intrinsic to our race's history. The science that is an expression of our highest gifts is also coarsening our perceptions.

There is a marked tendency today to attempt to circumvent this coarsening by a celebration of science as poetry. I must say that I regard this as an instance of the ailment. We cannot be edified by science unless we perceive the difference between science and poetry. Differently stated, the edifying dimension of science is philosophy, not poetry. I am a Platonist in this specific sense: poetry, science, or any human activity will corrupt us if it is separated from philosophy. It follows from this that philosophy will corrupt us if it is transformed entirely into science, poetry, or academic scholasticism. The reader will no doubt ask: what is philosophy? I am enough of a Platonist to wish to reply: philosophy is the attempt to answer that question. But let me put the point less obliquely. The task of philosophy is to preserve the delicate balance between man and the cosmos. This is of course not to say that science lacks delicacy. No Platonist is an enemy of science, but only, to repeat, of science separated from philosophy. Science is, or ought to be, an expression of delicacy; unfortunately, there are no scientific standards, in the modern sense of the term, of delicacy.

I have characterized contemporary analytical philosophy as an unself-conscious and deteriorated version of Hegelianism. This formula will not be pleasing to the analytical reader, who thinks of Kant, if he thinks of anyone, as his great predecessor. To this, there are two things to be said. The analyst's version of Kant tends to be a reductive one, in which the peculiarly Kantian transcendental elements, which distinguish Kant from Hume, are excised. Humean empiricism is then laced with Kant's conceptualism, and inoculated against subjectivity with a heavy dose of mathematical logic. Unfortunately, the virus is stronger than, and easily assimilates, the serum. Second, the analyst's motive in suppressing the transcendental dimension in Kant is to make philosophy as "objective" as possible. But there are no objects without subjects. Whether the analyst adopts behaviorism or semantics as his salvation, he inevitably invokes the subject of behavior or the witness of signs. It is, to put it briefly, the analyst's Kantian heritage that leaves him with no capacity to conceptualize the subject or witness, precisely because he is a Kantian minus the transcendental ego. He believes in concepts, but not in a conceiving subject, at least not as an appropriate subject for philosophical analysis. On this last point, to be sure, he is right, but not to his advantage. The absence of the subject, or its inaccessibility to conceptualization, or its "reification" via inappropriately applied concepts, is the main cause for the next-to-last act in the drama of philosophical analysis: its steady deterioration in a crescendo of technical frenzy.

Curiously enough, one aspect of this deterioration is a renewed interest in Hegel. It is true that the real motive underlying this interest is political rather than theoretical. The currently fashionable road to Hegel has been paved with Marxist (or quasi-Marxist) intentions. But nothing is more destructive of theory than political ideology. The Hegel of our academic salons is a distorted version, a fantasm of the original. This version is not strong enough to perform the one service that would awaken analytical philosophers from their dogmatic slumbers: namely, to persuade them that the only safeguard against subjectivism and objectivism is a dialectico-speculative logic. I trust, however, that I have made clear that this is not my solution to the analyst's plight. It is a solution that follows from the inner necessity of analytical philosophy, or the will to conceptualize. This will to transform the world into a concept would at least regain its health and strength if it were self-conscious. Kantian dualism at its best is not enough to revitalize a technological doctrine of reason. Hegel provides a reinterpretation of Kant within which dualism is transformed into something analogous to the Platonic balance of man and the cosmos. In other words, Hegel attempts to develop a conceptual logic of self-consciousness, which does not reduce the subject to an object or allow it to remain outside the boundaries of rational investigation. I prefer the Platonic original, but the Hegelian doctrine is a formidable attempt to transform the Platonic dream into an actual account of the whole. As such, it can be taken seriously in a way that analytical philosophy cannot.

This posing of the issue as a choice between Plato and Hegel is not an invitation to replace philosophy by historical dispute. I intend the formulation, like all of my historical examples, as a theoretical paradigm. And the paradigm is not one in which the choice is made. This is the feature of my paradigm that perhaps makes it most unfamiliar to those readers for whom theory is theory-construction, and philosophical progress is the solving of puzzles or the dissolving of problems. The paradigm is one of permanent debate. As a Platonist, I conceive of philosophy as dialogue, not system. We progress in philosophy by clarifying the conditions of the debate. Technical advances that contribute to this clarification are to be welcomed, but they must not be taken for a resolution of the debate itself. My chief criticism of analytical philosophy is that it restricts the range of philosophical dialogue, mistakes technique for theoretical understanding, is self-righteous about its own rhetoric (which consequently degenerates into scholasticism), and so contributes to the impoverishment of the human spirit. I have no objection whatsoever to analytical thinking. The combination of these two remarks provides the basis for a final summation of the positive aspects of this study.

I have tried to demonstrate that analytical thinking is inexplicable in its own terms, or that analysis turns upon synthesis, and still more broadly, upon what I have called intuition. This demonstration was intended to provide the means by which to dissect post-Fregean approaches to the central questions of being, non-being, existence, unity, and the like. I have hoped to show that these approaches are wrong, not because they can be replaced with more sophisticated technical analyses, but because they are unconscious instruments of a theoretical error. The positive aspect of my dissection follows directly: I claim to have taken a step forward, not by solving these problems, but by rendering them more visible. These problems make up the deepest stratum of our humanity. They have to be defended in each generation against the currently fashionable solutions, whether these be technico-theoretical or political. It is worth noting that the desire to dissolve philosophical problems is connected at a deep level with the desire to transform man into a post-historical being by way of political revolution. No sane man would deny that human beings are oppressed by historical arrangements, or that traditional philosophical problems are often irritating in their obscurity and, all too frequently, stimulate the formulations of charlatans. It does not follow from this that oppression will be removed by the suppression of history, an act that would presumably suppress human beings as well. Similarly, removing the basis for distinguishing charlatans from genuine critics of academic fashion is not an effective remedy against charlatanism.

The Limits of Analysis

In attempting to mark out the limits of analysis, then, I have not been motivated by the desire to impose a new system onto philosophical discussion. So too my presentation of the context of analysis as a daydream, and my defense of intuition in its several senses, is not offered as a new theory of how to philosophize, but as an account of what we actually do. The positive task of the philosopher is to fecundate his analytical skills with dreams, and to discipline his dreams with analysis. I cannot provide him with a manual of rules and regulations governing this activity. There are no rules and regulations for being reasonable, and certainly no rules and regulations for dreaming reasonable dreams. In philosophy, as perhaps in everything else, one communicates best his deepest dreams by enacting them.

NOTES

Chapter One

1. In S. Katz, ed., *Mysticism and Philosophical Analysis*, (New York: Oxford University Press, 1978), p. 201. (Bambrough's essay hereafter cited as IE).

2. See also my paper "Return to the Origin: Reflections on Plato and Contemporary Philosophy," *International Philosophical Quarterly* 16 (June 1976): 151–177.

3. In section 6, I will deny the Kripkean thesis that science discovers the essence of natural kinds and so makes original perception irrelevant. (A) Kripke vacillates on the relevance of pre-scientific perception and (B) if pre-scientific perception is irrelevant, we can construct nature at will and must do so in every possible world.

4. For examples of this point in a mathematical context, see the two papers by G. Kreisel, "Informal Rigour and Completeness Proofs" and "Mathematical Logic: What Has it Done for the Philosophy of Mathematics?" of which excerpts are reprinted in J. Hintikka, ed., *The Philosophy of Mathematics* (London: Oxford University Press, 1969), pp. 78–94, 147–152.

5. Consider especially impredicative definitions in which we need to know the totality before knowing that something belongs to it.

6. Davidson's views on the topic under discussion may be conveniently found in two papers: "Truth and Meaning," *Synthese* 17 (1967): pp. 304–322, and "In Defense of Convention T," *Truth, Syntax and Modality* (Amsterdam and London: North-Holland Publishing Co., 1973), pp. 76–85. See also the collection by G. Evans and J. McDowell, eds., *Truth and Meaning: Essays in Semantics* (Oxford: Clarendon Press, 1976).

7. "Truth Conditions and Criteria," *The Aristotelian Society*, supp. vol. L (Tisbury: Compton Russell Ltd, 1976), pp. 220–225.

8. An important exception to this tendency can be discerned in the writings of Max Scheler.

9. H. D. Sluga, "Frege's Alleged Realism," *Inquiry* 20 (1977): 235. Cf. also "Frege and the Rise of Analytic Philosophy," *Inquiry*, 18 (1975): 474, 477f.

10. For further discussion, see M. Dummett, "Frege as a Realist" in *Inquiry*, 19 (1976): 455ff; W. Marx, "Zur Bestimmung des Begriffes, 'Reines Denken' " in *Zeitschrift für Philosophische*

Forschung 28 (1974): 94ff; M. Sukale, *Comparative Studies in Phenomenology* (The Hague: M. Nijhoff, 1976).

11. At times Frege seems to deny explicitly a transcendental ego: "The concept has a power of collecting together far superior to the unifying power of synthetic apperception" (*The Foundations of Arithmetic*, trans. J. L. Austin [New York: Harper Torchbooks, 1960], p. 61 [hereafter cited in text as FA]). Nevertheless, the question remains whether the synthetic apperception constitutes the concept.

12. M. Dummett, *Frege* (London: Duckworth, 1973), p. 669.

13. Cf. E. Husserl, *Logische Untersuchungen*, (Halle: M. Niemeyer, 1928), par. 40ff.

14. *Translations from the Philosophical Writings of Gottlob Frege*, trans. P. Geach and M. Black (Oxford: Basil Blackwell, 1970), p. 151 (selections from *Grundgesetze*, vol. 1).

15. *Foundations of Arithmetic*, pp. 5, 19.

16. Ibid., pp. xix, 60ff. See also Frege, "Thoughts," *Logical Investigations*, trans. P. Geach and R. Stoothoff (New Haven: Yale University Press, 1977), pp. 17, 22.

17. "Thoughts," p. 24.

18. "Negation," Logical Investigations, pp. 31ff *et passim*.

19. "Thoughts," pp. 3–5.

20. Cf. *On the Foundations of Geometry*, trans. E. H. W. Kluge (New Haven: Yale University Press, 1971), p. 24.

21. *Foundations of Arithmetic*, pp. 19, 35.

22. "Selections from *Grundgesetze*, vol. 1" p. 145.

23. "On Sense and Reference" in P. Geach and M. Black, p. 60.

24. Ibid.

25. Many contemporary students of the Platonic dialogues are under the impression that Plato rejected his doctrine of conceptual, i.e., eidetic intuition in the so-called "late" dialogues, and in effect anticipated Frege's doctrines. It would take us too far afield to examine this intrinsically implausible thesis at length. However, one or two remarks are in order. It is right to observe that there is no reference to eidetic intuition in dialogues like the *Theaetetus, Sophist, Statesman,* and *Philebus.* But this leaves Plato in the same situation as Frege. How does the intellect grasp such eternal entities as the "greatest genera" of the *Sophist?* It is absurd to reply that these entities are acquired by diaeresis, since diaeresis is a *technē* and its products are human constructions. We must assume that they are acquired by intuition.

26. J. Piaget, *Le structuralisme* (Paris: Presses Universitaires de France, 1968) pp. 6f.

27. Ibid.

28. For example, in mathematical logic, a structure is a model or interpretation of a first-order language. The language and the model are constructions of forms and transformation-rules.

29. Here, I assume the intuitive obviousness of the phrase. In the next section, I turn to the problem of what it means to "have."

30. Piaget, *Le structuralisme*, p. 60.

31. "What is a Theory of Meaning?" S. Gutenplan, ed., *Mind and Language*, (Oxford: Clarendon Press, 1975), pp. 106ff, 113.

32. "What is a Theory of Meaning? (II)" G. Evans and J. McDowell, eds., *Truth and Meaning*, (Oxford: Clarendon Press, 1976), pp. 110, 128.

33. Ibid., p. 71.

34. Ibid., p. 104.

35. Ibid., p. 105.

36. Cf. S. Rosen, *Nihilism* (New Haven: Yale University Press, 1969), p. 46.

37. Cf. G. W. F. Hegel, *Wissenschaft der Logik*, ed. G. Lasson (Leipzig: Felix Meiner Verlag, 1951), Bd. 2, p. 254.

38. Cf. Rosen, *Nihilism*, pp. 51ff.

39. O. Ducrot, "Le structuralisme en linguistique," F. Wahl, ed., *Qu'est-ce que le structuralisme?* (Paris: Editions du Seuil, 1968), pp. 35f, 42f.

40. *Ontological Relativity* (New York: Columbia University Press, 1969), p. 84 (hereafter cited in text as OR).

41. I therefore disagree with the following assertion by Charles Parsons: "Quine's pegging of ontology to classical logic involves a realistic (as opposed to constructivistic or idealistic) conception of the existence of things" ("Ontology and Mathematics," *Philosophical Review*, 80 [1971]: 163f.).

42. J. Lyons, *Introduction to Theoretical Linguistics* (Cambridge: Cambridge University Press, 1968), pp. 58ff.

43. One should not confuse the hand-metaphor, which turns upon *haphē* (the official word for "touch" in *De Anima*), with *thigein* as used in *Metaphysics* Θ 10, and which carries the sense of "making brief contact" rather than of "having in one's grasp."

44. Cf. my article, "Thought and Touch: A Note on Aristotle's *De Anima*," *Phronesis* 6, No. 2 (1961): 127–137.

45. For a brief discussion of the historically crucial point in Descartes, see my "A Central Ambiguity in Descartes," in B. Magnus and J. B. Wilbur, eds., *Cartesian Studies* (Amsterdam: M. Nijhoff, 1969), pp. 17–35.

46. One needs to understand this in order to appreciate the current revival of intuitionism in modal logic. Cf. Chapter Two of this study.

47. C. Lewy, *Meaning and Modality* (Cambridge: Cambridge University Press, 1976), pp. 82ff.

48. For the remainder of this section, double quotes will designate an expression and single quotes a concept.

Chapter Two

1. *Metaphysics* A, 1, 981a24ff; A *Minor*, 1, 993b23ff; Z, 17, 1041a10ff.

2. Ibid., H, 1, 1042a17. The reader may wonder why I pass over primary substances or individuals, especially in view of the central role given to individual essences in contemporary modal logic. The answer is that, for Aristotle, knowledge of the individual is finally, or genuinely, knowledge of the species-form. To quote only from the most recent discussion of Aristotle's doctrine of essence by a writer who is familiar with contemporary as well as classical doctrines: "It is specific form that is responsible for the continued identity of (e.g.) the individual F through change over time, in that its persistence as numerically one and the same is its persistence as the same F," (M. Furth, "Transtemporal Stability in Aristotelian Substances," *The Journal of Philosophy*, LXXV, 11 [Nov. 1978]: 641). Cf. p. 638. I add in passing that Furth is quite right to challenge the traditional view that matter is Aristotle's principle of individuation (p. 643).

3. *Metaphysics* E, 1, 1025b14. The word *ousia* is difficult to translate; the traditional "substance" is not accurate, and "essence" is also used for the *eidos* or, more precisely, its *to ti ēn einai*.

4. Ibid., Δ, 7, 1017a22.

5. Ibid., Z, 1, 1028a10ff.

6. *Ethics* VI, 11, 1143a35ff; *De Anima* III, 4–7 *passim* and esp. 7, 431b3ff.

7. *Metaphysics* Z, 12, 1038a33.

8. Ibid., Z, 3, 1043b4ff; 1044a7ff.

9. Ibid., Z, 3, 1044a9.

10. Ibid., E, 3, 1043b1.

11. Ibid., Z, 17, 1041a10ff.

12. *Prior Analytics* I, 36, 48b2–4.

13. Γ, 3, 1004a9–16.

14. Ibid., I, 3, 1054b18ff.

15. Ibid., Γ, 6, 1011b18.

16. Ibid., Γ, 2, 1004a14.

17. Δ, 2, 1013b13–15.

18. *Physics* A, 7, 191a3ff.

19. Cf. *Metaphysics* E, 3, 1043b1: *to gar ti ēn einai tō eidei kai tē energeia hyparchei.*

20. "Frege as a Realist," p. 462.

21. Cf. F. Bassenge, "Das τὸ ἐνὶ εἶναι, τὸ ἀγαθῷ εἶναι etc. etc. und das τὸ τί ἦν εἶναι bei Aristoteles in *Philologus* 104 (1960), pp. 14–17 and 201–222 for a more adequate discussion of this expression.

22. For Aristotle, the "count" of individuals is relative to the specific form, whereas for Plato (according to Aristotle), each thing is a one, and hence is countable, irrespective of the nature of the measure. *Metaphysics* I, 2, 1053b9–16; 1054a9–19.

23. This hitherto standard etymology (suggested by Kurt von Fritz) has now been powerfully challenged by Douglas Frame in *The Myth of Return in Early Greek Epic* (New Haven: Yale University Press, 1978).

24. Cf. *Mind, Language, and Reality*, (London: Cambridge University Press: 1975), pp. 6, 16, 198, 219ff (hereafter cited in text as MLR).

25. Cf. Putnam, *Mind, Language, and Reality*, pp. 162f for another argument identifying conventionalism as a form of essentialism. Putnam, however, wishes to reject both positions.

26. Leonard Linsky, *Names and Descriptions* (Chicago: University of Chicago Press, 1977), p. 143. There is a useful simplification of Kripke's own simplified version of his semantics for a quantified modal logic in Linsky, pp. 130ff. See also Saul Kripke, "Semantical Considerations on Modal Logic," in L. Linsky, ed., *Reference and Modality* (London: Oxford University Press, 1971), pp. 63–72.

27. C. C. Chang and H. J. Keisler, *Model Theory*, (Amsterdam: North Holland Publishing Co., 1973), p. 3. On p. 4, the authors refer to the most intuitive sense of an interpretation of sentential logic as "a possible world." Since Kripke-models are models of intuitionistic logic, perhaps one should say "assertible or not" in place of "true or false."

28. Cf. Alvin Plantinga, *The Nature of Necessity* (Oxford: Clarendon Press, 1974), p. 248 for a distinction between pure and applied semantics.

29. Cf. Saul Kripke, "Naming and Necessity" in D. Davidson and G. Harman, eds., *Semantics of Natural Language* (Dordrecht, The Netherlands: D. Reidel Publishing Co., 1972), p. 344, n. 13. Kripke's essay hereafter cited in text as NN.

30. For extensive discussions, cf. the previously cited volumes by Linsky (*Names and Descriptions*) and Plantinga, as well as P. Gochet, *Quine en perspective* (Paris: Flammarion, 1978), pp. 165–184.

31. For analyses of these positions, cf. Plantinga, *The Nature of Necessity*, Appendix.

32. "Essentialism and Quantified Modal Logic" in *Reference and Modality*, pp. 73–87. Parsons's essay hereafter cited in text as EQML.

33. Cf. Plantinga, The Nature of Necessity, p. 245. One of my objections to Parsons is quite close to Plantinga's, although it was formulated before I read his book.

34. Ibid., p. 246.

35. Cf. Saul Kripke, "Is There a Problem about Substitutional Quantification?" in G. Evans and J. McDowell, eds., *Truth and Meaning* (Oxford: Clarendon Press, 1976), p. 342: ". . . if we are giving either a truth definition or an axiomatic recursive truth characterization for an object language, L, to say that we have thus given the semantics of L we must give it in an interpreted language we already understand. (This is a special case of the 'great fundamental principle' that definitions must be stated in language which is already understood.)" Kripke is arguing against the view that a meta-linguistic semantics of an object language is itself an uninterpreted formal language. His argument is directly applicable to my own discussion.

36. "Semantical Considerations on Modal Logic," p. 64: "Intuitively, we look at matters thus: K is the set of all 'possible worlds' . . ."

37. Parsons also says: "It seems natural to locate the source of necessities in the logical character of predicates (on a conventionalist view) or properties (on a 'naturalist' view) *rather* than in the objects of which they are predicated. Yet essential sentences cannot be verified on such a view" (p. 85). The word "natural" again conceals a philosophical problem involving the nature of intuition. Plantinga claims that *de dicto* is a sub-case of *de re* necessity (*The Nature of Necessity*, pp. 28f), but the word "intuition" does not even appear in the index to his book.

38. *Leibniz' Philosophy of Logic and Language* (London: Duckworth, 1972). Hereafter cited in text as PLL.

39. *The Guide of the Perplexed*, trans. S. Pines (Chicago: University of Chicago Press, 1963). pp. 206ff.

40. Ibid., p. 207.

41. For a brilliant discussion of the contradiction between the given and the constructed nature of experience in Carnap (whose thought underlies much contemporary discussion), see H. Caton, "Carnap's First Philosophy," in *Review of Metaphysics* 28, no. 4 (June 1975): 623ff.

42. Cf. Plantinga, *The Nature of Necessity*, chap. 1.

43. "Identity and Necessity" in S. Schwartz, ed., *Naming, Necessity, and Natural Kinds*, (Ithaca: Cornell University Press, 1977), p. 88.

44. The example of the unstable molecules comes from Michael Slote, *Metaphysics and Essence* (New York: New York University Press, 1975), p. 8.

45. It might be objected that one cannot apply canons of philological exactitude to what are basically spontaneous oral remarks. However, Kripke's lectures have been revised and modified by the author (NN, 342, n. 1), and this is the text we have. It is a text that has exercised an extraordi-

nary influence on contemporary analytical philosophy, and Kripke's uses of "intuition" are quite representative of the various uses of this term in the more carefully prepared literature.

46. Kripke is criticizing theories like that of D. K. Lewis.

47. W. V. Quine, *From a Logical Point of View* (Cambridge, Mass.: Harvard University Press, 1953), p. 8.

48. Cf. L. Linsky, *Names and Descriptions*, pp. 91 and esp. 143f.

Chapter Three

1. See *Set Theory and its Logic* (Cambridge: Belknap Press, 1963), pp. 28ff.

2. The reader will notice that this argument is like Kant's response to Hume's contention that we do not perceive a causal connection. The answer is that we do perceive such a connection, and analogous connections in the propositions by which we convey our denial that we perceive a causal connection. My argument is "like" Kant's, but not necessarily Kantian. It could also be Platonic.

3. A. Fraenkel, Y. Bar Hillel, A. Levy, D. van Dalen, *Foundations of Set Theory* (Amsterdam: North Holland Publishing Co., 1973), pp. 23–24.

4. P. F. Strawson, *Subject and Predicate* (London: Methuen, 1974), pp. 21, 26ff.

5. Pierre Aubenque interprets statements like "Socrates exists" to mean "Socrates is an instance of the species-form 'man' " (*Le problème de l'être chez Aristote* [Paris, Presses Universitaires de France, 1962], p. 170, n. 2). He draws the conclusion opposite to the one I give in the text above. As further evidence that my conclusion is actually justified by his interpretation, cf. p. 233, n. 1: "il est évident que, pour Aristote, il n'y a d'essence que de ce qui est (cf. Anal. post. II, 1, 89b34 . . .)." Aubenque does not seem to note in this context that to be an essence *of* what is, is other than to be "what is," i.e., exists. Note that, when Aristotle says science must determine, in the case of the centaur or the god, *ei estin ē mē estin*, if the usual analysis is correct, then there must be an *eidos* of the god. Otherwise put, since there is no *eidos* of the centaur, there is no centaur.

6. *Metaphysics* Γ, 1003b22ff.

7. This is why Aristotle is preferred to Plato by the early, "existentialist" Heidegger.

8. *Metaphysics* Z 17, 1041a16ff.

9. Cf. M. Dummett, *Frege*, pp. 278ff.

10. *Metaphysics* Δ 26.

11. Ibid., Δ 6.

12. *Nicomachean Ethics* K 4.

13. *Metaphysics* Δ 3, 1014a26.

14. Cf. S. Kripke, "Naming and Necessity," pp. 336ff.

15. Cf. *Nicomachean Ethics*, K, 5, 1175a12: "life is a kind of *energeia* . . ."

16. For further discussion of the alphabet-paradigm in Plato, cf. D. Gallop, "Plato and the Alphabet," *Philosophical Review*, 72 (1963): 364–376; and G. Ryle, "Letters and Syllables in Plato," *Collected Papers*, vol. 1 (New York: Barnes and Noble, 1971), pp. 54–71.

17. For an analysis of this myth, see my "Plato's Myth of the Reversed Cosmos" in *Review of Metaphysics*, September 1979, pp. 59–85.

18. In the Hebrew Bible, Moses sees an image of God, but hears his commandments as they are in themselves. This priority of hearing to seeing remains good in the Christian tradition, and plays an important role in contemporary philosophy thanks to the influence of Heidegger.

19. Cf. Richard Gale, *Negation and Non-Being*, APQ Monograph Series No. 10 (Oxford: Basil Blackwell, 1976), pp. 63ff.

20. *Ontology and the Vicious-Circle Principle* (Cornell University Press: Ithaca and London, 1973), p. 63.

21. "Ontological Commitments" in P. Benacerraf and H. Putnam, eds., *Philosophy of Mathematics* (Englewood Cliffs, N.J.: Prentice-Hall, 1964), p. 250.

22. Ibid., p. 254.

23. "On Referring" in *Logico-Linguistic Papers* (London: Methuen, 1971), p. 27.

24. Richard Routley, for example, in his =R* system, makes E an existence predicate, and introduces Π and ∑ as quantifiers over variables to which E has not yet been applied ("Some Things

Do Not Exist," *Notre Dame Journal of Formal Logic* 3, no. 3 [July, 1966]: 251ff). Singular existence statements like "Churchill exists" may be represented as E (c). "Something exists" is $(\sum x)$ $E(x)$. "Some things don't exist" is $(\sum x) \sim (Ex)$, and so on. $(\exists x) Ax$ is by definition $(\sum x) (A(x) \& E(x))$. And "a does not exist" is equivalent to "a is a referring expression without a suitable referent." Thus, "if a is a value of a variable bound by a $\sum$-quantifier or even of a variable bound by a $\forall$-quantifier, it does not, in general, follow that a exists" (Ibid., p. 275). Routley makes two assumptions of interest to us in his construction of $=R^*$. The first, that "exists" is an ontological predicate, is explicit. The second is not only explicit but quite visible: "to be," whether existentially or not, is to be something, i.e., something countable or nameable. But this means that Routley's analysis of negation is not substantially different from that of "Fregeans" like Russell, Wittgenstein, or Quine. I note here two crucial problems, often cited in the literature, that Routley's method seems to avoid. The first is the difficulty that if existence is a predicate, then $(\exists x) \sim Ex$ means "there is something such that it does not exist" (cf. L. Linsky, *Names and Descriptions*, p. 36). This ostensible problem is almost explained away by the English paraphrase, since "is" and "exists" are two different words whose senses are the same only to careless or willful ontological logicians. But the problem does not arise in Routley's system thanks to the two kinds of quantifiers. The second problem, cited by Linsky in conjunction with a remark about Meinong, but without a solution, is that there are no clear identity-conditions for non-existent objects (ibid., p. 154). I personally doubt that this is any more of a problem than that of defining identity-conditions for existent objects. However this may be, it does not arise for Routley, who has no difficulty in specifying the predicates appropriate to his non-existent objects. The objection could also be met, incidentally, by applying a criterion formulated by Ian Hacking against Quine: "Two possible states of affairs are the same if it is not possible that one should obtain without the other obtaining" ("Possibility," *Philosophical Review* 76 [1967]: 165).

25. Frege's definition of zero as the set of all objects that are not self-identical cannot be used as a concept of nothing in the sense of the text above, because it is itself intelligible only within a system of concepts that are defined in terms of objects.

26. G. E. L. Owen, "Plato on Not-Being," in G. Vlastos, ed., *Plato I: Metaphysics and Epistemology* (New York: Doubleday Anchor Books, 1971). Cf. Roland Hall, "Excluders," *Analysis* 20 (1959): 1–7.

27. Owen, "Plato on Not-Being," p. 246.

28. Ibid., p. 246.

29. "Sentence Meaning, Negation, and Plato's Problem of Non-Being" in G. Vlastos, ed., *Plato I*, pp. 273ff.

30. "Dialog mit Punjer über Existenz" in *Schriften zur Logik und Philosophie aus dem Nachlass*, ed. G. Gabriel (Hamburg: Felix Meiner Verlag, 1971), pp. 17ff.

31. Ibid., pp. 16f, 19.

32. W. V. O. Quine, *From a Logical Point of View* (New York: Harper Torchbooks, 1963), p. 8.

33. Linsky, *Names and Descriptions*, pp. 31ff.

34. *Tractatus logico-philosophicus*, in *Schriften*, vol. 1 (Frankfurt: Suhrkamp Verlag, 1969), 4.061.

35. Ibid., 5.512.

36. *Sein und Zeit*, 7th ed. (Tübingen: Max Niemeyer Verlag, 1953), paragraphs 40 and 58 *et passim* (hereafter cited in text as SZ). [The latest edition (1977) contains an unchanged text, supplemented by some (in my opinion) uninteresting marginal notes prepared from Heidegger's own copy.]

37. In addition to *Sein und Zeit*, see *Nietzsche*, Bd. 2 (Pfullingen: G. Neske Verlag, 1961), p. 50.

38. For relevant passages, see W. J. Richardson, *Heidegger—through Phenomenology to Thought*, 3rd ed. (The Hague: M. Nijhoff, 1974) and H. Feick, *Index zu Heideggers 'Sein und Zeit'*, 2d ed. (Tübingen: Max Niemeyer Verlag, 1968).

39. See "Was ist Metaphysik?" in *Wegmarken* (Frankfurt: Vittorio Klostermann, 1967), pp. 11f; *Nietzsche*, Bd. 2, pp. 51, 337, 383; *Zur Seinsfrage* (Frankfurt: Vittorio Klostermann, 1956), pp. 37f; cf. Richardson, pp. 204, 474 *et passim*.

40. *Holzwege* (Frankfurt: Vittorio Klostermann, 1952), p. 321.

41. "Replies" in *Words and Objections* (Dordrecht, The Netherlands: D. Reidel, 1969), p. 293.

42. *Nietzsche*, Bd. 2, p. 51.

43. Ibid., pp. 337ff *et passim*.

Chapter Four

1. Cf. H. Field, "Tarski's Theory of Truth," *The Journal of Philosophy* 69, no. 13 (July 13, 1972): 355. In order to carry out his program of reducing semantical to non-semantical notions, Tarski must make use of the semantic notion of "an adequate translation," which he does not reduce to a non-semantical notion. According to Field, this is not an "obvious" objection to Tarski's notion of truth characterization. "On Tarski's view we need to adequately translate the object-language into the meta-language in order to give an adequate theory of truth for the object-language; this means that the notion of an adequate translation is employed in the methodology of giving truth theories, but it is not employed in the truth theories themselves." Field does not raise the obvious question: what is the non-semantic basis for the validity of the methodology of giving truth theories?

2. G. S. Boolos and R. C. Jeffrey, *Computability and Logic* (London: Cambridge University Press, 1974), p. 183.

3. *Phenomenology and Logic* (Ithaca: Cornell University Press, 1977), p. 20 (hereafter cited as PL).

4. Speaking of the reflection principle of ZF set theory, Frank Drake says: "Now the *reflection principle* says simply that for any given formula Φ, we can find arbitrarily high levels of the cumulative type structure which reflect Φ" (*Set Theory* [Amsterdam-London: North Holland Publishing Co., 1974], p. 99). For discussion of related issues, cf. J. Mayberry, "On the Consistency Problem for Set Theory," *British Journal for the Philosophy of Science* 28, no. 1 (1977): 1–34.

5. For Frege, Russell, and others, of course, this means that numbers are indeed sets. But *which* sets these are, cannot be decided.

6. Cf. G. Deleuze, *Différence et Répétition* (Paris: Presses Universitaires de France, 1968), pp. 169–173 and 190–191.

7. In *Metaphysics* Γ,2, 1004b1ff, Aristotle distinguishes between philosophers on the one hand, and sophists and dialecticians on the other. The philosopher must give an account of everything, and so be wise; the sophist has a different way of life from the philosopher. This is a modification of the situation in the *Sophist*. The Eleatic Stranger does not distinguish between sophists and dialecticians (in the pejorative sense of the term).

8. Cf. also *Phaedo* 99d4ff., *Republic* 6, 510b4ff and the discussion of dianoetic *eikasia* in Jacob Klein, *A Commentary on Plato's Meno* (Chapel Hill: University of North Carolina Press, 1965), pp. 115ff.

9. Cf. L. Gäbe, *Descartes' Selbstkritik* (Hamburg: Felix Meiner Verlag, 1972), chap. 5, and esp. p. 63, for method as abstraction from experience. Gäbe also discusses the importance of optics in the development of Descartes's thought.

10. *Cratylus* 432b3f.

11. Cf. *Phaedo* 99e1ff.

12. Cf. G. Deleuze, *Différence et Répétition*, pp. 205ff.

13. The productive nature of diaeresis becomes unusually explicit in the *Statesman*. Cf. my paper, "Plato's Myth of the Reversed Cosmos."

14. Cf. Gäbe, *Descartes' Selbstkritik*, pp. 59ff. Gäbe brings out very well the connection between the classical doctrine of proportions and Descartes's method as described in the *Regulae*. The abstraction by this method from the "nature" of the body corresponds to the abstraction from the phenomenal properties of the perceived body in my own text.

15. This is not true of Quine, for whom theories, not propositions, come before the tribunal of truth.

16. I am of course not denying that there are nominalist revisions of Frege, but for my present purposes these intermediate species are irrelevant.

17. See, however, the very interesting article by J-L. Nancy, "Logodaedalus," in *Poétique* 21 (1975): 24ff.

18. Unless otherwise indicated, numbers in parentheses in this section will refer to page numbers in *Fichtes Werke*, ed. I. H. Fichte, Bd. 10 (Berlin: Walter de Gruyter & Co., 1971). I am citing from the *Wissenschaftslehre* of 1804 (hereafter cited as FW).

19. There is an extremely interesting "Fichtean" interpretation of Descartes's *Meditations*, and especially of the *cogito*, in H. Rombach, *Substanz, System, Struktur*, Bd. 1 (Freiburg and

München: Verlag Karl Alber, 1965), pp. 439ff. Rombach takes Descartes to be uncovering pure *Denken* or *Geist*, and hence the transcendental domain which Husserl criticizes Descartes for having overlooked in favor of a world-bound empirical ego. Rombach notes that if the Cartesian ego were world-bound, it would be extended and so imaginable but not thinkable (p. 458).

20. I am aware that use of the term "reflexive" raises logical problems for Fichte, comparable to the problem of the transition from consciousness to self-consciousness in Hegel. I employ this term merely as a convenience to the nonspecialist, to bring out the fact that, in Fichtean intuition, intelligence "sees" intelligence, not the determinate content as thought by the empirical ego. The logical problems intrinsic to reflection, although fascinating and important in themselves, are not relevant to my present purposes. Fichte was himself aware of this problem.

21. Cf. L. Brouwer, "Mathematik, Wissenschaft und Sprache" in *Monatschrift fur Mathematik und Physik* 36 (1929): 153–164; and B. van Rootselaar, "On Subjective Mathematical Assertions" in A. Kino, J. Myhill, and R. Vesley eds., *Intuitionism and Proof Theory* (Amsterdam, North Holland Publishers, 1970), pp. 187–196. I owe these references to David Lachterman.

22. Nietzsche, *Werke*, ed. G. Colli and M. Montinari, *Achte Abteilung*, 3 vols. (Berlin: Walter de Gruyter, 1974). I cite by volume, page, and fragment number: I, 34, 115; I, 37, 128; I, 112, 108; II, 33, 62. A typical formulation: "Der interpretative Charakter alles Geschehens. Es giebt kein Ereignis an sich. Was geschieht, ist eine Gruppe von Erscheinungen *ausgelesen* und zusammengefasst von einem interpretirenden Wesen." (Note: Nietzsche's spelling and punctuation in these fragments do not always follow the usual rules.)

23. For a typical statement of this point, cf. III, 162f, 184. The apparent world is in fact a perspective serving the survival and *Macht-Steigerung* of the individual. "Reality" is thus an active-reactive process of world-making, as enacted by each individual against the All.

24. This is one of Nietzsche's pervasive themes. Cf. I, 112, 108; II, 184f, 110; III, 111, 134, and esp. II, 435, 415: "Hier fehlt der Gegensatz einer wahren und scheinbaren Welt: es giebt nur Eine Welt," namely, a false one, for which we require lies in order to live in it.

25. III, 19, 21.

26. E.g., I, 13, 28; I, 13, 30.

27. I, 21, 59; II, 9, 3.

28. I, 138, 149: apropos the question, "What is it?" Nietzsche says, "Zu Grunde liegt immer 'was ist das fur mich?"

29. Cf. *Jenseits von Gut und Böse*, "Der freie Geist," par. 43: the philosopher of the future will say "Mein Urteil ist *mein* Urteil."

30. Logic, mathematics, and scientific order are all products of the will to power: I, 104, 90; I, 194, 16; II, 82, 144.

31. Cf. II, 59f, 106: the "reality" of the phenomenal world lies in the continuous repetition of similarities and relations, or in its logicized character; these are consequences of our perspective or perception. So the opposite of the phenomenal world is not the "true world" but "die formlos-unformulirbare Welt des Sensation-Chaos,—also *eine andere Art* Phänomenal-Welt, eine fur uns 'unerkennbare'." Cf. also III, 125, 152: "knowing" is a schematizing of chaos.

32. E.g. III, 168, 188.

33. This is the meaning of the famous remark that the world is an artwork giving birth to itself: I, 117, 114.

34. Cf. II, 121, 10: there is for Nietzsche a Dionysian yea-saying to the world as it is, "bis zum Wunsche ihrer absoluten Wiederkunft und Ewigkeit." Nietzsche's "realism" is thus inseparable from the divinization of "intoxication." This is Platonic: a mixture of *phronēsis* and divine madness.

35. This is not to say that Heidegger's interpretation is simply wrong. Cf. I, 320, 54: "*Das Alles wiederkehrt*, ist die *extremste Annaherung einer Welt des Werdens an die des Seins: Gipfel der Betrachtung.*"

36. Cf. I, 264, 3 and esp. II, 16, 38: the true is what is necessary for life.

37. Cf. *Ecce Homo*, "Warum ich so weise bin," beginning of par. 1: "ich bin . . . *décadent* zugleich und *Anfang.*"

38. *Die fröhliche Wissenschaft, Drittes Buch*, paragraph 109, in *Werke*, ed. K. Schlechta (Munich: Hanser Verlag, 1955), *Bd.* II, p. 115: "Der Gesamtcharakter der Welt ist dagegen in alle Ewigkeit Chaos. . . ." All quotations from Nietzsche's published works will be from Schlechta, with volume and page number.

39. *Also Sprach Zarathustra, Zweiter Teil*, II, 345. I generally follow the Kaufmann translation with some modifications.

40. *Menschliches, Allzumenschliches, Erste Abteilung*, par. 33; I, 757.
41. *Die Morgenröte, Zweites Buch*, par. 117; I, 1092.
42. Ibid., paragraph 119; I, 1094.
43. This standard view is attacked by Saul Kripke in "Outline of a Theory of Truth," *Journal of Philosophy* 72 (July–December 1975): 690ff.
44. *Die Morgenröte, Zweites Buch*, par. 118; I, 1093; paragraph 119 (*Erleben und Erdichten*), I, 1095.
45. Ibid., par. 119; I, 1095.
46. Ibid., par. 128; I, 1098.
47. *Also Sprach Zarathustra*, II, 297.
48. *Jenseits von Gut und Böse, Drittes Hauptstück*, par. 62; II, 623.
49. Descartes "consciously created a dream world, using constantly its images. Passing over the great dreams of 1619, what are the *Méditations* but a sequence of dreams, and what is the world of *Le Monde* but a dream of clear and distinct ideas where the ordinary world of common sense does not intrude? The very power of the Cartesian method is in the radicalism of this dream world of the thinking subject. . . ." R. Catesby Taliaferro, *The Concept of Matter in Descartes and Leibniz* (South Bend, Ind.: Notre Dame University, 1964), p. 2. There is an ingenious analysis of Baillet's report on Descartes's dreams of 1619 in R. Kennington, "Descartes' 'Olympica' " *Social Research* 28 (Summer 1961): 171–204. Kennington provides detailed reasons for regarding Baillet's summary as of an actual manuscript, and of the manuscript itself as a rhetorically concealed criticism of revelation and poetry in favor of mathematical philosophy. However, he fails to explain satisfactorily the fact that, in Descartes's "waking" interpretation of his dreams, revelation and enthusiasm, although distinguished from human knowledge, remain, like knowledge, within the scope of "the Spirit of Truth." One may agree with Kennington that this spirit is Socratic rather than Christian, without overlooking the role of daydreams, and rhetorical formulations of these dreams, for Socratic and Cartesian spirits. Cf. esp. pp. 197, 201ff.
50. Cf. Yvon Belavel, *Leibniz. Critique de Descartes* (Paris: Gallimard, 1960), p. 147.
51. Cf. A. Matheron, "Psychologie et politique: Descartes, la noblesse du chatouillement," *dialectiques* 6 (1974): pp. 85–87 and 93–95.
52. *Jenseits von Gut und Böse, Der freie Geist*, par. 30, II, 595.
53. For a flagrant example of Nietzschean poetics in contemporary analytical philosophy, cf. N. Goodman, *Ways of World Making* (Indianapolis and Cambridge: Hackett Publishing Co., 1978).
54. *Jenseits von Gut und Böse, Wir Gelehrten*, paragraph 211; II, 676.
55. Cf. *Nachlass*, III, 124, 14: "Parmenides hat gesagt, man denkt das nicht, was nicht ist—wir sind am anderen Ende und sagen 'was gedacht werden kann, muss sicherlich eine Fiktion sein.' Denken hat keinen Griff auf Reales, sondern nur auf. . . ."

Chapter Five

1. For an elaboration of this premiss, see my *Nihilism* (New Haven: Yale University Press, 1969).
2. *Phänomenologie des Geistes*, ed. J. Hoffmeister (Hamburg: Felix Meiner Verlag, 1952), p. 30.
3. "Von einem neuerdings erhobenen Ton in der Philosophie," *Theorie-Ausgabe*, Bd. 6 (Frankfurt am Main: Suhrkamp Verlag, 1974), p. 382.
4. *Kritik der reinen Vernunft* (Hamburg: Felix Meiner Verlag, 1956), B130. Hereafter cited as First Critique.
5. Unless otherwise indicated, numbers in parentheses in the text will refer to Kant, *Kritik der praktischen Vernunft* (Hamburg: Felix Meiner Verlag, 1952).
6. Cf. *Passions de l'âme*, ed. Rodis-Lewis (Paris: J. Vrin, 1955), Part One, Articles 40–41, 48, 50; Part Two, Articles 74, 111, 137.
7. Ibid., Part Three, Articles 152–153.
8. Cf. *First Critique*, B836.
9. L. W. Beck, A *Commentary on Kant's Critique of Practical Reason* (Chicago: University of Chicago Press, 1960), p. 245.

NOTES

10. Kant himself defends Platonism in the First Critique in the domain of "principles of morality, legislation, and religion" (B375). Platonic Ideas are for him telic archetypes (B374).

11. *Republic* VI, 508e; *Phaedo* 99c; *Timaeus* 28a–29a; *Laws* X, 903b–904b. *Kritik der Urteilskraft* (Hamburg: Felix Meiner Verlag, 1954), pp. 328, 360.

12. *First Critique*, B94.

13. Ibid., B851.

14. Numbers in parentheses now refer to the edition of the *Kritik der Urteilskraft* cited in note 10.

15. This is the theme of Pierre Aubenque, *Le problème de l'être chez Aristote.* (Paris: Presses Universitaires de France, 1962). More recently, it was defended by J. D. G. Evans, *Aristotle's Concept of Dialectic* (Cambridge: Cambridge University Press, 1977), esp. pp. 23f, 49ff.

16. Numbers in parentheses in the text will refer to pages in *Wissenschaft der Logik, Bd.* I (Leipzig: Felix Meiner Verlag, 1951).

17. For evidence and discussion, cf. my "Plato's Myth of the Reversed Cosmos" in *Review of Metaphysics* 32 (September 1979): 59–85.

18. Cf. Kant, *Kritik der reinen Vernunft*, B776.

BIBLIOGRAPHY

Alston, W. "Ontological Commitments." In *Philosophy of Mathematics*, edited by P. Benacerraf and H. Putnam. Englewood-Cliffs, N.J.: Prentice-Hall, 1964.

Aristotle. *Opera*. Oxford: Clarendon Press, 1956–64.

Aubenque, P. *Le problème de l'être chez Aristote*. Paris: Presses Universitaires de France, 1962.

Bambrough, R. "Intuition and the Inexpressible." In *Mysticism and Philosophical Analysis*, edited by S. Katz. New York: Oxford University Press, 1978.

Bassenge, F. "Das τὸ ἑνὶ ἑῖναι, τὸ ἀγαθῷ ἑῖναι etc. etc. und das τὸ τί ἦν ἑῖναι bei Aristoteles." *Philologus* 104 (1960): 14–47, 201–222.

Beck, L. W. *A Commentary on Kant's Critique of Practical Reason*. Chicago: University of Chicago Press, 1960.

Belavel, Y. *Leibniz. Critique de Descartes*. Paris: Gallimard, 1960.

Boolos, G. S. and Jeffrey, R. C. *Computability and Logic*. London: Cambridge University Press, 1974.

Brouwer, L. "Mathematik, Wissenschaft und Sprache." *Monatschrift für Mathematik und Physik* 36 (1929): 153–164.

Caton, H. "Carnap's First Philosophy." *Review of Metaphysics* 28 (1975):623–659.

Chang, C. C., and Keisler, H. J. *Model Theory*. Amsterdam: North Holland Publishing Co., 1973.

Chihara, C. *Ontology and the Vicious-Circle Principle*. Ithaca: Cornell University Press, 1973.

Davidson, D. "In Defense of Convention T." In *Truth, Syntax and Modality*, edited by H. LeBlanc. Amsterdam: North Holland Publishing Co., 1973, pp. 76–85.

———. "Truth and Meaning." *Synthese* 17 (1967): 304–323.

Deleuze, G. *Différence et Répétition*. Paris: Presses Universitaires de France, 1968.

Descartes, R. *Meditationes*. In *Oeuvres*, edited by Adam-Tannery, vol. 7. Paris: J. Vrin, 1947–1957.

———. *Les passions de l'âme*. edited by Rodis-Lewis. Paris: J. Vrin, 1955.

Drake, F. *Set Theory*. Amsterdam: North Holland Publishing Co., 1974.

Ducrot, O. "Le Structuralisme en Linguistique." In *Qu'est-ce que le Structuralisme?*, edited by F. Wahl. Paris: Editions du Seuil, 1968.

Dummett, M. *Frege*. London: Duckworth, 1973.

————. "Frege as a Realist." *Inquiry* 19 (1976): 455–492.
————. "What is a Theory of Meaning?" In *Mind and Language*, edited by S. Gutenplan. Oxford: Clarendon Press, 1975.
————. "What is a Theory of Meaning (II)." In *Truth and Meaning*, edited by G. Evans, and J. McDowell. Oxford: Clarendon Press, 1976.
Evans, G., and McDowell, J. eds. *Truth and Meaning: Essays in Semantics*. Oxford: Clarendon Press, 1976.
Evans, J. D. G. *Aristotle's Concept of Dialectic*. Cambridge: Cambridge University Press, 1977.
Feick, H. *Index Zu Heidegger's Sein und Zeit*. Tübingen: Max Niemeyer Verlag, 1968.
Fichte, J. G. *Fichtes Werke*. Bd. 10. Edited by I. H. Fichte. Berlin: Walter de Gruyter, 1971.
Field, H. "Tarski's Theory of Truth." *Journal of Philosophy* 69 (1972): 347–375.
Fraenkel, A., Bar-Hillel, Y., Levy, A., and van Dalen, D. *Foundations of Set Theory*. Amsterdam: North Holland Publishing Co., 1973.
Frame, D. *The Myth of Return in Early Greek Epic*. New Haven: Yale University Press, 1978.
Frege, G. "Dialog mit Punjer über Existenz." In *Schriften zur Logik und Philosophie aus dem Nachlass*, edited by G. Gabriel. Hamburg: Felix Meiner Verlag, 1971.
————. *On the Foundations of Geometry*. Translated by E. H. W. Kluge. New Haven: Yale University Press, 1971.
————. *Logical Investigations*. Translated by P. Geach and R. Stoothoof. New Haven: Yale University Press, 1977.
————. *Translations from the Philosophical Writings of Gottlob Frege*. Edited by P. Geach and M. Black. Oxford: Basil Blackwell, 1960.
————. *The Foundations of Arithmetic*. Translated by J. L. Austin. New York: Harper Torchbooks, 1960.
Furth, M. "Transtemporal Stability in Aristotelian Substances." *Journal of Philosophy* 75 (1978): 624–626.
Gäbe, L. *Descartes' Selbstkritik*. Hamburg: Felix Meiner Verlag, 1972.
Gale, R. *Negation and Non-Being*. Oxford: Basil Blackwell, 1976.
Gallop D. "Plato and the Alphabet." *Philosophical Review* 72 (1963): 364–376.
Gochet, P. *Quine en perspective*. Paris: Flammarion, 1978.
Goodman, N. *Ways of World Making*. Indianapolis and Cambridge: Hackett Publishing Co., 1978.
Hacking, I. "Possibility." *Philosophical Review* 76 (1967): 143–168.
Hall, R. "Excluders." *Analysis* 20 (1959): 1–7.
Hegel, G. W. F. *Phänomenologie des Geistes*. Hamburg: Felix Meiner Verlag, 1952.
————. *Wissenschaft der Logik*. Leipzig: Felix Meiner Verlag, 1968.
Heidegger, M. *Holzwege*. Frankfurt: Vittorio Klostermann, 1952.
————. *Nietzsche*. Pfullingen: G. Neske Verlag, 1961.
————. *Sein und Zeit*. Tübingen: Max Niemeyer Verlag, 1953.
————. "Was ist Metaphysik?" In *Wegmarken*. Frankfurt: Vittorio Klostermann, 1967.
————. *Zur Seinsfrage*. Frankfurt: Vittorio Klostermann, 1952.
Husserl, E. *Logische Untersuchungen*. Halle: M. Niemeyer, 1928.
Ishiguro, H. *Leibniz' Philosophy of Logic and Language*. London: Duckworth, 1972.
Kant, I. *Kritik der Praktischen Vernunft*. Hamburg: Felix Meiner Verlag, 1952.
————. *Kritik der Reinen Vernunft*. Hamburg: Felix Meiner Verlag, 1956.
————. *Kritik der Urteilskraft*. Hamburg: Felix Meiner Verlag, 1956.
————. "Von einem neuerdings erhobenen Ton in der Philosophie." In *Theorie-Ausgabe*, vol. 6, Frankfurt am Main: Suhrkamp Verlag, 1974.
Kennington, R. "Descartes' 'Olympica.' " *Social Research* 28 (1961): 171–204.
Klein, J. A *Commentary on Plato's Meno*. Chapel Hill: University of North Carolina Press, 1965.
Kreisel, G. "Informal Rigour and Completeness Proofs." In *The Philosophy of Mathematics*, edited by J. Hintikka. London: Oxford University Press, 1969.
————. "Mathematical Logic: What has it done for the Philosophy of Mathematics?" In *The Philosophy of Mathematics*, edited by J. Hintikka. London: Oxford University Press, 1969.
Kripke, S. "Identity and Necessity." In *Naming, Necessity and Natural Kinds*, edited by S. Schwartz. Ithaca: Cornell University Press, 1977.
————. "Is there a Problem about Substitutional Quantification?" In *Truth and Meaning*, edited by G. Evans, and J. McDowell. Oxford: Clarendon Press, 1976.

————. "Naming and Necessity." In *Semantics of Natural Language*, edited by D. Davidson, and G. Harman. Dordrecht: D. Reidel Publishing Co., 1972.
————. "Outline of a Theory of Truth." *Journal of Philosophy*. 72 (1975): 690–716.
————. "Semantical Considerations on Modal Logic." In *Reference and Modality*, edited by L. Linsky. London: Oxford University Press, 1971.
Lewy, C. *Meaning and Modality*. Cambridge: Cambridge University Press, 1976.
Linsky, L. *Names and Descriptions*. Chicago: University of Chicago Press, 1977.
Lyons, J. *Introduction to Theoretical Linguistics*. Cambridge: Cambridge University Press, 1968.
Maimonides, M. *The Guide of the Perplexed*. Translated by S. Pines. Chicago: University of Chicago Press, 1963.
Matheron, A. "Psychologie et politique: Descartes, la noblesse du chatouillement." *dialectiques* 6 (1974): 79–98.
Marx, W. "Zur Bestimmung des Begriffes 'Reines Denken.'" *Zeitschrift für Philosophische Forschung* 28 (1974): 94–105.
Mayberry, J. "On the Consistency Problem for Set Theory." *British Journal for the Philosophy of Science* 28 (1977): 1–34.
Nancy, J-L. "Logodaedalus." *Poétique* 21 (1975): 24–52.
Nietzsche, F. *Werke*. Edited by G. Colli, and M. Montinari. Berlin: Walter de Gruyter, 1974.
————. *Werke*. Edited by K. Schlechta. Munich: Carl Hanser Verlag, 1955.
Owen, G. E. L. "Plato on Not-Being." In *Plato I: Metaphysics and Epistemology*, edited by G. Vlastos. New York: Doubleday Anchor Books, 1971.
Parsons, C. "Ontology and Mathematics." *Philosophical Review* 80 (1971): 151–176.
Parsons, T. "Essentialism and Quantified Modal Logic." In *Reference and Modality*, edited by L. Linsky. London: Oxford University Press, 1971.
Piaget, J. *Le structuralisme*. Paris: Presses Universitaires de France, 1968.
Plantinga, A. *The Nature of Necessity*. Oxford: Clarendon Press, 1974.
Plato. *Opera*. Edited by J. Burnet. Oxford: Clarendon Press, 1900–15.
Putnam, H. *Mind, Language and Reality*. London and New York: Cambridge University Press, 1975.
Quine, W. V. O. *From a Logical Point of View*. Cambridge, Mass.: Harvard University Press, 1953.
————. *Ontological Relativity*. New York: Columbia University Press, 1969.
————. "Replies." In *Words and Objections*. Dordrecht: D. Reidel, 1969.
————. *Set Theory and its Logic*. Cambridge, Mass.: Harvard University Press, Belknap Press, 1969.
Richardson, W. J. *Heidegger—Through Phenomenology to Thought*. The Hague: M. Nijhoff, 1974.
Rombach, H. *Substanz, System, Struktur*. Freiburg and Munich: Verlag Karl Alber, 1965.
Rootselaar van, B. "On Subjective Mathematical Assertions." In *Intuitionism and Proof Theory*, edited by A. Kino, J. Myhill, and R. Vesley. Amsterdam: North Holland Publishing Co., 1970, pp. 187–196.
Rosen S. "A Central Ambiguity in Descartes." In *Cartesian Essays*, edited by B. Magnus, and J. B. Wilbur. The Hague: M. Nijhoff, 1969: pp. 17–35.
————. *Nihilism*. New Haven: Yale University Press, 1969.
————. "Plato's Myth of the Reversed Cosmos." *Review of Metaphysics* 33, no. 1 (Sept. 1979): 59–85.
————. "Return to the Origin." *International Philosophical Quarterly* 16 (1976): 151–177.
————. "Thought and Touch: A Note on Aristotle's *De Anima*." *Phronesis* 6, no. 2 (1961): 127–137.
Routley, R. "Some Things do not Exist." *Notre Dame Journal of Formal Logic* 3 (1966): 251–276.
Russell, B. *An Inquiry into Meaning and Truth*. Harmondsworth and Baltimore: Penguin, 1973.
Ryle, G. "Letters and Syllables in Plato." In *Collected Papers*, vol. 1. New York: Barnes and Noble, 1971.
Slote, M. *Metaphysics and Essence*. New York: New York University Press, 1975.
Sluga, H. "Frege's Alleged Realism." *Inquiry* 20 (1977): 227–242.
————. "Frege and the Rise of Analytical Philosophy." *Inquiry* 18 (1975): 471–498.
Strawson, P. F. "On Referring." In *Logico-Linguistic Papers*. London: Methuen, 1971.
————. *Subject and Predicate*. London: Methuen, 1974.
Sukale, M. *Comparative Studies in Phenomenology*. The Hague: M. Nijhoff, 1976.

BIBLIOGRAPHY

Taliaferro, R. C. *The Concept of Matter in Descartes and Leibniz*. South Bend, Ind.: Notre Dame University Press, 1964.

Tragesser, R. *Phenomenology and Logic*. Ithaca: Cornell University Press, 1977.

Wiggins, D. "Sentence Meaning, Negation and Plato's Problem of Non-Being." In *Plato I: Metaphysics and Epistemology*, edited by G. Vlastos. New York: Doubleday Anchor Books, 1971.

Wittgenstein, L. *Tractatus logico-philosophicus*. In *Schriften*, vol. 1. Frankfurt: Suhrkamp Verlag, 1969.

Wright, C. "Truth Conditions and Criteria." In *The Aristotelian Society, Supplementary Volume L*. Tisbury: Compton Russel Ltd., 1976.

INDEX

Absolute, the: in Fichte, 181–89, 198; in Hegel, 248, 255; in model theory, 255

Alston, William, 131

analysis: and being, 107; as a cognitive activity, 26–27, 217; context of, 10, 27, 35, 120–21, 127–28, 142, 149–50, 154–55, 159–60, 166, 174–75, 179, 190–91, 200, 216–18, 220–21, 235–36, 245, 259–60; meaning of, 7, 33; and nothingness, 135–37; and originals, 6; and self-consciousness, 178; and simple elements, 109–10; and structure, 29, 33; and synthesis, *xiii–xiv*, 7–10, 45, 218

analytical philosophy: and essences, 53–54; and existence, 104–5; and Fichte, 186, 189–90; and fundamental ontology, 44, 99, 197; and Hegel, 233–36, 241, 248–49, 252, 256, 258; and measurement, 152–54; and Nietzsche, 191, 200, 208–9; and nothingness, 132, 142, 147; and phenomenology, 16; Platonic and Kantian elements in, 8, 19–20, 45, 174–76, 189–90, 227, 258; and possibility, 103; and the rejection of intuition, 4–9, 50, 52–53, 58, 109, 118, 124, 142, 173, 175, 177; and rhetoric, *xiii*, 38, 121, 142–43, 153–54, 179, 221, 259; and semantics, 12; and unity, 108

Aristotle: on being, 98–99, 107, 115–16, 120, 139, 235; on essences, 59–64, 73; on the intellect, 36–37, 41–43, 59, 195, 222; on predication, 54–58, 113; and the principle of non-contradiction, 238–240; and the rejection of myth, 123–24

Bambrough, Renford, 4–6

being: and becoming, 193; and existence, 99–107, 109, 114–17, 129; homogeneity of, 235, 239; and nothingness, 142, 144, 146–48, 248; and ontology, 98; and thinking, 81, 223, 233, 234

belonging-to: and existence, 104–5; and intuition, 10, 135, 150; and predication, 23, 41, 52, 55–56, 66–67; *see also* having

Brouwer, L., 30, 186

Cantor, G., 105, 150

chaos, 193–208, 213; *see also* Nietzsche, F.

Chihara, Charles, 131

concept, 27, 137; concept of, 41–51, 53; in Frege, 23–25; world as, 219–56; *see also* Kant, I. and Hegel, G. W. F.

conventionalism, 66–67

copula, the: ontological sense of, 104–7, 113; traditional senses of, 100

Davidson, Donald, 12–15

Deleuze, G., 153

Derrida, J., 153